Zen Landscapes

Perspectives on Japanese Gardens and Ceramics

ALLEN S. WEISS

REAKTION BOOKS

Published by Reaktion Books Ltd
33 Great Sutton Street
London EC1V 0DX, UK
www.reaktionbooks.co.uk

First published 2013

Book design by Simon McFadden

The publishers would like to thank The Great Britain Sasakawa Foundation
for its support in the publication of this work.

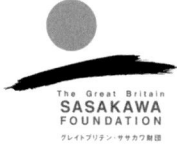

Printed and bound in China by C&C Offset Printing Co., Ltd

A catalogue record for this book is available from the British Library.

ISBN 978 1 78023 190 7

CONTENTS

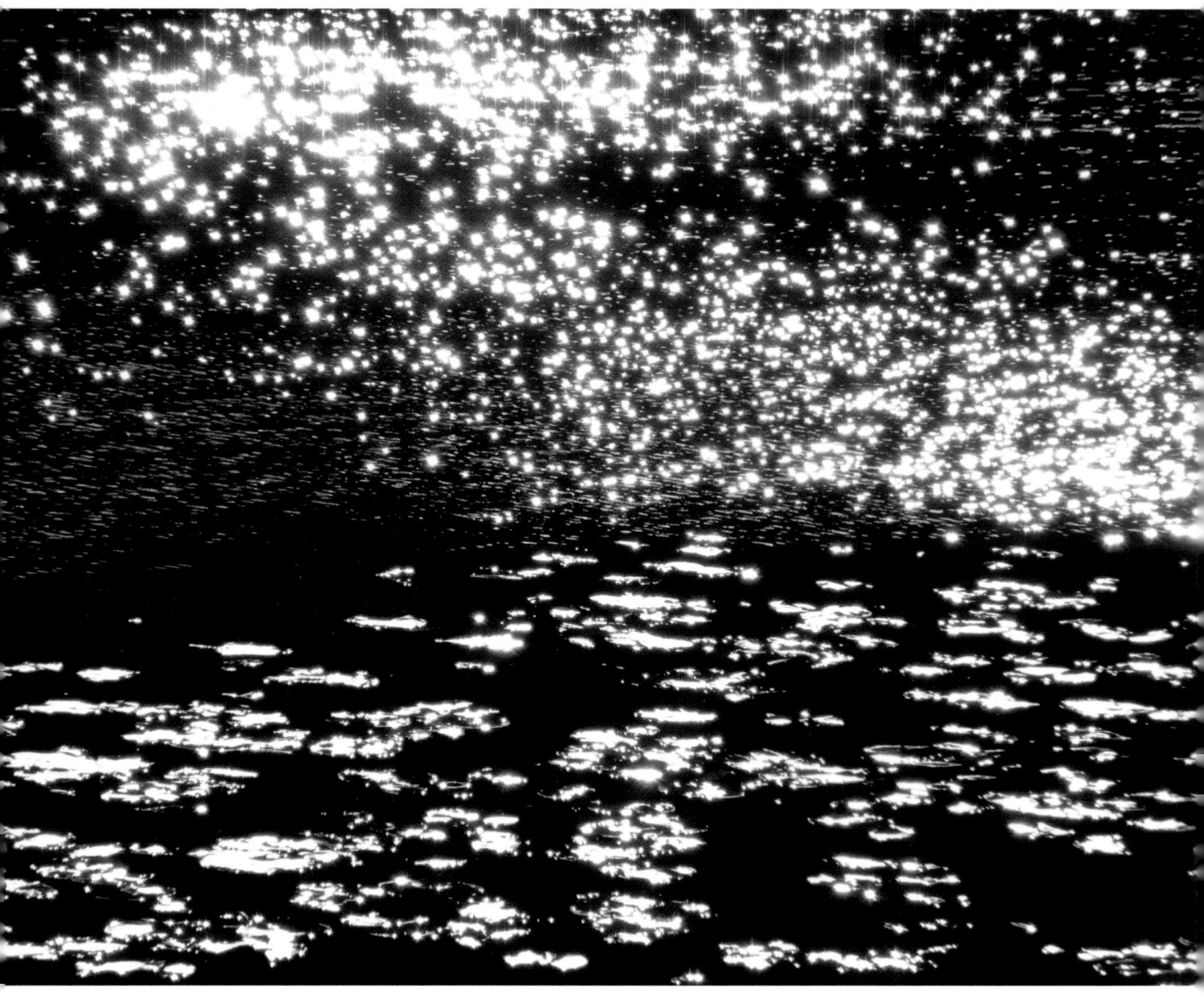

Ryōan-ji, Kyōyōchi Pond.

To understand the rose, one person uses geometry
while another employs the butterfly.

PAUL CLAUDEL,
L'Oiseau noir dans le soleil levant

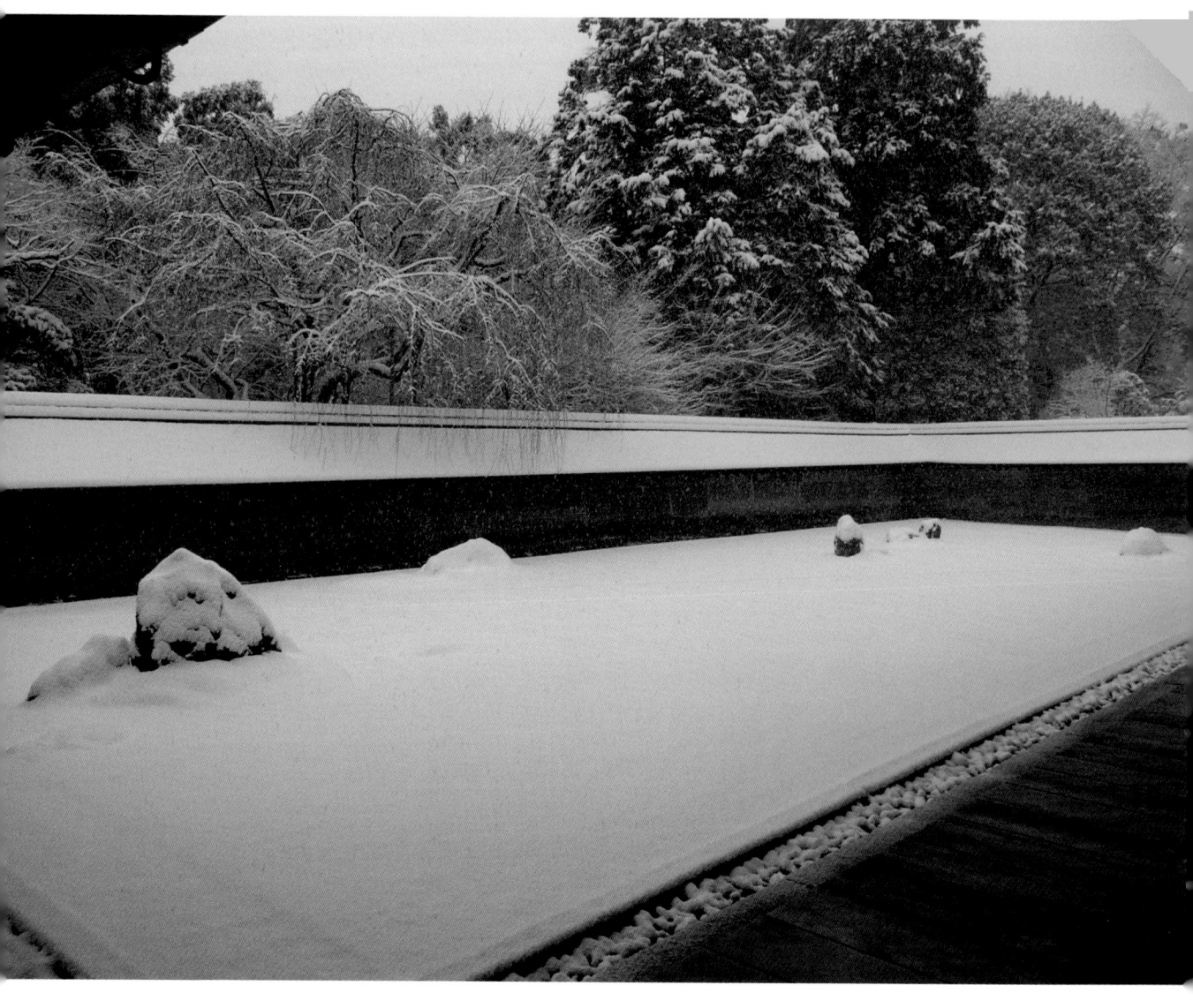

Ryōan-ji, snowstorm of 31 December 2010.

TRANSFORMATIONS OF VISION

The dry garden of Ryōan-ji in Kyoto is one of the most analysed and photographed works of art in the world. Thus, well before my first visit in November 2006, I felt I knew the garden intimately, and was thoroughly prepared to elaborate on the knowledge I had attained from dozens of books and hundreds if not thousands of images. As soon as I stepped onto the veranda of the temple overlooking the garden, I was stupefied, first by its sublime beauty and soon afterwards by the fact that it hardly corresponded to any description I had read of it. How could this be? Could all previous commentators have been so wrong? Could I have been so blinded by my own prejudices and paradigms? Could I have fallen into the textual trap of confusing image and description for the garden itself? Certainly my attraction to Japanese dry gardens stems from the fact that they corroborate my aesthetic principles, wishes and utopias. But might this passion, hitherto untested against its objects, have falsified my vision? I immediately suspected that my disorientation went far beyond mere culture shock. With each discovery about Japanese culture, my bewilderment seemed to multiply even as my knowledge expanded, and I seemed further from aesthetic enlightenment than ever, as Ryōan-ji led me to consider other art forms and other viewpoints: the stones had their antecedents in Chinese and Japanese painting; the surrounding walls evoked unglazed pottery surfaces; the stone borders hinted at the complicated issues of inside and outside in Japanese architecture; the sparse moss suggested the need for water in an otherwise dry garden, thus pointing to the essential role of atmospheric effects in Japanese art; the raked gravel stressed the role of stylization and stereotype in image and word; and the overhanging cherry tree evoked the crucial interpenetration of art and world. I was to discover that these correspondences were not mere free associations, but are deeply ingrained in Japanese aesthetics. After nearly two decades of meditation on Western gardens and landscape from the

Baroque through the modern and postmodern eras, I realized that I had to reorient my ways of seeing completely in order to be able to elucidate my initial astonishment before Ryōan-ji.[1]

As a result I offer here a certain number of principles, composed in the form of a 'Manifesto for the Future of Landscape', to give a sense of my attitudes and hopes – often against the grain of contemporary theory and practice – regarding landscape creation, appreciation and conservation.

1. The garden is a symbolic form, which suggests that symbols are as important as images to guide appreciation as well as restoration. The garden is earthly, but it also reaches to the heavens, and occasionally to the underworld.
2. The garden is never merely a picture, and the ground plan is usually misleading. The spatiality of gardens is plastic and dynamic, such that kinetics is of the essence. The garden is thus a synaesthetic matrix.
3. The garden is a Gesamtkunstwerk, a web of correspondences, a site that should encompass all the arts. Consequently, every garden must be continuously reinvented as a scene for contemporary activities.
4. The garden is simultaneously a hermetic space and an object in the world. Thus the 'formal' garden must remain open to the 'informality' of nature. Garden closure is a sociological and psychological phenomenon, not an ontological one.
5. The garden is a paradox, necessitating that complexity and contradiction should not be avoided, since the finest metaphors are often unstable and equivocal.
6. The garden is a narrative, a transformer of narratives, and a generator of narratives, such that a garden is all that it evokes. Consequently, tales and symbols are an integral part of gardens.
7. The unpeopled garden is either an abstraction or a ruin, suggesting that all aesthetic value has a use value that must be respected. The most complex landscape is the one most closely observed.
8. The garden is a memory theatre, which must bear vestiges of its sedimented history, including traces of the catastrophes that it has suffered.

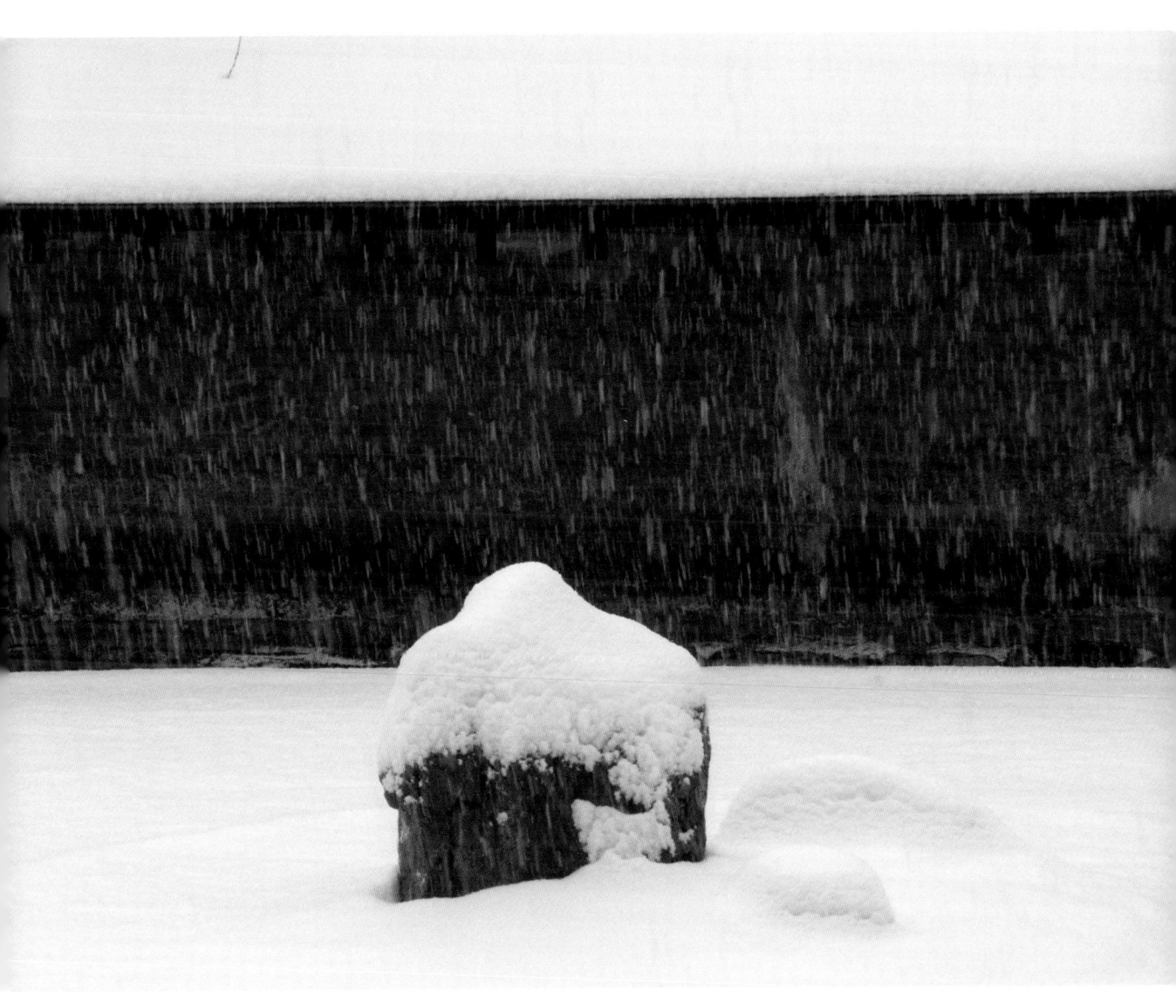

Ryōan-ji, snowstorm of 31 December 2010.

In the history of landscape, accidents are not contingent, but essential.

9. The garden is a hyperbolically ephemeral structure. Anachronism is of the essence, since a garden is all that it was and all that it shall become.

This summation is offered as a touchstone for the investigations that follow, not so much as a corrective to my initial perplexity before Ryōan-ji, but as a spur to new intuitions and as a conceptual guide to the seemingly disparate, but in fact crucial, relations between gardens and the other arts, notably ceramics and cuisine. If there is a constant across these pages, it is the theme of Zen; but this is not the subject of the book, but rather an ineluctable and illuminative thread.[2] Ultimately, every artwork bears its own phantasmic ontology, which must be distinguished from the cultural forms and symbols that ground the work. Throughout history and across cultures, the forms of and relations between representation and vision are constantly changing. Our ways of seeing must be no less adaptable, subtle and inventive.

THE FORMAL STAGING of the Japanese aesthetic sensibility is centred on the Zen-inspired tea ceremony, a sort of Gesamtkunstwerk which links painting, calligraphy, pottery, lacquer, woodcraft, architecture, design, poetry, cuisine, flower arranging, gardens and the gestural choreography of the ceremony itself in a highly ritualized event. Here, every art form informs all other art forms, and appreciation is a global experience. As Christine M. E. Guth explains:

> The true man of tea is measured by the skill with which he combines articles from his collection so that they form a harmonious ensemble in the tea room. This process, known as *tori awase* (selecting and matching), requires broad cultural knowledge, connoisseurship, and creativity. The host must consider the context: the season, the occasion, and the identity of the guest or guests. He must take into account the size, shape, texture, color, and material of each work of art . . . Although he must also keep in mind historical connotations such as the origins, history of ownership, and previous use of each article, he must use this knowledge creatively, so as to make each gathering a unique and memorable experience.[3]

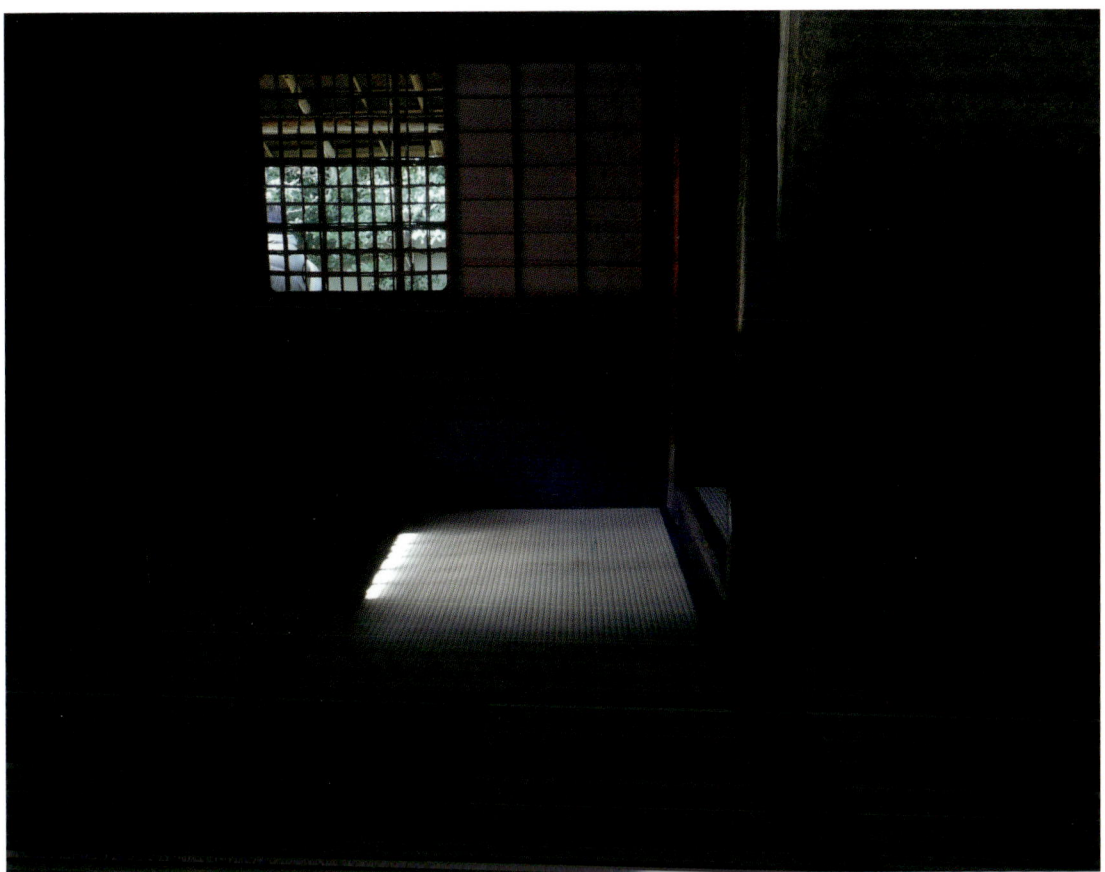

Kōtō-in, a subtemple of Daitoku-ji, tearoom.

Inspired by earlier Chinese Taoist and Buddhist types of tea ceremonies, Japanese forms of tea were first formulated by Ikkyū Sōjun (1394–1481), developed in the *wabi-sabi* style by Murata Shukō (1423–1502), elaborated by Takeno Jōō (1502–1555), to be finally systematized in what would become its modern form, still practised today, by Sen no Rikyū (1522–1591). Fundamentally, the tea ceremony is said to be nothing but *chanoyu*, meaning simply 'hot water for tea', a conceit suggesting that this art fundamentally exists not so much in the stylized gestures and the aesthetic disposition of objects, but rather as an ideal of appreciation, a model of connoisseurship, a form of intuition, a source of inspiration. But in fact it is an ultra-sophisticated combination of art appreciation, etiquette and spiritual discipline.

Zen Buddhism came to be at the core of Japanese culture for a number of reasons: the attractiveness to the rising warrior (samurai) class of a religion centred not on scripture and prohibitions but on volition and action; the fact that some Zen monks were widely travelled both within Japan and outside, and were thus a conduit of culture and trade; and that the egalitarian tea aesthetic fostered by the ceremony transformed certain temples into a social melting pot. Monasteries were repositories of art and learning, with many monks themselves being artists, and these temples already had aristocratic backing, and were thus integrated into the power structure. As tea became one of the ceremonial keys to Zen by the sixteenth century, this ceremony may be seen as a condensation of Japanese aesthetics, indeed as its predominant aesthetic paradigm, to such an extent that it has even been said that the spirit of tea is equivalent to the spirit of Zen. Tea is effectively the aestheticization of Zen, or, as the early tea afficionados used to say, 'tea and Zen have the same taste'.

In a more complex formulation, one could claim that tea is ritualized and spiritualized utilitarianism in the aura of simulated aestheticized poverty, where, according to Haga Kōshirō, a scholar of Zen and medieval Japanese history, 'a higher dimension of transcendent beauty is created by the dialectical sublation of an inner richness and complexity into the simple and the unpretentious'.[4] Zen has spiritual, material and social manifestations: the spiritual centred on the inner life, where corporeal discipline, ritualistic tasks, prayer, deep meditation and questioning (*kōan*) all aim towards self-enlightenment; the material concerning the aesthetics of tea, where shared appreciation of beauty guarantees collective harmony; and the social allowing the tea room or hut to serve as a sort of literary salon, where different classes in an otherwise rigidly hierarchical society had the rare opportunity of interacting.[5] In its ideal form tea is a spiritual exercise, while in its decadent form it often becomes little more than mannerism and snobbism, a cover for power brokerage and a pretext for art transactions. Though such decadence is not unexpected at certain historic junctures, it is nonetheless rather surprising to find accounts of hypercritical fault-finding among even the greatest of tea masters. This is certainly a sign of the difficulty of attaining spiritual heights, through tea or otherwise, and of the ease of sinking into commonplace worldly concerns. Rupert A. Cox stresses the complexities of the opposition between the spiritual and the material at the heart of

Zen culture – leading to many ambiguities and paradoxes – by analysing a series of crucial oppositions: religion / art; Buddhist world rejection / Confucian world affirmation; nobody / body; hermit / aesthete; discipline / etiquette; edifying experience / aesthetic form; enlightened / worldly; ascetic / aesthetic; existence / representation; immediacy / mediation; iconoclastic / iconophilic; formless / formal; non-verbal intuition / verbal or visual expression.[6] However, for numerous Buddhist schools, these oppositions are not absolute, and it is deemed thoroughly possible, even necessary, to realize enlightenment in both ordinary everyday experience and the arts. As Joseph D. Parker claims, 'the relation between the realm of enlightenment and nirvana is closely associated and even identified with the samsaric world of form and passionate attachments' whence, 'the efficacy of language and other cultural mediums for realizing Buddhist wisdom'.[7]

Zen stresses self-discipline, profound meditation and enlightenment through intuition by short-circuiting logic, metaphor, imagery, narration. The transcendental insights of Zen are illogical and paradoxical, but this does not negate the possibility of a deep sense of connectedness with objects and nature, nor does it obviate the foregrounding of metaphoric correspondences between all things and the interrelatedness between all arts. This is a form of spirituality without doctrine and scripture, where the bonds of tradition are loosened, or may even be altogether cast off, making Zen a veritable spur to creativity. In a sense, while its spiritual culture strives towards a non-metaphoric grasp of reality, the material culture of Zen offers a web of metaphors. A lifetime would not suffice to explore fully the subtleties of this aesthetic – geared to intuition, not demonstration, and thus immune to discursive proofs – but a consideration of its key terms may suggest how we can achieve a state of mind that would, if not guaranteeing enlightenment (*satori*), at least heighten our receptivity to Zen-inspired art.

The specialist of Zen culture Hisamatsu Shin'ichi writes of seven characteristics particular to the Zen sensibility: asymmetry, simplicity, austere sublimity or lofty dryness, naturalness, subtle profundity or deep reserve, freedom from attachment, tranquility.[8] Donald Keene reduces these to four pertinent features: suggestion, irregularity, simplicity, perishability.[9] Such schemas have been criticized for being too static and ahistorical, yet they can easily be amended by adding certain nuances, both formal and historical, that are simultaneously more complex and more direct. It is here that specifically Japanese aesthetic notions complicate the issue, since the forms taken by such consummate beauty proffer particular characteristics. It is often claimed that such terms cannot be translated. Of course, the same may be said for our own notions of 'art' and 'beauty'. The entire history of Western philosophy has attempted to clarify them, and they have only grown more complex as a result of all that study. What is crucial is to grasp the changing and polysemic significance and use value of these terms in their shifting historic context, rather than seeking impossible equivalent translations.

The infinitely complex combination of *wabi* and *sabi*, elaborated by Rikyū, and *shibui*, developed later in the history of tea during the Edo period (1603–1868), together set the proper psychological, spiritual and aesthetic attitude for appreciating Japanese art. The semantic density of these terms, along with their vast range of denotations and connotations, already implies existential richness and philosophical complexity. These terms designate complex aesthetic attitudes, which can be roughly parsed as follows. *Wabi* suggests the positive values of poverty and its attendant aspects of quietness, tranquillity, solitude, humbleness, frugality, unobtrusiveness, asymmetrical harmony, elegant rusticity. Haga Kōshirō expresses this sensibility by condensing it into three forms of beauty: simple and unpretentious, imperfect and irregular, austere and stark, and D. T. Suzuki refers to a joyful 'active aesthetic appreciation of poverty'.[10] *Sabi* signifies wear and patination by age and use as well as rust; it is a prime aspect of aesthetic sensibility inscribed in the Japanese language, since the word meaning to improve or to perfect, *migaku*, also means to polish or to rub. The patina on a bronze or the wear on a tea bowl will increase their value, as well might other sorts of imperfections or damage. Similar effects are also evident in architecture, as in the final coat of plaster that covers the interior of a *kura* (storehouse), which is traditionally covered with lampblack that is polished first with cloth, then with silk, and finally with the bare hand, to create a surface that appears like black lacquer. Another striking example of such artificially produced *sabi* is an ancient manner of adding lustre to wooden cabinets by polishing them with cloths dipped in used bath water, so as to rub the sebaceous secretions left in the water into the wood.[11] One might say, by analogy, that lichen and moss create the *sabi* of stone, while clouds constitute the *sabi* of the moon, and fog that of the mountains, adding to their beauty. *Sabi* consequently denotes a sense of familiarity, continuity, history, antiquity, and connotes a corresponding sense of passing and loss, loneliness and melancholy. By extrapolation, in its extreme instances, it evokes bleakness, chilliness, dessication, desolation, extinction.[12] *Shibui*, literally meaning astringency,[13] directly informs the representational modalities of the arts related to tea, denoting understatement, suggestion, restraint, modesty, discrimination, formality, serenity, quiet taste, refined simplicity, noble austerity. D. T. Suzuki goes so far as to claim that, 'in some ways, *wabi* is *sabi* and *sabi* is *wabi*; they are interchangeable terms', ultimately subsuming the formal into the spiritual, such that *wabi*, *sabi* and *shibui* are inextricably intertwined.[14] Beauty in Zen culture signifies an appreciation that spontaneously and intuitively incorporates all that is implied by these three terms. To interiorize these qualities is to approach a state of mind that can appreciate all Zen-inspired traditional Japanese art.[15]

The tea ceremony, circumscribed by centuries of ritualized gesture and iconographic codification, fundamentally seeks a state of mind guided by *wabi-sabi*, such that the material culture of Zen offers an allegory of its spiritual culture. That said, there seems to be no systematic correlation between aesthetics and enlightenment.[16] Tea is thus simultaneously an appreciation of material culture and a spiritual quest, all at once proffering an aesthetics, an ethics and an epistemology. Tea is both an artistic and a social event, each ceremony being a once-in-a-lifetime gathering – *ichigo ichie* (one time, one meeting) – seeking a harmony based on the mutual aesthetic proclivities of the host and guest. The gathering takes place in a tranquil abode, a sort of microcosm isolated from the world of everyday cares, where a sense of absolute equality and propriety reigns, established according to the basic precepts of harmony, respect, purity, tranquillity (*wa kei sei jaku*) – qualities otherwise expressed as reserve, reverence, restraint – which guide all considerations of beauty. D. T. Suzuki explains that these principles of harmony and reverence stem from Confucianism, purity from Taoism and Shintoism, and tranquillity from Taoism and Buddhism, which suggests that the global appeal of the tea ceremony in Japan might in part derive from its highly syncretic nature.[17] In the West, a dinner party may indeed turn out to be a 'once-in-a-lifetime' experience, but this is usually judged retrospectively, the sign of a particularly successful event whose transitory nature is bemoaned. In Japan, this sentiment of uniqueness is prospective, a goal rather than a result, where the transitory is cultivated and celebrated. This is accomplished by means of the thematic organization of the event, such that the sundry objects of the ceremony – the tea utensils such as the bowl, caddy, water basin and brazier; the flower arrangement, scroll painting or calligraphed poem (until the late nineteenth century, mainly writings by Chinese or Japanese Zen monks were so displayed); and the *kaiseki* meal that precedes the ceremony – all subtly allude to a particular theme and a specific season. Since the tea room is a place of heightened concentration, codified ritual, exquisite manners and refined aesthetics, the tea ceremony has a direct influence on the production and appreciation of art objects. Richard L. Wilson explains that 'in Japan, the art object is perceived not as autonomous, but as an inseparable part of a historical and social nexus. "Intrinsic" qualities of beauty or genuineness are secondary in importance to the authority of past and present owners and admirers.'[18] The ceremonial suitability of things, both artificial and natural, is as important as their intrinsic beauty, provenance, rarity. The beauty of an object is inseparable from the history of its use, and each tea ceremony deepens that history. Such is an aesthetic of use value in many senses of the term, from the primacy of functional objects to the centrality of gesture and the importance of ownership. Material culture here obtains a profound dimension.[19]

   Established in response to the luxury, magnificence, extravagance and ostentation of previous Chinese-inspired forms of tea favoured by the imperial court, the *wabi-sabi* aesthetic stresses the perfection of the utmost simplicity, the ideal being that of the hermit's hut in the mountains, a sensibility in line with the military austerity of the warlords who took power in the sixteenth century. Both aesthetics and connoisseurship in Japan are informed by these complex existential and conceptual matrixes, and Louise Allison Cort goes so far as to say that 'the *wabi* ceremony has claimed the Japanese imagination with a power that far outlasted its period of vitality. It has permanently affected the way in which Japanese think about material objects.'[20] Here, issues of authority, value and beauty refer to the originary moment – often fictively elaborated to the point of passing from history to myth – when the collaboration between Rikyū and Chōjirō (*d.* 1592), the founder of the Raku line of potters, established what have become the exemplary forms of both the ceremony and the tea bowl (*chawan*). According to Cort:

> Whereas appreciation of Chinese masterpieces of acknowledged value had been a largely passive activity, the selection of native Japanese pots, as well as more modest imported goods – Korean bowls and *namban* jars – presented an active challenge to the individual imagination. Each tea man's assemblage of utensils was a personal statement of taste. The role of the great tea masters – Jukō, Jō-ō, and Rikyū – was to discover and establish new possibilities for utensil types. Their experimental assemblages became the models that guided their students.[21]

Sen no Rikyū desired a uniquely Japanese pottery appropriate for the new form of the tea ceremony that he established so as both to escape from Chinese influences and counteract the growing ostentation that soon began to characterize tea under the regent Hideyoshi.[22] Following Jukō (Shukō), who sought out the indigenous and austere works from the Bizen and Shigaraki kilns in contrast to classic Chinese types, Rikyū worked, according to legend, with Chōjirō to develop an original form of pottery of the greatest simplicity, the subtlest irregularity, the most austere rusticity. Not only did this collaboration revolutionize the art of pottery, but it also transformed the very mode of connoisseurship and set a new aesthetic paradigm, since tea bowls would now be made, at least in part, according to the specifications of the tea master. Henceforth, creative intuition, rather than rote erudition, would guide the production and use of tea vessels. This shift from tradition to invention,

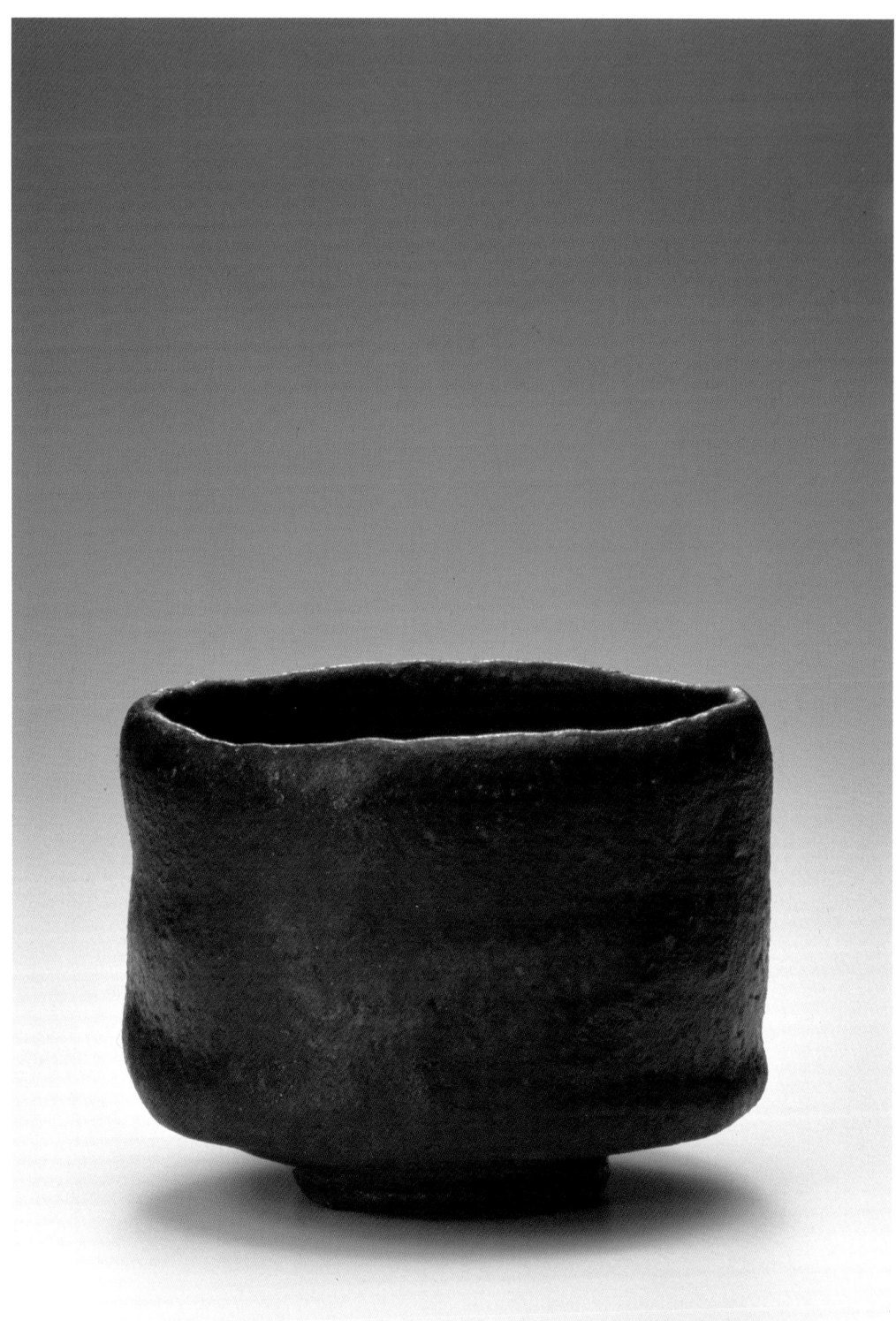

Chōjirō, Raku *chawan* named *Omokage* ('Profile'), late 16th century.

from a form of connoisseurship that was an erudite appreciation of an ancient foreign taste to one that foregrounded indigenous creativity, had both political and aesthetic implications, since it was a radically new source of wealth, power, beauty and knowledge. The rise of the centralized state concentrated power in the regent, with the sole exception of aesthetic judgement, which was the domain of the tea masters. This is doubtlessly the main reason for Rikyū's tragic fall: not only was he guilty of lèse-majesté, profiteering from the pottery trade and court intrigues, but the very essence of his activity as tea master and aesthetic counsellor of the new form of tea placed him in direct and profound conflict with Hideyoshi, who could not countenance Rikyū's aesthetic superiority. Rikyū revolutionized aesthetics by situating the discernment of beauty within the realm of immanence, such that the tea master's taste became the absolute arbiter of aesthetic value. Connoisseurship was transformed into a veritable creative act. It has remained such to this day.

TALES OF ORIGINS are useful in focusing on a specific issue and setting a specific paradigm, though we have long been wary of such myths and their ideological implications. However, it is not only the spuriousness of origins, but also the very intricacy of time itself, that complicates such research. This is a fortiori the case concerning landscape and gardens. The land artist Robert Smithson once famously claimed: 'You know, one pebble moving one foot in two million years is enough action to keep me really excited', an excellent reminder of the radical temporal differences separating the human and natural orders.[23] And even this pace is extremely rapid, if one considers the span of aeons (*kalpa*) in Buddhist and Hindu theology, where the largest unit of measurement is the great *kalpa*, lasting 1.28 trillion years, which may be visualized as longer than the time it takes a mountain of approximately 2,000 cubic miles – much greater than Mount Everest – to be completely worn down if every 100 years it is wiped once with a small piece of silk, or, in a more poetic formulation, the time it takes a rock brushed by an angel's wing every three years to wear away. In a less hyperbolic context, it must be stressed that anachronism is at the core of chronology and iconography, of symbolism and narrative.[24] That a garden element endures while everything surrounding it changes hardly makes of it an isolated, stable object. What appears as unequivocal presence is always a palimpsest of effects and forms, causes and effects, reality and myth, a dense web of significations and temporalities well beyond conscious comprehension and historical determination. One need only establish the chronology of each major detail of a garden to discover the site's complex and anachronistic structures. Or perhaps it would be more precise to use the term 'polychronistic' to describe better such relations. Of all art forms, gardens are most susceptible to the ravages of time, especially as their temporality is so finely, and often brutally, attuned to season and climate, history and catastrophe. All gardens must be considered according to their sundry, and often contradictory, transformations, such that the reality of any garden is one of complex, overlapping and often anachronistic temporalities.

Landscape history has long suffered from what I would call the 'curse of Hegel': due to their materiality and heterogeneity, gardens were relegated to the bottom of the hierarchy in this classical aesthetic system. However, in our contemporary post-postmodern moment, these are the very characteristics that make the garden a privileged site, where time is felt in its palpable presence. The changes wrought by time have both natural and artificial causes. The Princesse Palatine observed that during the reign of Louis XIV there was no place at Versailles that had not been modified ten times, stressing the rapidity of artificial change suffered by these gardens. Natural changes may be more immediate and catastrophic, or more subtle and considerably slower, such that we must consider the particular importance of extra-human timescales in Zen gardens, not only concerning the imperceptible growth and apparent stability of lichen, so intimately associated with lithic existence, but also the very formation of rocks themselves. The temporality of gardens is extremely complex, operating on several levels: natural, phenomenological, iconographic, historical. One must consider the very different time frames of daily and seasonal cycles, the changing light and meteorological conditions, the slowly growing moss, the even more slowly crumbling stone, and the hands of gardeners, whether they be creative or destructive.

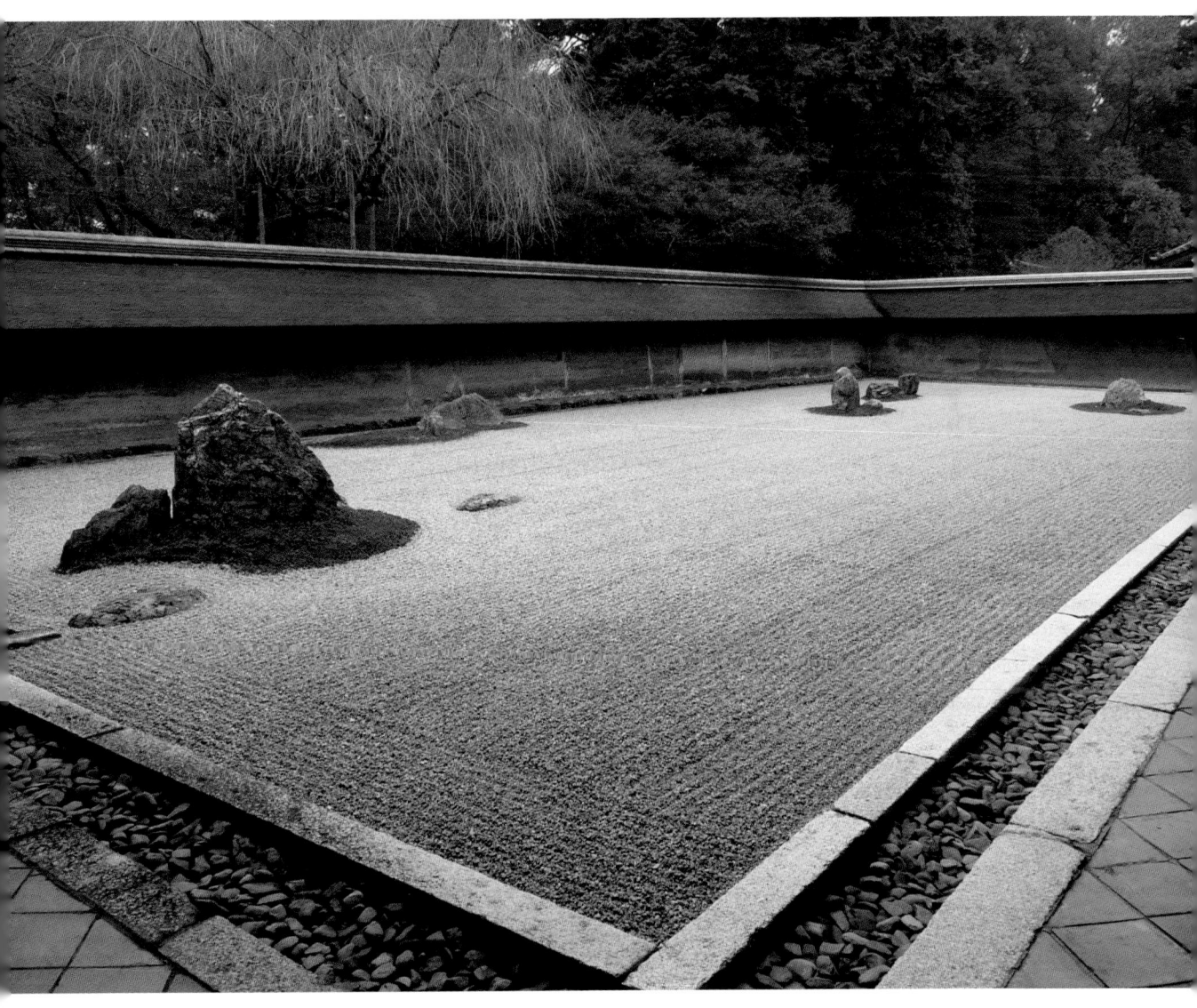

Ryōan-ji.

Kamigamo Shrine,
sand cones.

Ryōan-ji is a hyperbolic example of such perpetual and exceedingly slow transformation. Along with Versailles, Ryōan-ji is the most written about garden in the world: it would take an encyclopedia to chart out all its historical, formal and iconographic features. Mention of just a few of the salient moments will give a sense of the extraordinary richness of the garden's history and symbolism, and serve as a corrective to those many readings that simply stress purity, abstraction and emptiness. Not merely a religious and aesthetic site, Ryōan-ji (literally, Temple of the Peaceful Dragon) is also an icon suggesting ancient myths, an aid to contemplation, an image of utopia, a touristic distraction, a commercial enterprise, a site of power, a nexus of belief. In Japan, iconography is often complicated by the

Ryōan-ji.

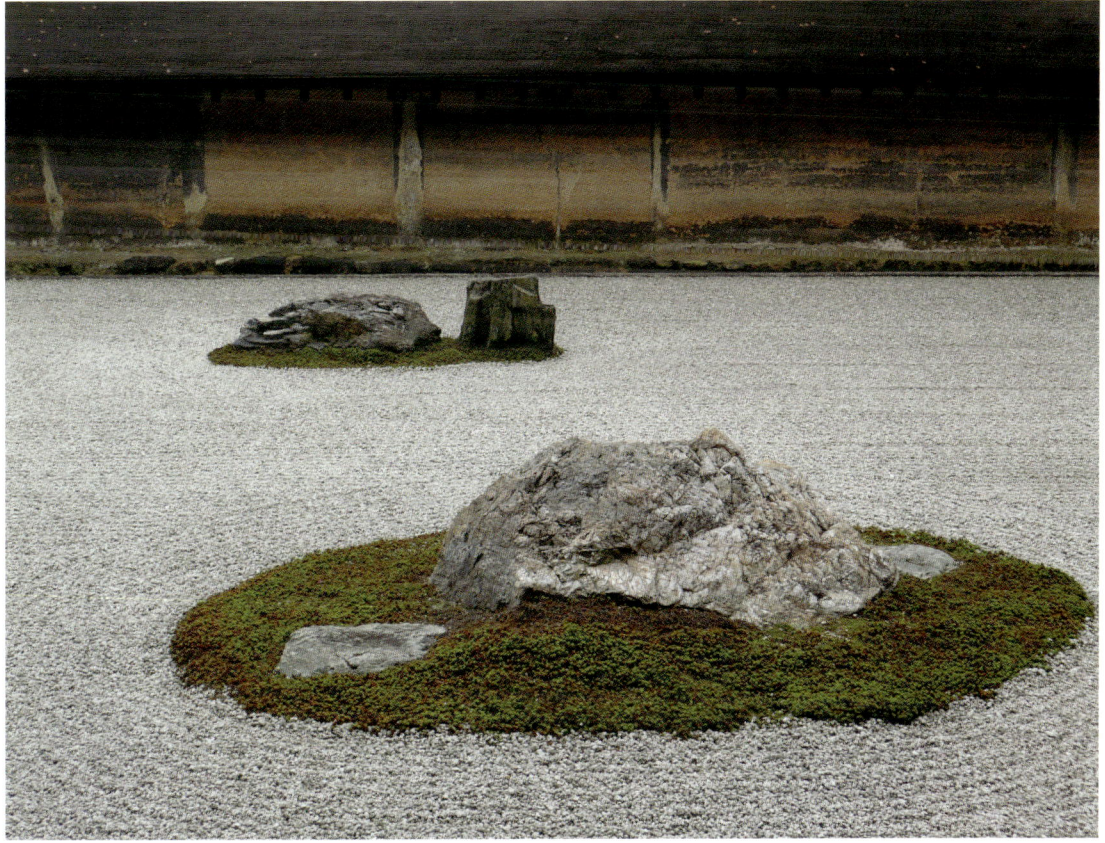

permeability between Shinto and Buddhism, between the various forms of Buddhism (for example, Pure Land, Five Mountains and Zen), and between the various schools of Zen (such as Rinzai Zen and Sōtō Zen). The iconography of the dry Zen garden is thus highly syncretic, and is hardly limited to the unrepresentable intuitions of Rinzai Zen that had become so important to Western artists in the second half of the twentieth century.

Given the longstanding and extreme syncretism of Shinto and Buddhism, one might surmise that the expanses of bare raked gravel in Zen gardens are derived from the empty sacred spaces of Shinto sanctuaries with their beds of gravel, piles of stones, sacred rocks and cones of sand, while the scenic rock formations have their distant origins in the utopias of Chinese Buddhism, often inspired by the specific Chinese landscapes refined in Song epoch (960–1279) painting. The influence of Chinese iconography is further complicated by three minor but fascinating curiosities: scholars' stones, dream stones and what the Japanese term *suiseki* (water stones). Scholars' stones, also known in the West as 'viewing stones', are called *qishi* or *yishi* in Chinese, which means 'fantastic rocks', names that carry connotations of the unusual, strange, wonderful, special. Like their larger homologues found in Chinese landscape gardens, they are often sculpted (unlike Japanese rocks, which are nearly always left in their natural state) to resemble the most extraordinary mountains of China, famously represented in painting and poetry. The stones, set on elaborate wooden bases and placed amidst the accoutrements on a writing table, are held in great esteem among Chinese scholars and collectors.[25] Dream stones, what the French term *pierres paysagées*, are rocks whose cross-sections reveal fantastic landscapes, on the cusp between abstraction and figuration. *Suiseki* are pebbles or small stones that evoke entire landscapes, selected according to the tenets of the *wabi-sabi-shibui* aesthetic, and mounted on fitted bases or even combined with bonsai. They are valued precisely for their representational associations, and their categorization (by shape, colour and surface pattern) recalls that of the much larger stones set in dry gardens: mountain stones, waterfall stones, island stones, shore stones and so on.[26] Yet in all cases, whether miniature or natural, the landscape has both practical value as a site for seclusion, solitude, meditation and the escape from

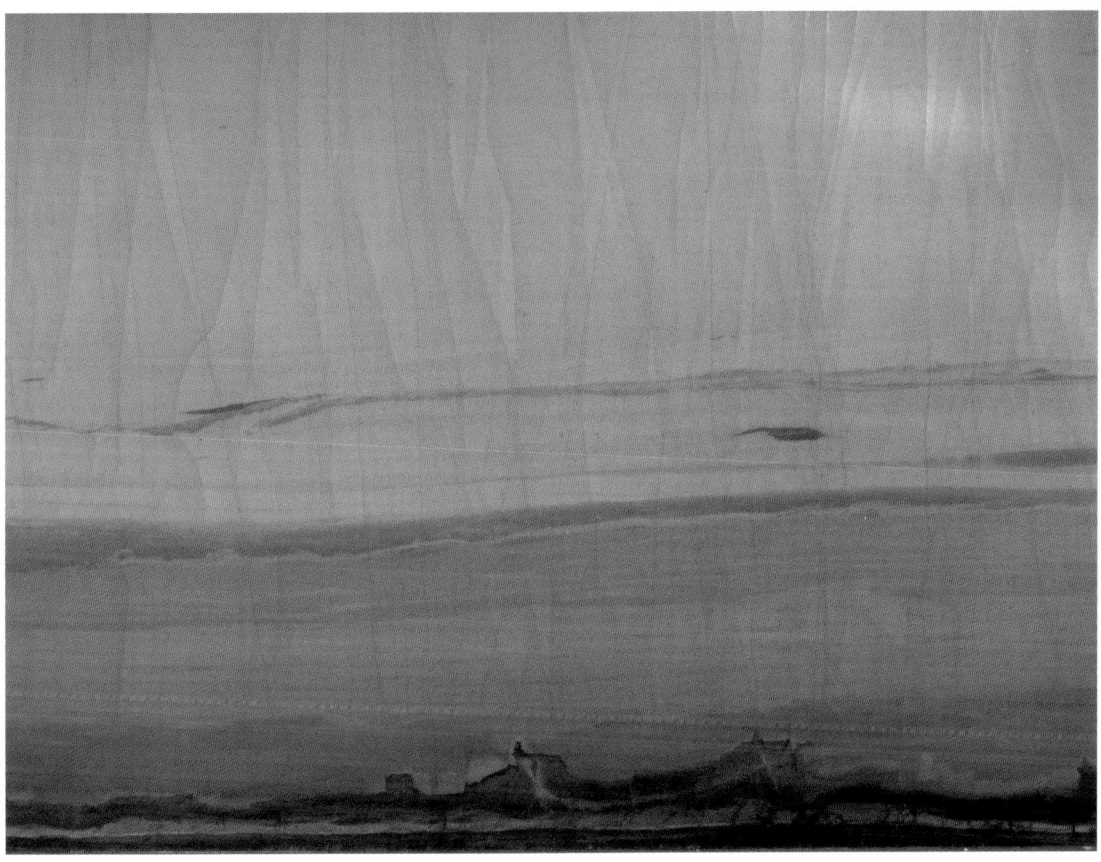

Dream stone.

mundane and courtly existence – a reclusion symbolized by the solitary hermit's hut – and a deep symbolic value, especially concerning mountains, as the realm of loftiness, transcendence and freedom, as well as of ghosts and spirits. Furthermore, as Joseph D. Parker explains, 'since it was not the exclusive domain of any particular religious, philosophical, or literary school, writing about the landscape was one site for the proliferation of various syncretic integrations of different intellectual traditions.'[27] Much the same might be said for the appreciation of landscape in all its manifestations, such as in gardens, poetry and pottery.

The stones of Ryōan-ji can benefit from such comparisons, which greatly complicate and enrich the interpretation of the garden. For example,

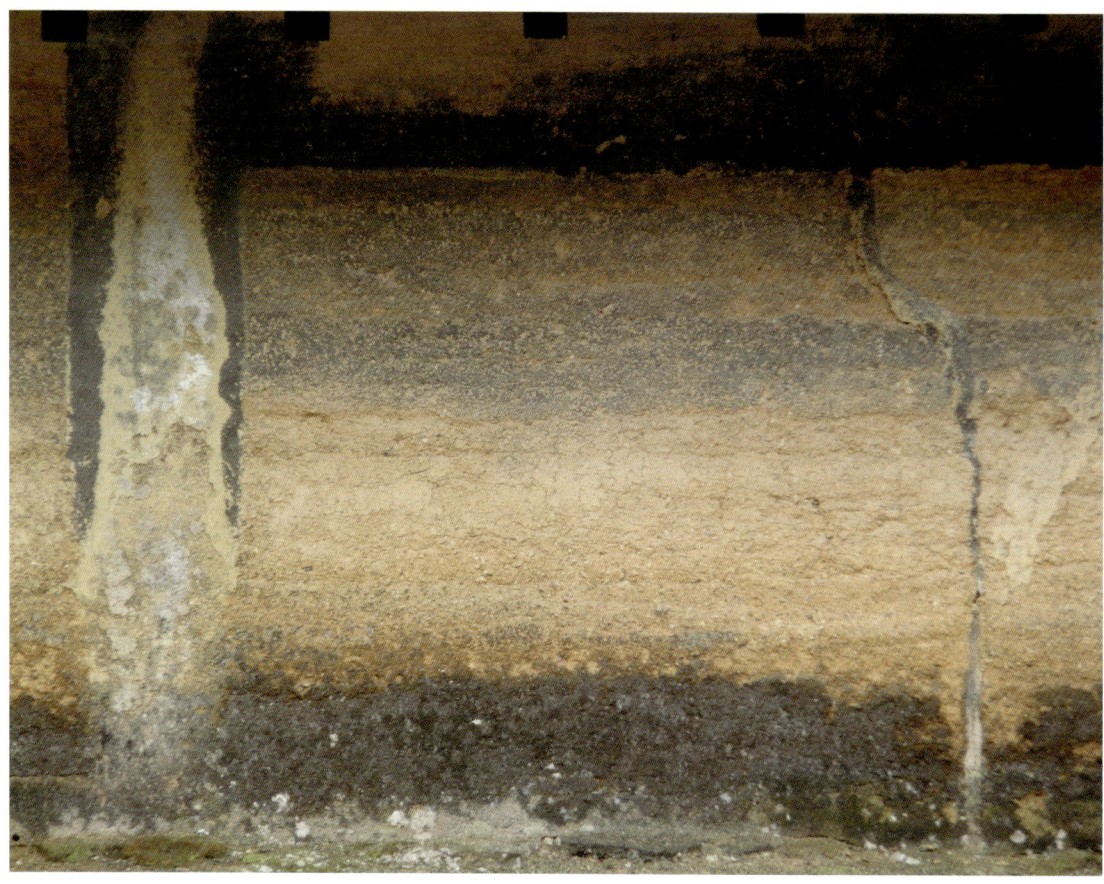

consideration of the aesthetics of dream stones might well inform the appreciation of the astonishing *aburabei*-style walls, made of clay steeped in oil, that surround the dry garden of Ryōan-ji and establish its cloistered space. Nearly all discussions of Ryōan-ji focus almost exclusively on its rock arrangements, and rarely is mention made of the walls, themselves national treasures, that surround the dry garden. Centuries of weathering have caused the oil to seep out in irregular mottled patterns, which along with a palimpsest of repairs makes these walls reminiscent of dream stones or, to make a more contemporary comparison, resemble certain paintings by Clyfford Still. But perhaps a more fundamental resemblance, in the Japanese context, is the distinct similarity to patterns on certain types of high-fired Bizen pottery. For what, after all, are these walls but a form of pottery, clay baked and aged by the sun, albeit rarely recognized as such? These walls are veritable lessons in Japanese aesthetics, instantiating the subtle relations

Ryōan-ji, detail of *aburabei* wall.

between figuration and abstraction, determinacy and indeterminacy, wilfulness and serendipity, denotation and connotation, revelation and suggestion. The walls of Ryōan-ji emblematize the slow, ever-changing effects of the weather over centuries, in stark contrast to the melancholy effects of instantaneous and ephemeral events. These walls constitute the irregular background against which appear the well-ordered forms of the garden, the chaotic ground of the sublime intuition.

Ryōan-ji provides perhaps the most extraordinary example of such aleatory art, but close examination reveals similar phenomena in many Kyoto temples. Another beautiful example exists at the little-known Saishō-in, a subtemple of Nanzen-ji, where the walls, set in a mountain gorge and thus subjected to extreme humidity, have been allowed to develop a thick coating of moss and lichen that has taken on fascinating patterns. Though not a catalogued treasure, nor even an indicated tourist attraction, the fact that this

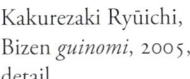

Kakurezaki Ryūichi, Bizen *guinomi*, 2005, detail.

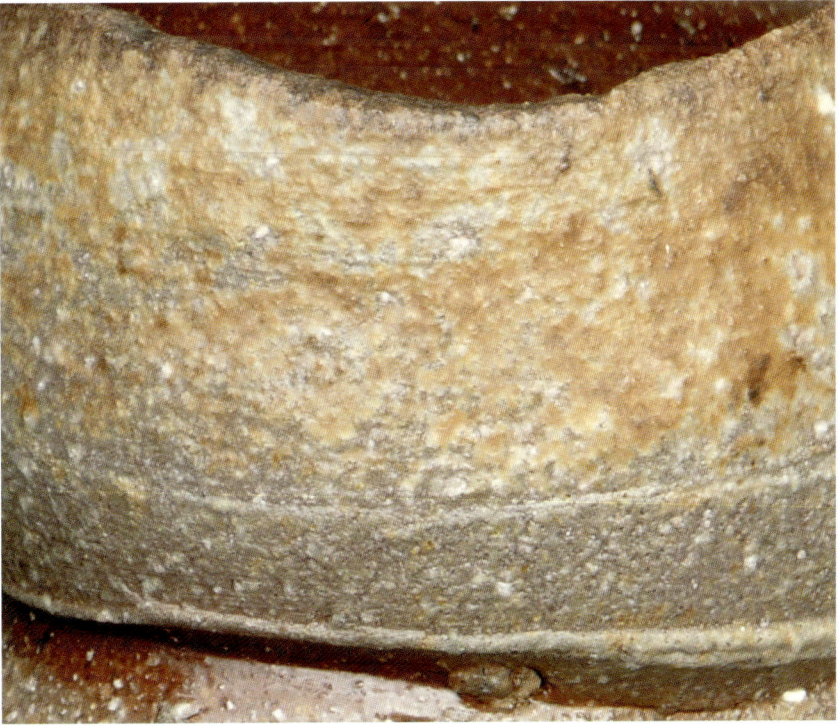

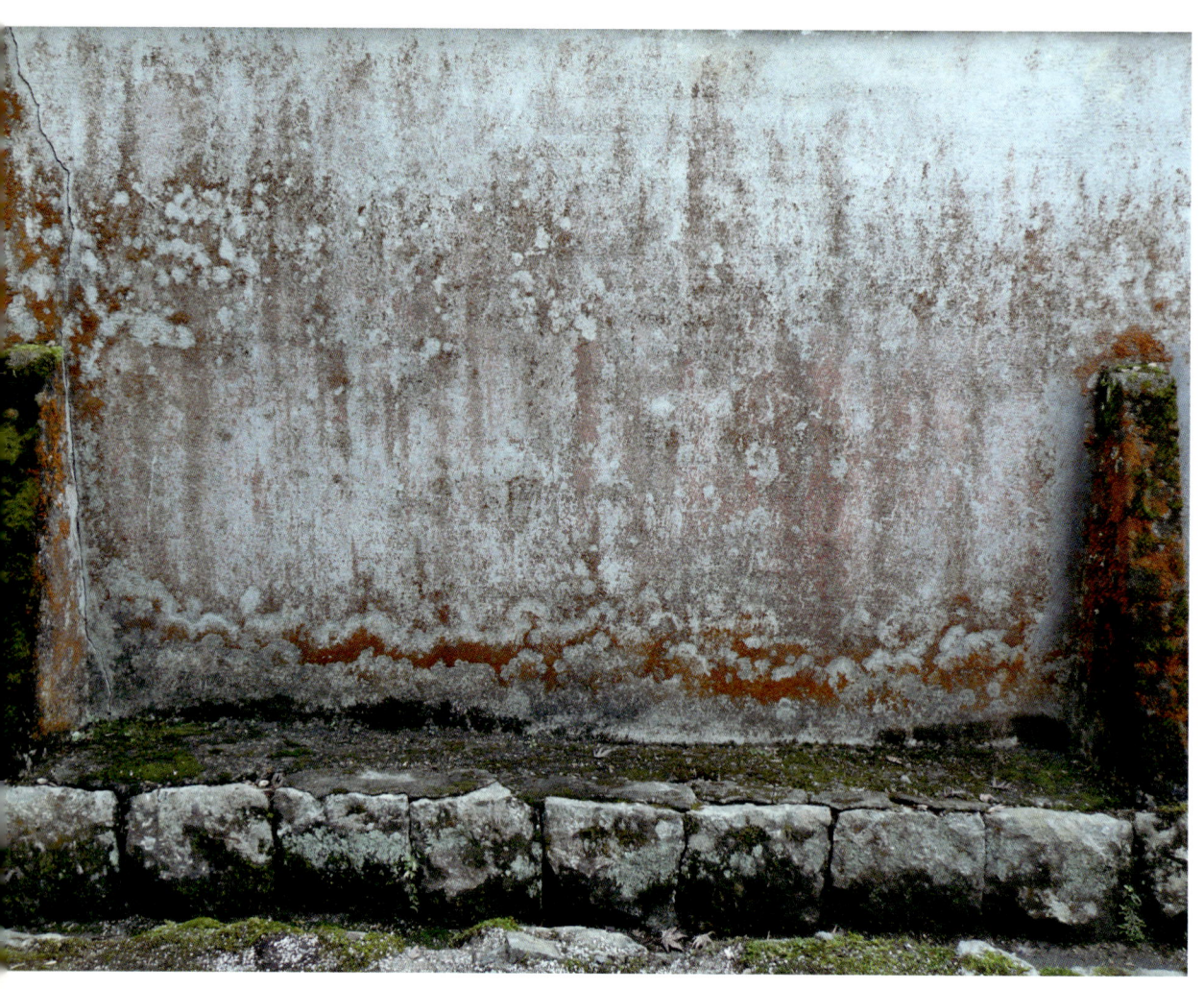

Saishō-in, a subtemple of Nanzen-ji, detail of wall weathering and lichen.

wall has not been renovated for many years attests to its aesthetic interest. Such effects, though rarely noted, are apparently treasured and can be found in many temples and residences. For example, consider certain stains on walls at Eikan-dō that resemble a form of Karatsu glaze derived from Choson (Korean) pottery, or several striking instances on the grounds of the Kyoto house of the landscape architect Shigemori Mirei. One would have to deduce that, given the cultural and theological compulsion to order, cleanliness and purity that generally reigns in Japanese society and even more specifically in Shinto and Buddhist culture – where cleanliness is a metaphor for enlighten-ment – all sorts of apparent degradation when left untouched might well be considered wilful aesthetic effects.

But not all essential transformations are natural. Gardens, one must remember, are not only perpetually tended, but also often replanted and occasionally completely transformed. The dry garden of Ryōan-ji has often been transformed by the human hand, though it would be practically impossible to determine how many times and in what manner. For example, Japanese temples, which in any case are renovated at regular intervals, are notoriously fire prone. The original abbot's quarters at Ryōan-ji burned down in 1797, and the building that now occupies the site is actually the abbot's quarters from Seigen-in, a subtemple of Ryōan-ji built in 1606 and moved, along with its paintings, as a replacement after the fire. The building is thus an architectural anachronism, indeed a discrepancy, in relation to the garden, created around 1499. Furthermore, if one were to believe old woodblocks, at certain moments in its history visitors were allowed to stroll *within* the dry garden, something we can hardly imagine today. The sixteenth-generation Kyoto gardener Sāno Touemon remembers playing among the stones in the dry garden of Ryōan-ji as a child before the Second World War. While this speaks more to modern neglect than aesthetic transformation, it nevertheless indicates the constantly changing aesthetics, use value and fame of the garden.[28] One might also wonder whether moss was always present, or how often overhanging branches were permitted to trouble the straight line of the walls, or whether the sand was always raked, and if the patterns have changed, as certain woodblocks seem to suggest. The other gardens surrounding the

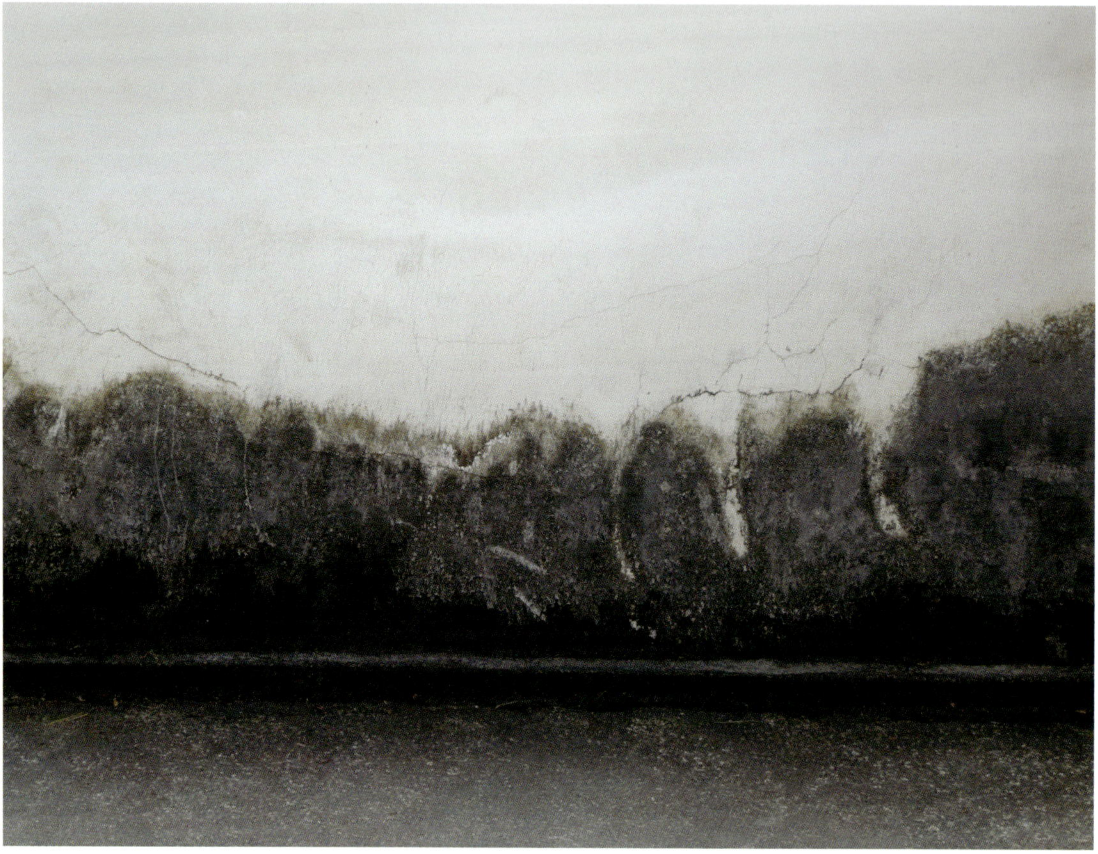

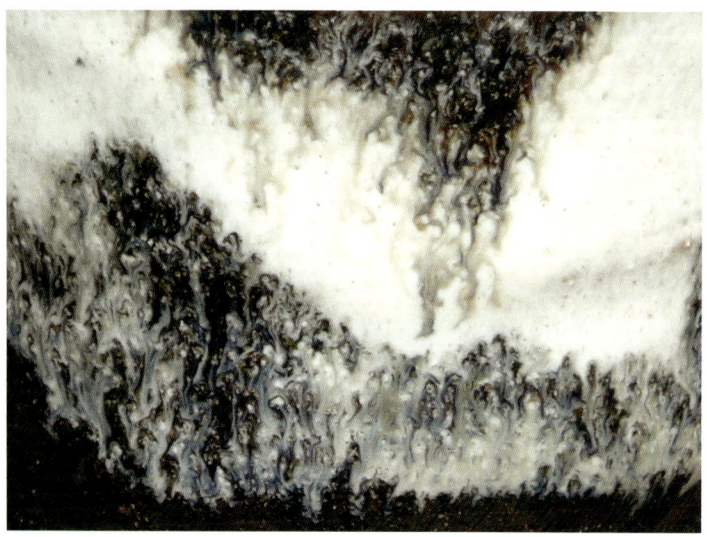

Eikan-dō, detail of wall
weathering.

Koie Ryōji, Choson
Karatsu *guinomi*,
2010, detail.

Shigemori Mirei house,
Kyoto, detail of
pavement weathering.

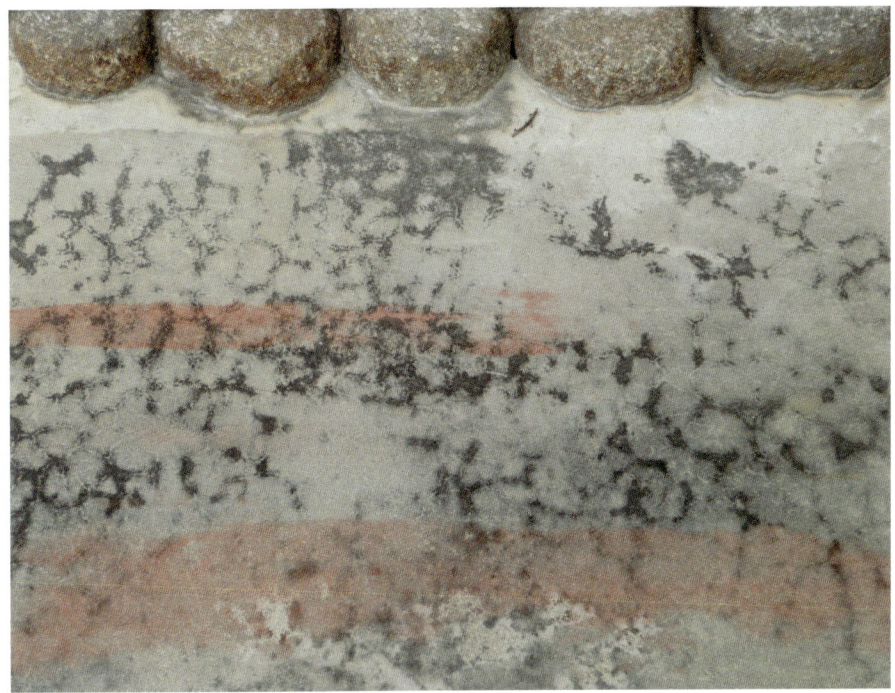

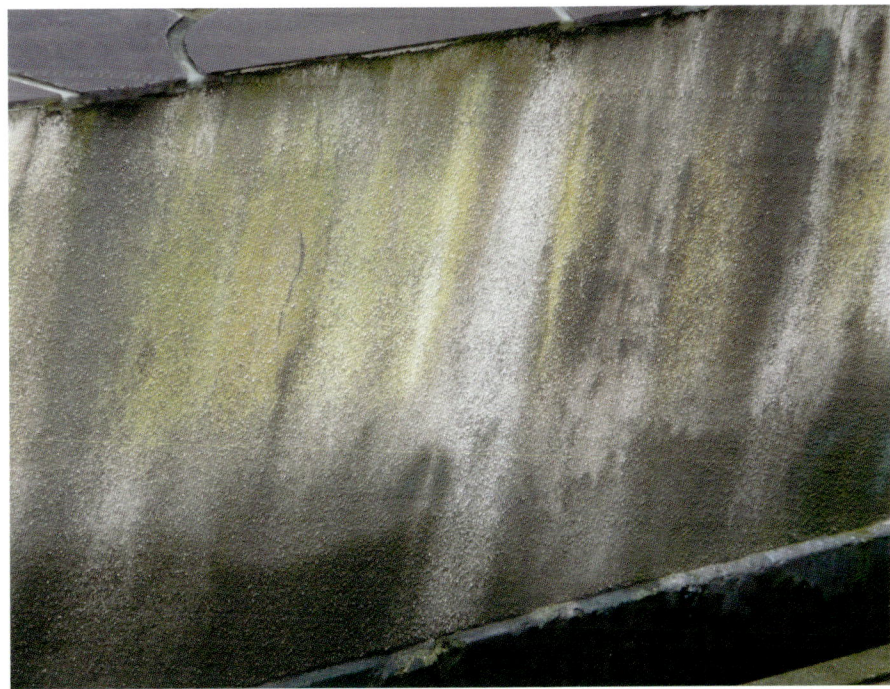

Matsuo Shrine, detail
of wall weathering.

abbot's quarters at Ryōan-ji have also often been transformed, but in fact the fame of the dry garden has so eclipsed the other parts of the site that the contiguous gardens on the other three sides of the temple building – a moss garden, a stone and moss garden and a pond that gives on to the tea house – are practically never analysed in studies of the temple.

But one change above all should hold our attention, especially since it has been generally neglected in Western studies of the dry garden. Concurrent with the political and social watershed following Oda Nobunaga's unification of Japan in the late sixteenth century, specific iconographic transformations celebrated the cultural achievements of the samurai, the new protectors of the monks.[29] The universal fame of Ryōan-ji is certainly in part due to its role as a symbol of the apogee of Japan's glory, just as the fame of Versailles endures as a hyperbolic expression of national unification, courtly splendour and divine royalty. Most important in these considerations of historicity and aesthetic anachronism is the fact that the iconography at Ryōan-ji was completely changed in 1606, when the sedate monochrome ink paintings of landscape, bird and flower motifs were replaced by extravagant, brightly coloured, gold-leaf-backed scenes of the Eight Immortals revered in Taoism. While the abbot's private quarters still housed the old monochromatic-style paintings, suggesting a theological continuity with more ancient forms, the new polychrome works exhibited in the ceremonial rooms catered to a radically different mentality, that of the considerably more ostentatious taste of the warlords. Temple paintings no longer served only as aids to solitary meditation but also became ornate elements of festive luxury. A new symbiosis developed between the sacred and secular worlds, exemplified by the tea ceremony and poetry readings. In this period when class barriers loosened such that aristocrats, samurai, priests and artists intermingled for the first time, the new polychrome style was prominently displayed in the public areas of the temple facing the dry garden, the site where the interchange between public and private, political and priestly, was most intense. Curator Onishi Hiroshi remarks:

> Thus Ryoanji's *shicchu* [the ceremonial room of the abbot's quarters]
> – very likely the first to have Chinese narrative themes in gold leaf –
> marks the culmination of a dialectical exchange between Zen monks
> and samurai patrons. The samurai leaders took over and remade images
> already prominent in Zen culture, while the Zen monks transformed
> their religious space as samurai influence flowed back into the Zen
> milieu.[30]

In this context of radical political and aesthetic transformation, the meditative, aesthetic and ceremonial use value of the dry garden could not have remained unchanged.

Dry gardens generally face a set of sliding wall panels (*fusuma*) in the temple rooms opposite them, panels that are often painted. In several famous instances, the iconography of the panels and the forms of the garden are homologous. A famous example is that of Jukō-in (a subtemple of Daitoku-ji). The stone arrangements of the main temple garden are strikingly similar to those in the painting by a follower of Kanō Eitoku (1543–1590), *Birds and Flowers of the Four Seasons,* set directly opposite the garden of the main hall of the abbot's quarters, called the Hyaku Seki no Niwa (Garden of the Hundred Stones). In fact, this work was painted in 1583, the year that Sen no Rikyū designed the garden facing the painting in collaboration with Kanō Eitoku, who made the preparatory sketches. Painting and garden are of a piece. In other instances, the rock arrangements in a garden may represent the exterior landscape, as is the case in Shinnyo-dō, where the silhouette of the garden's main stone arrangement almost exactly resembles the outline of the peak of Daimonjiyama, the highest mountain in the Higashiyama range of eastern Kyoto, framed in the garden by a captured view (*shakkei*). In the case of Ryōan-ji, the relation between such painted images and the gardens opposite them is almost never discussed, probably because the paintings disappeared long ago, having been removed from the temple and sold in 1895, during the time of the Meiji persecution of Buddhism, and only recently coming to light. These paintings, placed in the three rooms facing the garden (the public entrance, ceremonial room and patron's room),

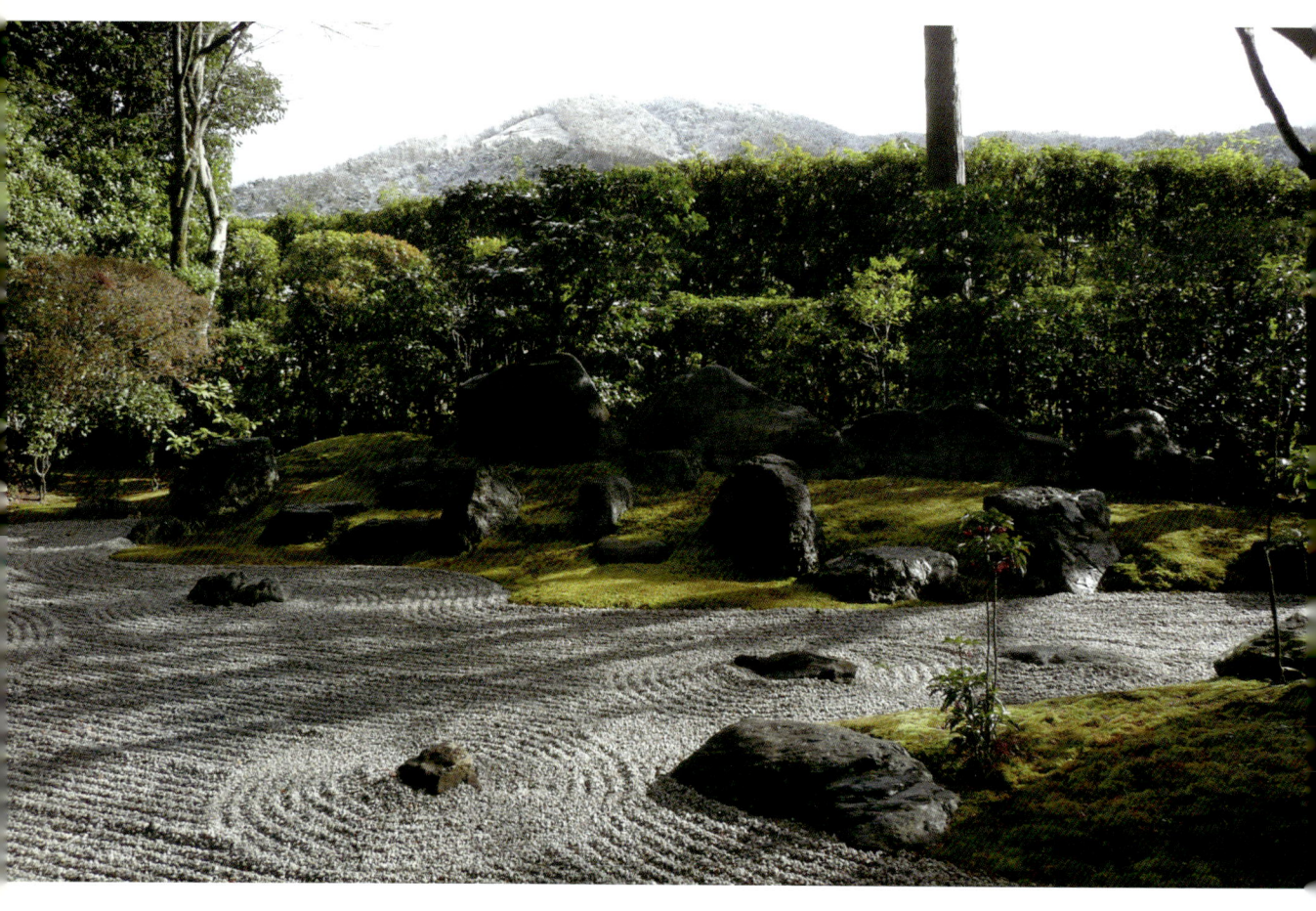

Shinnyo-dō, captured view of Daimonjiyama.

respectively represent motifs of *Tiger and Bamboo*, *The Chinese Immortals* and *The Four Elegant Accomplishments*. The relation of their iconography to the dry garden that preceded them is beyond the scope of this chapter, but it would be imprudent to assume that the meaning and use value of the garden remained unchanged faced with the radical iconographic shifts accompanying the political and social watershed following the unification of Japan. The jagged, irregular rock formations on the screens and in the garden are strikingly similar, and the empty gold background depicted in these paintings is aesthetically congruent with the empty fields of raked sand in the dry garden. Both scenes are supernatural, and thus obey different laws from those of the natural and human world. Insofar as this new iconography represents the idealized, utopian landscapes of the Chinese immortals, might not the garden be phantasmatically imbued with such utopian scenography, antithetical to the void that it so often represents in current interpretations influenced by Rinzai Zen?

This iconographic shift, as it reflects the groundbreaking social changes of the epoch, is not incidental to the garden, but essential to its very meaning. Even the most cursory examination reveals distinct similarities between the lithic outcrops depicted in these paintings and the stone formations in the dry garden of Ryōan-ji, suggesting that both are not mere flights of the artistic imagination, but rather creations informed by the lineage of a fully developed iconography. These correspondences are of prime interest, whether such images were contemporaneous with the creation of the garden as at Jūkō-in, or followed it as at Ryōan-ji. That a rock fresh from the Kamo River near Kyoto could represent an ancient Chinese utopia is not a sign of ideological misrepresentation, but rather of the profound richness of symbols, the syncretism of cultures and the labyrinthine meanderings of history. To neglect such correspondences is to misrepresent ideology and to falsify history. Such complexity, contradiction and paradox is typical of Zen gardens, which – even if radically different from the *roji* (dewy path) gardens created to lead to tea huts – fully partake in the aesthetic complexities of the Zen-inspired tea ceremony. As we know, Zen thrives on such paradoxes. These historical and cultural layers relate Ryōan-ji to a theological paradox, the terms of

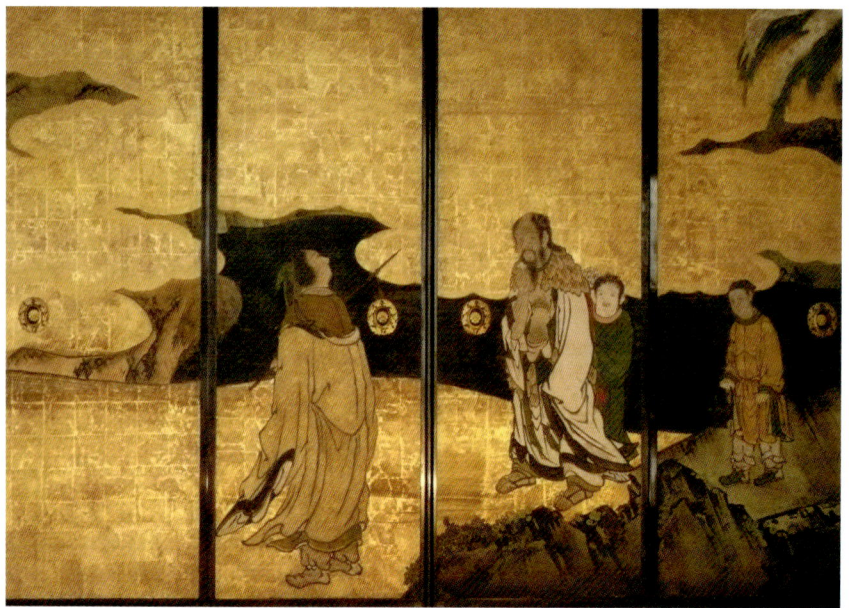

Circle of Kanō Eitoku, scene (left) and detail (opposite) from *Chinese Immortals*, c. 1606, Ryōan-ji.

which are a hieratic utopian iconography and a mystical naturalist iconoclasm, enriched by several strands of Buddhism, notably that of the Rinzai, Five Mountain and Pure Land schools, as well as Shintoism, Taoism and Conficianism somewhere in the mix.[31] Extreme syncretism is enriched by radical anachronism.

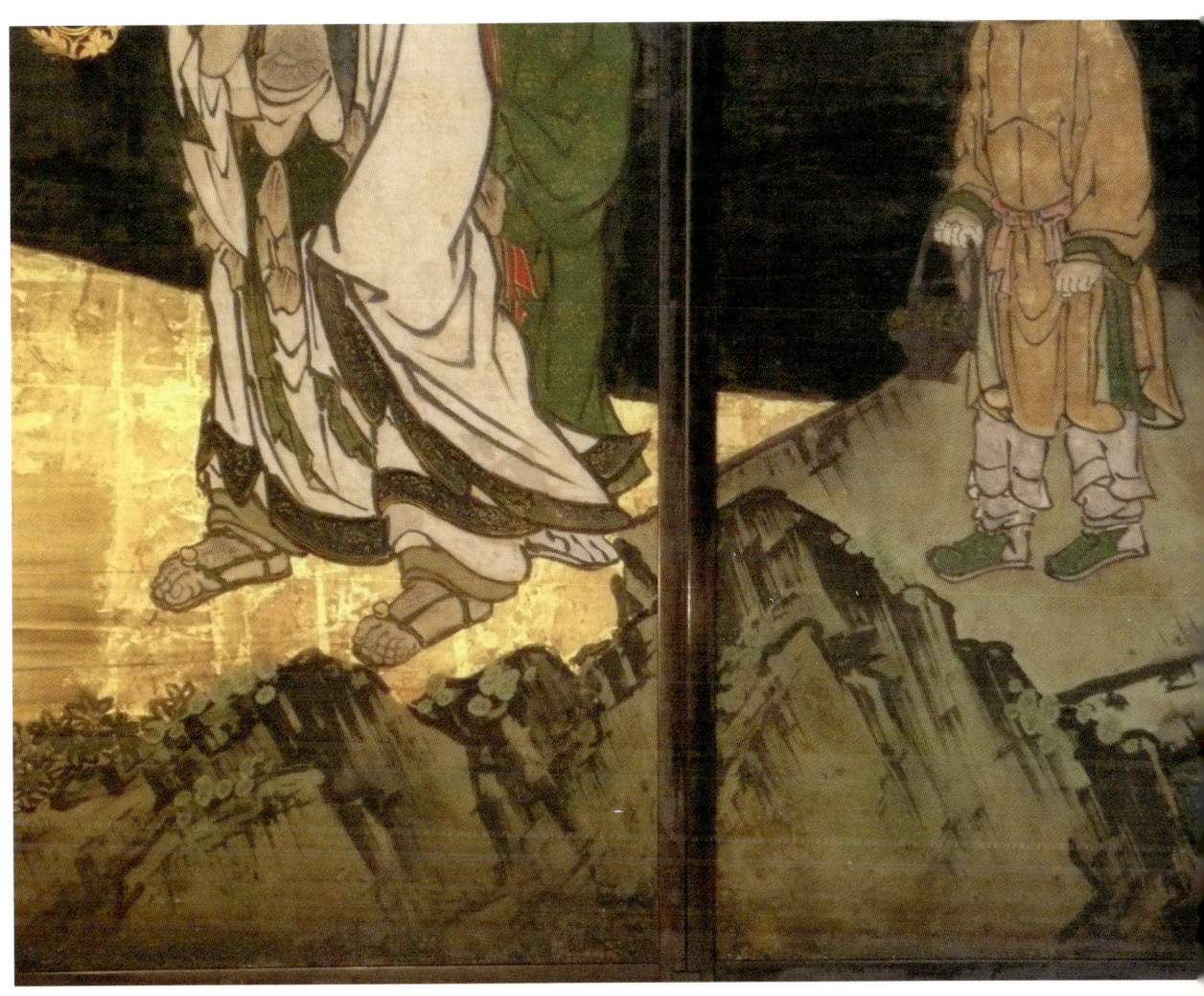

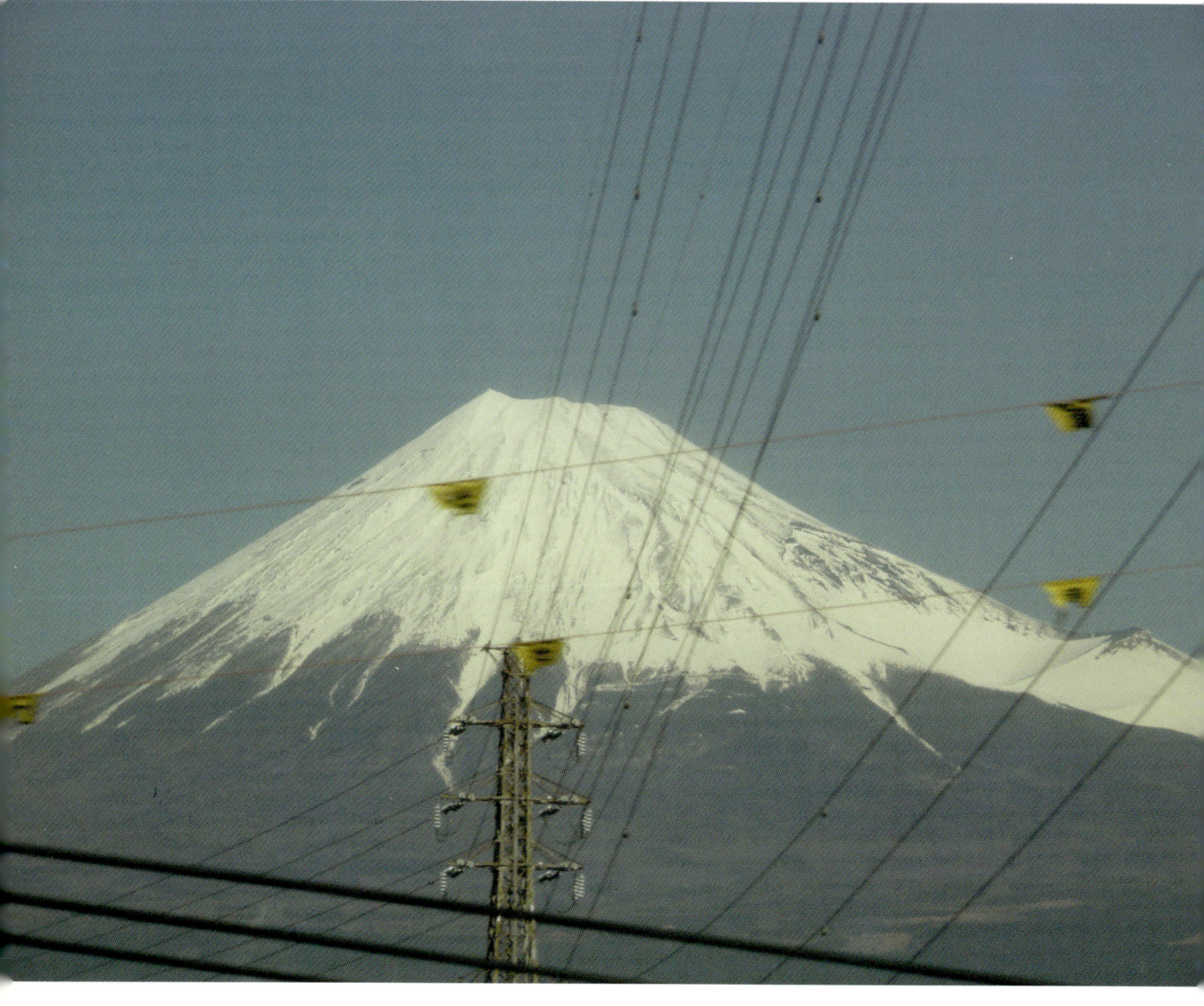

Fujisan.

ONE

TRANSIENT SYMBOLS

One of the classic Japanese tales adapted by the Noh theatre, *Ugetsu*, concerns the itinerant poet and monk Saigyō (1118–1190). One evening he arrived at a very dilapidated hut with a good part of the roof missing, and requested shelter for the night from the elderly couple who lived there. The man politely refused, explaining that their abode would be unworthy, but the wife, seeing that the traveller was a monk, wished to accommodate him. The problem was that the woman loved the moonlight so much that she did not want the roof repaired so the moonbeams could stream into the house, while the man preferred the patter of the rain and thus desired a suitable roof. As autumn was approaching, the situation became even more serious, since this was not only the best moon-viewing (*o-tsukimi*) season, but also that of the most delectable rains. The couple asked the monk:

> Our humble hut –
> Is it to be thatched, or not to be thatched?

The monk responded by saying that they had just composed a fine, though incomplete poem, in response to which they suggested that if he could complete the poem, they would lodge him, whereupon he proclaimed:

> Is the moonlight to leak?
> Are the showers to putter?
> Our thoughts are divided,
> And this humble hut –
> To be thatched or not to be thatched.

He was invited in, and as the night deepened, the moon advanced and finally entered the house. Soon afterwards they heard the sound of rain on the horizon, only to realize that it was in fact the rustling of leaves – a shower of falling leaves in the moonlight.[1] This poignant tale is a veritable allegory of Zen aesthetics, where paradox (the impossible simultaneity of moon and rain) is resolved by metaphor (leaves as rain).

Bashō, founder of the modern style of haiku, writes of the extreme love of nature among certain Japanese artists: 'Whatever objects he sees are referred to the flowers; whatever thoughts he conceives are related to the moon.'[2] Indeed, many critics claim that one of the most moving, indeed sublime, moments in *The Tale of Genji* is when Genji pays a night-time visit to one of his loves, to find the door ajar and the moonlight streaming in, prefiguring his entrance into the room. D. T. Suzuki beautifully evokes the Japanese love of the moon and its centrality in the Japanese imagination:

> The moonlight singularly attracts the Japanese imagination, and any Japanese who ever aspired to compose a *waka* or a *haiku* would hardly dare leave the moon out. The meteorological conditions of the country have much to do with this. The Japanese are lovers of softness, gentleness, semi-darkness, subtle suggestiveness, and everything in this category. They are not fiercely emotional. While they are occasionally surprised by earthquakes, they like to sit quietly in the moonlight, enveloped in its pale, bluish, soul-consoling rays. They are generally averse to anything glaringly bright and stimulating and too distinctive in its individuality. The moonlight is illuminating enough, but owing to the atmospheric conditions all objects under it appear not too strongly individualized; a certain mystic obscurantism pervades, and this seems to appeal to the Japanese generally.[3]

Though this estimation of the Japanese soul might not be evident while strolling today in Ginza, Tokyo's most prestigious commercial district, or in Shibuya, a forest of neon lights, the lunar attraction is the very essence of the Zen sensibility. Zen has even been defined as 'a finger pointing at the moon', as its eternally waxing and waning glow covers the entire world with a patina of spectral light. One of the classic autumn motifs is the full moon appearing through pampas grass, often seen in paintings and drawings, kimono patterns, decorated screens, lacquerware, pottery and even in food arrangements. For example, *tsukimi-wan* ('appreciating the full moon' soup) is a *dashi* and *shoyu*-based clear soup (kelp and bonito stock; soy sauce), usually served in a black lacquer bowl and garnished with a floating, paper-thin circle of daikon radish or grated yam shaped into a ball, on which are scattered a few bits of mitsuba or some other herb, or perhaps chrysanthemum petals or slivers of vegetable, arranged to look like the moon seen through wild grass. It is said that 'The moon is not pleasing unless partly obscured by a cloud',[4] or else seen through a stand of bamboo, the branches of a pine or, most traditionally, the grasses of autumn. Such eclipsing is emblematic of Japanese aesthetics, from the many screens that divide the space of the traditional house to the mud walls and bamboo fences that circumscribe the space of the Zen garden. This reveals the taste for incompletion and imperfection central to *wabi-sabi* aesthetics.

To say that iconography is codified is to imply that ways of seeing are classified, ordered, methodized, hierarchized, systematized. Such organization of images and perceptions does not limit aesthetic possibilities, but rather opens up many unexpected horizons. It is just as wonderful to learn to see as did the poets and painters in classic times as it is to discover new ways of seeing. No object, natural or artificial, falls outside this aesthetic purview, for our sense of nature is profoundly inflected by our culture. I have seen the dry garden of Ryōan-ji in full sunlight and in shade, in rain and snow, at dawn and dusk. And though I have seen photographs of it illuminated by moonlight as well as by electric light, I have never actually experienced it at night, and may never have the occasion to enjoy it under any moon, whether new or full. This should not, however, limit my appreciation, but rather expand it, since longing should be part of every aesthetic act. The moon can be enjoyed elsewhere, otherwise, in many ways that are sheer poetry. There exist, for example, numerous moon-viewing pavilions in Japan, perhaps the most famous attached to the Geppa-rō tea house located at the Katsura Detached Palace near Kyoto. One of the most popular rituals is to raise a cup of sake so that it reflects the first full autumn moon – the moon of great melancholy, marking the moment when life begins its decline – to then drink down the sake and the moon in the same draught. Though the moon often infiltrates the tea room, tea is not the only elixir in Zen culture.

Here, the highest aesthetic may reveal the greatest grace. Japanese monks and poets have a tradition of writing death poems, like that of the modern poet Baiko (*d.* 1903):

> Plum petals falling
> I look up – the sky,
> a clear crisp moon.[5]

The melancholy of passing captures the author in its motion, where for the only moment in the poet's life the instantaneous, unique event celebrated by the haiku is his own disappearance; where time passing and time transfixed are one.

DEATH IS GENERALLY deemed a taboo topic, and some make its avoidance an ethical imperative. In the words of Theodor Adorno, 'To write poetry after Auschwitz is barbaric.' The same may be said concerning Hiroshima and Nagasaki. And should we not again consider this injunction following the great Tōhoku earthquake and tsunami, and the nuclear catastrophe that followed at Fukushima?[6] One may, however, wonder about the limitation of Adorno's iconoclastic injunction to specifically poetry among all the arts, which may be partially explained by the fact that he was fundamentally more musician than poet. The most poignant rejoinder would be to cite Paul Celan's 'Todesfuge' ('Death Fugue', 1948), which suggests – utilizing a musical imagery that must certainly have moved Adorno – that one actually has an obligation to write such poetry, that only a more profound poetry of death can counter the death of poetry.

He shouts play death more sweetly this Death is a master from
    Deutschland
he shouts scrape your strings darker you'll rise then as smoke to the sky
you'll have a grave then in the clouds there you won't lie too
    cramped . . .[7]

The image of bodies gone up in smoke is common in Japanese culture, which has long practised cremation, as witnessed in *The Tale of Genji* at the moment when Genji laments the death of his wife, Aoi: 'No, I cannot tell where my eyes should seek aloft the smoke I saw rise, But now all the skies above move me to sad thoughts of loss.'[8] However, while in many cultures such immolation is an integral part of a ritualized work of mourning, in Auschwitz, Hiroshima, Nagasaki, the ritual was abolished, the mourning violated, the tomb not merely desecrated but annihilated. Such images must always be presented with the greatest of discretion and trepidation, yet they *must* be presented, over and over, not only so that we never forget, but also so that we can mourn, sublimate and plumb the depths of their horror.

    One of the most unexpected, indeed bizarre references to the catastrophe of Hiroshima occurs in Teshigahara Hiroshi's film *Ikebana* (1956), a documentary about his father, the ikebana master Teshigahara Sōfū who established the Sōgetsu (grass-moon) school of flower arrangement that revolutionized the art form by bringing it in line with the mid-twentieth-

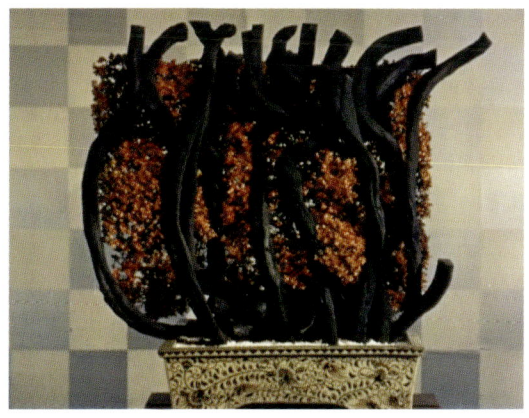

Still from *Ikebana* (dir. Teshigahara Hiroshi, 1956).

century avant-garde. The film is a somewhat whimsical presentation of this new form of ikebana, exhibiting the radically new forms sought by Sōfū, as revealed in the scene where he makes an arrangement consisting mainly of dead, calcinated branches and dried plants, the totality appearing as a stylized conflagration in a forest. The occasional use of such withered materials would be appropriate in traditional ikebana either for visual emphasis or to mark seasonal symbolism, just as dead branches and simulated lightning damage are used in bonsai (miniature plants) for verisimilitude and dramatic effect, and in other instances it might even produce a pleasant surprise, as Edward S. Morse explains regarding a bonsai of plum trees set in a garden:

> Before the evidence of life appears in the blooming, one would certainly believe that a collection of dwarf plum-trees were simply fragments of old blackened and distorted branches or roots, – as if fragments of dead wood had been selected for the purpose of grotesque display! Indeed, nothing more hopeless for flowers or life could be imagined than the appearance of these irregular, flattened, and even perforated sticks. They are kept in the house on the sunny side, and while the snow is yet on the ground, [they] send out long, delicate drooping twigs, which are soon strung with a wealth of the most beautiful rosy-tinted blossoms.[9]

But Teshigahara Sōfū displays the flowerless dead wood as the very core of the work, an icon of disaster, proferring a morbidity beyond the bounds of formal exigencies and good taste. At this point, however, the film suggests little more than a particularly idiosyncratic, and perhaps somewhat audacious if not contentious, gesture of formal innovation.

We might remember in this context that one of the classic statements on Japanese gardens, *Illustrations for Designing Mountain, Water, and Hillside Field Landscapes*, composed by the priest Zōen (fifteenth century), includes the following injunction: 'Bearing in mind the Five Colors of rocks, you must set them with full consideration of the relationships of Mutual Destruction and Mutual Production.'[10] This suggests that the power of nature as active principle, *natura naturans*, is always looming, and that certain forms of destruction are perhaps appropriate to the composition and elaboration of the dry Zen garden (*karesansui*, 'withered mountain water'). Indeed, many of the great Zen gardens were destroyed by fire, war, earthquakes and floods, and certain aspects of garden design are used to highlight the cyclical processes of the natural world, such as leaving tree stumps to disintegrate, rather than totally uprooting them as would ideally be done in most Western gardens. Decay and destruction are an integral aspect of Zen-inspired aesthetics, profoundly related to the temptation of the void. To see Teshigahara Sōfū's arrangement of dead branches simply as an innovative manifestation of modernism would be to miss its profound connection to classic expressions of melancholy.

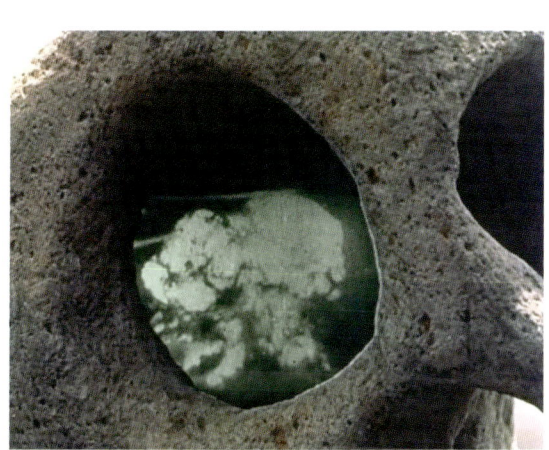

It is not until the final scene of *Ikebana* that, despite the seemingly innocuous and aestheticized subject-matter, we are witness to one of the most horrendous images of the twentieth century. The camera pans across a broad expanse of beach to reveal several sculptures by Teshigahara Sōfū, to pause finally on one of them and zoom in to the head shaped in the form of a skull. All of a sudden, in the hollow of the left eye socket, appears an atomic explosion, followed by a brief shot of Hiroshima in ruins, in all about thirteen seconds of film. Here we have symbol, icon and index of the greatest instance of annihilation in history: the eternal symbol of the death's head; the cinematic icon of an atomic explosion and the ruins of Hiroshima framed in the empty orbit; the luminous traces of the explosion itself that constitute the cinematographic index of all that was vaporized, burnt and irradiated by that nuclear holocaust.

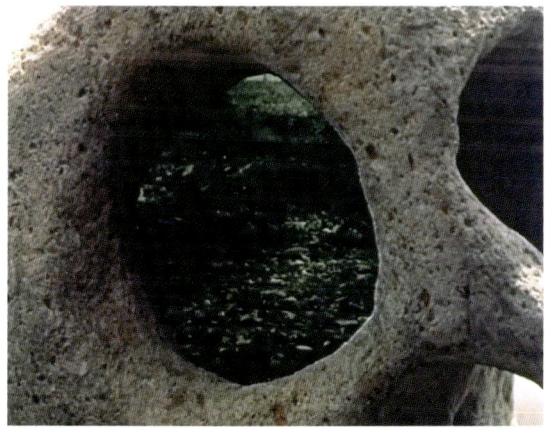

Two years after Teshigahara Hiroshi created this extraordinarily unsettling, indeed almost unthinkable montage – where the life-giving waves of the eternal ocean fade into the hyperbolic destruction of the instantaneous atomic blast – the great photographer Domon Ken published his book *Hiroshima* (1958), the harsh realism of which reveals the aftermath of the city's catastrophe. A year later saw the performance that launched Butoh, Hijikata Tatsumi's

Stills from *Ikebana*.

Kinjiki (Forbidden Colours, 1959), the spirit, iconography and choreography of which was profoundly influenced by these events.[11] One might go so far as to suggest that the nuclear holocaust in Japan signalled a radical rupture in the iconography and theatrics of death, divided between the superlatively aestheticized ghosts made visible in traditional Noh – with their resplendent costumes, entrancing masks, extraordinary choreography and fabulously convoluted plots – and the invisible radiation whose effects are horrifically symbolized in the ashes and contortions of Butoh, the 'dance of darkness'.[12]

A decade later, Hiroshima became the symbol of a revolution in architecture and aesthetics when Isozaki Arata exhibited the *Electric Labyrinth* installation at the Milan Triennale (1968), part of which was the collage *Hiroshima Ruined Again in the Future*, superimposed on a photograph of Hiroshima just after the atomic bomb had been dropped. This apocalyptic image of destruction and extinction is simultaneously witnessed by Isozaki as the death of all the utopias of the modernist avant-garde and as the sign of a new beginning in architecture and urbanism. 'Ruins are the style of our future cities',[13] he proclaims, explaining that the city is a process, and that its traumas must be depicted. Seeming to echo Zōen's injunction about mutual destruction and production, Isozaki explains: 'Bringing the city to be constructed back to the city that had been destroyed emphasized the cycle of becoming and extinction.'[14] In support of this claim, he refers to the aesthetic concept of *sabi*, the 'dried and emaciated', citing several classic Japanese sources.[15] *Sabi* signifies patination by age or use, connoting, as Donald Richie suggests, 'the bloom of time' and its corresponding feeling of melancholy; in extreme instances this feeling can be one of bleakness and desolation.[16] However, in traditional Japanese culture it is almost unheard of to make the ultimate extrapolation and directly relate the term to morbidity and death – not to mention its hyperbolic association with the atomic blast – as does Isozaki by associating *sabi* with the 'frozen landscape of death' at Hiroshima.[17] Such ghastly imagery is tantamount to a provocation, for who could bear the profoundly anti-aesthetic thought of nuclear fallout as the *sabi* of the earth?

Soon after the Great Hanshin-Awaji earthquake that devastated Kobē on 17 January 1995, the Japanese Pavilion at the 1996 Venice Biennale was

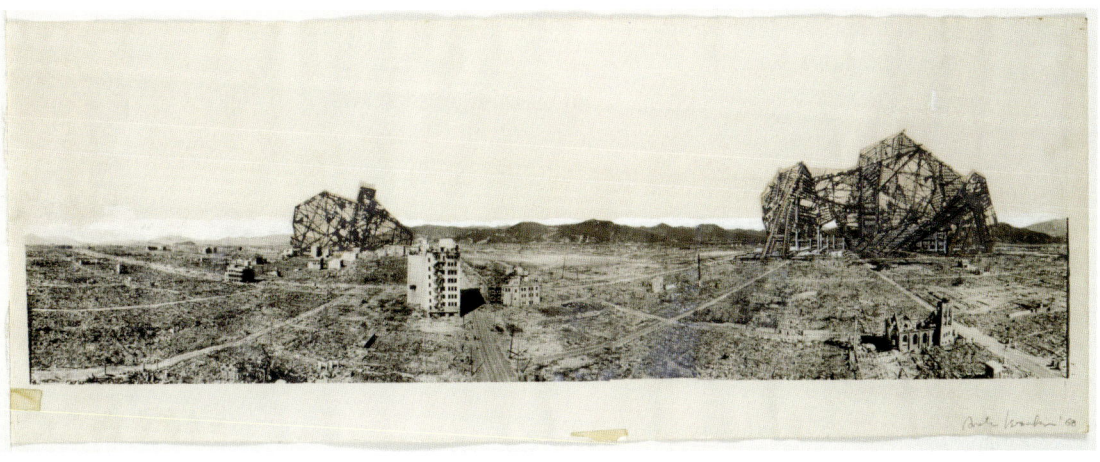

Isozaki Arata, *Hiroshima Ruined Again in the Future*, 1968, project, ink and gouache with cut-and-pasted gelatin silver print on gelatin silver print, 35.2 × 93.7 cm.

dedicated to 'Architects as Seismographers'. In this venue, Isozaki re-exhibited *Hiroshima Ruined Again in the Future*, explaining that, 'ruins were a source of the imagination'.[18] Might we suppose that the greater the ruin, the more profound the imagination? Might this not suggest a new or terminal manifestation of the sublime? Are we not confronted with a radically new form of temporality, measured in radioactive half-life? Isozaki sensed that we had already entered a new epoch in the history of landscape and cityscape, where the nuances and limits of metaphors and symbols had been radically transformed.

At times, the smallest is an allegory of the greatest. It is surely no coincidence that another of Domon Ken's best-known works is *Shigaraki Ōtsubo* (1965), a book on large earthenware jars that revolutionized the representation of pottery, with its high-resolution photographs and extremely detailed close-ups. Writing in the 1960s of pottery from the town of Shigaraki, literary and art critic Kobayashi Hideo describes the site-specific relationship between earth and pottery: 'The time I went to Shigaraki and gazed at the white earth and green forests of red pine, the idle thought drifted quite naturally into my mind that, if there were a forest fire here, it might well produce a gigantic Shigaraki pot.'[19] The art historian Louise Allison Cort glosses over this fantasy:

Chance, the absence of human will, is the manifestation of natural innocence. Yet nature, according to this aesthetic, possesses a will of its own: the pots emerge as the creation of the 'combat between the clay and the fire' within the kiln. Collectively, the features created by this awesome combat are termed the 'scenery' of the pot. Certain aspects of natural 'scenery' are felt to be embodied, transfigured, in the pot itself.[20]

The pot figuratively represents the earth while it is materially of the earth. Regarding a culture where pottery can evoke the sublime, it is hardly frivolous to relate this art form to even the greatest of catastrophes.

The very creation of pottery is a cataclysmic event, a violent transformation of earth. The mythopoetic dimension of this sensibility is explained by Bert Winther-Tamaki:

> The burning and vitrification of the clay in the kiln were imagined as a kind of condensation of the great spans of geological time that produce the rocky formation of the earth's crust. In this analogy, the ceramic artist travels back to a geological past, mimics the igneous processes of the earth, and then returns to the present to claim the products of 'superhuman time'.[21]

Thus pottery, in its most profound manifestation, is an allegory of the catastrophes of earth, fire, water. Certain types of unglazed, high-fired stoneware are particularly valued by pottery connoisseurs, and Murata Jukō, one of the originators of the Japanese way of tea, 'equates the appreciation of Bizen and Shigaraki wares with profound spiritual attainment'.[22] According to Cort, the appreciation of pottery concords with that of traditional poetry, insofar as 'the beginner was advised to start with a "correct and beautiful" style, progressing only gradually toward expression of images described as "cold" (*hie*) and "lean" (*yase*) or, in the ultimate refinement, as "dried out" (*kare*)'.[23] This suggests that only the most accomplished poets, which means only poets of a certain age, may allude directly to death, whence the rarity of

Koie Ryōji, Shigaraki
guinomi, c. 2008.

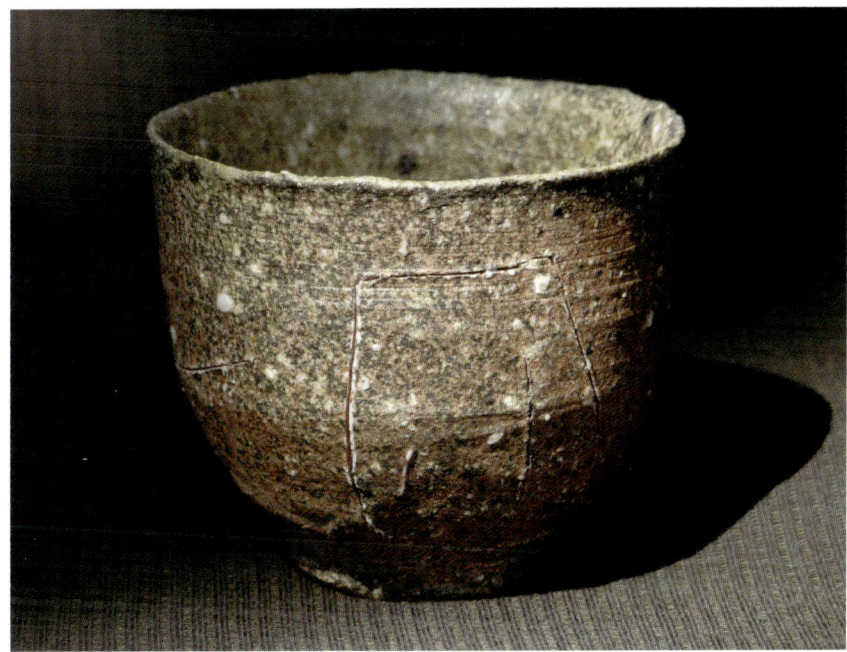

its expression. The highest spiritual attainment is thus in part a recognition of our own mortality or, as Inoue Yasushi expresses it in his historical novel *The Tea Master*, through the words of the tea master Shōō (Jōō): 'It is said that the quintessence of poetry is a cold, dry, exhausted universe . . . I would like that of tea to be similar.'[24]

Regarding the aesthetics of the tea ceremony, A. L. Sadler notes that in addition to the sundry shades of black and white, 'in decoration their most favored hues are Ash color, Tea color and Mouse color'.[25] This is so not only because such a dearth of bright colours is all the better to set off the ceramics and the flowers in the *tokonoma* (the alcove in the tea room where scrolls, pottery and flower arrangements are displayed), but even more profoundly because such are the colours appropriate to the sense of *wabi* rusticity and austerity. This ascetic sensibility corresponds to the 'dry' aesthetics of Zen gardens, which, like certain types of pottery, are valued precisely for their earthiness, austerity, irregularity, roughness. As signs of the solitude and melancholy central to the *wabi-sabi* aesthetic, the starkness of raw, troubled matter and lack of superfluous decorativeness are considered signs of heightened spirituality. Yet, however much the aesthetic of the 'dry' or 'withered' might suggest mortality, the visual representation of the morbid in tea culture is anathema. Rather, it exists in the most subtle allusions, referred to as *mono no aware*, the wistful thrill of the ephemeral, the melancholy of things passing, famously instantiated by the fall of a leaf or a petal, the melting of snow, the occultation by a cloud or fog, all gently signifying the transience of existence. It expresses both regret for time passed and relief in the Buddhist perspective of escaping from the worldy cycle of suffering. That the term *aware* occurs over a thousand times in *The Tale of Genji* is a sign of its importance. This refinement has been made familiar through the ages by the nearly obligatory presence of such references in haiku, poetry that revels in the evanescent without ever touching on the morbid. However, there exists one notable exception, the death poem (*jisei*), that final work composed as a parting gesture. In a sense, all manifestations of *mono no aware* are asymptotic to morbidity, just as all haiku are asymptotic to the death poem.[26]

In 1980 the potter Koie Ryōji created a work in India that consisted of 'firing' the ground with a blowtorch, a gesture that can be said to constitute a limit condition of pottery, if one takes into account the fact that while in English the word 'pottery' denotes the vessel-like form of the object, in Japanese *yakimono* ('fired thing') stresses the creative moment as the object passes through fire. One might well imagine, symbolically of course, that Koie would have been the ideal artist to have set that Shigaraki forest fire imagined by Kobayashi, in a gesture to celebrate the relation between human creativity and nature's agency. Koie sought the extreme limits of pottery by reformulating the question at the centre of the tradition: 'At what firing temperature does something become ceramic?' This resulted in the production of a provocative monument in Hokkaido, created by filling a long, 10-centimetre-wide groove with molten aluminium. When questioned as to whether this is *yakimono*, he responded: 'The aluminium was about 700 degrees centigrade, so the ground got burned. Therefore, it is yakimono. It is just a standing column, but it left a scorch mark on the ground. That's like "Scar Art".'[27] This modernist performance is also an indirect allusion to the very origins of pottery in Japan: Jōmon works from approximately 10,000 BCE and older, fired in outdoor bonfires at 600–900 degrees celsius.[28] Koie thus rethought the art of pottery according to the ontological limits of fire in relation to clay, the ultimate extrapolation of which is his series of anti-nuclear, anti-war pieces evoking the most extreme, deadly, horrific effects of fire. These include: *Testimonies* (1973), a trapezoid made of pulverized ceramics into which was inserted before firing a watch reading 8:15, the time of the nuclear explosion over Hiroshima; *No More Hiroshima, Nagasaki* (1977–present); *Chernobyl* (1989–present), a series of works, the one illustrated on page 194 consisting of pulverized Seto tea bowls on a brick base on which was placed a glass bottle that melted during firing; and *Anti-Nuclear Water Container* (1982), a white glaze *mizusashi* (water container), where the ironic rhetoric of the title attributes physically impossible prophylactic qualities to this work, while tacitly suggesting that the spiritual core of the tea ceremony can assuage the horrors of nuclear catastrophe. In the late fifteenth century a chief priest of Ryōan-ji made a claim that defined the Zen garden: 'Thirty thousand leagues should be compressed into a single foot.'[29] Half a millennium later, Koie would symbolically compress a nuclear catastrophe into a pot.

Paul Claudel, long-time ambassador to Japan and one of the French writers most attuned to the Japanese sensibility, wrote in *L'Oiseau noir dans le soleil levant* of the great Kantō earthquake of 1 September 1923, which destroyed Tokyo and caused over 140,000 fatalities, approximately the same number as the bombing of Hiroshima.

> Over there to the left, the immense redness of Tokyo, to my right the Last Judgment, above me an uninterrupted river of sparks and flashes. But that would not hinder the moon, waning and almost consumed, to rise in a silver archipelago. Soon afterward I see Orion appear in the sky, the great constellation that is the voyager's friend, the pilgrim of the sky that successively visits the two hemispheres. The moon began its course. Its hands stretch upon the sea, an ineffable consolation.[30]

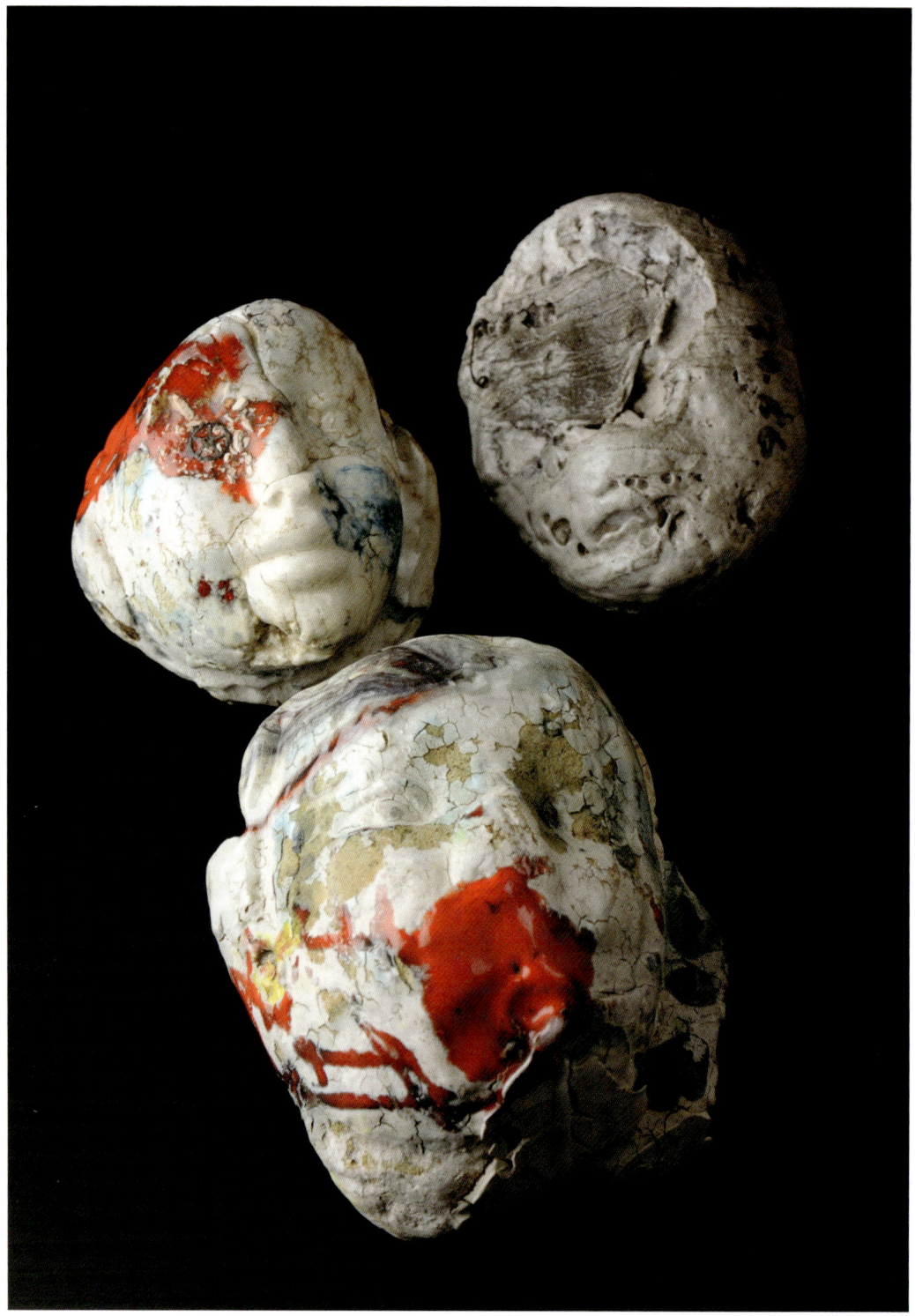

Koie Ryōji, *No More Hiroshima, Nagasaki*, 1977, ceramic sculpture, 15.5 × 18.5 × 13.5 cm.

That he can evoke the autumn moon at such a tragic moment is all the more poignant as he traversed the devastated landscape in search of his daughter, whom he believed to have been lost in the catastrophe. This moonlight is the *sabi* of the world, like the spectral ambiance of Noh, connoting the ineffable tragedy of death.

Among the most reproduced and celebrated images in Japanese culture, the full autumn moon has long been one of melancholy, as in *The Tale of Genji*, which opens with the emperor lamenting the loss of his favourite consort: 'When above the clouds tears in a veil of darkness hide the autumn moon, how could there be light below among the humble grasses?'[31] Here too the moon could have offered inexpressible solace, but in its stead we are granted another form of 'ineffable consolation': poetry. Claudel's moon, however, was not the full moon of traditional Japanese poetry, but a moon already waning: perhaps an omen of a new symbolism in the making. Claudel could not have imagined the nuclear tragedies to come in Hiroshima, Nagasaki, Chernobyl, Fukushima, nor the invisible evidence of radiation that would henceforth affect the future of landscape, nor the Butoh that would constitute a new *danse macabre*. But he already sensed that moon-beams could effectively counteract gamma rays.

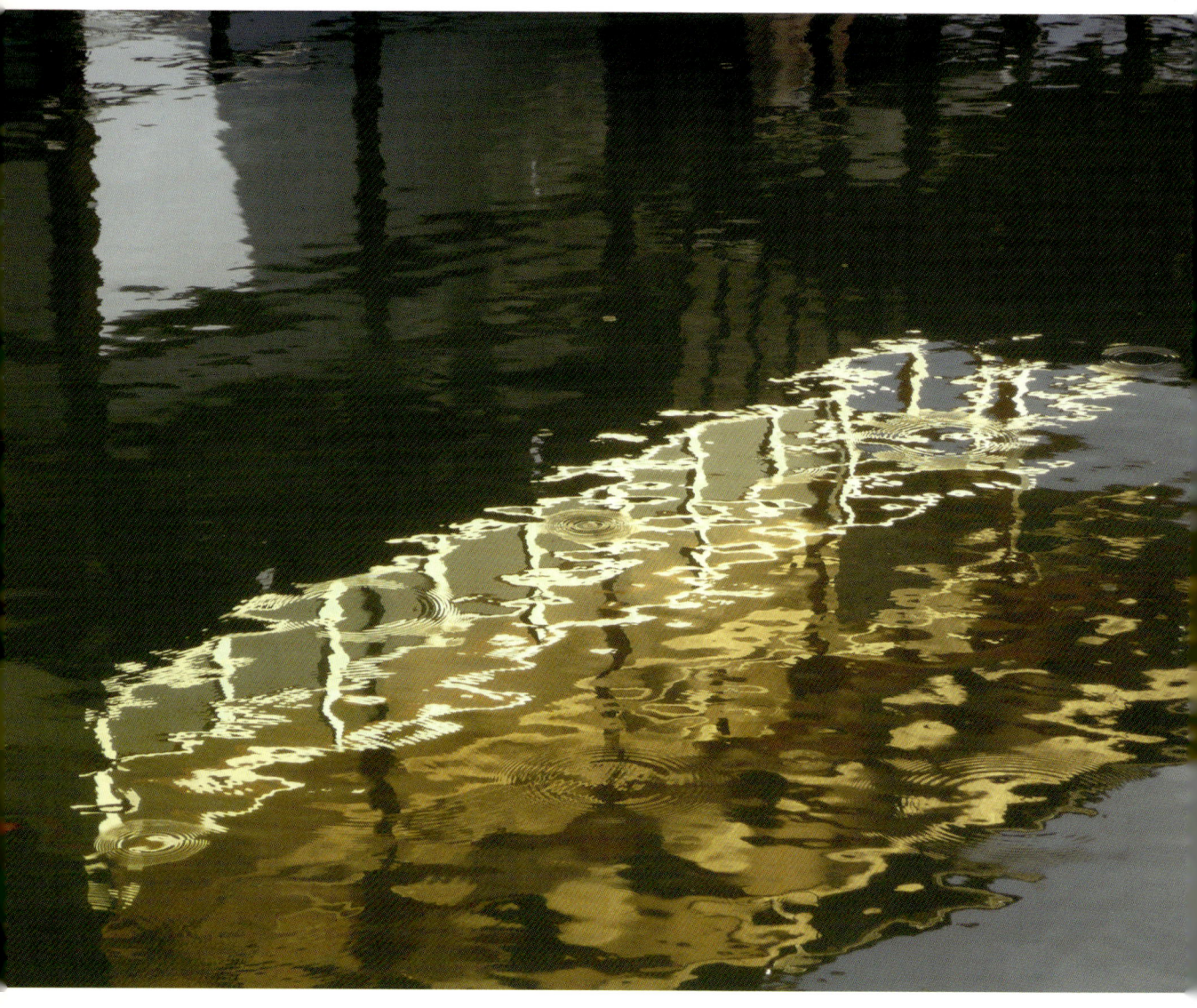

Kinkaku-ji (Temple of the Golden Pavilion).

TWO

ON THE CIRCULATION
OF METAPHOR

Charles Baudelaire famously asked: 'Have you ever noticed that a bit of sky seen through a vent, or between two chimneys, or through an arcade, gives a more profound idea of infinity than a vast panorama seen from a mountaintop?'[1] Large revelations often occur in very small spaces, and they are occasionally the result of a radical shift in scale and perspective. A few years ago Air France introduced the possibility of viewing a real-time video of the earth several miles below on long-distance flights, though these images were not very compelling. The following year, on a flight from Paris to Tokyo, this was replaced by pre-photographed European Space Agency (ESA) satellite images that did not coincide with the exact location of the aeroplane. Might somebody have realized that, due to almost inevitable cloud cover, real-time images are effectively often imageless, a blank white screen? Unlike the intriguing patterns in the aerial photographs by Yann Arthus-Bertrand, taken from altitudes low enough for details on the ground to be recognizable, the ESA photographs are experienced as abstract patterns, since they are scaled to views from an aeroplane flying at a standard cruising altitude of approximately 38,000 feet, from which most ground detail becomes unrecognizable. At one moment there appeared a photo of the confluence of the Amur and Zeya rivers in Siberia, striking for its astounding resemblance to the surface features of certain pieces of contemporary Oribe pottery. Within a certain aesthetic and experiential frame, the surface of the earth (reduced to an image) appears as a pottery glaze, while the surface of pottery (made of earth) appears as landscape. Such correspondences are distinctly more interesting than a blank video screen, essential as this might be to the avant-garde, as they instantiate the profundity, and unexpected postmodernity, of Gary Snyder's beautiful metaphor, 'the gleaming calligraphy of the ancient riverbed'.[2] In iconographic terms, such images (like the kanji for river, 川, *kawa*) – on the cusp between figuration and abstraction, representation and

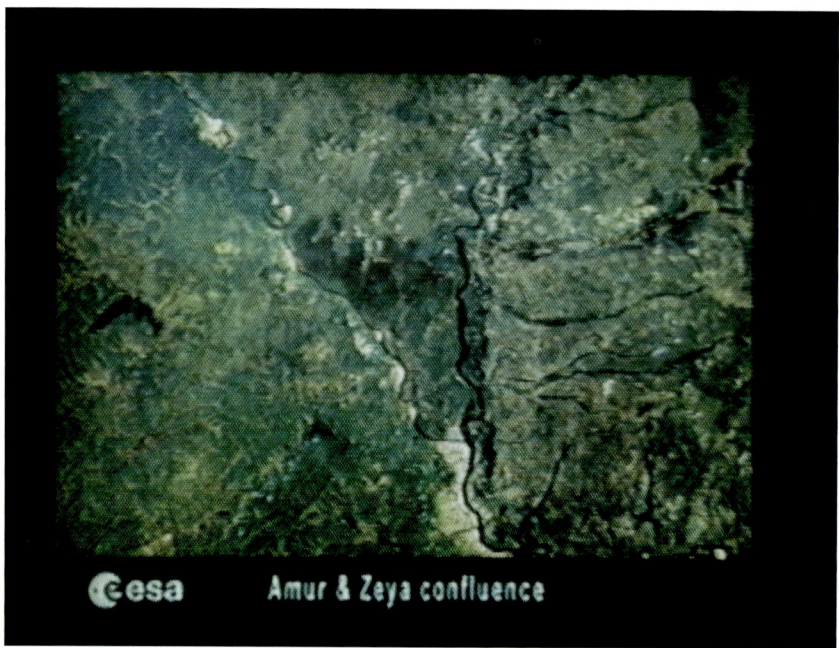

European Space Agency satellite photo of the Amur and Zeya rivers in Siberia.

reality, the virtual and the material – reveal the destiny of the aleatory trace, which can remain abstract and non-representational, or suggest letter or ideogram, hieroglyph or caricature, icon or image, according to the psychological and cultural predispositions of the viewer. For there exist material as well as cultural preconditions for all metaphorization. In Japanese aesthetics, meaning is sought in even the most random surface effects, those that most Western aesthetics would relegate to the realm of non-figuration. In the case of the ESA image, the reduction of scale, transformation of colour, and distortion of form caused by the display of high-resolution satellite photographs on a tiny, poor-quality LCD screen results in an extreme metaphoric condensation. As will be seen, this metaphor of ground for glaze is less subjective and less extravagent than might be imagined, for what is at stake here is the intransigency of materiality as it gets taken up within the circulation of metaphors.

Form is indissociable from matter. Semiology has taught us that every trace of human activity is simultaneously gesture, sign and symbol. Perhaps nowhere is this taken to such an extreme as in the experience of Japanese pottery, where manifestations of materiality, chance and symbolism are inextricably intertwined. Just as random patterns on pottery surfaces are often perceived as figurations of landscapes, an unintended crack may well suggest a calligraphic syllabic script (kana) or logographic character (kanji). In the case of a recent tea bowl by Kato Tsubusa that bears three roughly parallel vertical cracks, the pottery specialist and tea practitioner Umeda Minoru commented on it with one word, *yama* (山, mountain), since the form of the crack approximates that of the kanji. A crack (or any other surface detail) may be experienced on the empirical level, for what it explains about the materials and mode of production, or in relation to formal properties within an aesthetic context; it can also be read as a representational sign, or even as a manifestation of a Zen revelation. Like painting, pottery runs the gamut from simplicity to complexity, regularity to irregularity, and each work bears its own

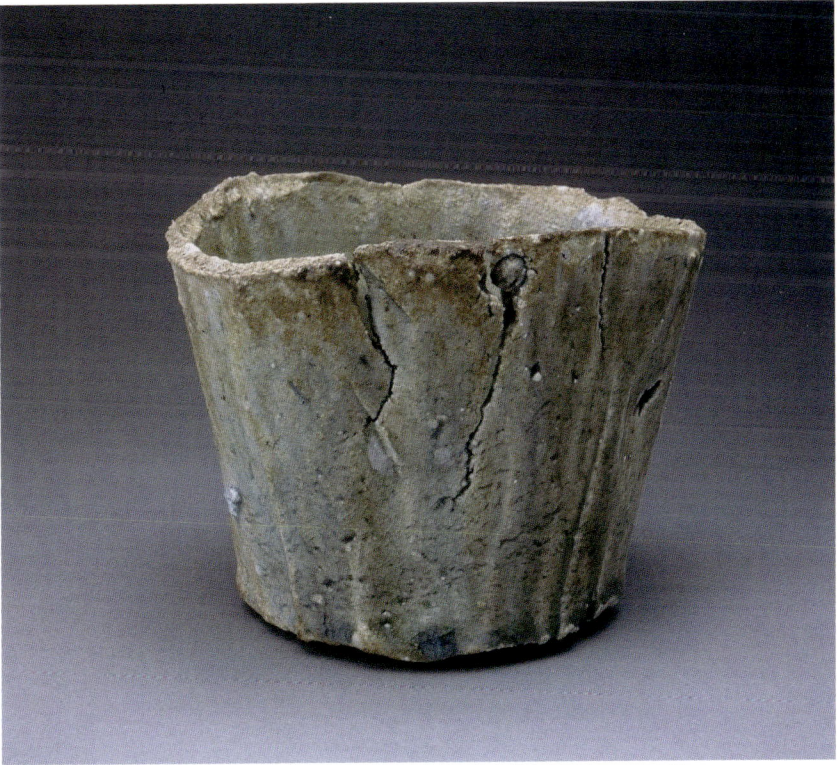

Kato Tsubusa, *chawan,*
c. 2006.

representational and symbolic possibilities. Suggestiveness, allusion and metaphor are of the essence. It is told that one of the Chinese emperors of the Song Dynasty, Huizong, would test the artists in the Imperial Painting Academy by proposing subjects drawn from classic poetry. One day he gave them the following verse: 'Lost in the green immensity, a red spot.'[3] One artist painted willows surrounding a garden pavilion with a woman dressed in red on a terrace; another depicted a forest of blackberries harvested by a sole woman; yet another showed a stand of pines topped with a red-beaked crane. But the winner of the contest was Liu Songnian, who created a seascape with the rays of the sun on the infinite horizon. Such minimalism was then rare in Chinese art, but it would come to have a vast posterity across the sea in Japan.

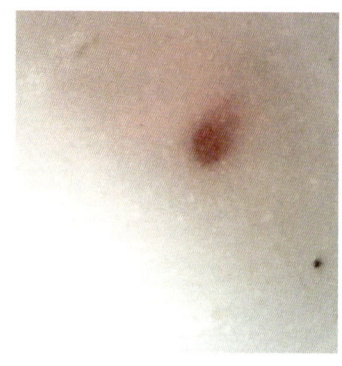

Kimura Nobuyuki, *guinomi, c.* 2008, detail.

It might be appropriate to begin this investigation of representation and narrative in the Zen garden with an even simpler image, perhaps the limit of iconicity: a red spot on a white background. While it may appear that this spot is abstract and informationless, it is actually rich in iconographic and narrative signification. For in Japanese aesthetics, metaphor exists within a complex and polyvalent circulation of images, such that iconicity is already narration. Writing of the varied arts of Japan, Maurice Pinguet explains:

> Its perfection resides in the fact that an empirical reality (a plum flower, the flight of a bird) . . . signifies that all being is contained within it, indivisible and everywhere equal to itself. Culture will be the development, varied by a thousand sensible figures, of the recognition that nature is deployed in the realm of being. Japanese art is nothing but the sum total of techniques adapted to this operation and conspiring with this evidence. Culture reveals that nature reveals being.[4]

At the core of this sensibility is an art of subtle allusions. And in most cases, the subtler the allusion the better, such that the single spot or line or crack existing at the extreme limit of figuration is highly valued. The context of the

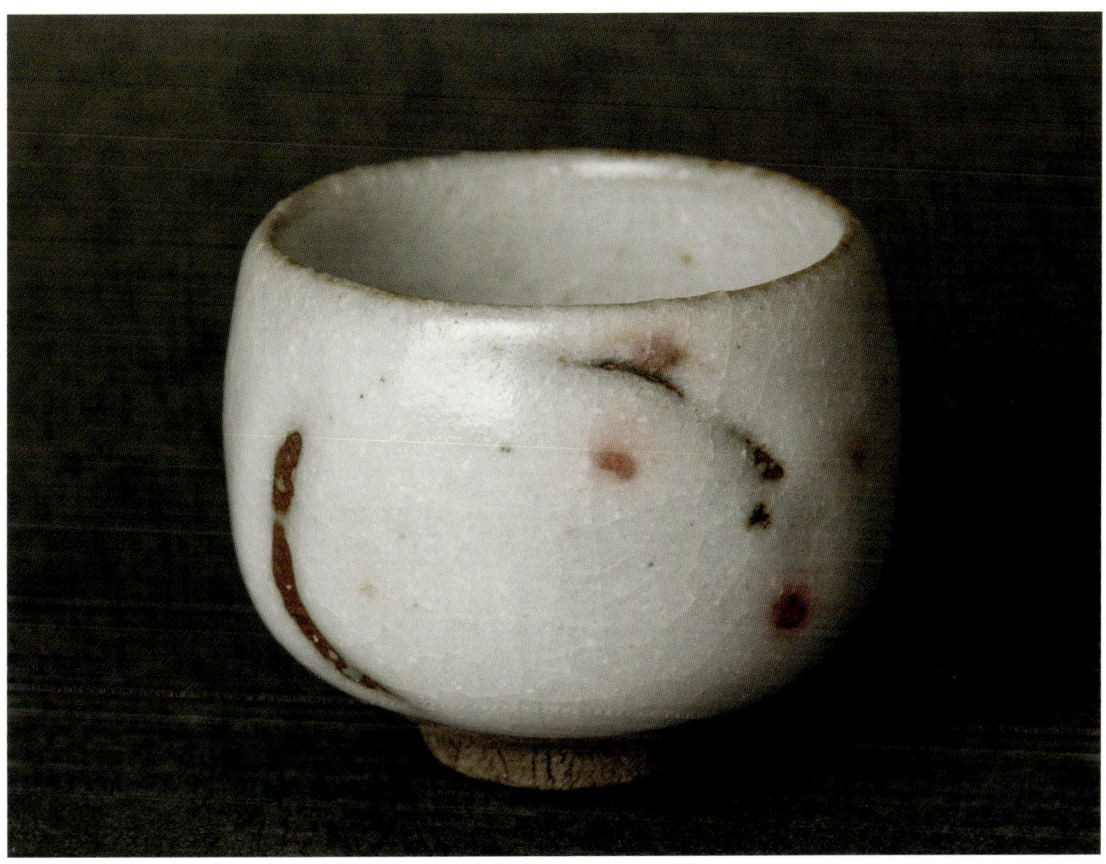

Kimura Nobuyuki,
guinomi, c. 2008.

apparently abstract red spot in question is the inside of a sake cup (*guinomi*) by the contemporary Kyoto potter Kimura Nobuyuki, with the outer surface depicting blossoming plum branches in the snow. Nearly all arts in Japan contain precisely coded seasonal markers, and this piece is no exception. The exterior suggests the very first signs of spring as the plum tree begins to blossom in the snow. As the cup is raised to drink, what at first glance seemed to be a purely abstract interior is recognized in its full iconographic intent, a plum blossom fallen on the snow, suggesting the very last throes of winter. As in haiku, this cup evokes a unique, ephemeral event within the context of recurrent natural cycles, grasped within a fully formed iconography and poetics.

The closest one comes in modern Western aesthetics to such a vast and densely interlinked system of resemblances and allusions is in Baudelaire's notion of correspondences, which attempts to establish an unsystematic, intuitive sensitization to the intricate and infinite play of metaphors that link all images, all arts, all senses, all the while joining transcendence to immanence.[5] While a century of modernism in the West generally depreciated representation and valorized abstract traces, Japanese culture continues to seek representational correspondences nearly everywhere, keyed to the ever-present seasonal markers that are nearly obligatory in haiku and that link all the arts. (The importance of word play in haiku, usually lost in translation, is crucial to the sense of correspondences, insofar as the double meanings thus obtained are in themselves expansive tropes.) Its most basic manifestation is the Japanese floral calendar, with vast symbolic implications and deep cultural resonances: pine (January), plum (February), peach (March), cherry (April), peony (May), iris (June), morning glory (July), lotus (August), seven grasses (September), chrysanthemum (October), maple (November), camellia (December).[6] But this is only the most schematized version: in fact, over 5,000 seasonal words have been catalogued in classic haiku, and one might even go so far as to claim that the great majority of nouns referring to the natural world have seasonal connotations. Furthermore, certain of the most significant natural phenomena, such as rain, have a very broad lexicon, so as to nuance description, imagery and allusion.[7] Over time and through poetic usage, most such words (and their corresponding images) have become codified, and thus regularly connote the same sentiments, to the point that there is an implied equivalence between seasons and emotions, or as Augustin Berque puts it, 'geomorphology is translated into configurations of spirit'.[8] Concerning the broader scheme of Japanese culture, as Joseph D. Parker explains, 'In much East Asian elite culture the landscape was traditionally an image of spiritual freedom, religious power, moral purity, and a political position transcendent to or outside of the ambitions and avarice of ordinary life.'[9] Otherwise stated, the landscape serves as a totalizing system of symbols for nearly all cultural values. This is true for both the literal landscape iconography as well as its major associations, such that

> In the classical literary traditions of East Asia the natural world was read historically or mythologically as a landscape inhabited by various well-known poets, as the residences of particular spirits or deities, or as the location of particular important historical events.[10]

Indeed, in much traditional poetry, such associations were of greater importance than the landscape imagery itself.

These translations or transpositions between seasons and emotions are highly codified, to the point of risking innumerable clichés. As actor Oida Yoshi explains, concerning the means of expressing emotion in the Noh theatre, 'If a person is sad, they don't talk about what they are feeling, but they might say, "Summer has gone. Winter will soon arrive. The autumn leaves are falling." Emotion is described through the phenomena of nature.'[11] Given their ubiquity, such markers effectively proffer the aestheticization of everyday life, and express the very depths of the soul. Murasaki Shikibu's classic *The Tale of Genji* abounds in such symbolism, and at one point the narrator thematizes such literary practices: when speaking of a princess living isolated in a particularly dilapidated and sad house, whose poetic imagination is far less than might be desired, he complains that 'Any lady living in a place like that should sometimes give poignant voice to her feelings by conveying the sorrows she knew so well in terms of the fleeting moods of plants, trees, or the sky.'[12] Here, the world is often personified, as in this poignant expression of melancholy, also from *The Tale of Genji*: 'In the waning light the very sky seemed inclined to weep, shedding a hint of rain.'[13] Augustin Berque sees the very structure of the Japanese language as accentuating its symbolic and existential rapport with the natural world: the imprecision of the grammatical subject – which can either be decentred and shifted towards a collective identity, or can disappear altogether – facilitates forms of expression where subjectivity is mediated by the surrounding environment, where the human is expressed by the natural, and where nature is consequently elevated spiritually.[14] This feeling towards nature is both aesthetic and religious for, as Paul Claudel so well expresses the matter:

> In Japan, the supernatural is thus nothing other than nature, it is literally supernature, that region of superior authenticity where raw facts are transferred into the domain of signification. It [the supernatural] does not contradict [nature's] laws, but underlines their mystery.[15]

The great tea master Kobori Enshū (1579–1647) specifically uses such symbolism to express the essence of tea, which he describes as 'the mists of spring, the cuckoo hidden in the fresh green leaves of summer, the loneliness of the evening sky in autumn, and daybreak in the snow of winter.'[16] The contextualization of the red plum spot is rather simple, given the high degree of codification of seasonal effects and their application to pottery. One may consult, for example, the entry for February in a modern tea diary such as Sasaki Sanmi's *Chado: The Way of Tea*. Most of the sweets (*okashi*) for that month symbolize red or white plum blossoms, such as the *yuki no ume* (snow on plum), which consists of red bean jam wrapped in thin rice cakes and sprinkled with fine flour. The author specifically associates this cake with a poem by Sōyō:

> The plum blossom is covered with snow but its fragrance covers all.[17]

Furthermore, this tea master's favoured pottery dishes for February are of Oribe, Raku and Karatsu, often approximating plum blossoms in form, image and colour.[18] One often finds such symbolism throughout *kaiseki* meals (the cuisine associated with the tea ceremony, destined to become Kyoto's, and more generally Japan's, haute cuisine).[19] Murata Yoshihiro, chef of Kyoto's Kikunoi restaurant, makes a March dish he calls *kakure ume* (hidden plum), where he represents the plum blossoms against the last snow by covering a large pink *umeboshi* (pickled Japanese plum) with a sauce made of *shirako*, white milt, in this case of sea bream.[20] The iconographic coherence obtained by seasonal imagery creates a resonance between the microcosm of the restaurant or tea room and the natural environment.

The profundity of this sensibility, with its vast metaphoric range, its labyrinthine sense of time, and its synaesthetic form of perception, is beautifully illustrated by a passage from Michaël Ferrier's novel, *Sympathie pour le fantôme* (2010), in a passage that takes place in a Tokyo bar at the moment that the bartender offers, as the *pièce de résistance* of a series of dishes accompanying the protagonist's sake drinking, a simple *umeboshi*, here preserved in alcohol. The drinkers are at first somewhat surprised by the paucity of the offering, a shrivelled, washed-out, wasted plum, but they soon come to realize its rarity, being told that it has been marinating for 70 years:

> I taste . . . Slowly, progressively, at the back of the mouth, then in more distant vaults – the canal of the throat, the stalls of the lungs – its song rises like that of a timid cricket . . . Its flavor is extraordinarily powerful and profound, an acidity at first muted, then fresher, peacefully unfolding. The scents slowly invade me . . . The plum came from afar, it went back centuries, ages, Niagaras of time. You think you are eating it but in fact it is devouring you, it comes to seek you out, to stalk you in the deepest recesses of your palate. You are dispersed from within, drawn out toward your openings – mouth, ears, tympana – that suddenly start to feel, to shudder, to roar . . .
>
> Then, entire strata rush by: Time, with its veins, its marblings, its alluvia . . . Not that of social plans and reforms, checkbooks and calendars . . . real Time, the time that unfolds at the end of time . . . Simultaneously, your entire body begins to exist as never before: five senses, your voice changes, and your smile sparkles like a rain storm. Your nostrils palpitate. Your nose has wings, your ears pavilions. You become bird, insect, butterfly.
>
> Profoundness of the plum. One has to search far for words, not only haphazardly in dictionaries but also in the infinite range of interior treasures, one's entire portable lexicon, whose very existence was previously ignored: peaks, plains, musical staffs. A poem of elegance at the tip of the tongue and on the edge of the nerves.[21]

Not only does this plum serve to reveal the depths of the protagonist's soul and to offer an allegory of the plot – in which certain people lost to history, the phantoms of the title, are revived through art – but it also reaches beyond the seasonal metaphor to plumb the depths of time itself. Here, the excessiveness of metaphor – which, in its explicitness, hyperbole and lack of attachment to a codified poetics is radically different from the aesthetics of the haiku – leads to revelation.

These examples of plum blossoms and fruit reveal how the complexity of iconography reinforces the profundity of narration. But there is another key factor that must be taken into account: unpredictability. Given the extent to which the aleatory is valorized in Zen-inspired aesthetics, it is often difficult to determine whether mimetic effects are established by creative premeditation or through retrospective contemplation. Not pure chaos, but a partially controlled ordering of chance, a fluctuating tension between the infinite and ineffable formal complexity of the macrocosm and the finite though indeterminate materiality of the microcosm. Perhaps sculptor Isamu Noguchi said it best when, speaking of stonework in his last writings, he insisted: 'chance no chance, mistakes no mistakes'.[22] The *wabi-sabi* aesthetic derived from the tea ceremony and central to Japanese aesthetics emphasizes irregularity, asymmetry, rupture, accident, breakage, erosion. Such effects are most evident in pottery, where a crack, slip or glaze may be seen to represent a mountain or a cloud. To seek random images in irregular and dilapidated surfaces is not unlike Leonardo da Vinci's suggestion of finding images by staring into a fire in a hearth or by throwing a paint-soaked sponge at a wall and investigating the consequent patterns; or eighteenth-century painter Alexander Cozen's technique of discovering landscapes in decomposing walls; or the passion for *pierres paysagées* or Chinese dream stones; or seeing images in clouds. In the West, such randomness is related to the Romantic aesthetic of incompleteness and potentiality, which valorizes sketches above oils because of the extent to which they leave a great part of the aesthetic act to the spectator's imagination, a similar rationale to that behind the Japanese admiration for ink drawing. The difference is that the Japanese have both a millennial tradition of seeking such effects (inspired by even earlier Chinese art), and a vast catalogue of forms to codify such imagery, which is not incidental but essential to their arts. Indeed, one of the key descriptive terms of

Cloud in the form of Fujisan, Kyoto, December 2009.

Japanese pottery is *keshiki*, which refers to the 'landscapes' suggested by the varied surface irregularities caused by firing certain types of pottery: stains, breaks, cracks, vitrification, flash marks, ash deposits, finger impressions and so on.[23] Such landscapes do not, therefore, stem from the sort of free association typical of the unlimited and unrestricted semiosis characteristic of much Western modernism, but rather from a traditional aesthetics based on a vast set of poetically validated associations. In the context of tea, such 'landscapes' are not merely Rorschach tests revealing private symbols, but additions to a venerable history of poetic imagery. Just as pottery often conjures up landscapes, natural scenes may well evoke pottery, in a particularly site-specific manner. For despite the current tendency to use commercially produced clays, all the great kilns are associated with particular types of local clays, which in themselves bear visual suggestions and symbolic resonances. As Louise Allison Cort put it so well: 'The fifteenth-century tea men who first brought those jars into their tearooms knew how to read the landscape, just as they could read shadings of ink on paper and see mountains and streams. In their mind's eye, they saw the valley that had made the jars.'[24] Such is a poetics of the earth in its primal form.

Consider the range and limits of such metaphoric complexity: 'Sekishu once placed some water-plants in a flat receptacle to suggest the vegetation of lakes and marshes, and on the wall above he hung a painting by Soami of wild ducks flying in the air.'[25] Here, the heterogeneous combination of the real and the represented in a single image does not create a sort of meta-representation, but rather suggests that the world consists of many levels of reality, both hidden and revealed. A different sort of hybridity is manifest in the entrance hall of the famed *ryōkan* (inn) Chikurin-in Gunpou-en, which seems to be decorated with two large vases containing elaborate flower arrangements. While one of them is indeed an ikebana arrangement in a light-blue vase, the other is in fact an illusion, a dark vase posed in front of a screen depicting white flowers which appear to be placed in the vase.[26] The difference between these two flower 'arrangements' is a lesson in Japanese metaphoricity, which has long existed in the art of ikebana. We find another such arrangement by Teshigahara Sōfū in his book *This Boundless World of Flowers and Form*: an arrangement created for the Kyoto temple Kanchi-in consisting of pine, persimmon and white camellia in a Shigaraki vase set before an ink painting by Miyamoto Musashi so that one of the lateral branches of the ikebana is positioned to make it appear that some of the nearly abstract images on the painting are part of the flower arrangement.[27] These sorts of illusions and allusions must not be forgotten regarding the arts of tea and of the table, where pottery is an integral part of the culinary scenography, and where each piece is ideally chosen in relation to such wonderfully complex sets of elements.[28]

This aesthetic thus values both abstraction *and* figuration, production *and* reproduction, the unique presentation of sheer materiality *and* the categorical representation of images with all their allusions and connotations. While most names of tea huts stem from literary sources, the given poetic names (*mei*) of tea utensils such as bowls, water jars, tea caddies (*chaire*) and scoops may be inspired either by literary allusions – whether from Zen aphorisms or court poetry – or by physical qualities. To name an object, whether univocally or equivocally, is to situate it within a symbolic and historical matrix and, not coincidentally, this act of naming also adds a surplus value to the work by seemingly attaching it to famed historic people and places. Consider, for example, the celebrated tea bowl Fujisan (one of eight *chawan* designated as National Treasures) created by the legendary painter and potter Hon'ami Kōetsu (1558–1637), on which a subtle effect of slip and ash glaze vaguely resembles Mount Fuji seen through the fog. Zen aesthetics are exemplified by suggestion and allusion, valorizing the attenuation of the literal by the indistinct, the shadowy, the obscure, the hazy. It is precisely such vagueness that motivates this type of representational sensibility, illustrated by the perennial Japanese fascination with forms obscured and rarefied by fog and mist, smoke and shadow, rain and snow. The state between the choate and the inchoate, that moment when images emerge or disappear, the cusp between figuration and abstraction, is particularly appreciated. This is an art of the incipient and the potential, manifested spatially by incompleteness and temporally by the suggestion of continual transformation. The desire for iconicity, the very anticipation of recognizing an image, creates a tension and dynamism in our perception of the object, transforming it into a partially open work, full of figurative potential.

Whereas the satellite photo described earlier evokes the earth as pottery, in Fujisan the pottery surface recasts a formed handful of earth as mountain and atmosphere. On the macrocosmic level, a tiny pottery crack may well symbolize the effects of the great earthquakes that regularly ravage the Japanese peninsula, a metaphor that, after consideration of our satellite image, no longer seems so audacious. At stake here is the representational quality of traces, where the potency of visual (and auditory) metaphors does not necessarily depend on the degree of verisimilitude, but rather on the differences between terms, forms, materials. This is well expressed by the philosopher Paul Ricoeur:

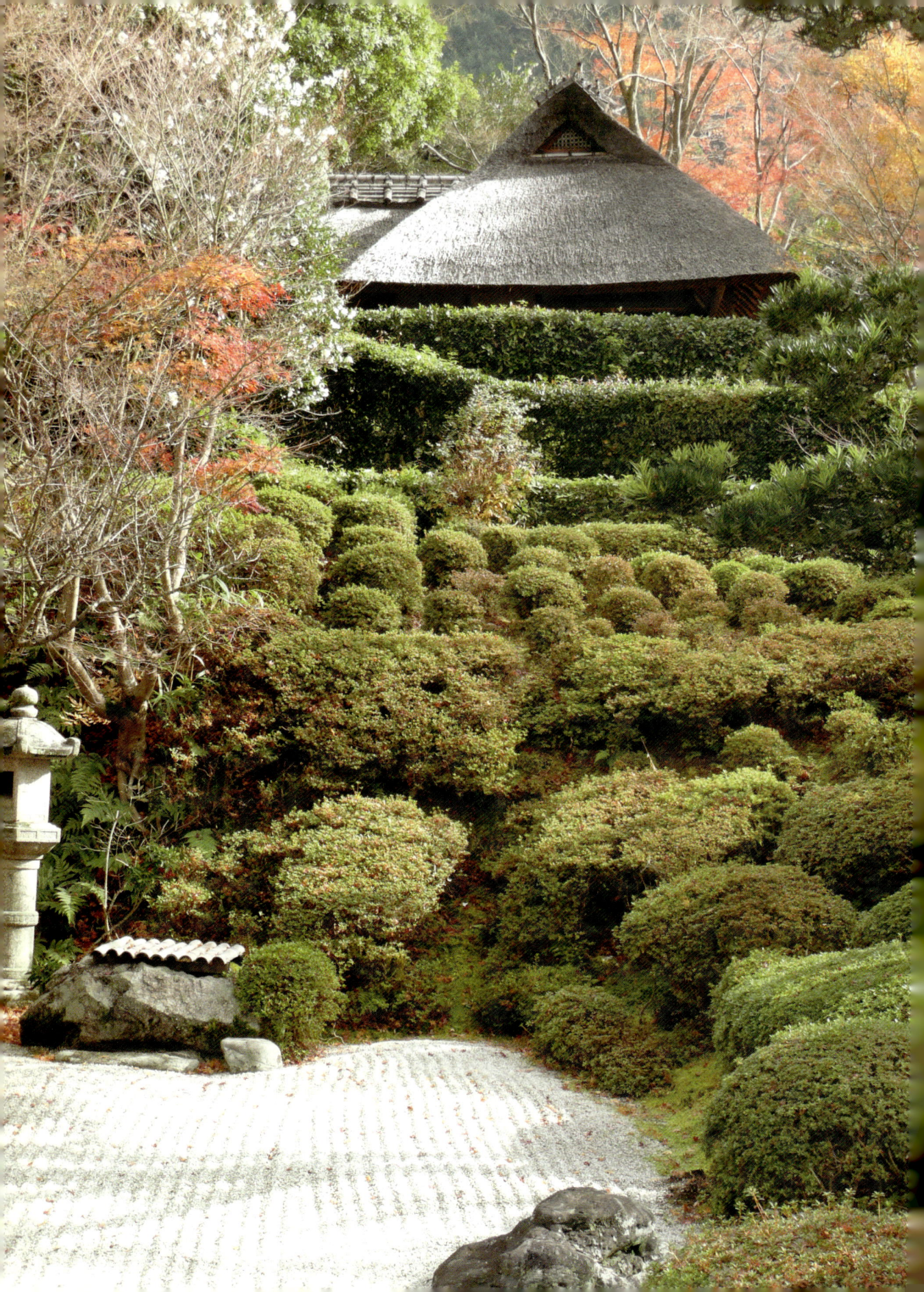

If we continue to translate *mimesis* by imitation, what must be
understood is the contrary of the copy of a preexisting reality,
and we must rather speak of creative imitation. And if we translate
mimesis by representation, we must not understand by this word a
redoubling of presence, as we can still hear in the Platonic *mimesis*,
but the cut that opens the space of fiction.[29]

This is instantiated throughout the Japanese arts, and the resultant equivocation between abstraction and figuration constitutes an ineluctable aspect of
Japanese aesthetics. It is inscribed in the very structure of Japanese writing,
which contains both syllabic script and logographic characters, composed of
three principle forms: formal block or regular (*kaisho*), informal semi-cursive
or rounded 'running hand' (*gyōsho*) and cursive 'grass writing' (*sōsho*). The
limit of equivocation between, indeed conflation of, word and image is
found in *ashide-e* (reed-script picture), drawings where the brushstrokes
simultaneously serve as representational elements (reeds, water in motion,
stones and so on) and kana in the cursive style. Thus Japanese calligraphy
articulates visual and conceptual forms, creating a fundamental ontological
equivocation, and a consequent principle of correspondence, at the very core
of Japanese imagery and thought.[30]

    This complex, refined and open-ended sense of representation will even
have consequences concerning the most mimetic forms of reproduction,
namely imitations (and counterfeits) of pottery. While the archetypes established by the early tea masters, notably Rikyū, remained ever-present within
the tea schools established by Rikyū's descendants, they would have been
continually refined. Rikyū's taste would thus become, according to Joseph
Kitagawa, a sort of '"grammar" which structures new expressions and experi-
ences'.[31] Tradition would be superseded by novelty, which would become
new tradition in turn. Eventually, however, what began as creativity would
fall into mannerism and sterile repetition, as is often the case following
aesthetic revolutions. Thus any object directly related to Rikyū is of prime
importance. Yet given the minute number of such objects, reproductions
of famous teabowls, a practice engaged in by the Raku workshop over the

Konpuku-ji, topiary
in the form of wooded
hills, with Bashō-an
hut in the background.

centuries, became essential for numerous reasons: ensuring the transmission of traditional pottery techniques, marking commemorations and homage, disseminating the orthodox taste of Rikyū, creating a community of practice, elaborating aesthetic symbolism and spiritual aura, maintaining the authority and continuity of tea institutions, establishing associative contact with past tea masters, offering readily available models for further creativity, determining social status, generating market value. Morgan Pitelka explains:

> Reproduction helps us to understand the operation of tradition itself. Far from being a reductive, derivate act, reproduction serves to sustain and support tea practice; it is neither a purely creative nor conservative process, but one that enriches, extends, diversifies, and preserves tea culture in varying degrees depending on context, period, and practitioner.[32]

For example, Kaga Kōetsu, a famous red Raku *chawan* created by Hon'ami Kōetsu, was frequently copied, even by so famous a potter as Ryōnyū (1756–1834), the ninth-generation head of the Raku household. It is clear by comparing these reproductions that absolute fidelity to the original was not essential, but rather the reproduction of the general shape, colour and distinguishing details. Indeed, such reproductions were often made from hearsay, without the possibility of ever having examined the original piece. It could thus be said that the relationship between archetype and copy in such cases is metaphoric, with a transfer of only certain pertinent and distinguishing elements, without any desire for integral reproduction. Such is imitation as creation.

This suggests that the key to understanding all forms of representation, as well as the paradoxes thereof, entails the contradictory exigencies of *mimesis, metaphor, correspondence* collateral with *rupture, metamorphosis, disintegration.* Japanese aesthetics maintain an imperative to create a circulation of metaphors between the various arts, all the while stressing the ephemeral effects of passing time.[33] Several factors determine the degree and mode of representation stemming from an art object's material uniqueness: its utilization as a design element (within the strict limits of the tea room environment); its position within the representational field (in relation to the other objects in the tea ceremony); and its performative use value (in the choreography of the tea ceremony).

This complex notion of representation, linked to considerations of temporality, is also crucial to considerations of gardens, since their fundamentally seasonal existence implies constant transformation – both linear change and cyclical degradation followed by restoration – and thus perpetual iconographic mutation. This richness is best made apparent by conducting the mental exercise of matching the sundry elements of a given garden, as they change through the year, to the total catalogue of seasonal words in haiku. This will clearly reveal how metaphoricity is founded on temporality, or rather on a palimpsest of temporalities guided by the seasons and open to aleatory effects. Thus the aesthetic perception of gardens necessitates attunement to unique material forms (design), to their ever-changing appearance over time, and to recognition of how such forms are experienced and formalized through poetic allusion.

Yet it should not be assumed that such hyperbolic attention to detail suggests that there is a single appropriate manner of viewing such gardens. Zen implies multiple levels of interpretation, all valid in different manners. There exist what Gregory P. A. Levine calls a religious, mystical, devotional eye, with its 'temple effect', and a secular, scholarly, historical, pleasure-seeking eye with its 'museum effect'. Both of these, in their own way, are motivated by 'eye-opening effects', that is, viewing protocols which configure specific ways of approaching such scenes and objects.[34] Each person arrives with different beliefs, different expectations, different protocols of viewing. Where one finds in Zen gardens the living presence of nature, another seeks a revelation of the transcendental void, while a third discovers sublime beauty. One need not become a Buddhist monk seeking enlightenment (*satori*) to appreciate the Zen garden, yet, as for all art, the form and depth of appreciation depends on what one brings to the scene. These temples and gardens are thus simultaneously sites of meditation, magic, devotion, knowledge, curiosity, and even commerce, play, profanation.

The crucibles of Japanese aesthetic form and practice have long been tea rooms or pavilions, many of which are to be found facing gardens within Zen temples, a fact that causes further aesthetic complications. A glaring misunderstanding with vast implications is the anachronistically modernist desire to see Ryōan-ji as purely abstract and beyond iconographic determination, as has been the case with Bruno Taut's writings from the 1930s, which inaugurated the Western disregard of Ryōan-ji's iconography. Taut's high-modernist appreciation of this garden, as well as of the Katsura Detached Palace, was formulated in the light of functional, minimalist, anti-decorative modernist imperatives. (Philip Johnson is said to have burst into tears on seeing Ryōan-ji. His emotions were certainly inspired by Taut's vision.) In the modernist West, one's perception, fortified by anti-representational concepts and prejudices, is often arrested by the beauty of abstract imagery, while in Japan the same image might well function as what could be termed a 'metaphoric relay'. Typical of this abstractionist misinterpretation, which has practically become the standard reading of Ryōan-ji, is that of Thomas Hoover, who writes in *Zen Culture*:

> Unlike Daisen-in, the garden at Ryōan-ji is not a symbolic mountain scene. It is instead a work of abstract art on a canvas of sand which goes beyond a symbolic representation of a landscape scene to provide a distillation of the very universe. It is internationally regarded as the very essence of Zen, and it is almost impossible to describe, in either words or pictures.[35]
>
> . . .
>
> Between them, the gardens at Daisen-in and Ryōan-ji encompass the range of *kare sansui* gardening in Ashikaga Japan. The first is a symbolic landscape of parched waterfalls and simulated streams drawn in monochromatic granite; the second, a totally nonrepresentative abstraction of stone arrangements in the sand-covered 'flat garden' style.[36]

This perceptual confusion is confounded by a conceptual particularity, the fact that of all the classic Zen-inspired dry gardens, Ryōan-ji is one of the

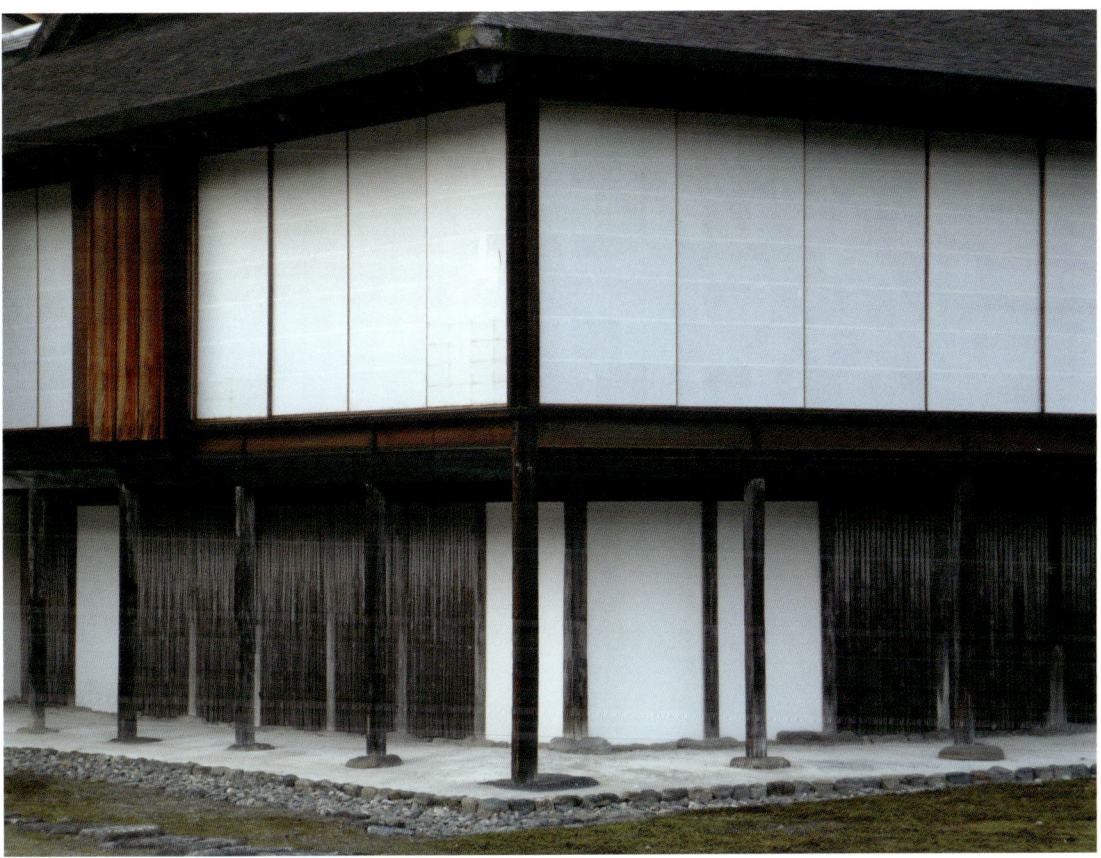

Katsura Detached Palace, *shoin* (main building).

rare ones in which the stones are unnamed, whence its iconographic ambiguity. This is surely one of the factors that led to the Western view of this garden as abstract and minimal (rather than a representation of mountainous islands on a vast ocean, as is the usual reading of the stones set on raked gravel in a dry garden), an interpretation congruent with the precepts of international modernism.

In comparison, the extraordinary garden at Daisen-in (a subtemple of Daitoku-ji) is composed of approximately 100 stones, all of which bear names, variously denoting stone types, unique stones or use value: Buddha's foot-impression stone, turtle's-head stone, immovable stone, *zazen* (seated meditation) stone, splash of waves stone, Dharma stone, bright mirror stone, dragon's-head stone, tiger's-head stone, hermit's-head stone, white cloud stone, waterfall stone, pearl stone, and so on. Concerning the specific value and meaning of stones, François Berthier notes: 'Just as the landscape suggested by the garden at Ryoanji is abstract, the one at Daisen-in is given quite concrete expression', a claim clarified by his explanation concerning Ryōan-ji: 'It is precisely because the significance of this garden remains vague that it is so rich in meaning: it is because it is shrouded in mystery that it offers everyone a large margin of fantasy.'[37] In fact, this 'vague' significance should suggest the broad scope of metaphoricity rather than a lack of it; it should highlight the tension between iconography and abstraction, not nullify it; the argument should remain within the bounds of iconology, and not slip totally into the psychology of fantasy.

The comparison between these two gardens is striking since not only are the stones of Ryōan-ji unnamed but, as has often been remarked, they are not particularly beautiful or unusual specimens. To the contrary, not only does Daisen-in contain a huge number of stones, all of them named, but many are particularly beautiful. However, this does not necessarily suggest that the iconography of Daisen-in is either unified, coherent or intuitively recognizable. While the symbolism of certain stones and arrangements is immediately apparent (as in the case of easily identifiable forms and configurations found in many gardens, such as the turtle island and the crane islet, the waterfall rock, the treasure boat stone), others are iconographically more obscure (like the bright mirror stone, the water imp stone, the pearl stone). While some stones help establish the scenography (such as the treasure-boat stone, the presence of which suggests that the expanse of sand on which it appears is a huge river leading out into the ocean, or the waterfall rock which lends dynamism to the scene), the sum total of the myths and imagery behind the stones of Daisen-in is certainly beyond the comprehension of all but the most learned specialists, and in any case it does not amount to either a coherent myth or a coherent scene. Rather, the names serve several functions that are not necessarily concordant: to stress the individuality of each stone; to organize the iconography of the scene; to suggest symbolic or mythic significance. The mystery of Ryōan-ji exists because its symbolic value is under-determined; that of Daisen-in exists because it is exceedingly complex and over-determined.

It has been suggested that Ryōan-ji is a sort of concrete *kōan*, that Zen exercise of question and answer intended to foster enlightenment by circumventing logic and thrusting one into immediate reality. The reduction of this garden to abstraction and minimalism suggested by many modern authors eliminates the equivocation and paradox central to Zen, and diminishes the garden's complexity and mystery by limiting interpretive possibilities and rationalizing its irrational characteristics. Simply stated, the iconography of Ryōan-ji is implicit, not explicit; allusive, not evident. One of the key Zen principles is *yūgen*, the mystery behind the suggestiveness that permeates Zen art, the sense of wonder at the profound and poetic mystery of the world, explained by D. T. Suzuki as follows: '*Yūgen* is a compound word, each part, *yū* and *gen* meaning "cloudy impenetrability" and the combination meaning "obscurity", "unknowability", "mystery", "beyond intellectual calculability" but not "utter darkness"'.[38] However, this in no way suggests that such mystery necessarily obviates consideration of the mythical, representational and iconographic foundations of this garden. Rather, it would seem to offer a yet more profound sense of representation.[39] Indeed, even *yūgen* itself has its emblematic icons. Augustin Berque explains how for Zeami (1363–1443), who elevated Noh to a spiritual practice, an evening snowfall particularly evoked 'the obscure attraction of the unformulated', while the Zen master Dōgen (1200–1253) understood such snow to be the very symbol of negation, 'the emblem of the concepts of *kū* (the void) and *mu* (nothingness, or rather absence)', the very ground of being symbolized precisely as that cold, empty, desolate world that is the epitome of *wabi-sabi* beauty.[40] The beauty of such imagery is evidenced in *The Tale of Genji*:

> The snow was very deep now, and more was falling. The waning light set off pine and bamboo prettily from one another, and Genji's face took on a clearer glow. 'More than the glory of flowers and fall leaves that season by season capture everyone's heart, it is the night sky in winter, with snow aglitter beneath a brilliant moon, that in the absence

of all colors speaks to me strangely and carries my thoughts beyond this world; there is no higher wonder or delight. Whoever called it dreary understood nothing.'[41]

This also obtains in relation to material culture. While moss on rocks and the moon partially hidden by clouds, akin to the patina cherished as *sabi*, are related to *yūgen*, so too may be artificial effects, as William Theodore de Bary explains:

> To achieve the end of *yūgen*, art had sometimes been stripped of its color and glitter lest these externals distract; a bowl of highly polished silver reflects more than it suggests, but one of oxidized silver has the mysterious beauty of stillness, as Seami [sic] realized when he used for stillness the simile of snow piling in a silver bowl. Or one may prize such a bowl for the tarnished quality itself, for its oldness, for its imperfection, and this is the point where we feel *sabi*.[42]

A related image is that of ice, as the fifteenth-century *renga* poet Shinkei (1406–1475) explains: 'Nothing is more beautiful than ice. The thin crust of morning ice on the stubbled rice fields, icicles hanging from eaves of aged cypress bark, the feeling of withered trees and grasses locked in hoar frost.'[43] One can cherish an object or an effect, an image or sheer materiality: each has its own poetry and its own mystery.

The laws of non-contradiction do not hold in Zen: temptation of the void indeed inspires iconoclasm, but this in no way implies that it does not simultaneously admit iconography. One particularly influential valorization of abstraction was accentuated and disseminated by D. T. Suzuki's famed lectures at Columbia University, where his interpretations of iconoclastic Rinzai Zen tended to dissimulate – for an American audience on the verge of rejecting representation – the long and complex iconographic history of other forms of Buddhism, as well as non-Buddhist thought, that had long informed the arts in Japan. Rupert A. Cox notes the problems that arose from this reductivist version of Zen:

It is the Zen character of the arts which is stressed in Suzuki's writings, to the exclusion of all the other religious, social and political influences that we know about from the historical record. Through the theory of pure experience, all of the arts in Japan are made to appear to be the natural expressions of Zen thought, and therefore of the authentic spirituality of the Japanese.[44]

Later, an even more extreme and reductive version of this position was brought to the awareness of a broad art-world public by Suzuki's most famous student, John Cage, whose theory and practice of indeterminacy in the arts is a direct offspring of the Zen tradition. Finally, this viewpoint culminated in the Deleuzian-Cagean position of the philosopher-musicologist Daniel Charles, who espoused a radical denial of iconography by a priori excluding 'anthropo-morphic' readings so as to dismiss all representational possibilities.[45] There is an anecdote that Cage, a great lover of Ryōan-ji, suggested that the positions of the stones were not chosen according to carefully determined aesthetic,

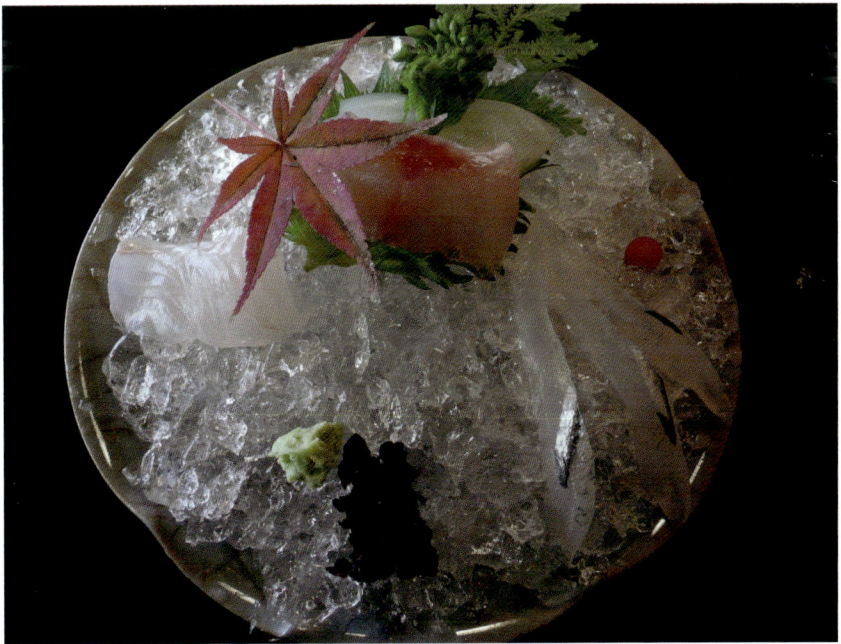

Ryozanpaku restaurant, Kyoto, 2009, sashimi.

symbolic or metaphysical calculations, but that the emptiness of the sand permitted them to be placed anywhere whatsoever. This Duchampian supposition reveals more about Cage than about the Zen garden. In 1983 he created the first of several versions of a musical composition entitled *Ryoanji*, and in 1992 he produced *Where R = Ryoanji*, a series of graphite-on-paper works consisting of fifteen pebbles randomly placed on a page and encircled to create the graphic elements. This schematic representation of the garden in fact eliminates the tension between abstraction and figuration, as well as the iconographic mystery, both of which contribute to the richness of the garden.

Cage had always said that he wished to work not in imitation of nature, but in imitation of nature's processes. However, given the infinite complexity of natural systems, it would be impossible to prove if he ever succeeded, and we thus cannot assume that any of his works, the Ryōan-ji-inspired pieces included, had been created in this manner. Yet it was not nature, but men, who created Ryōan-ji, and we simply do not know how the gardeners conceived this site. In any case, Cage had no intention of imitating the gardeners, since this would have entailed a vast project of historical, mythical, ritual and iconographic analysis that was certainly antithetical to Cage's modes of production, and which would have been a hyperbolically representational process. In fact, it is not a foregone conclusion that the process of creating Ryōan-ji the garden and *Where R = Ryoanji* the drawings have anything in common other than a final count of fifteen stones on a more or less blank slate. The immediate extrapolation of Cage's claim about the random placement of the stones would be that any fifteen stones arranged in any manner on any flat surface would be the aesthetic equivalent of Ryōan-ji, and the ultimate extrapolation would be a *reductio ad absurdum* confusing singularity with genre, such that any disposition of a given number of objects on any empty field would be aesthetically equivalent. The problem is that Cage valorized the indeterminacy of the process over the equivocation of the object. Perhaps this situation arose from the fact that Cage identified with the creator rather than the spectator, valuing process over object. He sought the potential indeterminacy of the creative moment, all the while ignoring the determinate indeterminacy separating abstraction and iconography. Yet, paradoxical as it

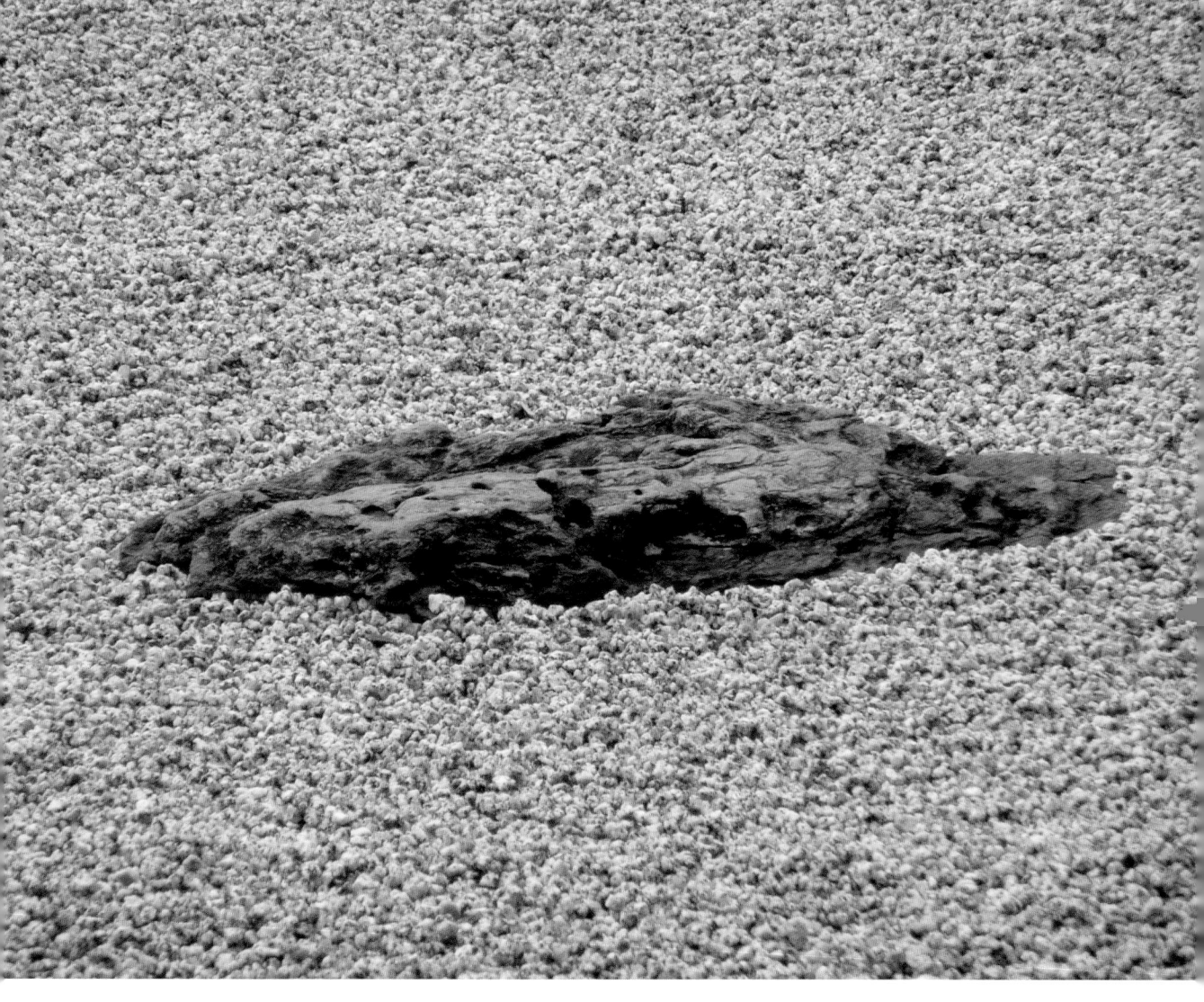

Ryōan-ji.

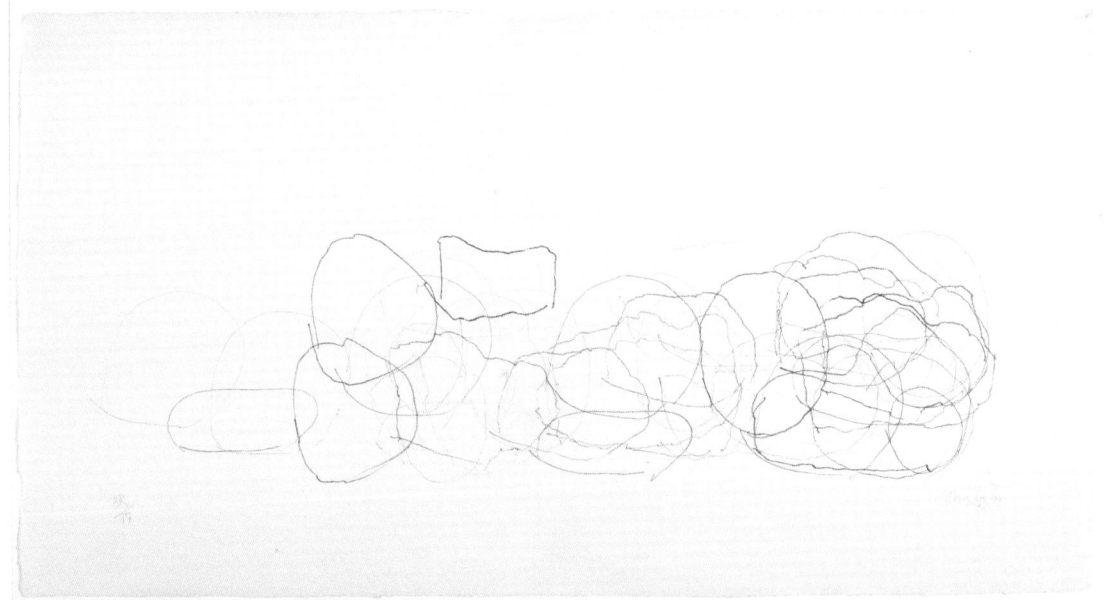

may seem, one may indeed attempt to establish an iconography of the void, just as twentieth-century musicology has established an inventory of silences.

Part of the beauty of the Zen garden – and in particular the sublime beauty of Ryōan-ji, which exemplifies an extreme sublimation of such forms – rests precisely on equivocation, as Günter Nitschke explains:

> In the opinion of garden expert Mirei Shigemori, the *kare-sansui* garden reflects two aesthetic ideals fundamental to Muromachi thinking: *yugen*, a profound and austere elegance concerning a multi-layered symbolism, and *yohaku no bi*, the beauty of empty space.[46]

Somewhat atypically, according to his reading, Shigemori stresses the symbolic depth of *yūgen* rather than its sense of mystery, ineffability and unspoken connotation. But what he makes clear is its relation to the void, perhaps the ultimate mystery. Such is not the difference between representation and abstraction, but rather between two levels of representation: that of the world and that of the void, the latter of which is also contingent on varied symbolic

John Cage, *3R/17* (*Where R = Ryoanji*), 1992, pencils on handmade Japanese paper, with computer-based I Ching score, 25.4 × 48.3 cm.

levels. At stake are types of metaphors and degrees of metaphoricity. The Zen garden is equivocally symbolic. That Ryōan-ji has been referred to as a 'garden of emptiness' (*mutei*) is hardly proof of its abstraction, since emptiness is both physical and metaphysical, as Zen masters and Western philosophers have long taught. Nitschke claims that 'it belongs to the art of the void', but he is also aware of the aura of symbolism that surrounds this nothingness.[47] A prime goal of theology is to reconcile us with this void, whether through anguish or joy. The void may be pure nothingness, or it may be the empty spaces between objects and the empty time between events, the *ma* that operates as both spatial gap and temporal interval creating a perfect natural balance. Furthermore, the iconography of the dry Japanese garden shares one major feature with that of painting and calligraphy, the elaborated background on which the figures are set. Just as the empty fields of raked gravel gain significance from texture and patterning, Japanese *washi* paper – flecked with mica and gold, threaded with silver, watermarked, patterned, coloured – reaches extraordinary heights of creativity. Here the 'void' takes on a very palpable, even sensual, form. The void may be metaphoric or it may be real. Emptiness may be a sign of iconoclasm, or yet another icon.

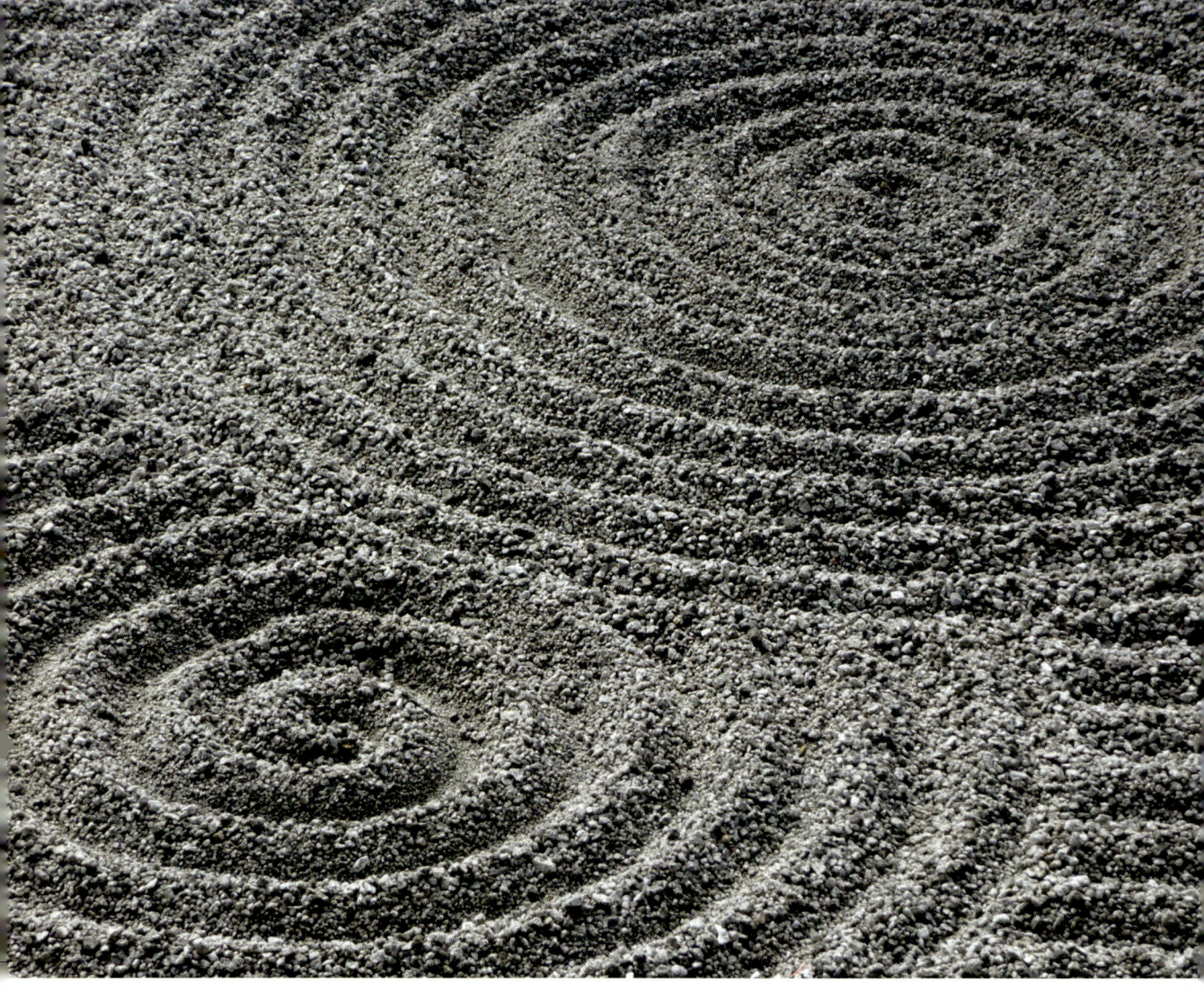

Tōfuku-ji, raked sand.

THREE

ZEN MOUNTAINS, ZEN WATER

The Teramachi shopping mall in Kyoto is the epitome of a certain contemporary vision of Japan: a supercharged, unbridled consumerism couched in an empire of signs. With the exception of its Shinto shrines, this mall consists of storefronts with few decorative touches other than the mostly inexpensive merchandise on display. However, in this aesthetically bleak environment, one shopkeeper could not resist the centuries-old impulse typical of Kyoto, to have a small garden at the front of the shop. The traditional Kyoto shop and house (*machiya*) is a narrow and elongated structure that generally has three gardens: one in the front, one in the rear, and a courtyard garden – the *tsuboniwa*, a small garden (measuring at least two *tatami*, that is, 3.3 square metres) enclosed within the architectural structure. Innumerable Kyoto restaurants have at least one small garden; whether in the entrance or the courtyard, in the window or an alley, just a few square metres suffice. So the shopkeeper designed a sort of Arte Povera garden: a small stone placed alongside a clear bowl of water with plants floating in it, all set on a chair surrounded by several potted plants, the largest of which contained eleven light pebbles set on the soil, and sundry pebbles and large glass beads strewn on a ledge behind. This is an ephemeral garden, since it was necessarily dismantled every evening before the shop closed. Moving in its simplicity and frugality, this bricolage landscape reveals the minimal conditions of a garden: stone, water, plant. One finds, for example, in Zuihō-in (a sub-temple of Daitoku-ji) an iconographic source for such a garden: a bonsai set between a pottery water basin and a small stand of decorative grass.[1] Is this a garden? A metaphor of a garden? A plan for a garden? Or simply disparate objects related by garden-inspired circumstances?

The small chair-garden in Teramachi might not be extraordinary, but it nevertheless reveals a striking power of the reductive imagination. One limit of such abstraction exists in Myōshin-ji – head temple of the Rinzai Zen sect,

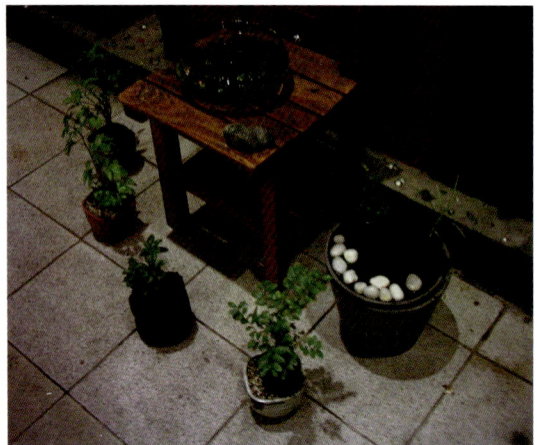 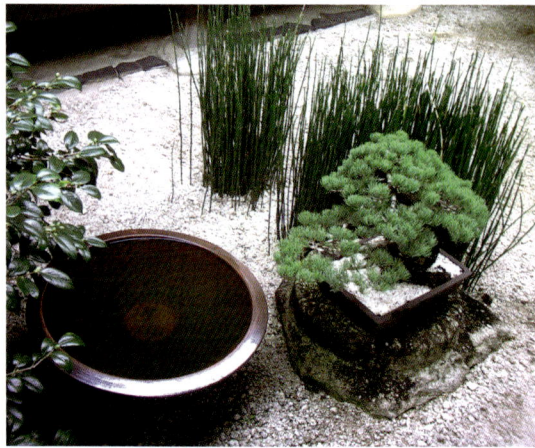

Portable garden at Teramachi, Kyoto, 2006.

Zuihō-in, a subtemple of Daitoku-ji.

of which Ryōan-ji is dependent – where the entrance to the subtemple Zakke-in is flanked by two absolutely minimal parterres, almost certainly mid-twentieth-century creations. On the left, a flat, square, white stone set into an L-shaped bed of small white pebbles; on the right a thicker, irregular, black stone set into a rectangular bed of small white pebbles. The use of what resemble paving stones as major garden elements is remarkable, for the focus on cut stone is rare in traditional Japanese gardens, having come into vogue only with the influence of modernism. Is this hyperminimal play of binary oppositions – L / I; double rectangle / single rectangle; white / black; regular / irregular; thin / thick; smooth / scored; white-on-white / black-on-white – mere decoration? Or rather the zero-degree *karesansui*? Or perhaps a three-dimensional conceptualization, an ideal prototype, of the dry garden? Whatever the case, this courtyard is a veritable lesson in stones, since it reveals the diverse practical and symbolic uses of rocks: as border, marker, path, parterre, cairn, sculpture and even sacred object, for there is an altar before which is set a small piles of stones, as if in offering to the gods (visible on the right of the photograph on p. 89). The apparent minimalism of these dry, stony parterres belies the actual complexity of such gardens, which must always be approached according to their play of scale, surroundings, climate, motion, temporality and so on. Otherwise we experience an abstracted picture, not a living landscape. This setting thus simultaneously reveals

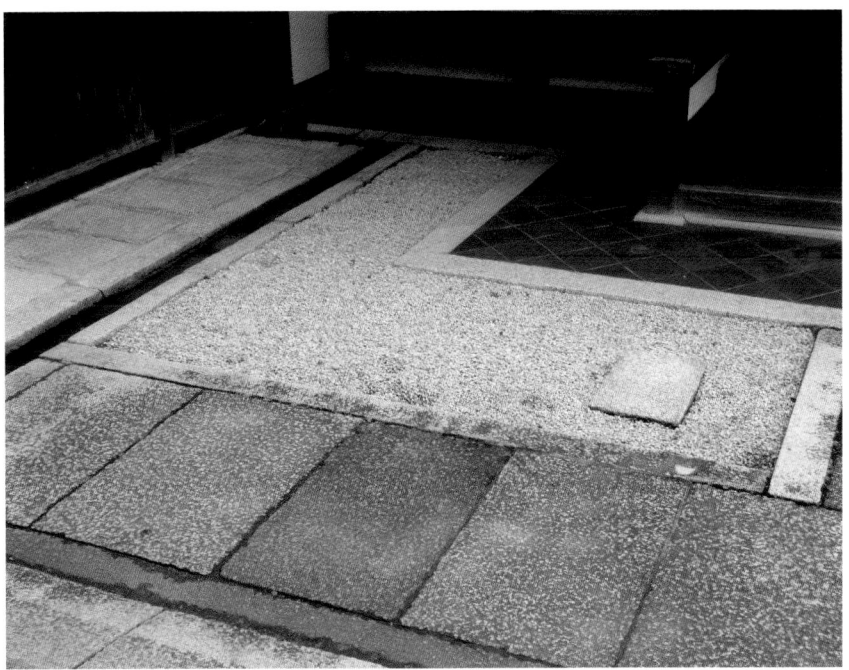

Zakke-in, a subtemple
of Myōshin-ji.

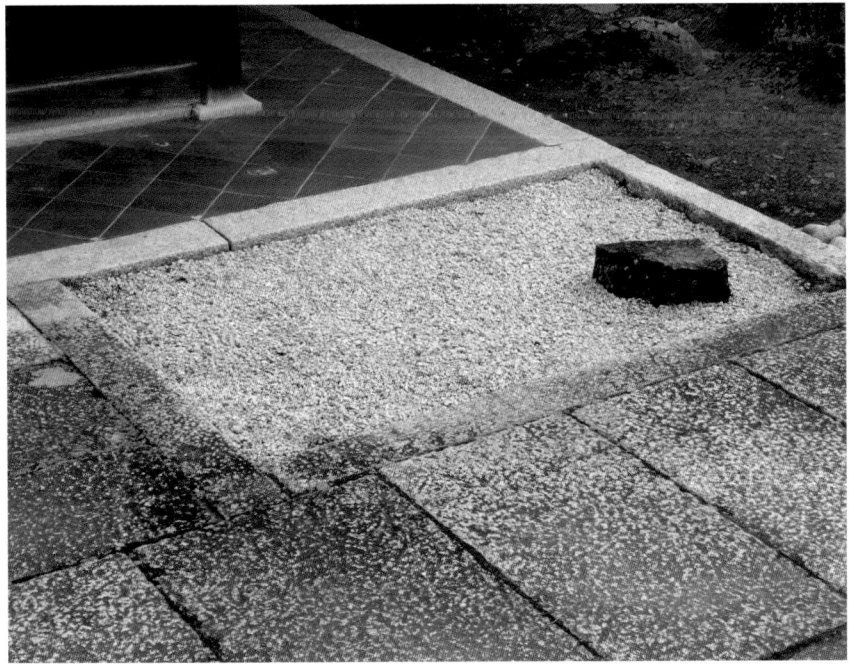

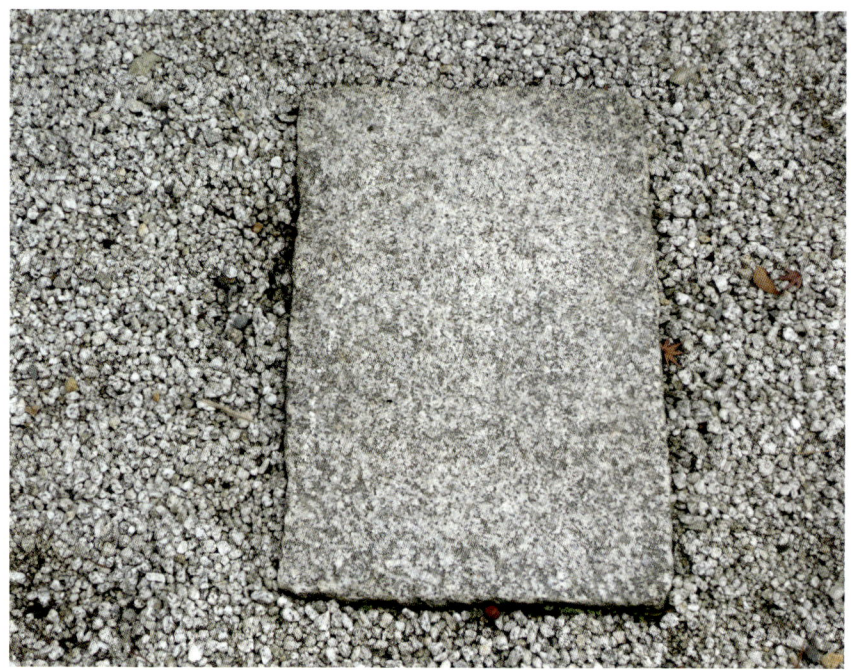

Zakke-in.

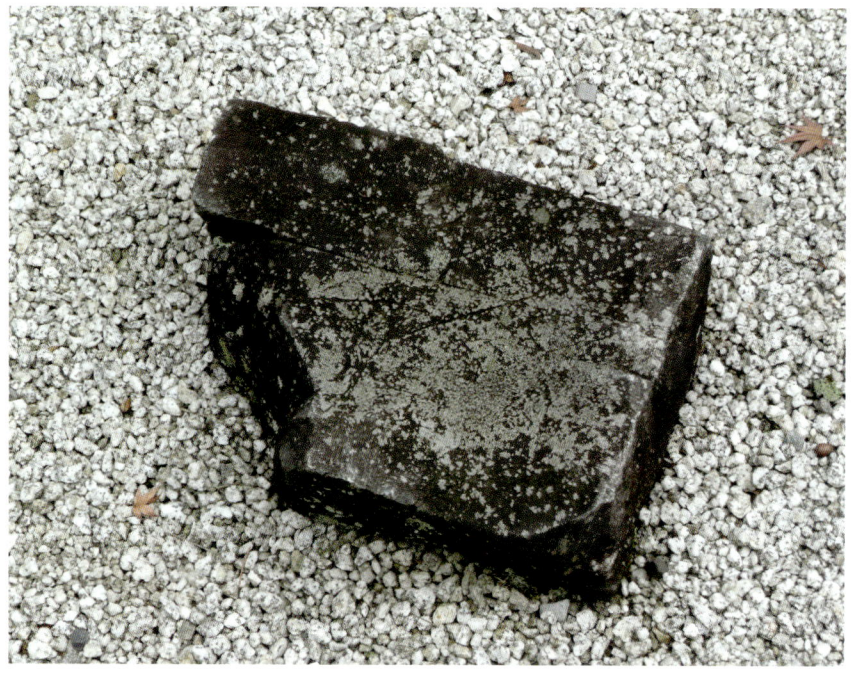

the minimal conditions of a dry garden and the maximal conditions of
visibility, instantiating the claim that 'the richest site is that which is
most closely observed.' But what are we willing to call a 'garden'? Might
it be the smallest framed unit, whether the frame be physical or conceptual?
If we can see a 'garden' in a plate of food or on a work of pottery, might
we not be obliged to reconsider our manner of observing the natural
landscape? At what point in such discussions could we delete the quotation
marks from the word 'garden'? This garden in Zakke-in is most certainly
a lesson in the art of observation, revealing that what may appear to
be the simplest is in fact the most profound. Is this not a typically
Zen intuition?

Zakke-in.

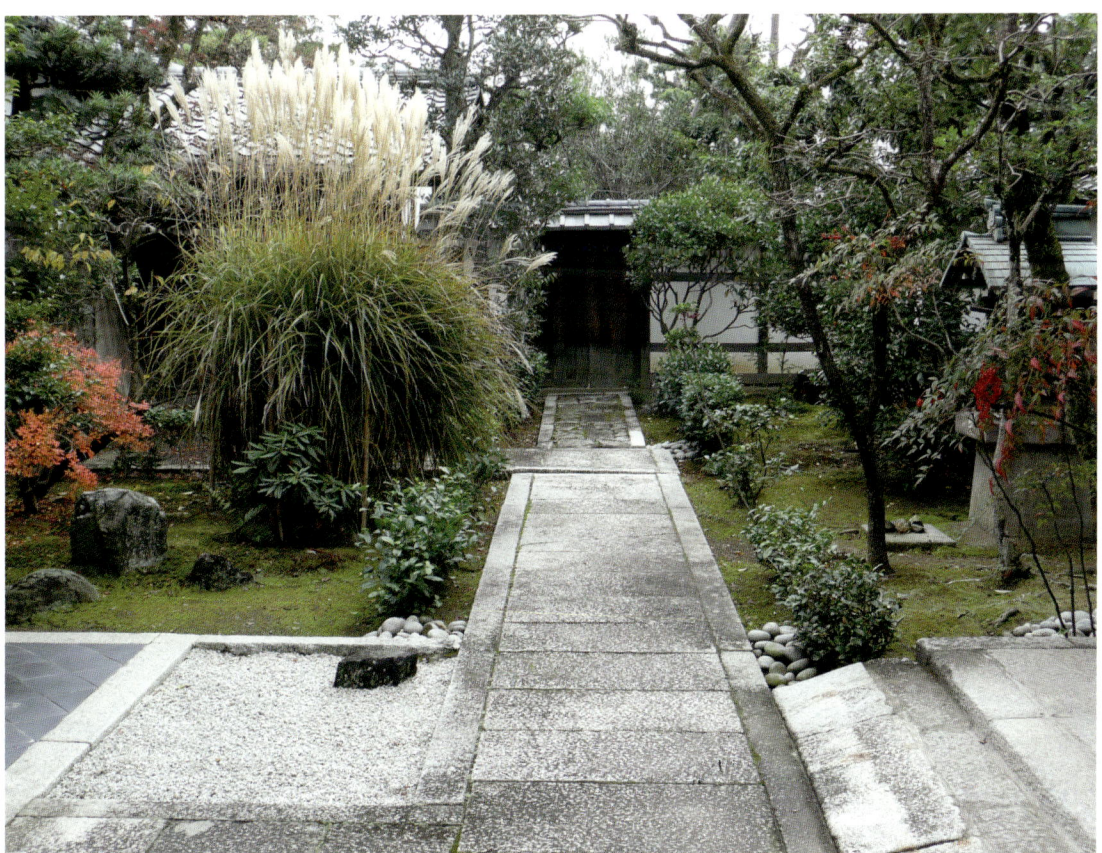

The unequivocal focus of the Zen garden is stones. We find stones alongside stones, stones on stones, stones representing mountains, stones crushed to gravel, and often just single exceptional stones that all by themselves constitute a landscape. Lafcadio Hearn, the great nineteenth-century interpreter of Japan, describes the particularly Japanese passion for stones:

> Curious, this child love of stones! Stones are the toys not only of the children of the poor, but of all children at one period of existence: no matter how well supplied with other playthings, every Japanese child wants sometimes to play with stones. To the child-mind a stone is a marvelous thing, and ought so to be, since even to the understanding of the mathematician there can be nothing more wonderful than a common stone.[2]

One might add that this remains true for the adult mind, especially in Japan, where certain stones are raised to the level of priceless treasures, and where the sense of the earth permeates all aesthetics. Hearn also says, 'Only a very great mind could answer all a child's questions about stones.'[3] In *Le Geste et la parole*, the French prehistorian André Leroi-Gourhan shows how the Palaeolithic origins of art stemmed from a fascination with regularity within an overbearingly irregular, chaotic world:

> Figurative art as such was preceded by something more obscure or more general which corresponds to the deliberate vision of forms. The unusual within forms, a powerful incentive toward figurative concern, existed only from the time when the subject confronted an organized image of his universe in relation to the objects which enter into his field of perception.[4]

Such found objects include highly regular things, such as seashells with their complex mathematical forms, polished pebbles which appear as if already reassuringly domesticated (imbued with a natural *sabi*, one might say) and the occasional crystal with its magical optical qualities. Such is an art of fascination, and the contemplation of these objects is a form of meditation and self-reflection. 'These concretions directly touch the depths of man's reflective thought. It is mysterious and even disquieting to discover in nature a sort of congealed reflection of thought of which the unusual is the incentive.'[5] A uniquely formed pebble may well have evoked the very first aesthetic reactions among humankind.

In Chinese and Japanese cosmology – be it Taoist, Buddhist, Shinto or animist – stones are not mere inanimate objects, but rather concentrations of cosmic and telluric energy (chi) flowing in different patterns throughout the universe. Zen master Dōgen insists that pebbles are sentient beings that participate in Buddha's nature, and according to Shinto tradition, the natural or artificial rock arrangements of certain sites have the function of attracting the *kami*, those supernatural creatures that inhabit the surrounding forests and mountains. Indeed, the very first 'garden' might be deemed the fields of gravel or sacred rocks (*iwakura*) related to the *kami*, cordoned off by *shimenawa*, ropes used to delimit and protect sacred rocks and trees. Such age-old theories of panpsychism have recently been reconsidered on the subatomic level by contemporary science. One theorist suggests that 'the rock's innards "see" the entire universe by means of the gravitational and electromagnetic signals it is continuously receiving', and further proposes that, 'if you are poetically inclined, you might think of the rock as a purely contemplative being'.[6] In short, agency is distributed everywhere in the universe.

In both Japanese culture and the earlier Chinese culture that inspired it, rocks are thus valued for both force and form, as Günter Nitschke explains:

> Hence individual rock settings became more than simply imitations of famous natural sights or metaphors of mountains and islands within a garden; they now expressed the energetic constellations of nature. They offered the garden-maker a symbolic language in which to state the most profound truths of nature which lay beneath its aesthetic surface.[7]

Rocks are of such great aesthetic importance that one classic Chinese book of painting teaches: 'In order to learn to paint, one must invariably learn

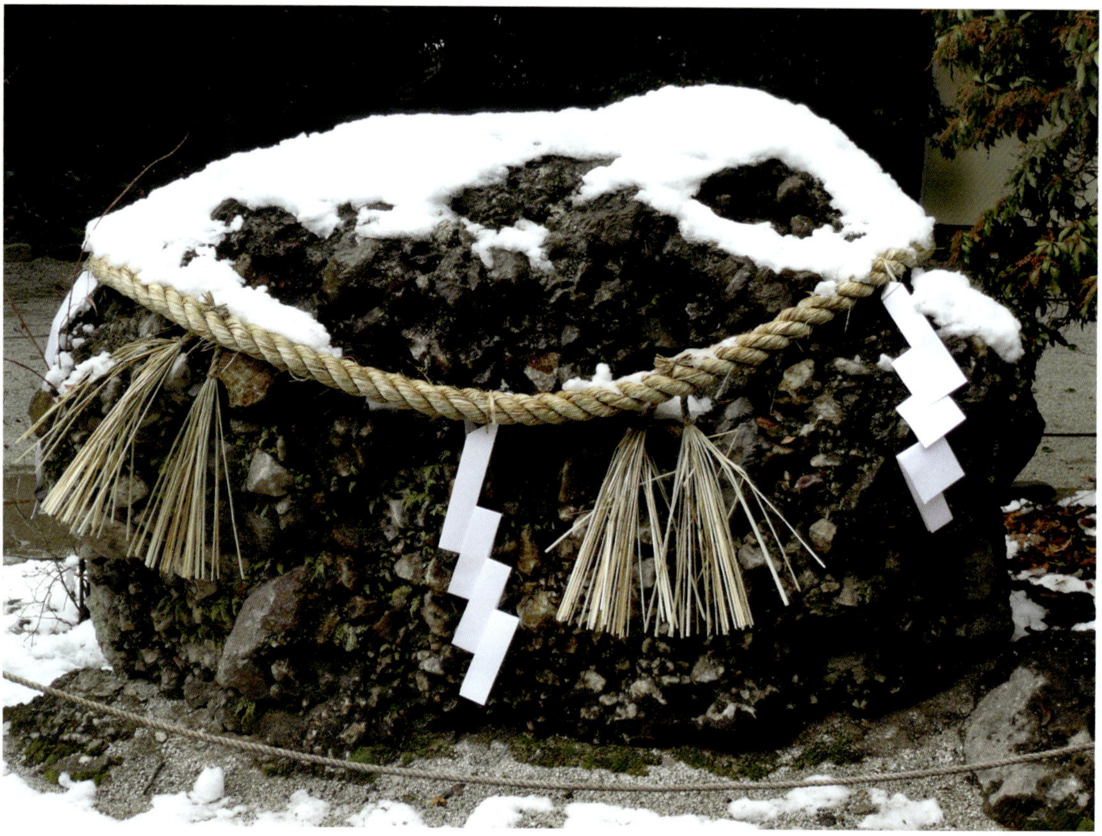

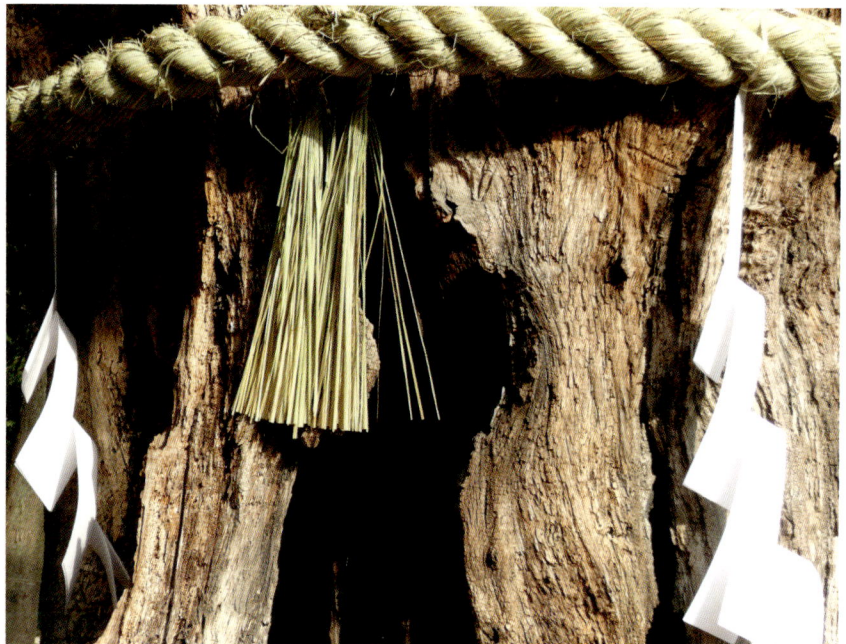

Shimogamo Shrine,
sacred stone.

Shimogamo Shrine,
sacred tree.

how to paint rocks. Of all the techniques of using the brush, none are more difficult than those required for rocks, and no subject calls for a greater range of techniques than rocks do.'[8] Not only have the forms of many different types of mountains been enumerated in the annals of Chinese painting, but there also exists a specific repertory of brushstrokes for representing different aspects of mountains, such as 'coiled up clouds', 'hatchet marks', 'devil's face', 'skeleton's skull', 'sesame seeds', and so on.[9] The iconicity of such painting extends down to the very form of the brushstrokes. (We might compare European Renaissance depictions of clothing, with their intricate folds and extravagant decorations, as a prime sign of painterly virtuosity, though in the West, for centuries every effort was made to guarantee the invisibility of the brushstrokes.) In classic Chinese art, the artist first learns to draw stones and rocks, much as the Western artist begins with the human figure. Indeed, following Taoist cosmology, the rock is seen as a dynamic entity, as François Cheng, writing of mountains in Chinese culture, explains:

> Moved by breath, nourished with fog and wind, it is capable of metamorphosis. Poets and painters baptised it with the beautiful name, 'root of the clouds.' Constantly transformed by the energy of the ground and the sky, it offers multiple facets and incarnates multiple attitudes: placidity and torment, tenderness and savagery.[10]

With changes in perspective and lighting, framing and atmospheric conditions, the physiognomy of rocks and mountains is transformed at every instant, becoming as fluid as water. Conversely, Loraine Kuck claims that for certain gardens such as Joei-ji in Yamaguchi prefecture, credited to Sesshū (1420–1506), the painter who revolutionized Japanese art, the choice of rocks in the garden was made so as to simulate his particular form of brushstrokes.[11] Painting and stone thus exist in reciprocal iconic relation down to the very level of the brushstroke.

The Chinese love of rocks may even be surpassed by that of the Japanese. Bernard Rudofsky makes a good point (his sarcasms notwithstanding) in claiming that

Maybe we ought to envy the imaginative powers of a people who can distinguish rocks by one hundred and thirty-eight names (if only two sexes); that will court and covet rocks of special appeal, kidnap them, wrap them in silks and brocades like the most precious of sweethearts, and carry them in triumphal procession to their new abode.[12]

We might remember that in the European tradition, the relics of saints and their spectacular receptacles have long received exactly the same sort of devout, and often criminal, attention. Rudofsky is clearly referring to a specific incident in Japanese history when Nobunaga, the warlord who began the unification of Japan, had a rock garden created at one of his palaces in Kyoto. Regarding the transfer of that particularly coveted stone from one garden to another: 'Nobunaga had the rock wrapped in silk, decorated with flowers, and brought it to the garden with the music of flute and drums, and the chanting of the laborers.'[13] At the other extreme there exist, according to Zōen, the 'unnamed', 'worthless' or 'discarded' rocks, ones that do not have any specific characteristics that warrant naming but that are nevertheless essential in garden composition, whether to enhance the naturalness of the formal composition, to create dynamic balance or to highlight a more prominent stone.

The contemporary landscape architect Marc Peter Keane expresses the manifold aspects of this passion well, writing of the early creators of the dry garden:

they had no word for gardening, simply the expression *ishi wo taten koto*, 'the art of setting stones'. Setting stones was so entirely fundamental to the act of garden building that it defined the process, and through the medium of the stone the designers of that era wove various meanings into their gardens. They set a stone and called it Shumisen, Japanese for Sumeru, the central mountain of Buddhist and Hindu cosmology; they set another and called it Fudō-myōō, the Buddhist deity who purges the world of evil; they set still another to evoke the image of a windswept ocean shore and express allegorically the waste and abject loneliness felt by lovers denied their love; and they set stones of specific colors around their home to balance the flow of life-energy based on rules of an ancient Chinese geomancy. The stones were animated with meanings potent and diverse, and yet beyond all those cultural affections, they also remained a testimony to communal work and, deeper still, a symbolic link back to the wilderness. Beyond the superficial sculptural beauty of the stones and the great material value placed on them in later years, the ancient messages lay enfolded within them, informing all else, the way a primordial reptilian center remains at the stem of our brains.[14]

Zōen's *Illustrations* enumerates 57 named rocks, reduced from the 361 of Chinese tradition and from the thousands in certain Indian manuscripts. Rocks are categorized into types according to structure, function (scenic and sensory effects) and symbolism (Taoist, Shinto, Confucian, Buddhist): side rocks, lying rocks, wave-repelling rocks, water-cutting rocks, stepping stones, shadow-facing stones, ducks'-abode rocks, hovering-mist rocks, human-form rocks, mirror rocks, reverence rocks, demon rocks, vengeful-spirit rocks, taboo rocks, triadic Buddhist waterfall rocks, and so on.[15] In practice, the total number of named stones is countless. Specific rocks may symbolize mountains, both mythological and real, most often Shumisen and Fuji. Rocks may represent other natural objects as well, like the waterfall rocks (*taki-ishi*) common in Zen gardens, so named because their striated vertical surface patterns suggest cascading water. Notable rocks are often given unique proper names, such as Twofold World Rock, Rock of the Spirit Kings or Dragon's Abode Rock. In comparison, while stones do have symbolic resonance in Christian iconography, their significance has hardly touched the popular imagination, and has been lost to all but specialists. Steve McCaffery explains:

> The identification of stone as the figure of Christ was a persistent theme throughout the Middle Ages. In his *Summa de exemplis et similitudinibus rerum*, and with a fecund demonstration of what Saint Jerome calls *tropologia libera*, Giovanni di San Gimigniano devotes forty chapters to

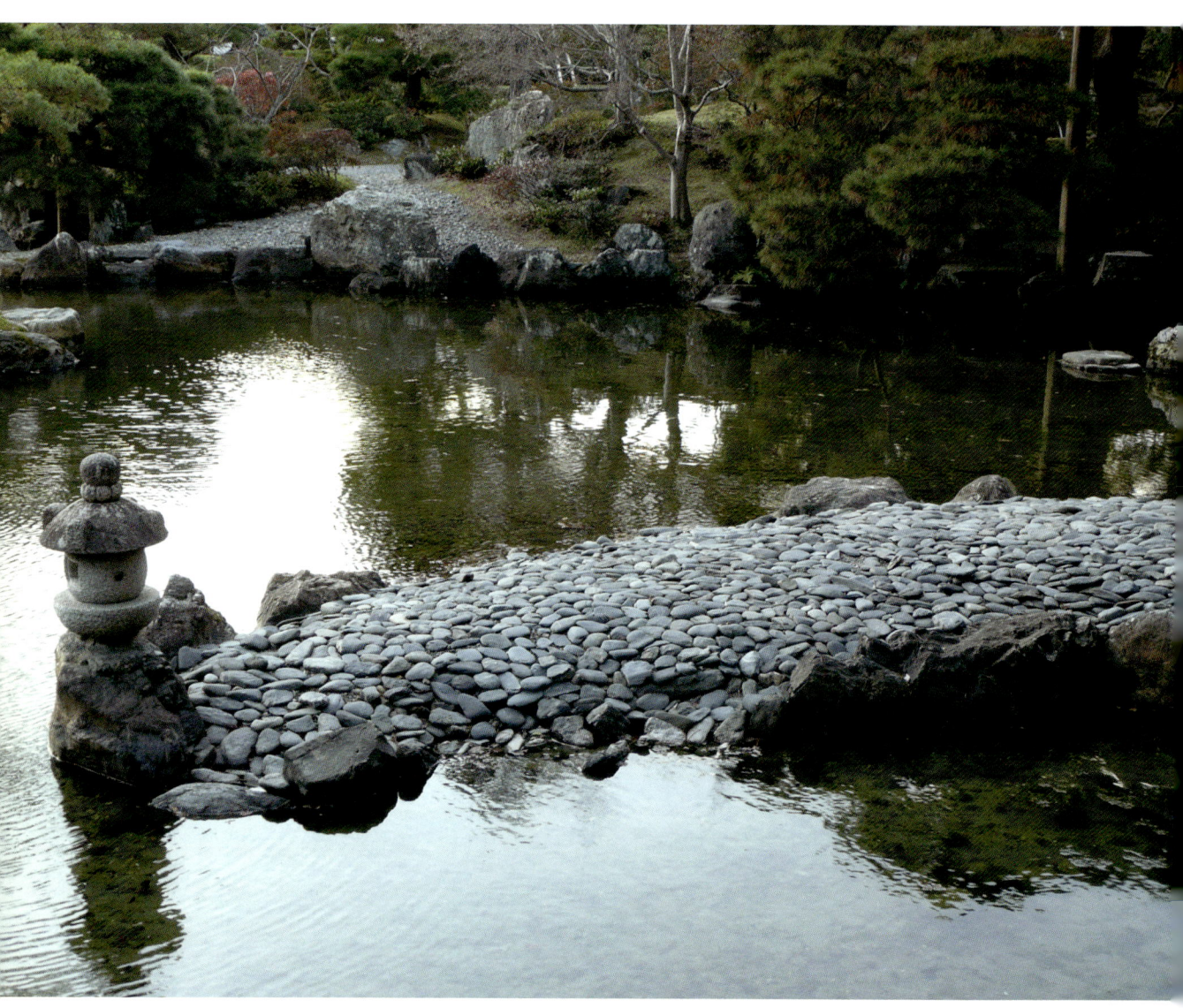

Katsura Detached Palace, Kyoto, stone arrangement in the form of Amanohashidate.

the significance of stones. All stones are figures of Divine love; marble is a figure for Beauty, Goodness, and Prudence; Mary is chalcedony and her virginity asterite; and Christ is chrysolite.[16]

Contemporary Western customs regarding birthstones have become a pale version of what was once a rich theological symbolism.

Some Zen gardens are representations of the natural landscape, especially the rocky shores of the Inland Sea and the environs of the five mountains surrounding Kyoto.[17] Perhaps the most famous example is the pebble arrangement in the pond set before the Shokin-tei tea house at the Katsura Detached Palace in Kyoto, which is in the image of the great sandbar Amanohashidate, one of the three great scenic views of Japan, located in Miyazu Bay in northern Kyoto prefecture. Indeed, Japan itself is basically a huge stone that rises from the ocean, and Mount Fuji has long been a formal archetype in all the Japanese arts. Conversely, our means of viewing the landscape are always inflected by art. The Zen garden was influenced by the natural landscape as seen through both the poetry and iconography of Chinese Song dynasty landscape painting, which featured representations of China's extraordinary mountain ranges and incredible rock formations, not unlike the manner in which the English picturesque garden was influenced by Italian, French and Dutch landscape painting. (The English garden might have developed quite differently if British collectors of the epoch had been more enthralled by those Italian Renaissance paintings which depicted fantastic rock formations.) Thus Japanese Zen gardens are informed not only by Chinese, Korean and Japanese landscapes, but also by their traditions of landscape painting. Furthermore, a favoured representational technique is the literary landscape, such as the garden in the Katsura Detached Palace that represents a landscape described in *The Tale of Genji*. Another famous example is the garden of Tenryū-ji (Kyoto), where, as Itoh Teiji notes, the pond and its rock arrangements suggest a painting in the style of the Chinese Northern Song dynasty, while its famed captured view of Arashiyama with its blossoming cherry trees resembles a traditional Japanese painting of the *yamato-e* style.[18] Painterly templates, however hybridized in style and iconography, are of the essence.

Japanese and Chinese gardens are informed both by natural landscapes and by their idealized representation in landscape painting, with mountainous islands central to their iconography. But since perception is always culturally conditioned, and there is no untutored 'natural' vision, no 'artless' sight, one must always seek the cognition behind the perception, the myth behind the image, which in Japanese gardens are derived from Chinese fantasies of mythological paradises: Taoist paradises such as the Isles of the Immortals, also known as the 'Turtle Islands'; Buddhist utopias such as Amida's Western Paradise; and Mount Sumeru, the *axis mundi*, represented in gardens by rocks called Shumisen. As in so many myths worldwide, the mountain is considered to be the primal manifestation of form, the origin of the cosmos emerging from amidst universal chaos. It has sacred value and iconographic privilege. Curiously, in terms of the broader metaphoric value of stones, it should be noted that in Zōen's list, at least twenty refer to water-related effects, while only three represent mountains, which in itself suggests the highly metaphoric value of such rocks. Zōen's *Illustrations* divides all stones into five major 'colours' or types, organized according to the five elements (wood, fire, earth, metal, water) such that wood stones are tall and vertical, and are usually placed at the back of groupings; metal stones are low and vertical, related to wood stones; fire stones arch dynamically towards the sides, and are placed on one of the sides towards the front of the arrangement; water stones are flat and horizontal; and earth stones recline, and are used in the foreground.

These sundry forms of landscape metaphoricity are extraordinarily concentrated in ceramics, that art form which most sensually and most directly links the hand of artist and collector to the earth. Indeed, glaze and scorch patterns that resemble landscapes are simply referred to by the term *keshiki* (landscape). The transformative alchemy of ceramics parallels and symbolizes the geological work of creating rocks and mountains. Stony landscapes are decomposed over the centuries into clay, which is then fired to once again become stone. In the kiln, the extraordinarily violent interaction of the elements conspires to create new forms: the earth and water that make up clay are transmogrified by the forces of air and fire to create stone, whence

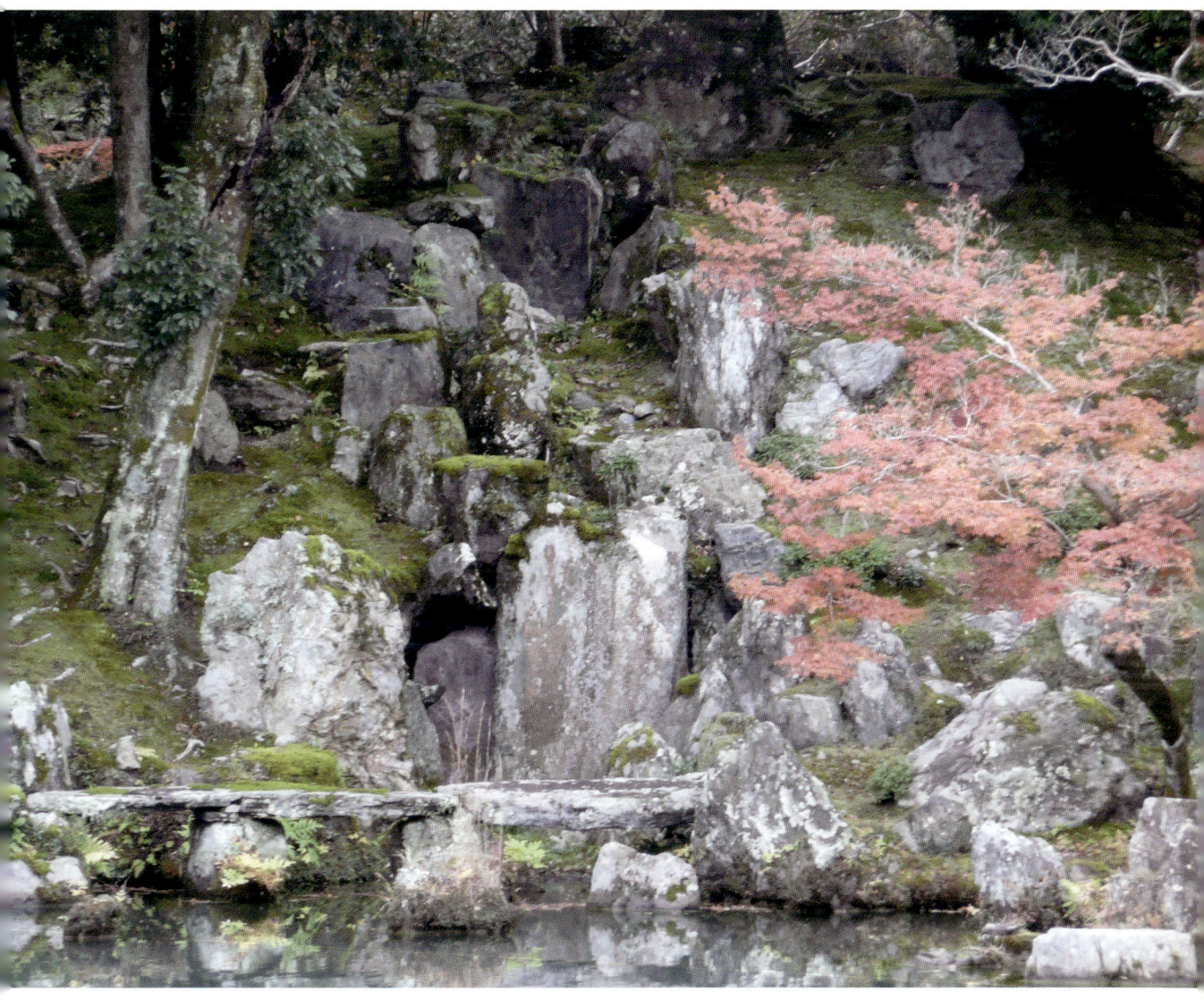

Tenryū-ji, dry waterfall.

the term 'stoneware' for high-fired works. The hyperbolic instance of this passion for clay is the preference among many pottery lovers for unglazed stoneware, most famously Bizen and Shigaraki works, where the immediate action of fire and ash on undecorated clay is most evident.

This connection to the earth was deeply felt by Isamu Noguchi, whose pottery, along with that of Picasso, was among the major post-war influences on Japanese ceramics. He expresses this in an almost mystical account of his identification with nature:

> A fine balance of spirit with matter can only occur when the artist has so thoroughly submerged himself in the study of the unity of nature as to truly become once more a part of nature – a part of the very earth, thus to view the inner surfaces and the life elements.[19]

In 1952 Noguchi embarked on an intensive period of pottery production, while living in the Kamakura compound of Kitaōji Rosanjin, the great potter, calligrapher and restaurateur. Perusal of the catalogue of Noguchi's landmark exhibition of 1952 at the Museum of Modern Art in Kamakura is revelatory, for not only are the pieces categorized by regional pottery types (Bizen, Karatsu, Kasama, Seto, Shigaraki), but of the 119 pottery objects, 77 are either Bizen or Shigaraki. His preference for these austere and undecorated styles reveals a keen interest in the immediate relations between the landscapes of pottery and of the earth. Indicative of this proclivity was his studio at Kamakura where, dug out of the cliffside, Noguchi left the back earth wall in its raw state, leaving the scars of the heavy metal machines that hollowed out the space and letting soot accumulate over time.[20] The aesthetic relation between pottery and the immediate environment of studios and kilns is worthy of extended study. Noguchi's subsequent career is interesting in this regard, since after his last intense foray into pottery he concreted on sculpture based on Japanese stones, circumventing the allegorical relation between kiln and nature to go directly to the source. There exists, however, one late work that serves as an allegory of this choice, and of the artistic sublimation of matter in general. While working at the American Academy in Rome in 1962, he created *Lessons of Musokokushi*, in honour of Musō (1275–1351), a Zen priest reputed to have created two of the most famous gardens in Kyoto, Tenryū-ji, site of the first 'borrowed view' in Japan, and Saihō-ji (Kokedera, the Moss Temple), which contains a grouping of stones believed to be the earliest dry waterfall arrangement. *Lessons of Musokokushi* consists of five rock-like moulds of clay that were formed on the floor and then cast in bronze, resulting in a work that recalls so many *karesansui* rock groups, and to which Noguchi referred as 'my own Ryoanji'. Yet here the earth is transmogrified into metal, the landscape disappears, and the bronze 'rocks' are destined for the museum. What remains is but a simulacrum of Noguchi's favourite materials, those that constitute the Japanese earth.

This should remind us that pottery may function as either pure material surface or as a *tabula rasa* for calligraphy and painting. A fascinating example of purely material metaphoricity is a series of *guinomi* created by Jeff Shapiro, an artist now based in upstate New York who long worked in Japan, where the cups appear as igneous stones, suggesting the correspondence between kiln and volcano. He explains the technique:

> It is carved from a chunk of clay that is placed over a simple cylindrical form and then carved and scraped to make the outside and inside shape. The surface in this case is from two glazes. The light color is a shino glaze and the black is a black oribe that I heavily reduce to give it the slightly 'volcanic' look. It is fired in the small down draft wood fired kiln . . . The approach to making the guinomi and other work is to keep a strong organic characteristic aspect to the work but to transcend this into something that is my own and perhaps more abstract.[21]

There also exists another technique for creating a similar effect termed *koge*, where the work is buried in embers for a prolonged period so that texture is developed as ash continues to deposit while running into the ember bed. Further ash saturation leads to *ishi-koge*, which, as the name suggests, is a rock-like appearance.[22] The lesson here is diametrically opposed to that of the *Lessons of Musokokushi*: ash turned to stone decorates the stoneware

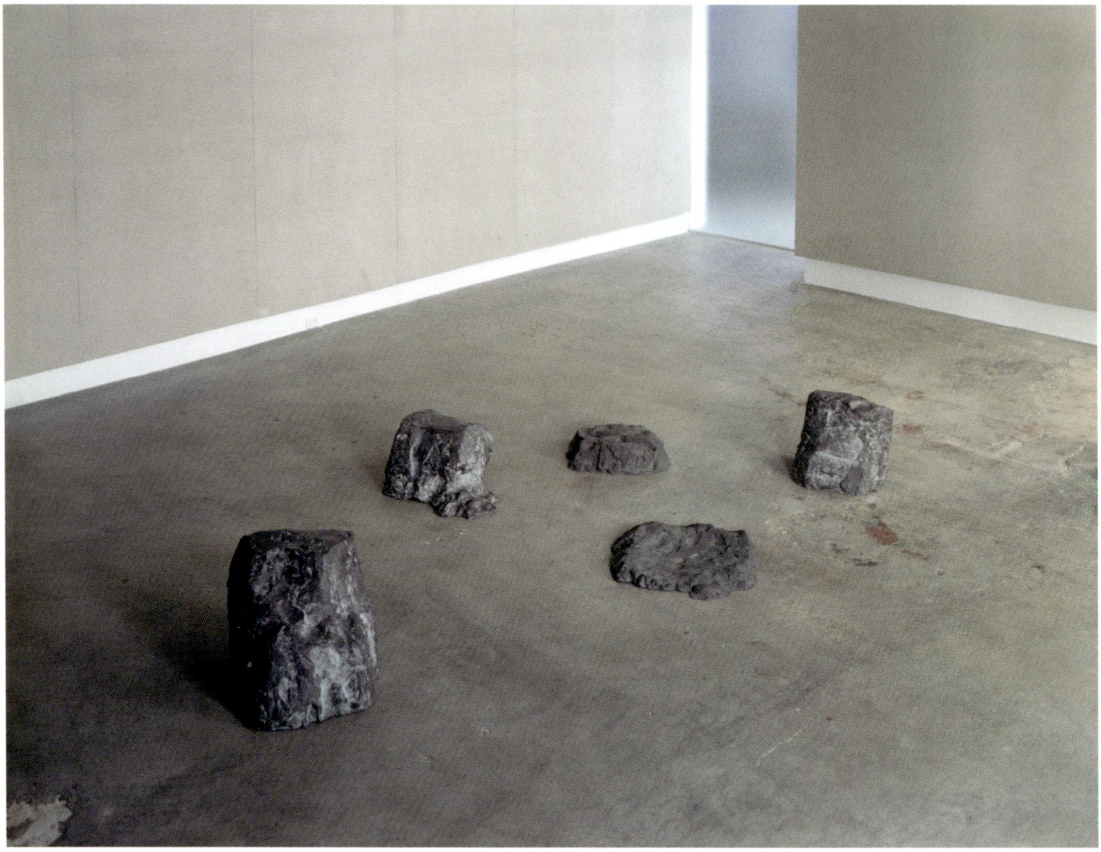

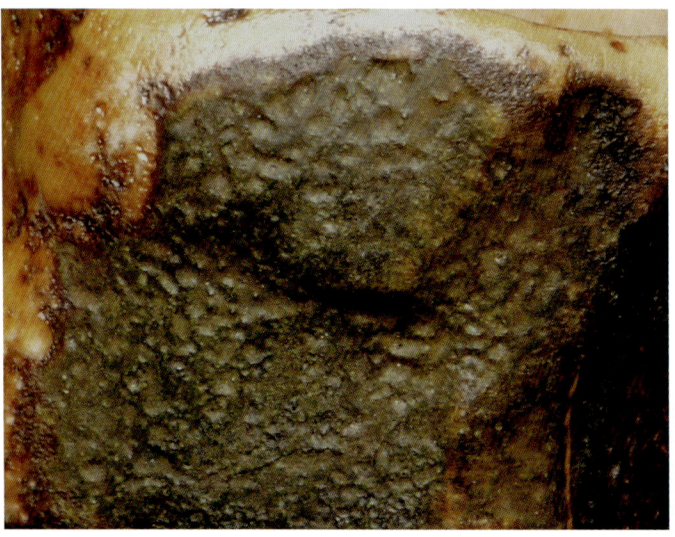

Isamu Noguchi, *Lessons of Musokokushi*, 1962, bronze.

Jeff Shapiro, *guinomi*, 2008, detail.

surface in imitation of stone. A simulacrum that is a sign of pure materiality, a tautology that marks the confluence of the object and its representation. Not unlike the soot on the walls of Noguchi's studio at Kamakura, it reveals what he calls 'the shadow of materiality'.[23] Is this shadow anything other than *sabi*, proof that even stone suffers that beauty and that melancholy caused by the passing of fire and time?

Given the primacy of the lithic in Zen gardens, one of the key antinomies of the dry garden is that its symbolism is so profoundly aquatic. The very notion of a 'sea' of sand or a 'waterfall' rock, a contradiction in terms, is particularly appropriate to the Zen spirit of paradox. For in the Zen garden – where landscape is never dissociated from metaphor, symbolism, transcendence – contradiction is of the essence, as both metaphysical underpinning and design feature. Indeed, the great twentieth-century garden historian and landscape architect Shigemori Mirei insists that 'until one can silently meditate on it, until one can hear the sound of waves emanating from the entire garden, one has not understood the garden at Ryōanji'.[24] The ancient Japanese word for garden is *shima* (island), and the term for landscape is *senzui* or *sansui* (literally 'mountains and waters', from the Chinese *shanshui*). This amalgam of mountain and water, vertical and horizontal, rugged opacity

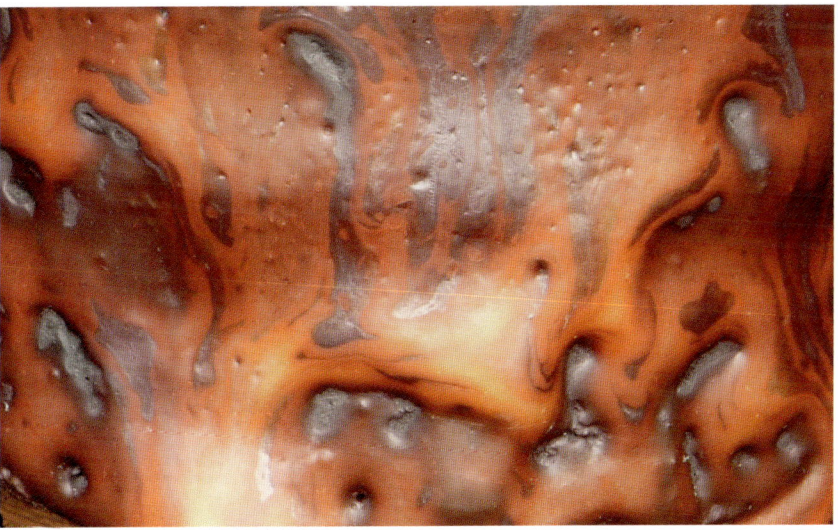

Yamada Kazu,
Shino 'dancing fire'
glaze *guinomi*,
c. 2010, detail.

and liquid smoothness, volumetric and planimetric, alludes to the key component of the Zen garden. Gary Snyder states it most succinctly:

> Mountains and Waters are a dyad that together make wholeness possible . . . There is an obvious fact of the water-cycle that mountains and rivers indeed form each other . . . that landforms are a play of stream-cutting and ridge-resistance and that waters and hills interpenetrate in endlessly branching rhythms . . . 'Mountains and waters' is a way to refer to the totality of the process of nature.[25]

Indeed, as Augustin Berque explains, the gods reside in the depths of both the mountain forest and the sea: 'This homologue is directly expressed in language by the doublet *oku/oki*: the "bowels" of the mountain, *oku*, and the "high sea," *oki*, come from the same verbal root. Thus, from one part to the other of the ecumene, the mountain and the sea bipolarise the sacred.'[26]

The precedent for this symbolic and visual conflation of water and rock is already found in the Chinese antecedents of Japanese art. According to ancient Chinese cosmology, far too complex to examine here in detail, the reciprocity between water and mountain is a function of the void. Things are metaphysically transformed by passing through the void, a process pictorially represented, in the Song landscape painting that so influenced Japanese aesthetics, by the function of the blank canvas. Here, water and mountain do not exist in rigid antithesis, but rather in fluid reciprocity, where the cloud is a condensation of water that takes on geological form as it incarnates the dynamics of the real, such that 'water can virtually evaporate into clouds and inversely clouds can virtually fall back as water, and mountains are finally capable of changing into waves and waves of forming mountains.'[27] This has long been noted by painters. To give one example among many, consider the words of Wang Chih-yuan of the late Qing dynasty:

> A rock is certainly a stable entity. And yet one must represent it like a presence as mobile as breath, as fluid as water. This is not easily expressed in words, and the painter must feel it. The Ancients called

Matsuo Shrine, waterfall, garden created by Shigemori Mirei, 1974.

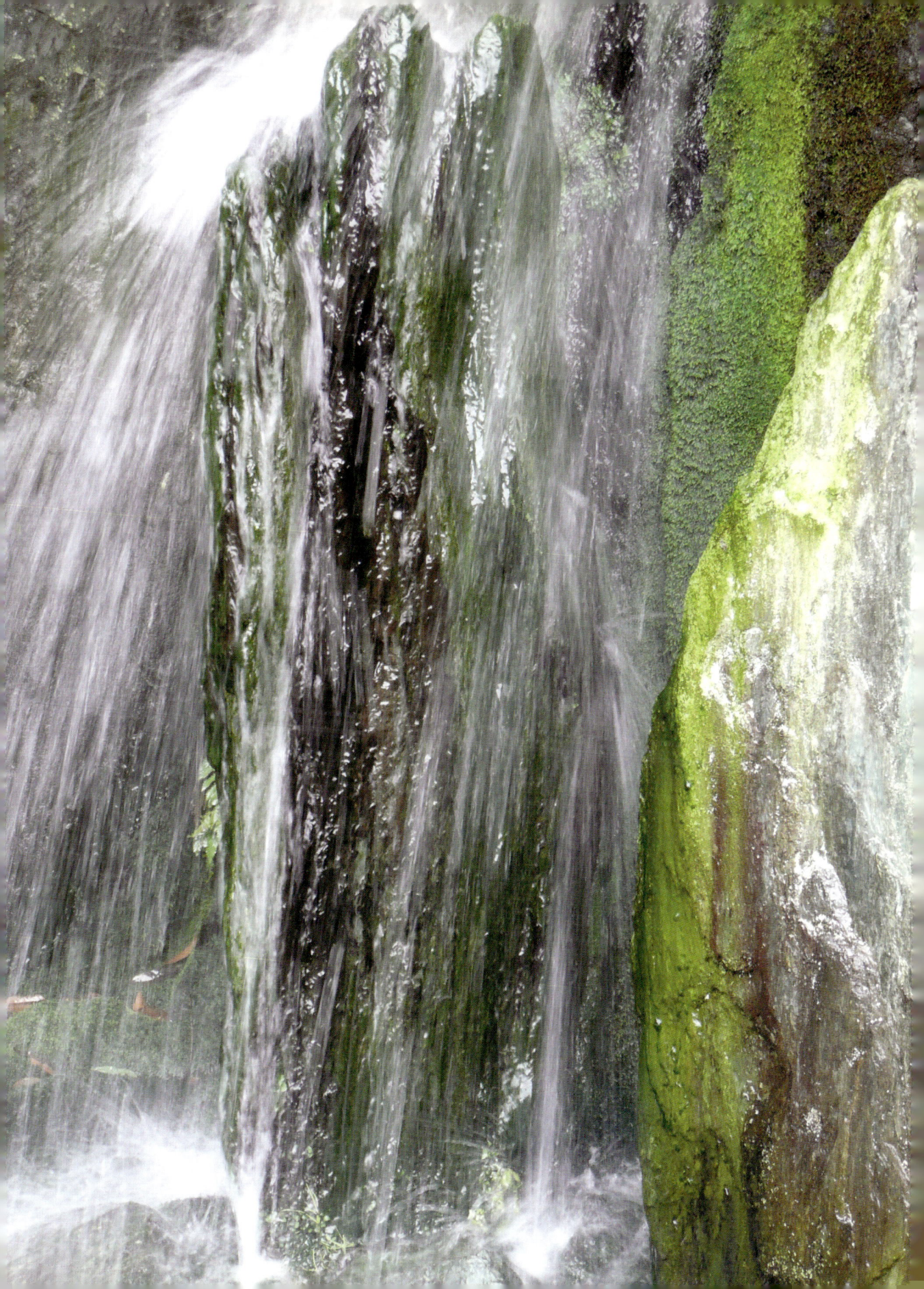

mountains 'the roots of the clouds', so as to say that these mountains, with their tormented or joyful, fantastic or peaceful aspects, seem to change their physiognomy at every moment. One sees by this that the spirit of the mountain is entirely one of mobility and fluidity.[28]

The articulation of mountain and cloud is effected by yet another form of water: mist and fog. Not only does fog create that sense of indistinctness and mystery central to Chinese and Japanese art, but it also plays a cosmologically transformative role, establishing an active, dynamic principle within the scene. Thus, as another painter of the same epoch, Tang Tai, put it: 'It is not so much a matter of imitating nature as of taking part in the very process of Creation.'[29]

   Cognizance of vast formal homologies is crucial in approaching the Zen garden. Metaphor, abstraction and stylization are always a matter of degree, and they all make up what we generally call representation. However, incompatibilities and contradictions may be of more interest than resemblances. The famed Zen adage attributed to the Chinese master Qingyuan Weixin is particularly apt in this context: before enlightenment, mountains are mountains and waters are waters; during the quest for enlightenment, mountains are not mountains and waters are not waters; after enlightenment, mountains are just mountains and waters are just waters. Such is the very structure of metaphoricity and literalness. We might well apply this adage to the stones (mountains) and raked gravel (sea) of Ryōan-ji, in order to reveal the profound polysemy of this garden, and to insist that it can simultaneously represent utopia and the void, energy and ocean, landscape and painting. For in art, especially Zen art, the Aristotelian laws of non-contradiction no longer hold. This might well explain a fundamental irony in Ryōan-ji, the fact that the bed of gravel on which the stones rest prefigures what the stones will one day themselves become, mere sand.

   The metaphoricity of the *karesansui* is vast, and the void is but one aspect of its symbolism. On this model, perhaps the most minimal garden of all is to be found in Tokai-an, a subtemple at Myōshin-ji: the rectangular space merely contains gravel with a simple wave pattern raked into it, and no other stones. Only the pebble-covered areas at Shinto shrines are simpler, as they do not even have the raked patterns, but it would probably be anachronistic to call these 'gardens'. However, such simplicity does not obviate the possibility of representation, as Zōen explains in *Illustrations*, by going so far as to suggest that sand alone may suffice to create a landscape scene:

> Another type of shoreline scenery is the ebb-tide beach, which has no striking features but simply creates the impression of the tide constantly ebbing and flowing. Here, if just by spreading fine and coarse grades of sand and without setting any rocks you can visually re-create a single scenic ambience.[30]

This paradoxically aquatic effect of dry gardens is well described by art historian Yoshinobu Yoshinaga: 'The garden is an attempt to represent the innermost essence of water, without actually using water, and to represent it at that even more profoundly than would be possible with real water.'[31]

Without appreciating such ambiguous and contradictory metaphors and representations, essential iconographic features are lost, and these gardens are reduced to purely formal enterprises. Furthermore, a typically Zen equivocation also disappears by eliminating the sense of wet dryness and dry wetness. Historically, it is certainly not without importance that gardeners have always used aquatic metaphors in describing the *karesansui*, and many of those who have contributed to renewing the study of these gardens continue to see them according to such metaphors. This long history turns the stone–water metaphor into a conceptual palimpsest. Consider, for example, the captions to Mizuno Katsuhiko's *Landscapes for Small Spaces,* from which is collated the following expressions: 'stream that meanders', '"river" of white sand', '"sea" of the main garden', 'ripples from a single drop of water', 'mighty ocean', 'the sea and rocks bordered by "waves" representing islands'. Noguchi characteristically cuts to the essence of the matter: 'Stone in nature is the thing which undergoes the least change, and water the most change – because of this contrast they belong together.'[32] Indeed, the very notion of a 'sea' of sand or a 'waterfall' rock, a contradiction in terms, is particularly appropriate to the Zen *kōan* spirit of illogic and paradox.

The extraordinarily complex arrangement of stones and shrubs at Daisen-in (a subtemple of Daitoku-ji), perhaps the most condensed and complex of all dry Zen gardens, represents in stones and pebbles a waterfall that cascades under a small bridge to divide into two branches of a river flowing in one direction out towards the open ocean where there floats a 'treasure ship' stone, in the other direction to a pool. Here, relative scale is a function of iconography and not perspective, such that the ocean to the right is not much larger than the stream to the left, and the varied use of stones and pebbles suggests the need of a typology to differentiate such effects: the large, irregular, striated, vertical stone (*taki-ishi*) demarcating the waterfall; the small regular pebbles representing cascading water; the slightly larger, slightly more irregular pebbles delineating the white water where the waterfall breaks under the flat stone of the bridge; the wave patterns of the small white pebbles depicting the flowing waters of the river. Perhaps most astonishing of all, at the left side of the garden, the small white pebbles of the flowing river end in a basin, formed by a circle of medium-sized stones filled with large black pebbles, the latter representing deep, still water, with several ferns and a stone in the centre. (Here the central stone seems to be not a metaphor, but just a stone.) This represented pond is juxtaposed to a large stone with a hollowed top (it is impossible to determine whether this hollow is natural or artificial, and such ambiguity is of the essence), in which there often rests a small pool of rainwater: a real, miniature 'pond' alongside a figurative one.[33] One might compare Ryōan-ji, where the real and the figurative are similarly juxtaposed, since the border of the dry garden – two parallel rows of rectangular stones within which are set a larger and darker grade of pebbles – is actually a drainage ditch, into which the 'ocean' threatens to overflow during the next high tide. This is the threshold between macrocosm and microcosm, cosmic and worldly, metaphor and reality.

What are we to make of all this dry, overly stylized water, notably at Ryōan-ji, with its dramatic relation between ripple patterns – longitudinal across the garden, concentric around the rock groups – seeming to illustrate

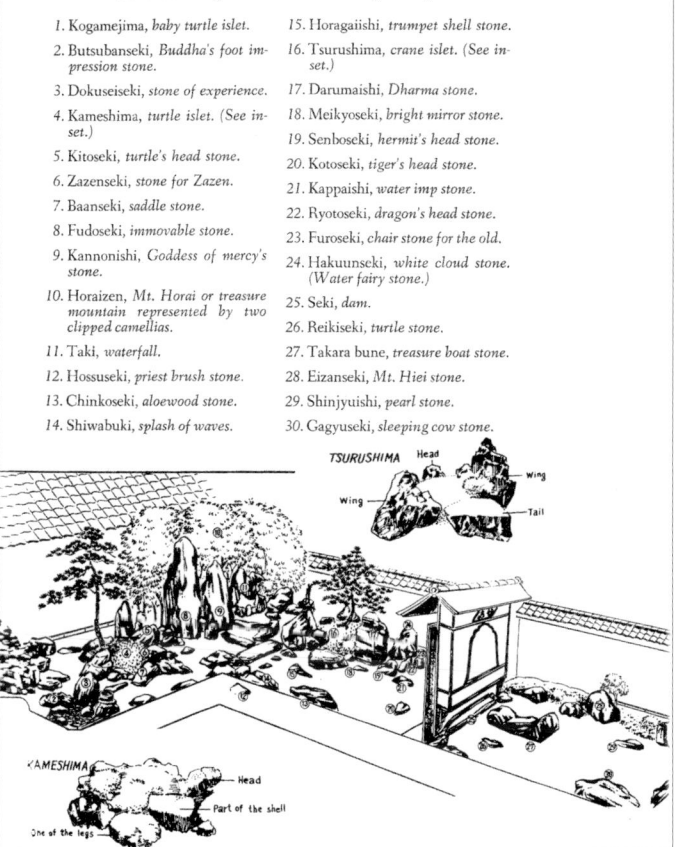

12. *The drawing shows rocks in the Zen garden of Daisen-in.*

1. Kogamejima, *baby turtle islet.*
2. Butsubanseki, *Buddha's foot impression stone.*
3. Dokuseiseki, *stone of experience.*
4. Kameshima, *turtle islet. (See inset.)*
5. Kitoseki, *turtle's head stone.*
6. Zazenseki, *stone for Zazen.*
7. Baanseki, *saddle stone.*
8. Fudoseki, *immovable stone.*
9. Kannonishi, *Goddess of mercy's stone.*
10. Horaizen, *Mt. Horai or treasure mountain represented by two clipped camellias.*
11. Taki, *waterfall.*
12. Hossuseki, *priest brush stone.*
13. Chinkoseki, *aloewood stone.*
14. Shiwabuki, *splash of waves.*
15. Horagaiishi, *trumpet shell stone.*
16. Tsurushima, *crane islet. (See inset.)*
17. Darumaishi, *Dharma stone.*
18. Meikyoseki, *bright mirror stone.*
19. Senboseki, *hermit's head stone.*
20. Kotoseki, *tiger's head stone.*
21. Kappaishi, *water imp stone.*
22. Ryotoseki, *dragon's head stone.*
23. Furoseki, *chair stone for the old.*
24. Hakuunseki, *white cloud stone. (Water fairy stone.)*
25. Seki, *dam.*
26. Reikiseki, *turtle stone.*
27. Takara bune, *treasure boat stone.*
28. Eizanseki, *Mt. Hiei stone.*
29. Shinjyuishi, *pearl stone.*
30. Gagyuseki, *sleeping cow stone.*

TSURUSHIMA Head Wing Wing Tail

KAMESHIMA Head Part of the shell One of the legs

Diagram of Daisen-in, a subtemple of Daitoku-ji.

the laws of wave mechanics? (A modernist version of these ripples created by Shigemori Mirei at Tōfuku-ji uses spirals instead of concentric circles, offering yet another metaphor and another contradiction, as the spirals may be construed as whirlpools, accentuating the dynamism of the waters in this motionless arrangement.) These wave patterns seem to be contradictory, because only waves seen from high altitudes appear motionless, yet those at Ryōan-ji, still as stone, are within touching distance. This would seem to indicate a conflation of viewpoints: the real, proximate, human viewpoint (close enough so that the waves should be moving, but are not) and an ideal viewpoint, either of a human on a high mountain crest (or today in an aeroplane), or that of a deity in the heavens, far enough to still the waves.[34] But more profoundly, the stillness and timelessness of these unchanging forms is troubled by the suggestion of an originary moment. The circular patterns around the rock formations seem to represent that very instant, that eternally irrevocable event – unique and decisive like a calligraphic mark – when the stones rose from or were cast into that great, empty, primal, wave-filled sea: an ever-present representation of the mythic creative instant when the stones were posed once and for all eternity. While on one level they represent waves surrounding islands, on another they are the patterns of energy emanating from the stones themselves. The wave patterns seen as manifestations of originary

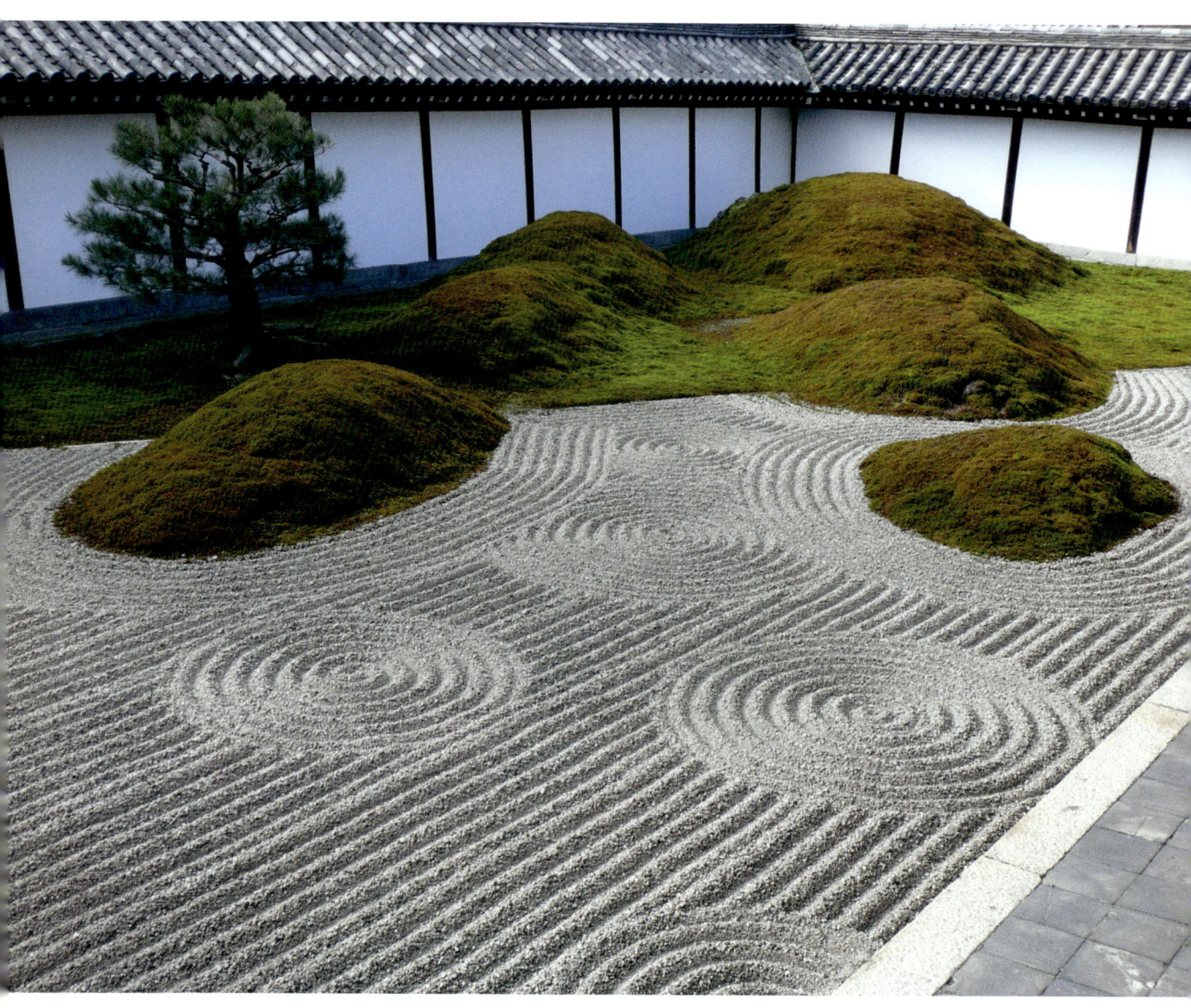

Tōfuku-ji, Abbot's Hall, garden created by Shigemori Mirei, 1939.

telluric energy in Ryōan-ji are more primal than the metaphoric ocean they are said to represent. Frozen time, or eternal stillness? Permanence or transcience? It is as if the horizontal waves were those of the chaos before creation, and the circular ones traces of the origins of the world, both existing in contradictory perpetuity. Such is the space of dry water, still waves, proximate distance — the space of the impossible, the space of paradox, the space of Zen enlightenment.

The hyperbolic dryness (and metaphoric wetness) of the *karesansui* at Ryōan-ji is counterbalanced by two ponds. One enters the temple complex in full view of the vast and beautiful Kyōyōchi Pond, with its 'water-dividing' stones that prefigure the forms of the dry garden and its metaphoric aquatic quality. Then, though rarely mentioned in studies of the site, just a few metres away from the famed dry garden, on the opposite (north) side of the abbot's quarters, near the tea hut, is a small lotus pond, a tiny wetland to counterbalance the metaphoric vastness of the dry sea of its infinitely more famous counterpart. Also rarely mentioned is the fact that the dry garden of Ryōan-ji is contiguous to a modest moss garden, perpendicularly situated on the west side, and connected by the veranda that surrounds the entire building. The subtle transition between the two gardens, utilizing low shrubbery to blur the threshold that separates them, is an articulation of both real and metaphorical relationships: both disparities and correspondences are manifest.

The moss garden, like the dry one, is itself a genre among Japanese landscapes. The minuscule amount of moss that covers parts of the rocks in the dry garden exists in stark contrast to the luscious bed of moss that covers the entirety of the adjacent garden. The moss and lichen of the 'dry' garden – a veritable contradiction in terms, since abundant water is necessary for the growth of plants of the Musci class – appear as accidents, stains, imperfections, living shadows on the rocks perpetually exposed to the open sky. But this is already an improper qualification, since the core of Zen depends on the perfection of imperfection. Rather, these 'stains' should be seen as an integral part of the beauty of the rocks, their *sabi*. To the contrary, in the adjacent garden, moss is of the very essence, living its existence in perpetual shade. The function of the moss and lichen in these two gardens highlights differences in

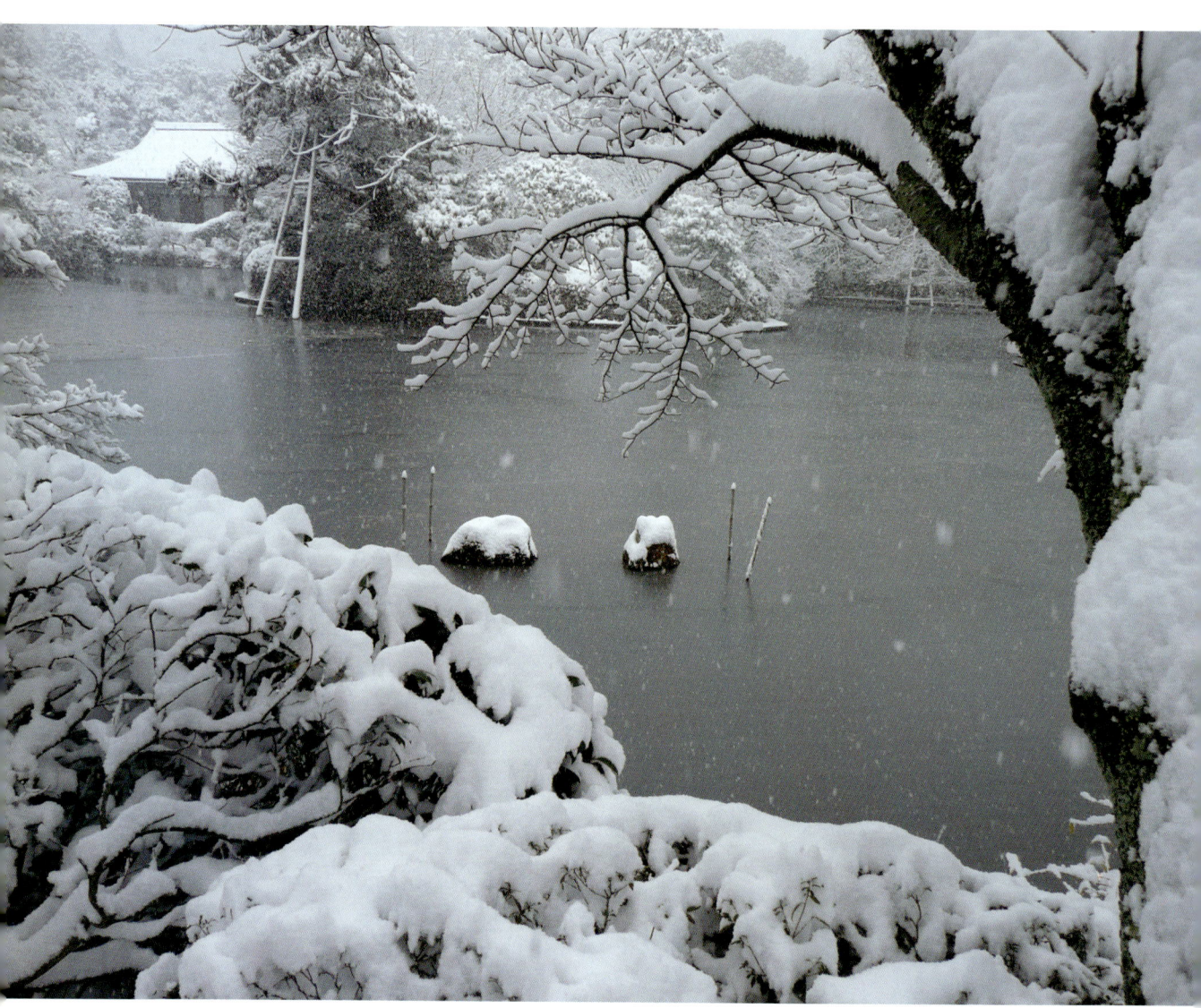

Kyōyōchi Pond, Ryōan-ji, 'water-dividing' stones, 31 December 2010.

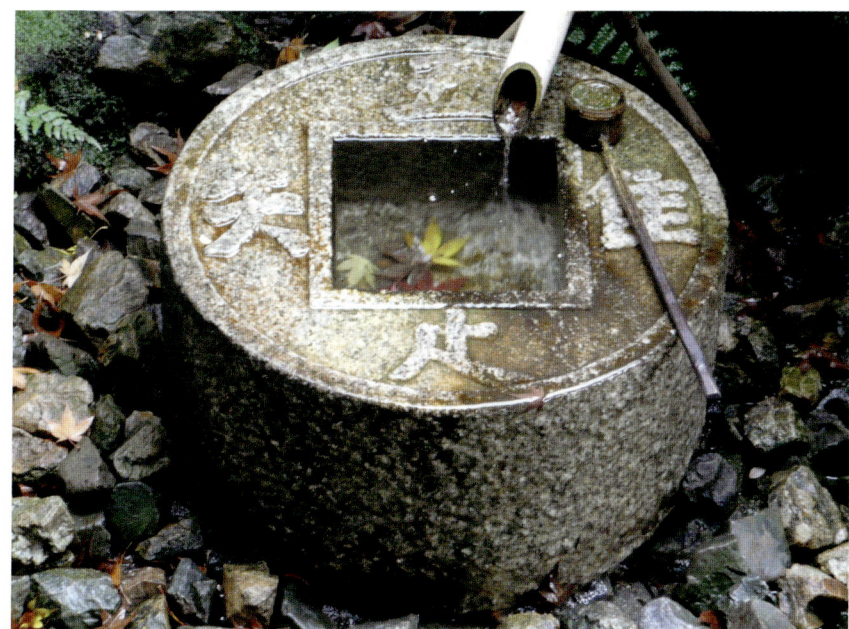

Ryōan-ji,
chōzubachi (laver).

Ryōan-ji,
moss garden.

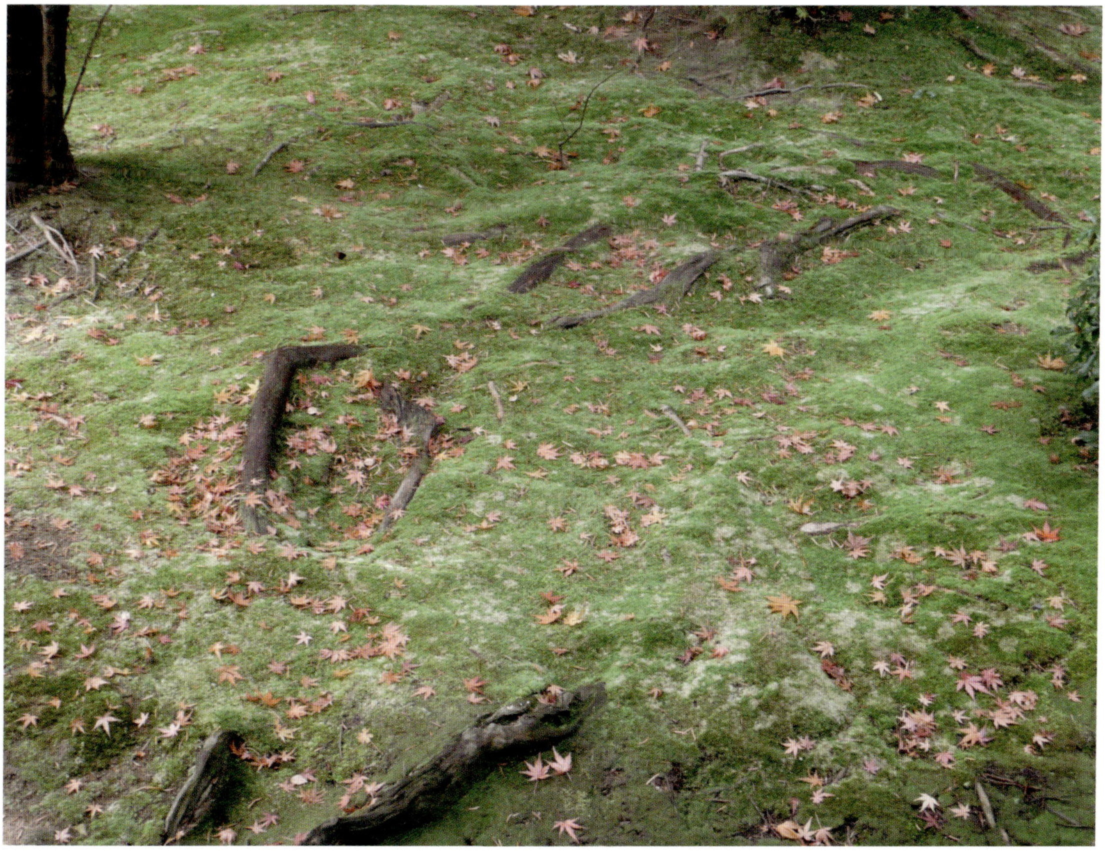

scale, quantity, quality, design: from the living, weathered patina on a few rocks to an entire ground covering. Furthermore, compared to the simplicity of this moss garden – barely more than an irregular lawn – can one really speak of the *karesansui* as 'minimal'?[35]

IT IS SAID that in the dry garden of Ryōan-ji, at the moment one attains *satori*, the sound of water can be heard. The relation of the sound arts to landscape offers many fascinating anecdotes. During the Showa period (1925–89) there existed the custom of gathering during early summer at the Shinobazu-no-ike pond in Tokyo's Ueno Park to listen to the sound of lotus flowers blooming. This is described by the musician and composer Imada Tadahiko:

> However, the frequency of that sound is approximately 9–16 Hz. As we normally hear sounds within a frequency range from 20 Hz to 20,000 Hz, people were unable to actually hear the sound of the bloom of a lotus flower. But they loved and wanted to listen to that phantom sound. The experience was a kind of communal auditory hallucination.[36]

Musicologist David Toop comments on this particular experience: 'A prime listening site can be extraordinarily revealing. Minute actions click into focus. The clarity can slow pulse rate and perceived time. But loneliness may loom into view, also, and the deathly absence of significant activity.'[37] Perhaps, since the sound of lotus flowers blooming is so close to the threshold of audibility, for some it is audible, for others inaudible; or perhaps it depends on the particular flowers, or the acoustics. Witness the opening of Kawabata Yasunari's short story 'The Hat Incident' (1926): 'It was summer. Every morning the lotuses in Ueno's Shinobazu Pond opened their flowers with a lovely bursting sound.'[38] What is foregrounded is the threshold between *listening for* and *listening to*: since the sound in question is just at the threshold of human auditory sensitivity, the event is not only about flower music. The extreme concentration demanded by this exercise teaches one to hear the entire soundscape, such that background sounds are foregrounded, and the usually unheard sonic subtleties of the environment become the subject of attention. This is therefore a festival, striking in its extreme minimalism, that teaches one to hear anew, not unlike John Cage's famous Zen-inspired silent composition *4′33″* (1952), in which the musicians are instructed to make no sounds whatsoever, such that the ambient noise constitutes the music. We need to rethink the entire environment of the Zen garden according to such Zen-inspired ways of listening.

In fact, the 'ocean' of sand about to spill over into the drainage ditch at Ryōan-ji has as its archetype the ever-present overflowing rice paddies characteristic of the Japanese landscape, which in turn is encountered in many other forms, for example, the way sake is often served in contemporary restaurants, either overflowing a crystal glass into a wooden box (*masu*), or overflowing the wooden box into a saucer. (What is standard practice in one cultural context may be disconcerting in another. In one Kyoto restaurant I witnessed a waiter who consistently poured red wine precisely to the brim in a standard wine glass, forming a meniscus without ever letting the wine overflow. The visual effect was as striking and unexpected as the oenological effect was disquieting.) The horizontal plane is materialized at the rim in an evanescent shimmering of liquid, while the vertical line of the receptacle is dynamized by the overflow, forming a small pool at the base, like the overflowing of wells, fountains, sculptures, baths, basins, hollowed rocks and lavers (*chōzubachi*), everywhere apparent in Japanese architecture and gardens.

One of the most stunning examples of such dry water is to be seen in Teshigahara Hiroshi's 1964 film adaptation of Abe Kōbō's novel *Woman in the Dunes* (1962), in which the protagonist is held prisoner in a town situated in deep sand pits located on a beach, where the constantly flowing, spilling, falling, whorling sand acts just like water, a continuous cascade from the beach into the pit, with the constant menace of burying the occupants alive. The perpetual removal of the sand is the major preoccupation of the inhabitants, a veritable task of Sisyphus, setting the existential theme of the tale. And in case the spectator does not quite get the metaphor, at one point, to protect the dinner table from the sand leaking through the roof, the woman

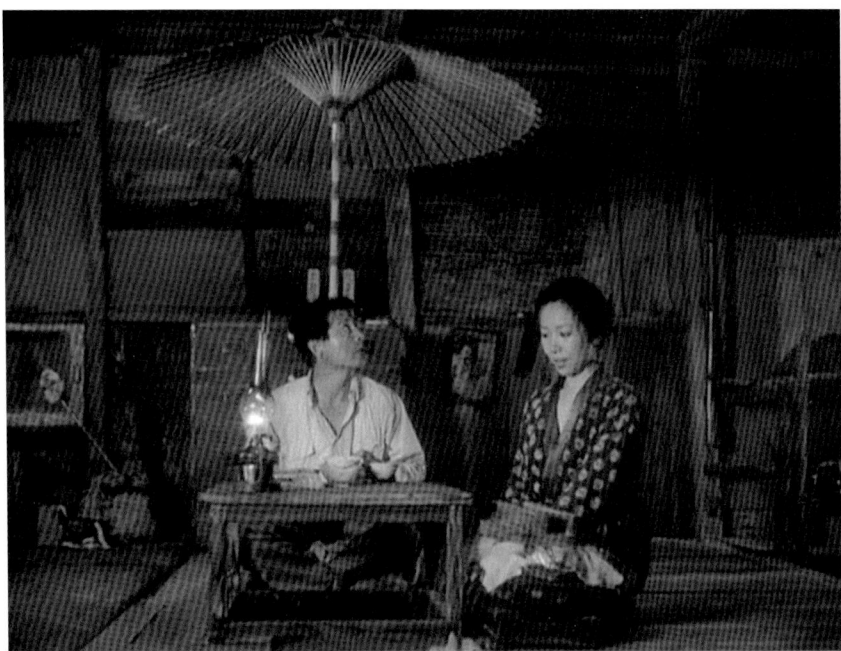

Still from *Woman in the Dunes* (dir. Teshigahara Hiroshi, 1964).

of the house opens an umbrella above the table, and afterwards she washes the dishes not in water, but sand. Teshigahara writes of this experience: 'In the course of struggling with the sand, I realized that sand flows like liquid, possesses will, and represents beauty and solitude. My creativity was stirred by the struggle with the sharply pointed, stinging sand.'[39] The composer Takemitsu Tōru, rather than using a blatantly aquatic soundtrack like his composition *Water Music* (1960) – a work of *musique concrète* based on a variety of water sounds, creating effects not unlike those of a water zither – devised a more dramatic and abstract score. One particularly subtle and disquieting aspect of this manifestation of the sand-as-water metaphor in *Woman in the Dunes* is the fact that whereas on a sandy beach one hears the blending of both sand and water sounds, in the film – where water is the most precious commodity in the terribly arid landscape – the visual cues suggest sand-for-water, while the soundscape is one of pure sand and wind.

Writing of the age-old question of the origins of music, Leonard Bernstein claimed: 'I believe that from the Earth emerges a musical poetry, which is by the nature of its sources tonal.'⁴⁰ This also obtains in Japan, where the relations between music and natural sounds have been highly codified according to very precise seasonal symbolism, as famously expressed in *The Tale of Genji*, when during a discussion about the relative merits of spring and autumn, Genji praises the latter: 'To my mind, autumn with its touching beauty weaves the instruments together with cricket songs to make the music truly sublime.'⁴¹ Such music takes many forms, some of them paradoxically aquatic. One of the most beautiful, though relatively unknown, types of Japanese sonic installations is the *suikinkutsu* (water zither cave), said to have been invented by the great tea master Kobori Enshū (1579–1647). The water that is used to purify the hands and mouth before the tea ceremony overflows from the *chōzubachi* (laver) into the *tsukubai* (the stone arrangement in which the laver is placed), and is then evacuated into the *suikinkutsu*, a small buried jar or chamber, where the water drips into a pool at the bottom, creating sounds akin to those of the *koto* or *kin*, types of zither. As the guests kneel down in a gesture of ablution, they are met with a mysterious aquatic music emanating from the earth. The *suikinkutsu* is usually made of pottery, with an irregular unglazed surface that causes numerous droplets of water to form and drip in irregular patterns, thus creating a complex sonic environment, where the earth resonates with the song of water. This aleatory music, as if of liquefied earth, variously serves as purification of body and soul, anticipation of the pleasures of the tea ceremony and prefiguration of the rare sounds that punctuate the stillness of the tea hut.

It is said that while the tea ceremony should be performed in total silence, so as to increase awareness of the setting and performance, there are still the three sounds of tea: the clink of the lid on the kettle, the tap of the tea bowl on the mat and the clink of the teaspoon on the tea bowl – metal on metal, pottery on straw, wood on pottery – a sonic combination of the materials intrinsic to tea.⁴² But there is yet another sound, metaphoric and metonymic, one that links inside to outside, microcosm to macrocosm: the strains of the boiling kettle, as described by Kawabata Yasunari in the following scene from *Snow Country*:

The innkeeper had lent him an old Kyoto teakettle, skillfully inlaid in silver with flowers and birds, and from it came the sound of wind in the pines. He could make out two pine breezes, as a matter of fact, a near one and a far one. Just beyond the far breeze he heard faintly the tinkling of a bell.[43]

This passage recalls (and might well be based on) another, from Okakura Kakuzo's classic, *The Book of Tea*:

The kettle sings well, for pieces of iron are so arranged in the bottom as to produce a peculiar melody in which one may hear the echoes of a cataract muffled by clouds, of a distant sea breaking among the rocks, a rainstorm sweeping through a bamboo forest, or of the soughing of pines on some faraway hill.[44]

Occasionally this sonic trope is inverted – a sign of its equivocation and sonic polyvalence – as is the case in the account of Hideyoshi's great tea ceremony at Kitano, where he summoned all the tea masters of the country to appear with their best wares for a ten-day outdoor festival. After the first day, however, a rebellion broke out, and the rest of the event was cancelled, the tea booths taken down and, following a contemporary account: 'the glade resumed its wonted quiet. And only the sound of the wind in the pines, which again resumed their sovereignty over the landscape, remained to recall the bubbling of a thousand kettles.'[45] Here the natural metaphor takes precedence over the cultural one, with the sound of the wind in the pines being the most renowned of all, perhaps best heard in *Matsukaze* (wind in the pines), one of the most famous compositions for shakuhachi flute.

In *The Tale of Genji*, the *locus classicus* of so many paradigms of Japanese art, on one hot summer night we find Tamakazura, one of Genji's favourites, listening to him play the *wagon*, a form of *koto*. Amazed at his beautiful touch, she wondered: 'What wind can be blowing, then, to make it sound so beautifully?'[46] A note in the recent annotated English translation explains that in the *Shūishū*, an eleventh-century anthology of court poetry,

the reciprocity of natural and cultural forms is constantly evoked, as in the
verse by Saigū no Nyōgo, referring to another string instrument: 'The sound
of the pines on the mountain wind mingles with the music of the *kin*; and,
for this concert, which string was tuned to which?'[47] These sonic tropes from
Japanese poetry and music set the emotional and metaphoric stage for the
performance of the tea ceremony. D. T. Suzuki also evokes such sounds:
'The breeze passing through the needles of the old pine tree harmoniously
blends with the sizzling of the iron kettle over the fire.'[48] The sizzling kettle
indeed onomatopoetically harmonizes with the sound of the breeze, but
here Suzuki is more philosopher than poet, and hears no correspondences
between sounds, seeks no poetic resonances and imagines no musical
variations. Ultimately, one could go so far as to say, as Dairin Sōtō taught
his pupil Jōō, the great tea master: 'Realize that the taste of tea and the taste
of Zen are the same and absorb the wind in the pines. Then will your mind
be undefiled.'[49]

Japanese poetry depends on such sonic correspondences. Listening for
the mimetic music of the world, where one of the central sonic figures of this
infinite matrix of interconnections and resemblances is the sound of water,
we conceive of the kettle as both musical instrument and proto-synthesizer.
In this regard, the particular sounds of the *suikinkutsu* are described with
a specific vocabulary, like the attack, sustain and decay of musical tones:
the attack of the first drops caused by the splash of the ladle upsetting the
normal water flow, the crescendo of the cataract and the final diminuendo
as the water settles back into its normal trickle. But any description of the
suikinkutsu must not remain totally abstracted from the environment in
which it is found, and thus should be imagined within the broader soundscape of a Zen temple, with the ambient sounds of the wind, birds, crickets,
chants, gongs and perhaps even the sudden *clack* of a deer scarer (*shishi-
odoshi*) – a pivoted bamboo tube that slowly fills with water delivered by a
spout, and which suddenly falls back on a rock or basin with a sharp sound
(not unlike the percussion in Noh theatre) once the centre of gravity is
surpassed – all serving as external counterpoint to the rarefied sounds
of the inner sanctum of the tea room. The deer scarer, with its unique timbre

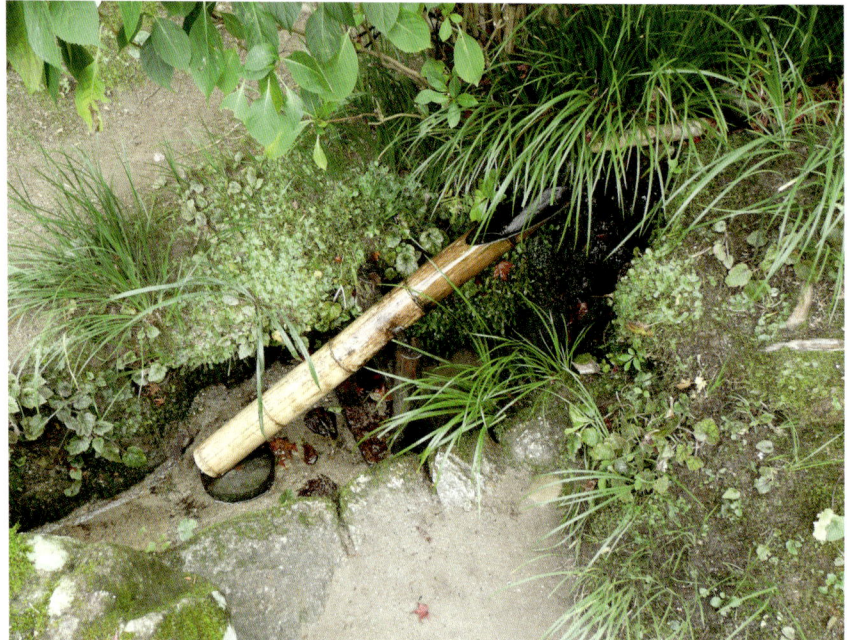

Shisen-dō, *shishi-odoshi* (deer scarer).

and constant metre, provides a sort of sonic frame for the more diverse and aleatory sounds of the garden, a single metred beat set against the infinite sonic complexity of the world. Once again, the work of John Cage is useful in grasping these issues in a Western musical context. In the late 1940s, before beginning his studies under Suzuki, Cage realized that rhythm need not be bound to metrics, to a sense of temporal regularity: 'Rhythm is not at all something periodic and repetitive. It is the fact that something happens, something unexpected, something *irrelevant*.'[50] Rhythm, in its broadest definition, is the temporal relation between any two sound events whatsoever (no matter how many other sounds, or how much silence, or how much time or space, intervenes between the two), and relations between different sounds are not so much polyrhythmic as what one might call 'hetero-rhythmic'. Rhythm has to do with framing rather than counting.[51]

The most famous *suikinkutsu* extant is to be found in the Enkō-ji temple in Kyoto. However, the changes wrought by modernization – vastly increased ambient noise and intensive tourism – have resulted in a radical transformation of the social and symbolic functions of this instrument, as well as changes in its form. No longer does it offer an occult surprise for the happy few chosen to attend a tea ceremony, since for the vast majority of tourists it has been turned into the mere curiosity of an unusual musical instrument. The secret, symbolic, esoteric sounds previously linked to the tea ceremony have been transmogrified into a public sonic event, a new form of music. This change is allegorized in the revised form of the instrument. Previously, the entirety of the *suikinkutsu* was underground, an invisibility that led to astonishment; but now wooden bamboo tubes have been inserted into the echo chamber to amplify and transmit the sound, so as to counter the noisy ambiance. Ironically, this tube system also serves as a barrier, so that the laver cannot be approached and utilized, a situation reinforced by the fact that the ladle that normally would be laid across the bamboo support spanning the *chōzubachi* is usually absent. The *suikinkutsu* thus loses its surprise effect just as the *chōzubachi* is deprived of its purifying function.

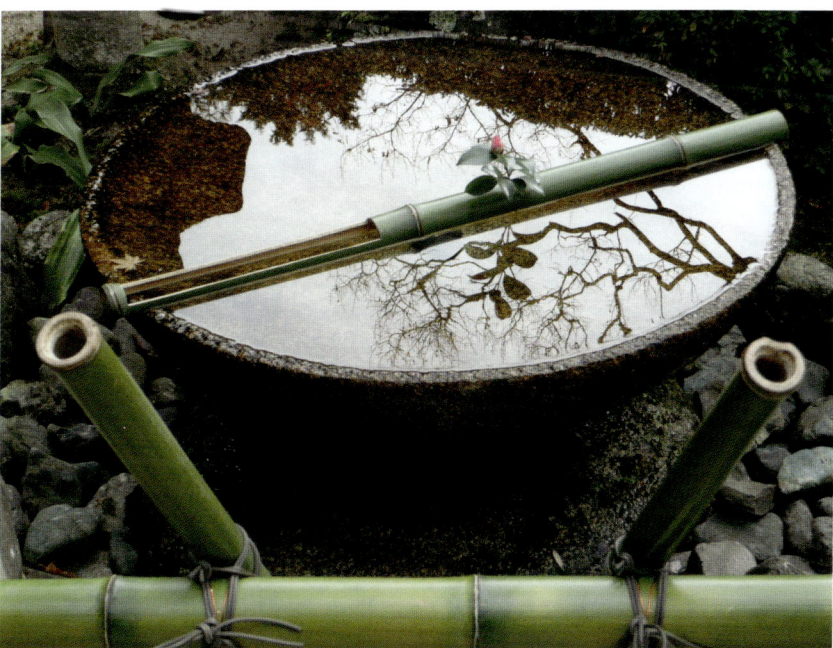

Enkō-ji, *suikinkutsu* (water zither).

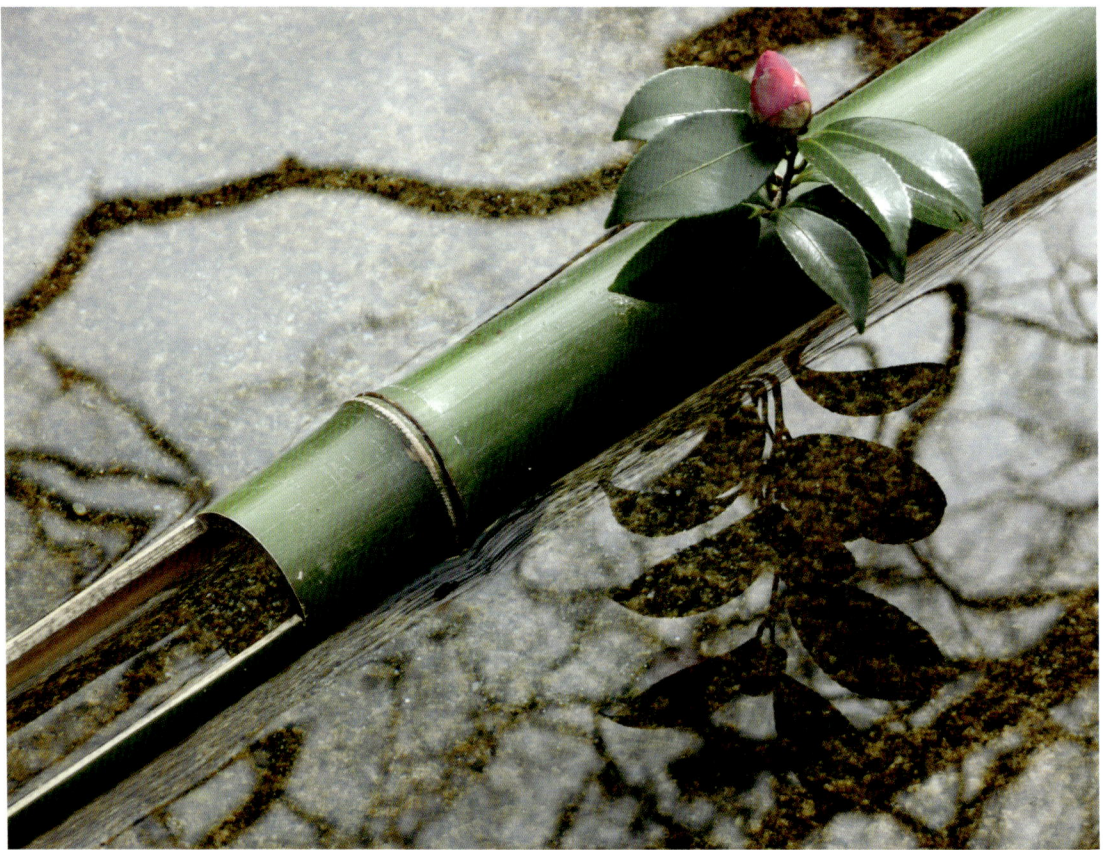

It is no longer the splashing of the ladle into the water that creates the music, but rather the water's constant flow. We experience modern music, not poetic correspondence.[52]

Enkō-ji, *chōzubachi* (laver).

These sounds can be heard on a beautiful electroacoustic composition by Steven Feld, *Suikinkutsu*, which begins with the 'raw' recording of the sound that lasts 2 minutes 41 seconds, and continues as a constructed sound environment. Feld describes the composition:

I made the recording in august when there was maximum interaction acoustically between the water frequencies and the 2–zemi cicada species that paint all that zzzzzzzzzzzz acoustic humidity . . .

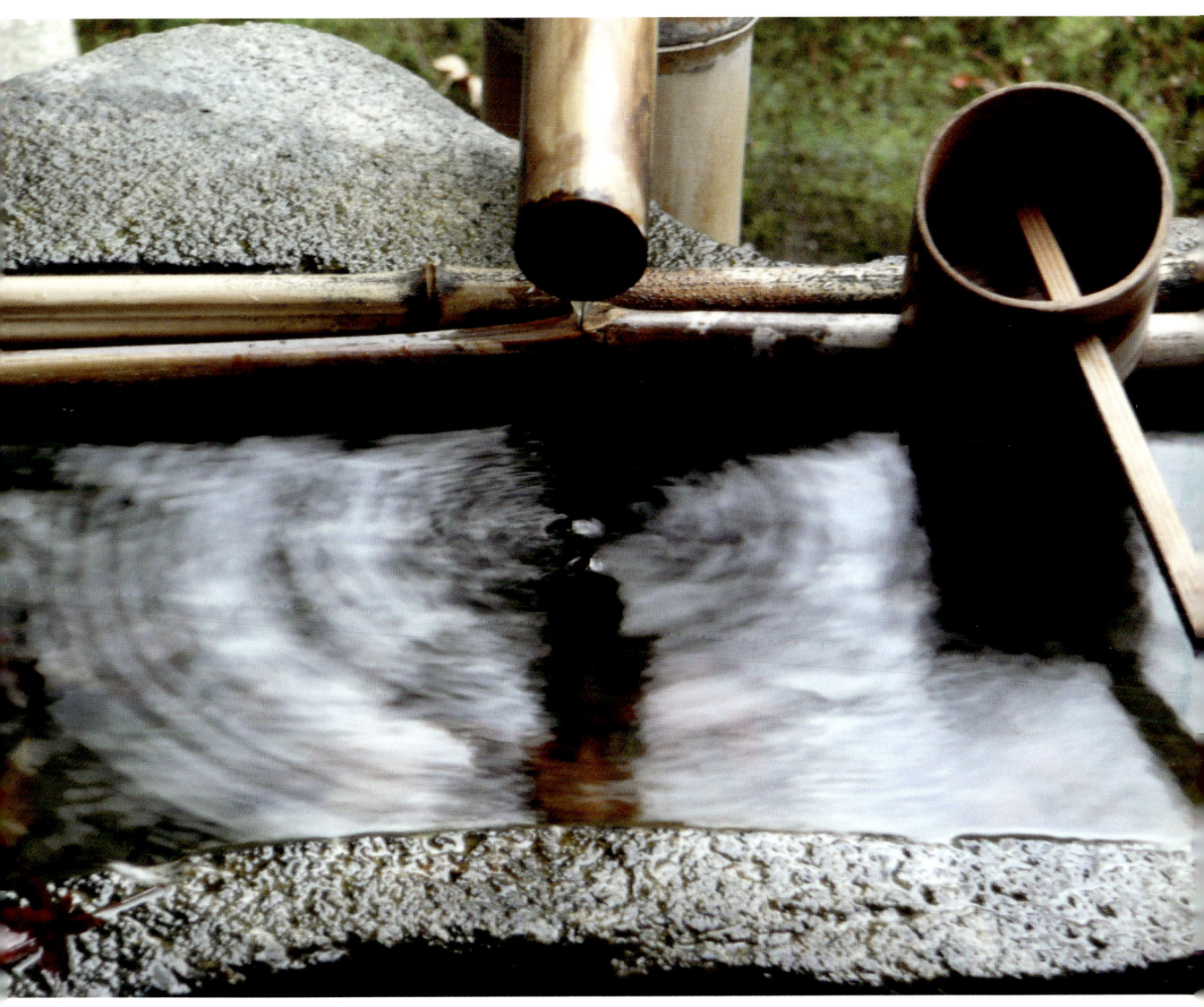

Kennin-ji, *chōzubachi*.

zzzzzzz is my acoustic memory of aburazemi and kumazemi i think that recording is a bit more dominated by kumazemi zzzzzzzzzz.[53]

The mixing procedure consisted of a Cage-inspired cut-up of seventeen different lengths sampled from the original raw recording and interwoven onto eight tracks through a randomizing programme, 'successfully catching the intensity of the cicadas interacting with the drips, and the relationship between rhythmic random and the suggestion of a dance time'.[54] The poignancy of the combination of water and cicada (whose tones signify the end of summer and the onset of autumn, that melancholic season) is evident to every lover of tea, as we are reminded by the sounds that accompanied Sen no Rikyū's final tea ceremony preceding his suicide, described by Okakura Kakuzo: 'The singing kettle, as it boils over the brazier, sounds like some cicada pouring forth his woes to departing summer.'[55]

Japanese art and aesthetics are imbued with equivocation and paradox, and our description, rhetoric and criticism should demand no less. This conclusion is thus inspired by one of the classics of Japanese literature, Bashō's *The Narrow Road to the Deep North*. At one point he describes his visit to the temple Ryūshaku-ji near Obanazawa in Yamagata prefecture:

> As I moved on all fours from rock to rock, bowing reverently at each shrine, I felt the purifying power of this holy environment pervading my whole body.
>
> In the utter silence
> Of a temple,
> A cicada's voice alone
> Penetrates the rocks.[56]

Written before the massive rock formation that faces the locked door of Ryūshaku-ji, this poem is a prelude to meditation. The sound of the cicada as it is absorbed by the rock redoubles the silence, and the fact that the temple door is locked stresses the sacredness and isolation of the precinct.

But unlike the cicada's cry that enters the stone, the poet could only stand before the gate. Both the water music of Enkō-ji (an aquatic music that emerges from the earth) and the cicada chant at Ryūshaku-ji (an entomological music that penetrates the earth) are signs that one need prepare oneself to enter a higher spiritual plane (where the powers of the earth permeate the body). Such spiritual music stems from the vibrations of both stone and water, which in Japan may very well be the same thing.

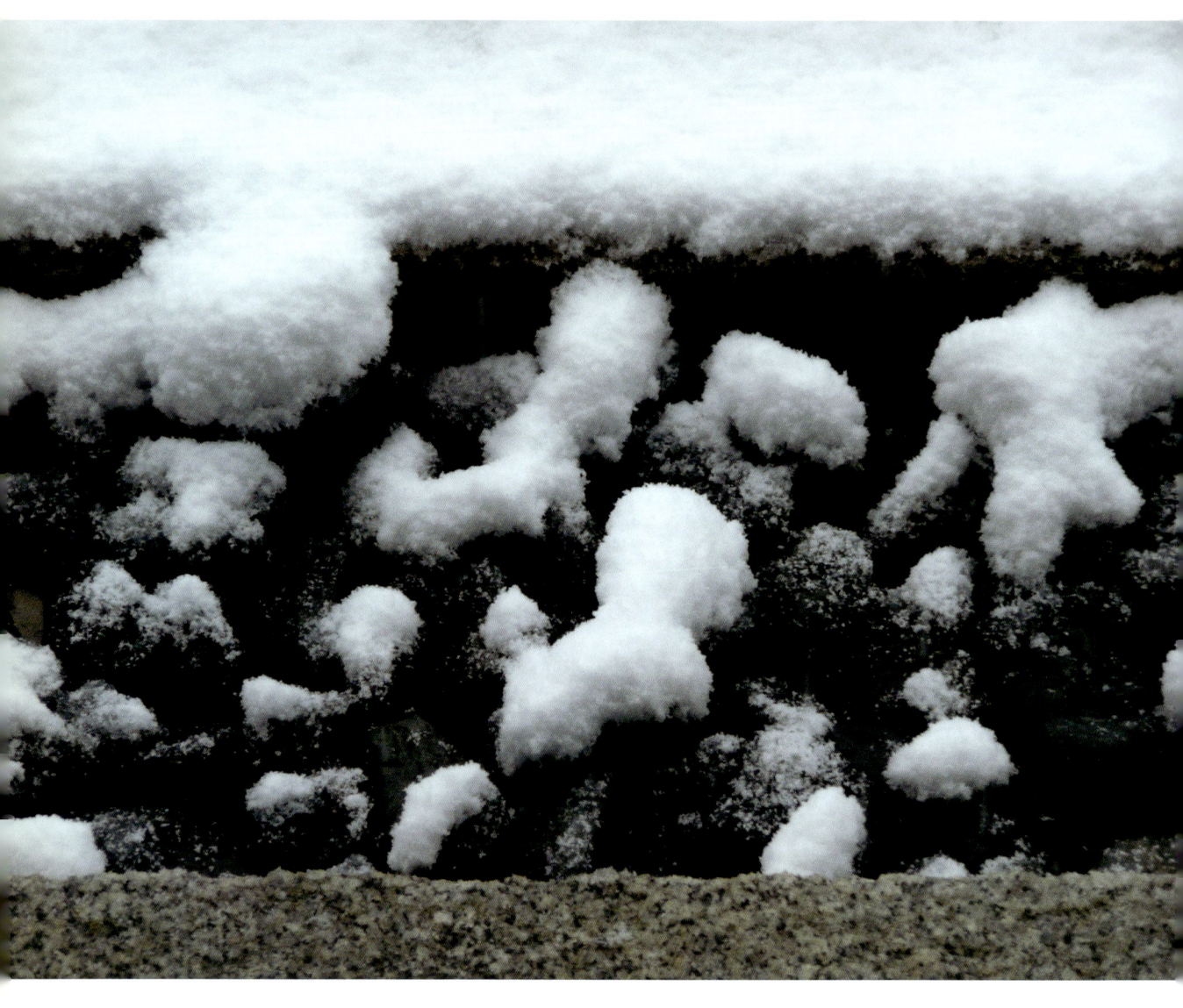

Ryōan-ji, detail of dry garden border in snow.

FOUR

CRACKS

Every stone has a destiny, thus every stone should have its chronicler. A garden is a matrix of individual objects linked by aesthetic intent and material circumstance, and while the ensemble is experienced according to a common temporality, each object has a different history, usually pre-dating the existence of the garden. There is a particular stone in my garden at Dogwood Ridge on Long Island, New York, which attracted my attention several years ago. It is light brown, slightly larger than the largest tea bowl, quite nondescript: the sort of stone that generally remains unnoticed, unless it is simply deemed an eyesore and tossed on a stone heap or discarded in the woods. It was almost certainly deposited here during the glacial drift of the Pleistocene epoch, somewhere between 1,500,000 and 12,000 years ago. Granted, this is a very vague estimation, but the reality of rocks is often as obscure as the souls of men. Once left on this ridge, it probably lay undisturbed for millennia, especially since the slightly hilly terrain was never propitious to farming, until the moment in 1966 when the ground was broken to build a house. From that time on, this stone suffered the worst destiny of any rock on the property, since it found itself directly under a drainpipe at the corner of the house. Month after month it directly receives streams of run-off rainwater; winter after winter it is encased in ice, thawed, encased again and again, until the rains of spring begin a more clement cycle, only to have the summer heat bake it for weeks on end. One day about a decade ago I noticed that the stone had split in two, and it has fascinated me ever since, not unlike the large split rocks that have begun to appear in contemporary Zen-inspired gardens created by Masuno Shunmyo and in the sculptures of Izumi Masatoshi, first apprentice and then long-time collaborator of Isamu Noguchi.

There is the accidental of the instant and the accidental of the ages. Even the strongest rock, the greatest mountain, will wear and crack over

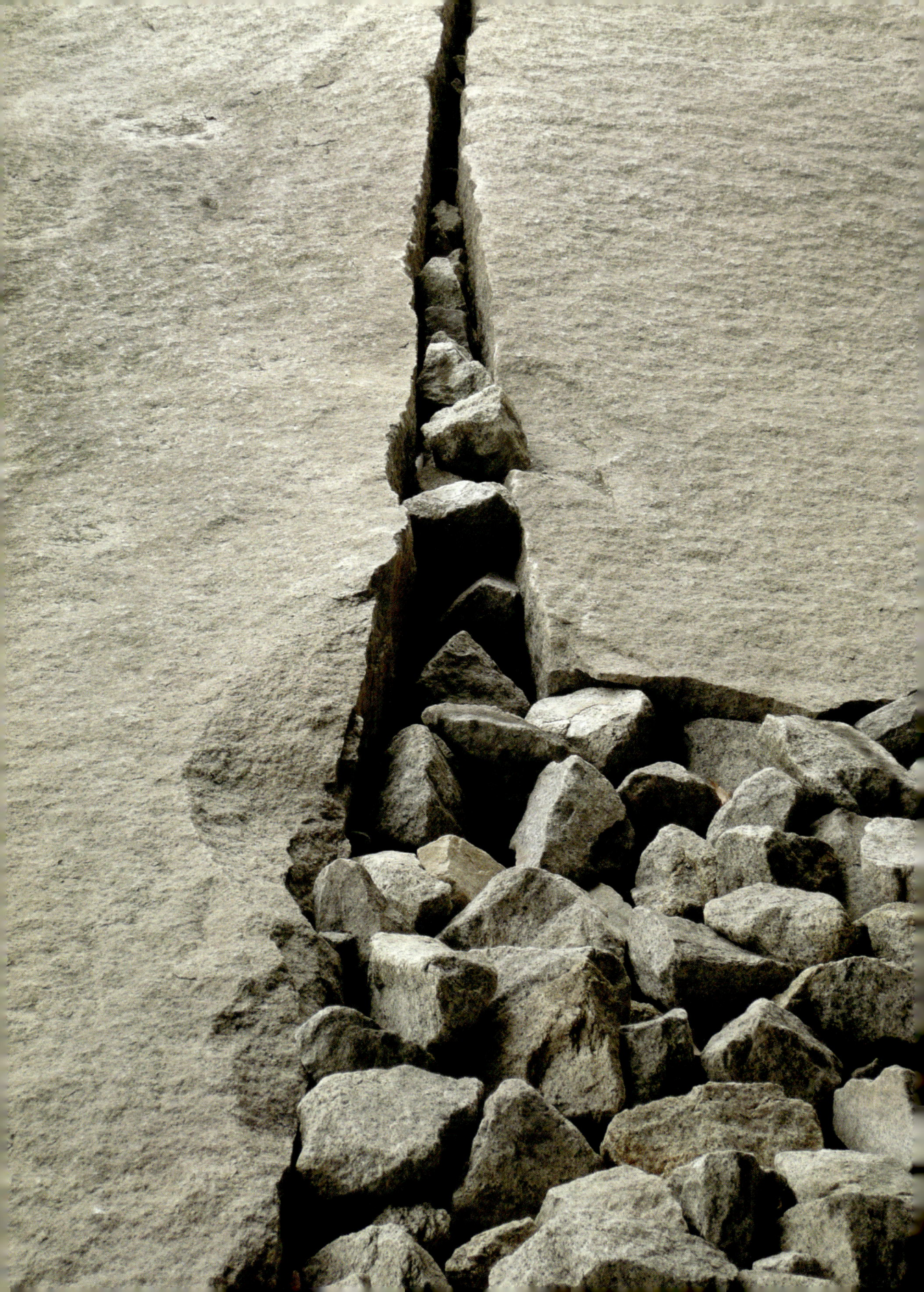

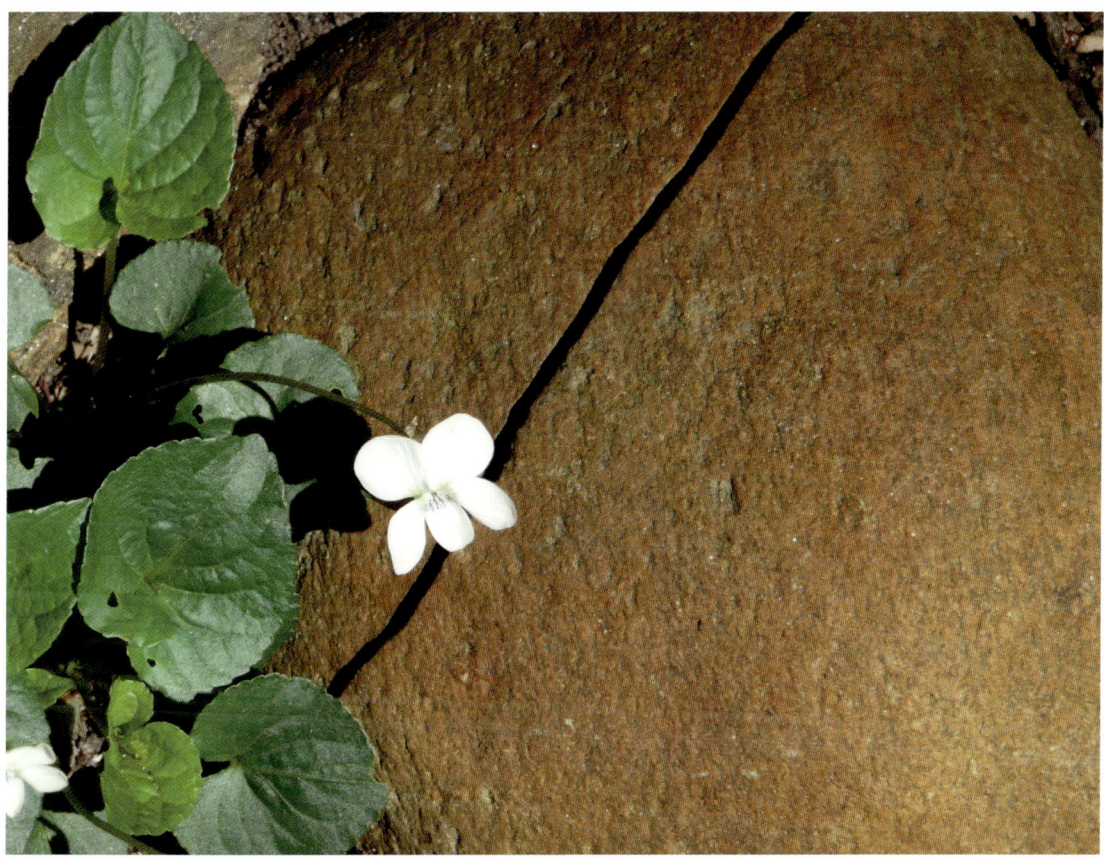

Dogwood Ridge,
New York, stone.

Masuno Shunmyo,
Canadian Embassy
garden, Tokyo, 1991,
detail.

time, eventually to be reduced to rubble, then sand, then dust: such is the
pathos of stone. For example, the ocean of gravel at Ryōan-ji is delimited
by a complex border of stones and gravel whose function is drainage. Of all
the rectangular stones that delimit this ocean, one is cracked through and
through. This garden is given extraordinary daily care, motivated by many
reasons: the rigours of monastic practice, where ritualized gestures make of
quotidian tasks like sweeping and cleaning a meditative experience; the acute
attention to detail and the devotion to the highest attainments of craftsmanship typical of Zen aesthetics; the Zen equation of the mundane with the
spiritual; and the extraordinary aesthetic ideals this garden has come to
exemplify, accentuated by the fact that it is a Historic Monument of Ancient

129

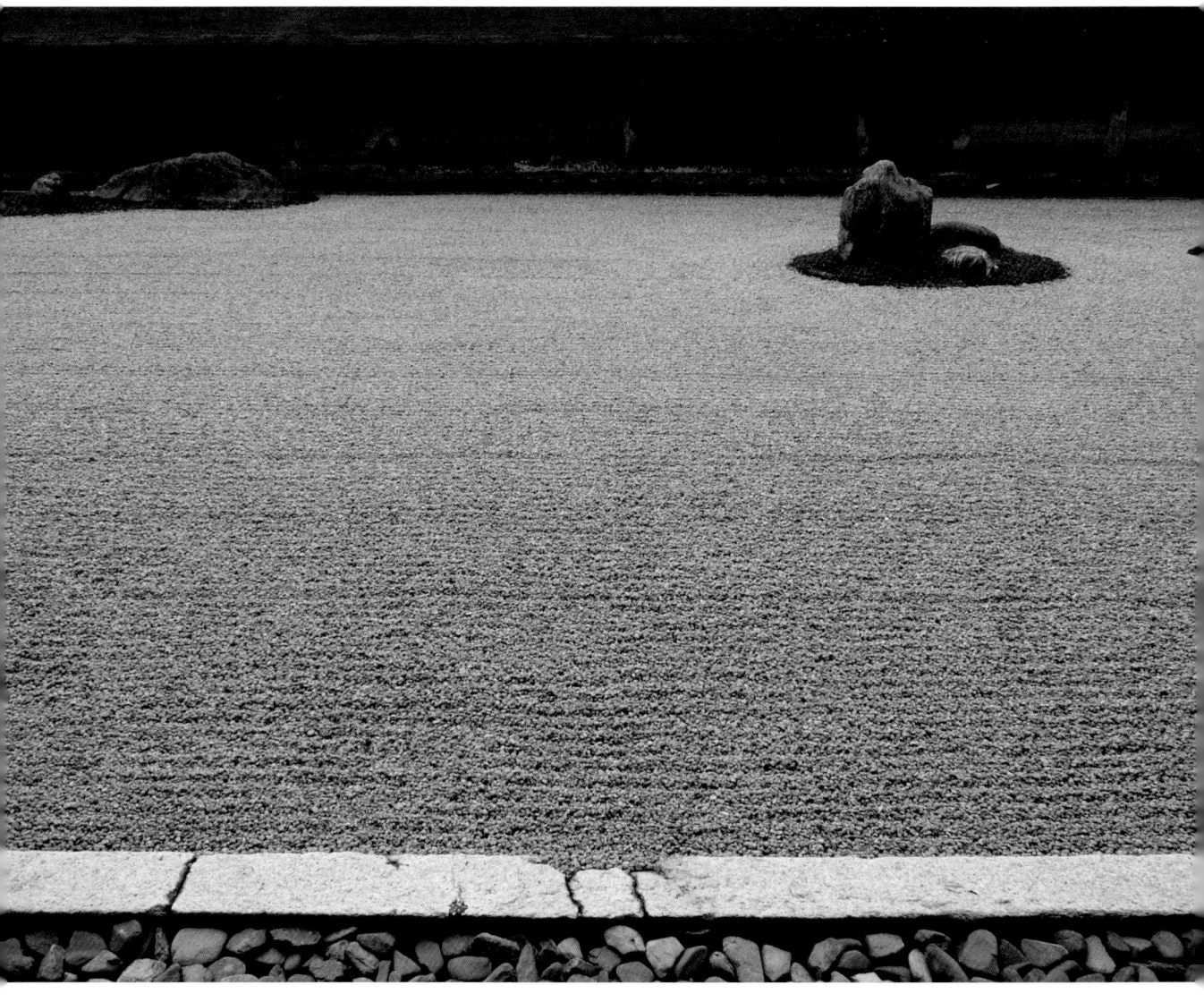

Ryōan-ji.

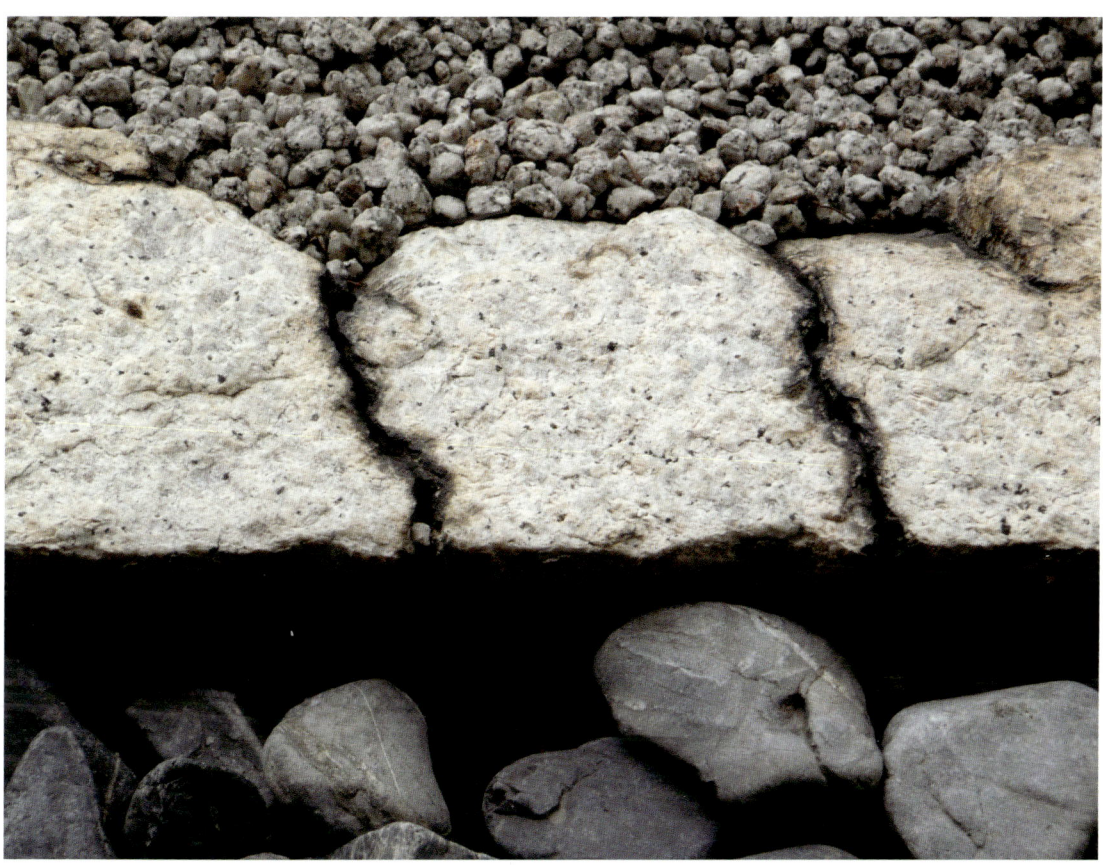

Ryōan-ji, detail.

Kyoto, a UNESCO World Heritage Site and, along with Versailles, probably the most famous garden on earth. These factors all suggest the appropriate manner of approaching the garden. Thus it is impossible to imagine that this cracked stone was left there by chance, and the fact that the crack has remained after the latest round of renovations is a further sign of its significance. Of what might it be an allegory? What does it tell us about Ryōan-ji? About aesthetic temporality? About ourselves? For what is the ephemeral in the face of centuries, of eternity?

Though the *karesansui* is highly composed and artificial, it would be an error to presume that its existence is merely that of *natura naturata*, of a nature purely passive and manipulated. We should remember that Zōen

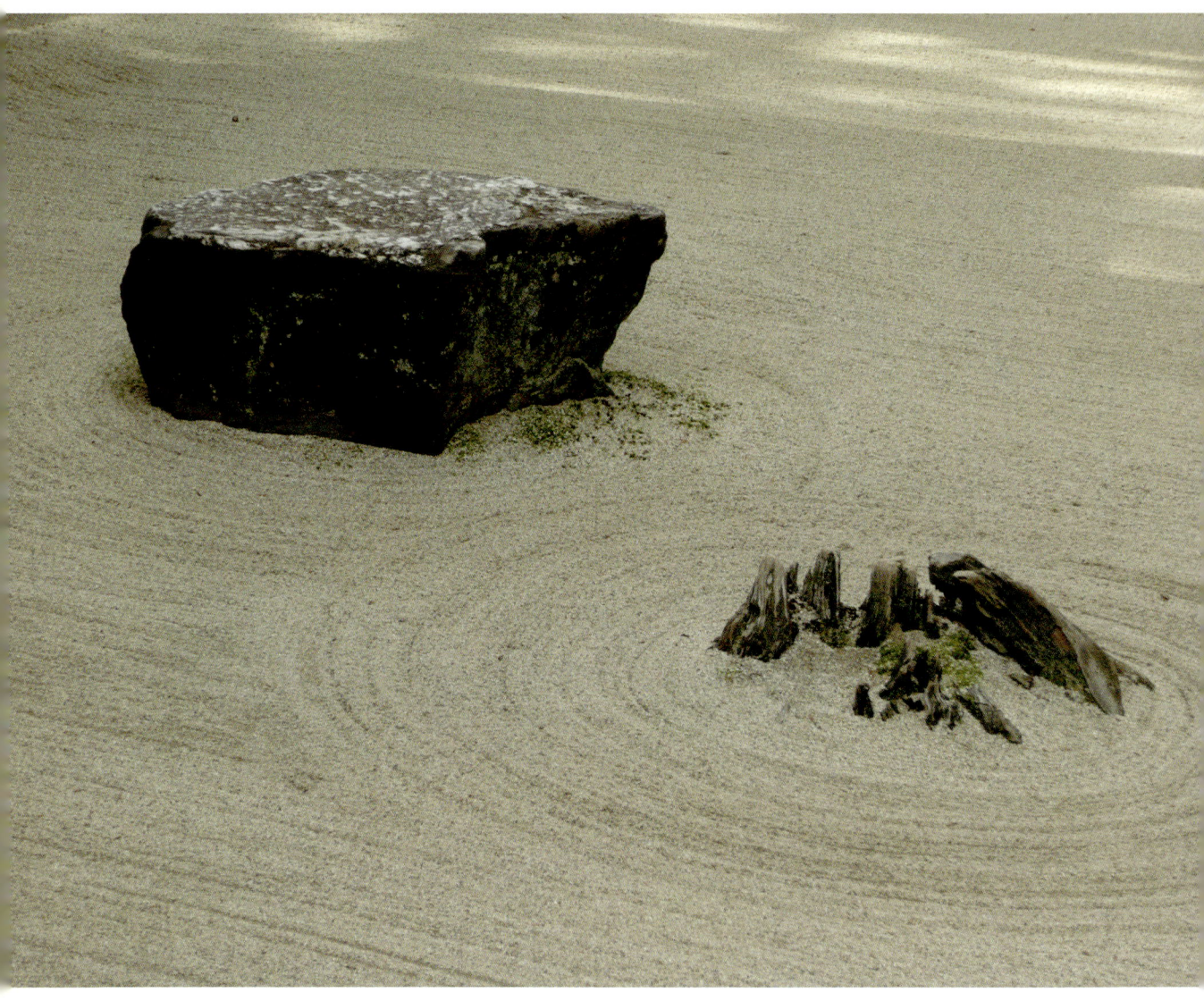

Shisen-dō.

begins the *Illustrations* with the injunction: 'Bearing in mind the Five Colors of rocks, you must set them with full consideration of the relationships of Mutual Destruction and Mutual Production.'[1] The power of nature as active principle, *natura naturans*, is always looming. While many of the greatest Zen gardens were indeed simply destroyed by fire, war and climate, in some rare instances catastrophe brought a garden to be seen, quite literally, in a new perspective. The case of Tenryū-ji is an extraordinary example. This was the first Japanese garden, created by Mūso Soseki in the fourteenth century, to have included a *shakkei*, a borrowed view, with the mountain Arashiyama framed within the garden composition. By the modern epoch the trees beyond the pond had grown so tall that they obstructed the borrowed view of the mountain, completely transforming the appearance of the garden. But on 21 September 1934 a terrible storm ravaged Kyoto, taking down most of the old growth on that hill, so as to reveal the mountain and bring the garden back to its originally conceived state.[2] It is also believed that the extensive moss covering of Saihō-ji (Kokedera, the moss temple) was not part of its original conception, but is rather a result of the garden's neglect in the nineteenth century during the Meiji restoration, when Buddhism was devalorized as a result of the promotion of Shinto in the name of national cohesion and modernization. This in no way detracts from its aesthetic value; on the contrary, it is one more example of the supreme value of serendipity in Zen-inspired Japanese art.

Destruction and decay are appropriate markers of time in gardens. One stunning and unique object is to be found in a small, informal garden attached to a shrine in the village of Okiradai in the Hakone region near Mount Fuji: a tree had rooted around a stone (what in bonsai is called *sekijoju*, the roots surround a rock), and was cut off at the base of the trunk to create what appears to be an octopus grasping the stone. Here, frozen temporality is in the service of bizarre iconography. Another typical sort of example is to be found in many of the gardens of Zen temples in Kyoto: the trunks of felled trees are not uprooted, but rather left to decompose slowly in a form of negative growth, sprouting fungi, lichen, ferns, moss. Even such apparently extemporaneous and informal gestures are coded, though in a

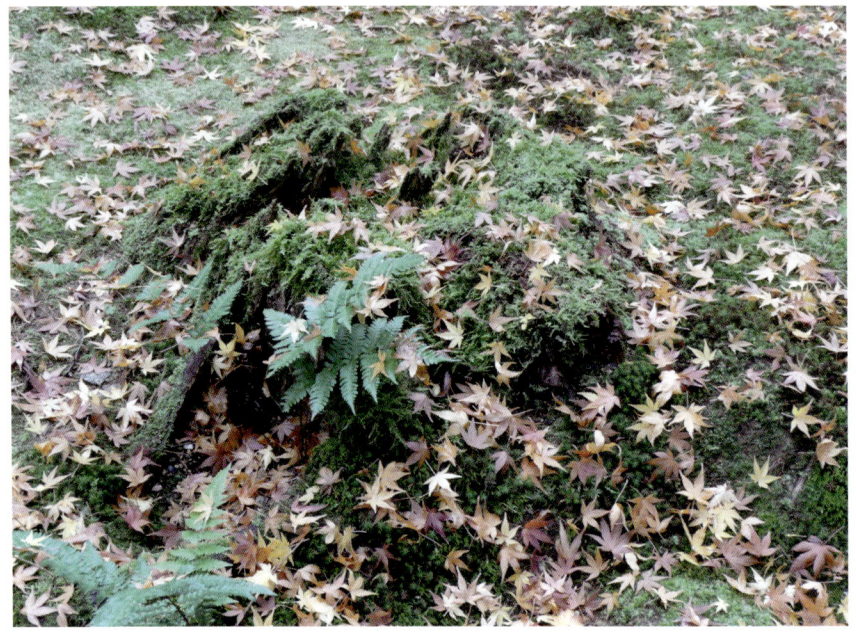

Ryōan-ji.

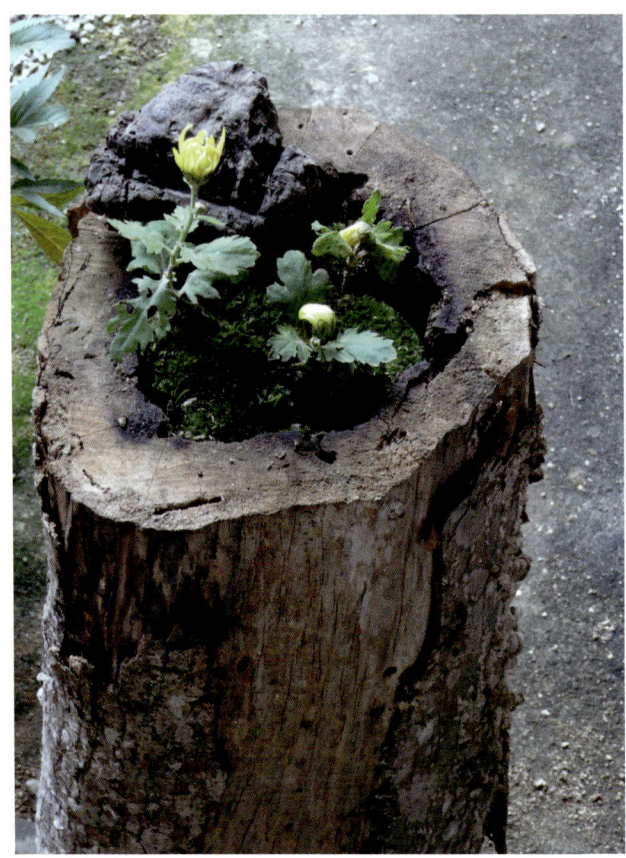

Manshu-in.

mysterious aesthetic, as Zōen informs us in his *Illustrations*: 'The stump of
a willow tree may be left there to view, but the stump of a pine tree must
be speedily dug up and disposed of.'[3] Perhaps this is because pine is a symbol
of eternity, thus a dead pine would be a symbolic contradiction in terms.
Every garden has its own cycles of growth, decline and decay. Our experience
of landscape temporality is one of varied scales, where the instantaneous,
ephemeral, enduring and eternal simultaneously organize our vision and
determine our mood.

   It has often been suggested that to show the perfection of the stone
arrangement at Ryōan-ji one should imagine moving any one of the stones,
such that the resulting disequilibrium would reveal, *a contrario*, the unalterable

Daitoku-ji.

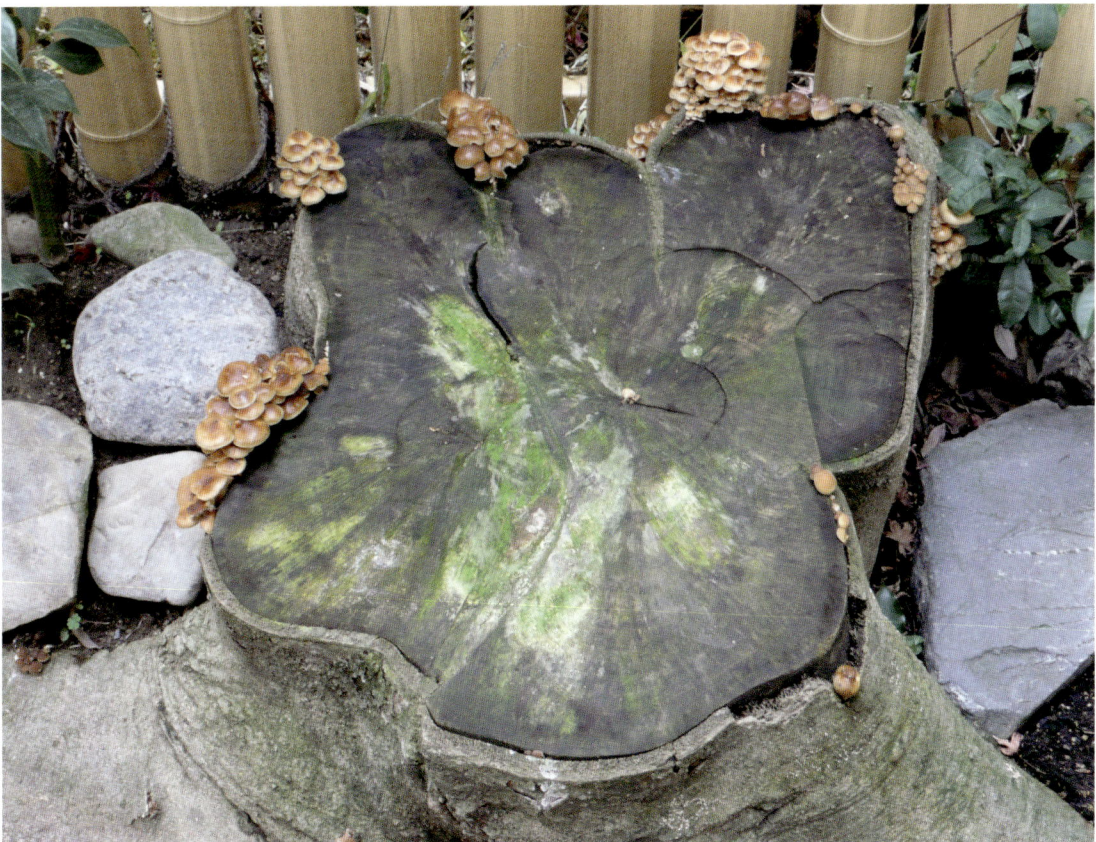

genius of the garden. Whether or not this be the case, one might consider the following fantasy, a sort of mental experiment. Imagine the day, perhaps after a great frost, when one of the stones would be found completely fissured, half of it remaining standing and the other half lying flat on its side, thus creating a new pattern with sixteen instead of fifteen stones. This haphazard event would have monumental consequences in the history of art, and the subsequent curatorial and theoretical debate would reveal immense conceptual rifts in the theory and practice of preservation and conservation. Should the two pieces be left as they are? Would it depend on the beauty of the broken pieces? Should the fallen piece be removed, and the standing part retained, or vice versa if a better pattern were thus attained? Should the two pieces be invisibly mended? Or restored like fine pottery with gold-filled lacquer? Or perhaps with red lacquer, alluding to the sacred gateways (*torii*) that punctuate the Japanese landscape?[4] Or should the stone be replaced with a homologue? Or with a stone completely different, so as to mark the historic moment of the rupture?

A writer of my acquaintance lives in the Mouzaïa neighbourhood in Paris. Like the nearby park Les Buttes Chaumont, celebrated in Louis Aragon's *Paysan de Paris* (1926), all the buildings in this neighbourhood are built on the unstable ground of abandoned gypsum mines, and the fragile geological substratum of Mouzaïa cannot support buildings higher than two or three storeys, and even then stability is a question. This is why Mouzaïa has more the atmosphere of a quiet provincial village than a part of Paris. One day the writer's house began to split in two. The standard solution was quickly applied: structurally, the exterior was discretely wrapped with steel strapping; cosmetically, the interior was plastered and repainted. One of the most inventive writers in the French language chose one of the least inventive architectural solutions to a not uncommon problem. Here, the ghost of Gordon Matta-Clark, who made his aesthetic fame by sawing an entire house in half, certainly did not hover. For restoration in the West is almost always a matter of dissimulating damage and recovering original forms, or at least their semblance.

In Japan things are otherwise, inspired as they are by Zen Buddhism, whose wisdom teaches that all is incomplete, imperfect, impermanent. One startling example following the Great Hanshin earthquake in 1995 that ravaged Kobe is Miyamoto Katsuhiro's *House Surgery* (1997), where the highly visible structural support of the collapsed building transforms a rather banal two-storey wooden house into an architectural curiosity. Considerably more expensive than demolition and rebuilding, the house was reconstituted and supported by a steel skeleton carefully fitted into the damaged areas, with the steel then painted white to accentuate the forms of both destruction and intervention. As Murielle Hladik suggests, 'All the while conserving the traces of history and the transparency of spaces, Miyamoto creates a new scenography: a staging of time, a memorial of the earthquake, and a revival.'[5] While the practical and economic exigencies of architecture rarely permit such aesthetic follies, it is true that in Japan – a country ravaged throughout its history by earthquakes, fires, floods, wars – the architectural tendency is to rebuild rather than to repair, a paradigm of which is the famed Great Shrine at Ise, which is dismantled and totally reconstructed every twenty years. There does exist in Japan, however, a venerable aesthetic of visible repairs, exemplified on a much smaller scale by the fact that repairs on Japanese pottery are customarily not made with the invisible mends required by Western restorers but rather by *kintsugi*, using a filling of *urushi* lacquer mixed with 23-carat gold dust so as to highlight the crack, as is the case, for example, of the famous Seppo (Snowy Peak) tea bowl, created by Hon'ami Kōetsu, which not only exhibits a spectacular fissure, but where the gold-lacquered repair itself has cracked over time. One wonders about the aesthetic value of this cracked crack. Taking this as an inspiration, could one not imagine, for the damaged Paris house, the possibility of not hiding the crack

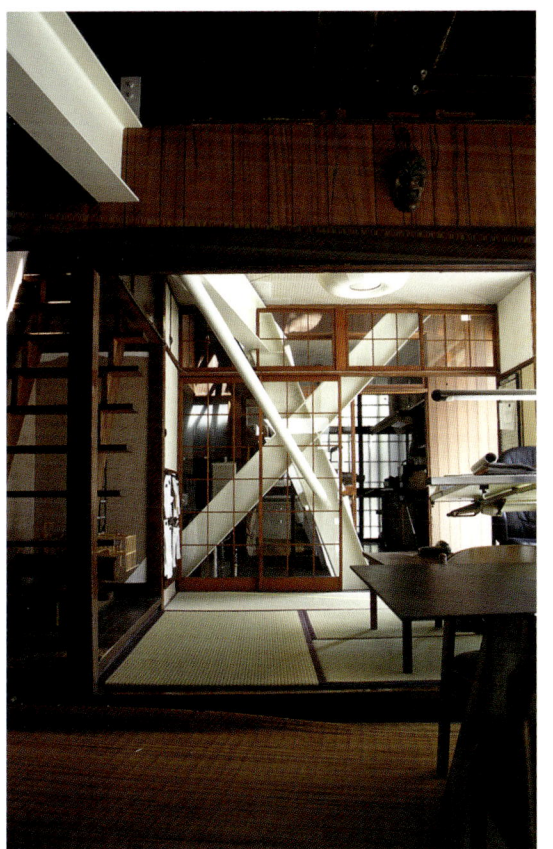

Miyamoto Katsuhiro, *House Surgery*, 1997, interior.

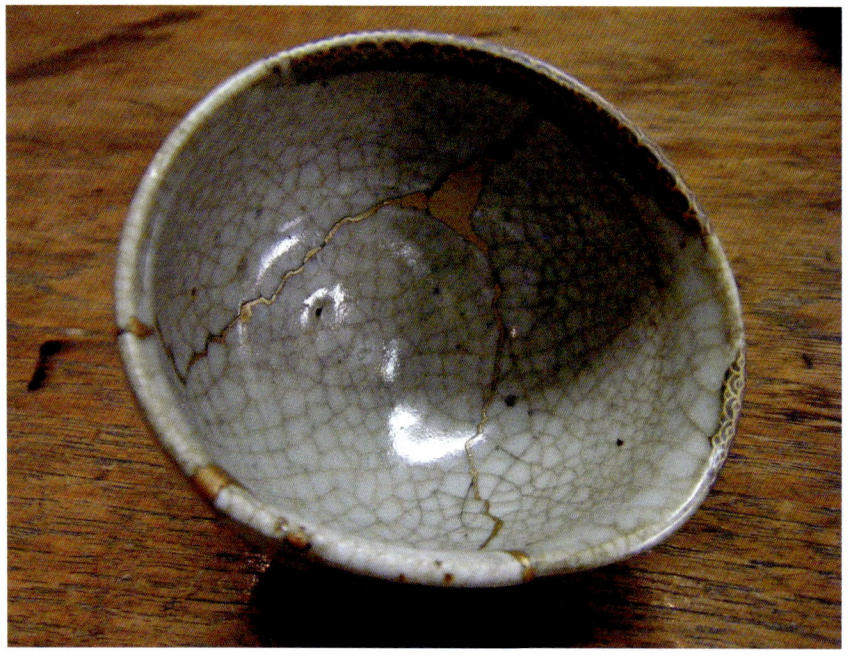

Seto-garatsu *guinomi*, early 17th century, with *kintsugi* repairs.

under a coating of white plaster and paint, but rather colouring the plaster gold or blood red or sky blue?

Japanese *wabi-sabi* aesthetics valorize irregularity, damage, weathering, dilapidation, such that the effects of time and use enrich rather than dimin-ish the artwork, adding to the symbolism rather than detracting from the value. A crack may constitute the lasting trace of an instantaneous event, even a catastrophe: a tiny pottery fissure may well evoke both the effects of the great earthquakes that regularly ravish the Japanese peninsula and the fact that the process of creating pottery – separating and crushing the earth, exposure to extreme temperatures, immersion in water – metaphorically resembles earthquakes, fires, floods and the horrific ravages of war. That the source of the nuclear disaster at Fukushima was a cracked containment vessel is hardly beside the point. However, a crack may be just a crack, although some cracks are more perfect than others. There is a wonderful anecdote to this effect. One of the bamboo vases created by Sen no Rikyū was slightly cracked, and was consequently named Onjōji, after the cleft bell of the

Onjōji temple overlooking Lake Biwa near Mount Hiei. It was passed on to his grandson, Sen Sōtan, and once when a guest commented on the fact that it was leaking onto the floor of the *tokonoma* during a tea ceremony, Sōtan replied that this was in fact the very essence of the vase. Others have even gone so far as to insist on the aesthetic and contemplative values of the tiny pool of water that resulted from this leakage. Though this tale is almost certainly part of the hagiography surrounding Rikyū's memory, it nevertheless serves as a fine allegory of the fact that what appears accidental and imperfect in Western art is essential for Zen-inspired works, and perhaps nowhere are such effects, revealing the perfection of imperfection, more evident than in the art of pottery.[6]

We should note in this context the strong, ancient and indeed essential Japanese sense of what structuralism has termed 'the materiality of the signifer', which in the West consciously came to the fore at the height of modernism, but which had in fact existed in Japan, at least on an intuitive level, ever since the origins of its arts. For example, the most ancient Japanese pottery already reveals many of the characteristics that would come to be appreciated in *wabi-sabi* aesthetics. Zen-inspired art valorizes and generalizes certain tropes particular to the art of pottery, notably all that signifies imperfection. Indeed, the crack is a fundamental aesthetic effect in Zen, the point where human and non-human agencies combine, articulating the contingency of chance material effects with intentional aesthetic determinations. Manifest-ations of materiality and chance are often linked, as when a spontaneous, non-intended crack reveals the interior of the clay beneath the glaze, a desired effect. Aleatory and partially indeterminable firing effects on pottery are thus highly valued, and certain subsequent damages, occurring even after centuries of use, are occasionally considered to be aesthetic (and not merely contingent) features. The crack is simultaneously sign and event, the avatar of ephemeralness and impermanence and the symbol of *mono no aware*, that melancholy of things passing central to so much Japanese art, and one might even say to the very constitution of Japanese psychology and epistemology.

The sense of the ephemeral is all the more poignant when expressed by juxtaposing the fleeting with the enduring, the intimate with the cosmic.

Indeed, the most lasting might be symbolized by the most fragile, like the archetypical metaphor of water representing stone central to garden symbolism. In his book on the Zen gardens of Kyoto, the twentieth-century painter Higashiyama Kaii writes with great fondness of a passage in the *Man'yōshū*, an eighth-century anthology of poetry, which expresses great joy at the construction of a mountain of snow planted with flowers.[7] One might imagine the mountain in this winter scene planted with plum blossoms so that, as it melted, it would slowly be transformed into a flower-strewn pool to signal the imminent approach of spring. For we must remember that the ephemeral and the evanescent do not only imply the instantaneity of passing with its uncanny threat of oblivion, but also the sense of anticipation and longing that bring hope of renewal and joy. Those seasonal markers everywhere evident in Japanese culture express such temporal complexities, like a woman who, in a gesture considered to be stylish, might choose a plum pattern for her kimono while snow is still on the ground, ever so slightly before the plum trees have actually begun to blossom. Human agency in the arts is inextricably and mysteriously intertwined with a natural causality that has definite aesthetic effects, and is thus often aided by the vastly more powerful, often incalculable and even incomprehensible agency of *natura naturans*, with the sublime always on the horizon.

A crack may mark the initial formation of an image from the non-figurative matrix of matter, and even constitute a sign that inaugurates the possibility of language. According to gestalt theory, the most primal dimension of the aesthetic field, from which all modes of representation arise, exists at the level of non-objective disordered scribbling.[8] At this primal level where signification originates, a figure (be it a crack, tear, scratch or scrawl, however seemingly meaningless or ambiguous) is differentiated from a chaotic ground, focused on, and eventually endowed with value, even significance. Signification might subsequently take either figurative or linguistic forms (or both simultaneously), and the role of the aesthetic sensibility is to maintain the tension, the equivocation, between abstraction and representation, between materiality and image. Ultimately, whether such traces are wilfully created or serendipitously discovered makes no difference:

production and recognition are equal components of the aesthetic sensibility, which arises from the delight in pure material form merged with the quest for meaning. The contemporaneity between figure and ground, form and chaos, sense and nonsense is the paradox at the core of aesthetics, indeed of human existence itself. Might not Zen enlightenment comprise a form of intuition where these oppositions are no longer incommensurable.

Broken forms suffuse Japanese imagery, since common types of brush-strokes in ink drawing are the *haboku* (broken ink) or *hatsuboku* (flung ink) styles borrowed from ancient Chinese calligraphy and painting. There also exists for pottery a typology of aestheticized cracks, increasing in size from the glaze crackling on many types of pottery, notably celadon, to minute cracks caused by the clay shrinking around tiny bits of stone (*ishihaze*), an effect particularly appreciated on Shigaraki pottery, to hairline and small cracks, and finally large see-through fissures, even gaping holes caused by extreme erosion. At one extreme is celadon pottery, characterized by highly refined and subtle transparent crackle glazes, produced in numerous colours, the most famous resembling jade. Created in China and reproduced by Japanese kilns in the seventeenth century, celadon was a staple of the tea ceremony in both countries before the inception of a uniquely Japanese form of the ritual inaugurated by Sen no Rikyū.[9] If one might refer, in contemporary terms, to the overall crackle patterns of celadon as stochastic, the opposite extreme would be represented by the dramatic, singular, unique crack. Intentional damage is also permitted, for example in the case of the tea bowl alternately known as Shumi (Mount Sumeru) or Jūmonji (Cross), which was a large, plain Korean bowl that the tea master Furuta Oribe (1545–1615) wished to adapt to the tea ceremony, but found too large. He proceeded to break it apart with vertical cuts, work it down to size, and glue it back together with red lacquer, whence the cross.[10]

There is another anecdote, perhaps apocryphal, but no less telling, that accentuates the radical differences between Chinese and Japanese aesthetics. One day the tea master Jōō was going to a ceremony with Rikyū, and as they passed in front of a shop Jōō noticed a beautiful vase, albeit too symmetrical due to its two identical elaborate handles. He said nothing, planning to return on his own to purchase it. But later that day he found the vase gone, because Rikyū had the same idea. Soon afterwards, he was invited by Rikyū for a ceremony and, realizing that this vase would most probably be used, he hid a hammer in his kimono, planning to break off one of the handles so as to 'perfect' the vase. On arriving, he saw the vase in the *tokonoma*, bearing only one handle and the rough patch where the other one had already been broken off.[11] Rikyū ostensibly did this to destroy the symmetry, but as a side benefit the gesture also created an attractive single rough spot on the otherwise smooth surface, which in turn exposed a small patch of clay, revealing its 'flavour'.

The *chawan* considered by some tea practitioners to be the finest in the world is the sixteenth-century Korean bowl known as Kizaemon-Ido, now a Japanese national treasure. According to the scholar of Japanese folk art Yanagi Sōetsu, this bowl is said to contain the essence of tea. Having begun its life as a humble rice bowl, its unassuming simplicity brought it to the peak of appreciation in the tea ceremony. Over the centuries it became cracked through and through, and it was repaired in a most 'unaesthetic' manner. This has obviously not impacted on its aesthetic value, and might well have added to it.[12] Such gestures eventually became mannerisms in the annals of tea. It is told that Ōkōchi Kimbei, the father of the Edo period daimyo Matsudaira Nobutsuna, predicted the demise of the tea master Oribe, as recounted by cultural historian Kumakura Isao:

> Oribe was the kind of person who damaged the treasures of the realm. If, for example, he did not like the shape of a certain hanging scroll, he would deliberately cut it shorter. Or if the tea bowls and caddies were perfect and without flaws, he would purposely break and repair them and declare the broken and repaired articles to be interesting.[13]

In fact, broken pottery is a veritable commonplace in the annals of the tea ceremony; the list is almost endless. A few examples paraphrased from Sadler's *The Japanese Tea Ceremony* will suffice:

When Matsudaira Tadanao, the Lord of Echizen, was presented with a valuable tea caddy by the shogun Hidetada in appreciation of his victory in a battle at Osaka, he showed it to his men and, since there was no way to share the bounty, smashed it in obvious displeasure at the gift, and offered to distribute the pieces to his soldiers.

A tea master once invited Rikyū to a ceremony where he used a tea caddy named Sessan, and was so disappointed that Rikyū did not appreciate it that he smashed it against the hearth. One of the guests gathered the pieces and had it mended, and then invited Rikyū to a ceremony where he used it. The piece received much praise, and it was subsequently returned to its former owner.

The farmer Dōroku was a tea man who owned a valuable Chinese tea caddy much admired by Shōō and Rikyū. On his deathbed, he broke the rare work, realizing that the inheritance of this piece might be a source of discord between his sons.

Rikyū, always in search of rare tea implements, reported to Hideyoshi one day that he saw a beggar who had a fabulous kettle. He was instructed to obtain it at any cost, but the beggar refused all demands, protesting that if he gave away his only kettle, he could not boil water for his tea, whereupon he smashed the kettle which broke in two. Rikyū brought the two pieces to Hideyoshi, who had it mended, and was so thrilled with the result that he had three copies made: one for himself, one as a gift for Rikyū and another for Hosokawa Yūsai, with the original to be returned to the beggar.

The daimyo Tokugawa Yorinobu had a tea caddy that was considered one of the three greatest treasures of the empire, given him by his father Ieyasu. One day, one of his retainers, Shigeyoshi, known for his drunkenness, insisted that the official in charge of this work show him the piece, and no sooner had it appeared then he fell over it, breaking it with the hilt of his sword. When this was reported to the daimyo, he simply ordered that it be glued together, and that the official not be reprimanded, since Shigeyoshi was a fine soldier who could be counted upon, and after all the tea caddy could not shoot an arrow or wield a spear.[14]

While these tales serve obvious allegorical purposes, each one also reveals a profound truth about the aesthetics of tea.[15] We can well understand why one of the most treasured pieces of Japanese pottery is the Momoyama epoch Iga ware water vessel (*mizusashi*) named Yabure-bukuro (Broken Pouch, an Important Cultural Property now in the collection of the Gotoh Art Museum), a source of continued inspiration for Japanese potters. The several intersecting gaps that seem to split apart the extremely rugged surface of this piece's sagging form prove to be surface effects. The poetry of the piece plays in part on the impossibility of a split pouch to perform effectively its function of holding water, a veritable Zen paradox, and in part from the fact that the piece is at the limit between form and formlessness, as the sag is a result of the collapse of form from the extreme heat of the kiln. A quite different type of example would be the *chawan* by Chōjirō named Vestige (in the collection of the Raku Museum). This tea bowl is of the utmost simplicity, except for a small, nearly geometric form – resembling the irregularly shaped wooden plugs used to repair floorboarding – encrusted (or perhaps carved) just under the inside lip. This is the 'vestige' that gives the work its name and its mystery, for we do not know of what this form is a trace, or whether it might be a symbol. Is it a valuable though unidentifiable relic for which the bowl serves as support, or the simulacrum of a repair that serves as an allegory of imperfection as perfection?

This might well lead us to imagine a catalogue of pottery imperfections that could inspire a room in a 'museum of accidents' such as that imagined by Paul Virilio. Indeed, some styles of pottery seem to be a compendium of accidents. The great twentieth-century potter Hamada Shōji claimed:

If a kiln is small, I might be able to control it completely, that is to say, my own self can become a controller, a master of the kiln. But man's own self is but a small thing after all. When I work at the large kiln, the power

Ryōan-ji, floor repairs.

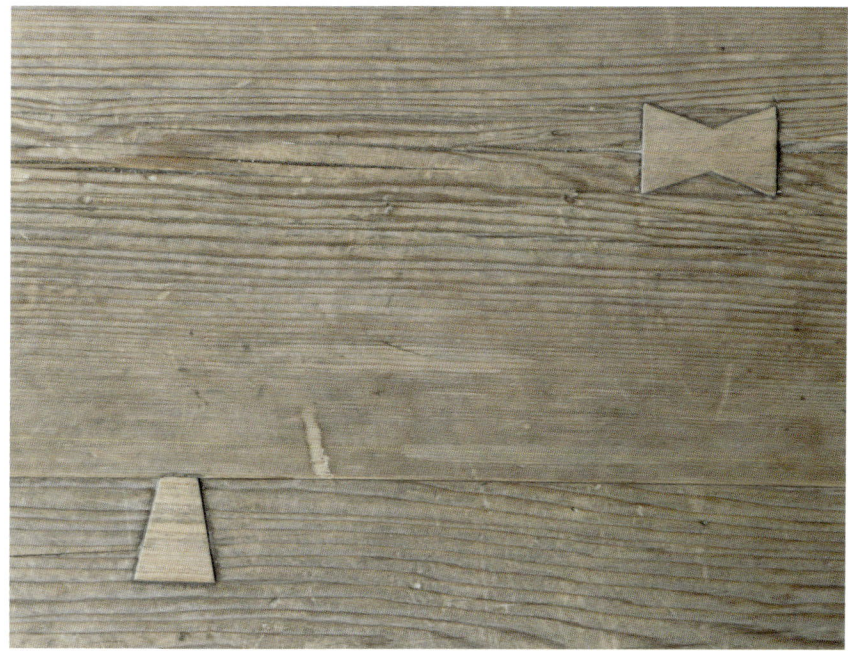

of my own self becomes so feeble that it cannot control it adequately. It means that for the large kiln, the power that is beyond me is necessary.[16]

This sensibility has continued to inform pottery appreciation in Japan. For example, the film-maker Teshigahara Hiroshi, who created pottery as well as practising tea and ikebana, explains his interest in the former:

> Things made of clay are easily broken. When the piece is on the point of being broken and yet retains its integrity – this is the point at which it is beautiful. Regular artisans try to avoid that extremity and aim at achieving perfect stability. But I do not. I aim to bring the work to the most dangerous, unstable point.[17]

Despite his highly experimental tendencies (or perhaps precisely because of them), this echoes the attitudes of many of the great potters of the past. Pottery specialist Robert Yellin recounts:

I've seen many a sixteenth century Momoyama period guinomi repaired with gold and/or lacquer and often such pieces are very expensive. I had a client once who purchased a Shigaraki guinomi and loved using it. However one day he dropped it while rinsing it and it shattered into many pieces. He was distraught, yet I told him not to frown and send the pieces to me. He did and I then sent them to my fabulous crafts-man restorer and in a few months time the guinomi was sent back with brilliant gold threads bonding the guinomi back together again. Upon seeing this the client was overjoyed, saying it was even more beautiful than before and now he was going to intentionally break all his collection! Of course I advised him against that.[18]

Earlier forms of repair include metal staples, which rust over time, conflating the two senses of the term *sabi*.

There is an extraordinary tale of broken pottery in Cees Nooteboom's novel *Rituals* (1980). One of the protagonists, a secretive Eurasian named Philip Taads, is obsessed by Raku pottery, and seeks to obtain a perfect example of a tea bowl by one of the Raku masters. One day Taads sees, in the window of an antique store, the object of his quest, a bowl by Raku IX (Ryōnyū, 1756–1834), which he purchases for a princely sum, an act that leads to a totally unexpected and horrific denouement. The synaesthetic description of the bowl holds the promise of the full joys of the tea ceremony:

> The bowl had the same color as the dead leaves, all dead leaves together – the gleam of candied ginger, sweet and bitter, hard and soft, the luxurious fire of decay. It was a wide bowl, almost clumsy, not made by man but born in an unnameable prehistory.[19]

The description is particularly rich: mention of the prehistoric is a means of signifying the rarity and value of the bowl; the colour of dead leaves is both a seasonal marker and a cryptic premonition of things to come; the ginger gleam denotes its *sabi*; the mention of fire alludes to the non-human agency of the kiln that participated in its creation. But the end is not what might be expected. After inviting the protagonist and the antiques dealer to a ceremony featuring the rare bowl, he proceeds to another, very different ceremony all by himself. In an immaculate, totally empty room he smashes the bowl to bits. Its description is now quite different, symbolizing the tragedy in all its morbidity:

> But in the middle of the floor, broken into a hundred pieces, there lay what could only be the raku bowl, smashed with great force. On the gleaming, gold-colored mat the fragments lay scattered like bits of congealed and withered blood.[20]

He then commits suicide by drowning. The trajectory of the *chawan* from traditional antique gallery to tea room to destruction chamber (not coincidentally similar to the white cubes of modernist museums and galleries) is an allegory of the destiny of traditional tea pottery in the modern age: a recommodification that eventually leads to the withdrawal of works from circulation, whence the ruination of use value and the degradation of an entire aesthetic.[21]

Rituals is profoundly influenced by Kawabata Yasunari's *Thousand Cranes* (1952). In this novel, with a plot too complex to summarize here, the interpersonal relationships are symbolized by works of classic tea ceremony ceramics, the most important of which were also made by Ryōnyū. Most notable is a Shino *chawan* that bears the lipstick traces of Mrs Ota, the lover of both the protagonist Kikuji and of his deceased father. Following the death of Mrs Ota towards the end of the novel, her daughter Fumiko, after making love with Kikuji, shatters the precious *chawan* and then disappears, perhaps having committed suicide. The pathos of the event is expressed by the claim that the protagonists' lifespan constitutes but a very short moment of the bowl's existence, and the works of pottery appear practically as characters in their own right: 'Seeing his father and Fumiko's mother in the bowls, Kikuji felt that they had raised two beautiful ghosts and placed them side by side.'[22] Though Fumiko acted like Taads, wishing the broken bowl to represent death, Kikuji tries to put the pieces together, and finally saves them for some unstated and perhaps as yet unknown future purpose. Perhaps this act symbolizes the desire for Fumiko's return, all the while serving as an act of mourning for Mrs Ota.

The ends of *Rituals* and *Thousand Cranes*, from the point of view of the tea bowl, can be interpreted in two ways. Stated in the postface to *Rituals* is the fact that in 1591 Sen no Rikyū was forced to commit suicide by Hideyoshi, a tale that is one of the foundational myths of tea culture, a summit of pathos. Rikyū assembled his closest friends for a final tea ceremony in which he utilized his most precious objects. Afterwards, he distributed these priceless works to his friends as parting gifts, saving for himself only the *chawan* – which we may well imagine was made by Chōjirō – which he smashed to smithereens so that it could never again be used, and then committed ritual suicide. Clearly, the suicide of Nooteboom's protagonist echoes that of the greatest of tea masters, though the ceremony and the decor differ radically. Such is an anti-ceremony, fostering not the social harmony and aesthetic contemplativeness of traditional tea, but rather an isolation, exhaustion and exclusion unto death.

It must not be forgotten that before the age of photographic reproduction, unless seen in person, a famous artwork could only be known through poetry, literature or hearsay, and one might live an entire lifetime hoping to drink but once from a particular bowl. The fact that each tea ceremony is conceived as a once-in-a-lifetime event, and that the minimalist Japanese aesthetic ordains that only one or at most a few precious objects be visible at once, means that the presence of any given artwork becomes an extremely rare event, a manifestation of *mono no aware*. Contrary to today's rampant mediatization, before the modern epoch, the more famous a tea bowl, the rarer its manifestations. Such is a ritual of anticipation and imagination, of nostalgia and recollection. While a bowl lasts long after the ceremony, we may never see it again. The general tendency has been to imagine the ephemeral symbolized by such classic figures in Japanese haiku and music as the fall of a petal, the wind through the pines or the leap of a frog. But mountains too crumble, and pottery cracks: the difference is one of temporal scale. It is the role of art to relate these varied temporalities to the time of our lives. The irony of Taads's mysterious suicide is that the tea ceremony that preceded it celebrated not life's fleetingness, but death's imminence, which are not necessarily the same things. Fumiko, on the contrary, drank what might have been her last tea from a bowl bearing her mother's lipstick traces, and broke the bowl to symbolize a double disappearance, that of her mother and herself, a double rupture with Kikuji, as recompense for the shame of succumbing to him. Kikuji is left with an extraordinary Shino water jar, previously described as being, 'soft . . . like a dream of a woman.'[23] In fact, he is left with the dream of two women, as well as with a certain nostalgia, one of the prime functions of tea utensils.

But there is another possible interpretation, more subtle, otherwise perverse, yet equally attuned to the complex aesthetics of Japanese pottery. What if such breakage were the ultimate emblem of the aesthetics of imperfection? What if we were to imagine these *chawan* fully reassembled (as are many precious antiquities, reconstituted from a myriad of fragments), such that the shattered forms remained visible through gold-filled mending, an emblem of Taads's and Fumiko's shattered lives? What if such already supreme rarities became even more unique by the imprint of a mortal gesture, fixed for future generations both by a morbid tale and a virtuosic repair? But all this is, of course, literary fantasy. Consider rather a real example, a sake cup (*guinomi*) by the contemporary Japanese artist Kuwata Takuro (*b.* 1981). The *guinomi* is often referred to as a mini-*chawan*, and it participates indirectly in the aesthetic of the tea ceremony, influenced to this day by the exigencies of the *wabi-sabi-shibui* aesthetic. (That the term *shibui* has recently taken on the sense of 'cool', much to the consternation of trad-itionalists, is perhaps not without interest.) Japanese art rarely totally escapes the aesthetic demands of tea, whether through direct lineage or in determined reaction. While tea ceremony utensils tend for the most part to follow a more or less classic and traditional aesthetic, other forms of pottery have been left freer to explore more unrestrained modernist and postmodernist prerogatives. This piece, by a young and as yet relatively unknown artist, represents an extreme limit of the art of pottery, insofar as it condenses, epitomizes and hyperbolically transforms certain of the crucial aspects of the Japanese sensibility: handmade quality, formal irregularity, exploration

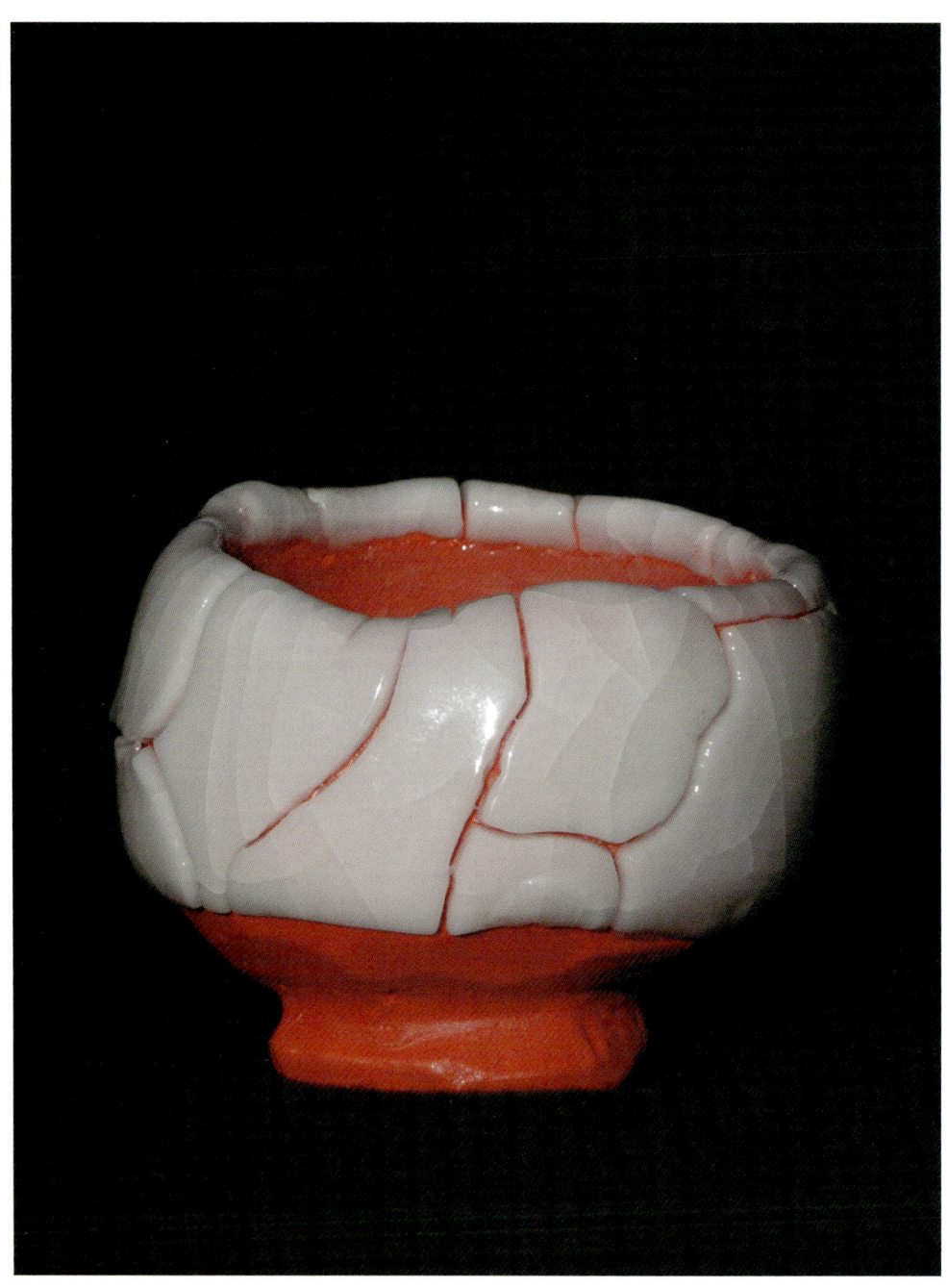

of materiality, efficient utilitarianism. Yet this *guinomi* is almost unthinkable in the context of all but the most avant-garde tea ceremony sensibilities, and it can be said to exemplify an anti-*shibui* aesthetic: self-conscious uniqueness, design-oriented formalism, audacious inventiveness, overstated brashness, affected artificiality, almost kitsch taste. The nearly dayglo colour offends all classic chromatic sensibilities; the contrast between the white glaze and orange-red surface is harsh and unaccommodating; the layer of white glaze (almost an independent entity, both crackled and cracked, nearly as thick as the cup itself) appears as a hyperbolic pastiche of classic crackle, fissure and breakage. More at home in the white space of a gallery or the shiny steel and black marble decor of a high design restaurant than among the soft woods of traditional Japanese architecture, its artificial colour suggests neither blood nor autumnal tints. It partakes of the Japan of endless flashing neon signs and high-contrast advertising colours, not of the realm of wood and lacquer celebrated in Tanizaki Jun'ichirō's *In Praise of Shadows* (1933) and in so many nostalgic novels. It is difficult to say if the piece is ironic or excessive, but it is certainly a work of pure mannerism, and one might well imagine sipping sake from it in Miyamoto Katsuhiro's *Zenkai House*. It evinces not the *shibui* of traditional understatement but the cool of postmodern hyperbole.

Kuwata Takuro, *guinomi*, 2009.

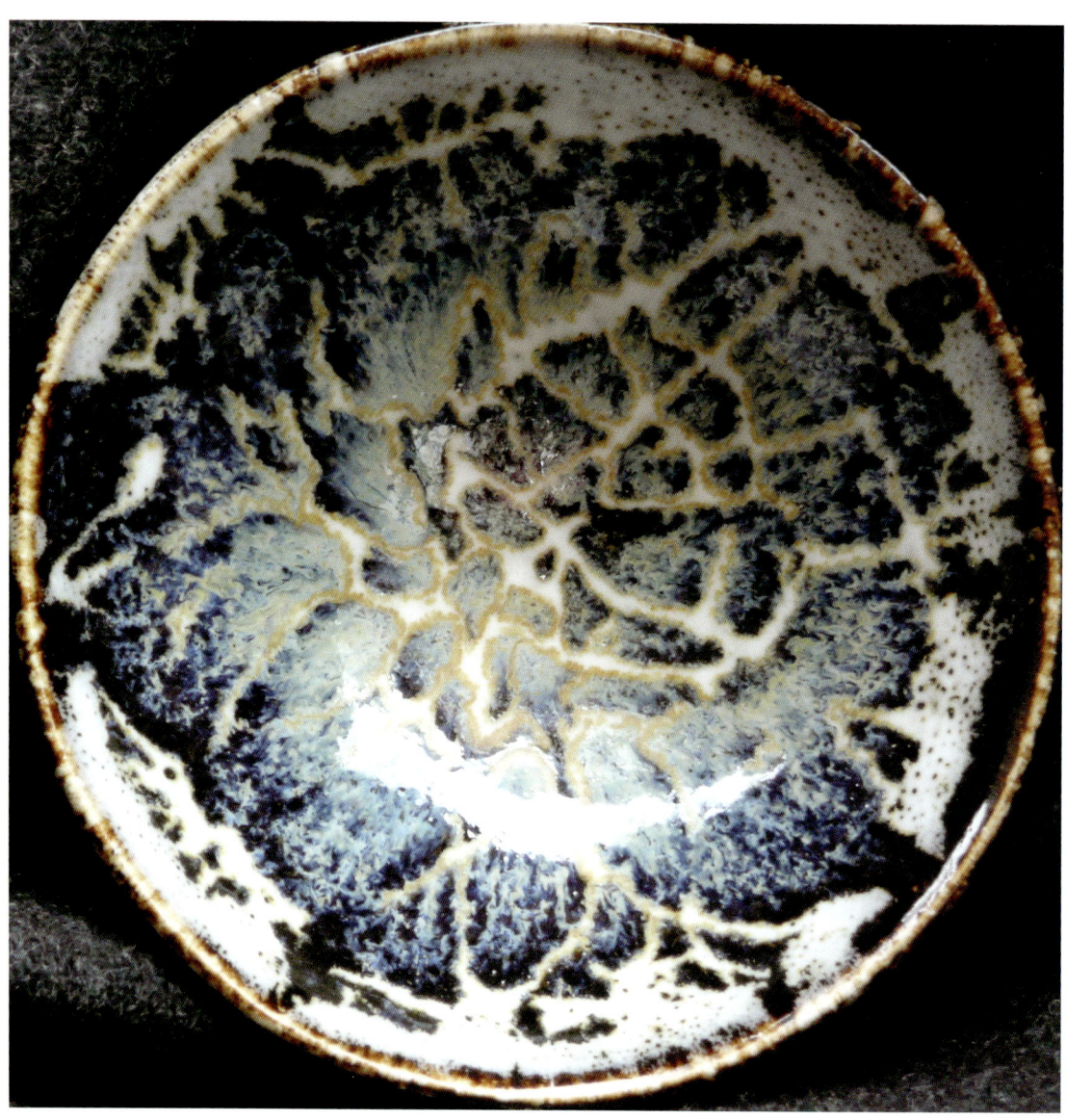

Kimura Moriyasu, 'sky tenmoku' *sakazuki* (shallow sake cup), *c.* 2010.

FIVE

POTTERY LANDSCAPES

In the West, wine drinking is a transparent affair. The enthusiast well knows that in order to appreciate the colour of the wine, the only acceptable glass is one of absolutely clear crystal. The purist will even frown on the finest cut glass, since the added sparkle denatures the visual experience. This is why drinking from the rarest vessel, be it a Tiffany Favrile floriform goblet or a Gallé cameo glass beaker, a silver chalice or the Holy Grail itself, is oenologically superfluous, even counterproductive. Such beautiful glasses are too fragile, too rare, too decorative. Their particular beauty detracts from that of the wine, such that their use is pure ostentation. The ideal is, as M.F.K. Fisher so astutely put it, 'glasses no more ornamented than the bubbles they imitate'.[1] In Japan, the opposite is true, for it is the wine, sake, that is crystal clear, giving centre stage to the drinking vessels. There are most notably three forms of pottery sake cups: the largest, the *guinomi*, exists in a great variety of shapes, often similar to both the larger and taller *yunomi* teacup and the classic *chawan* of the tea ceremony; the *choko* (*o-choko*), which resembles in size and function a shot glass; and the saucer-shaped *sakazuki*. The *guinomi* shares most of its aesthetic characteristics with its larger and more famous counterpart, the *chawan*, though while the *guinomi* and *choko* are about as small as a drinking vessel can comfortably be, the *chawan* can only be held comfortably in two hands.

The tea bowl is near the top of the Japanese aesthetic hierarchy, making it an object of the utmost prestige.[2] However, though the *guinomi* is often referred to as a mini-*chawan*, its use is neither codified nor ritualized, governed not by arcane ritual refined over centuries, as is the case for the *chawan*, but by the commonplace rules of quotidian etiquette and politesse. Thus the *guinomi* may be of any shape and quite variable in size, as long as it can contain sake and be pleasant to drink from, while the *chawan* must easily permit wiping and whisking, and the tea must form an attractive pool and be easy to consume. Removed from the aesthetic expectations demanded by the tea ceremony, the *guinomi* is less bound to tradition and thus more amenable to experimentation. In behavioural and gestural terms, even though sake is offered sacrificially at both Shinto shrines and Buddhist temples, sake drinking is a secular activity circumscribed by the contingencies of the gastronomic context. One might add that the intoxicating effects of sake are most certainly deritualizing, to say the least. The *guinomi* exists as an individual entity (not as a type, as is the case for most Western wine glasses), which makes all the more unfortunate the recent trend of serving sake in Western-style crystal glasses.[3] Pottery sake cups share all the aesthetic principles of the tea bowl, though to different effect. The value of a tea bowl is in part determined by the manner in which it highlights the colour and texture of the frothy, light green tea (*macha*) particular to the ceremony, thus traditionally limiting the acceptable chromatic spectrum. (Rikyū basically reduced the possibilities to red and black.) On the contrary, the practically colourless transparency of sake, permitting all forms, motifs and colours, makes it the ideal liquid to reveal the beauty of the cup itself. The *chawan* is best admired empty, the *guinomi* is most intriguing half full. Here, the same aesthetic reveres both the opaque and the transparent, the brightly tinted and the colourless, the stimulating and the intoxicating, plenitude and the void.[4]

Certain philosophers would insist that to grasp any single object fully, one must know the entire universe. This holistic approach is central to Japanese aesthetics, where each and every art form shares certain central principles, most notably a strong link to the seasons. Each season, divided into three parts for added refinement, is figured by highly coded norms of motif, colour and form, often expressed in the most subtle allusions, metaphors and correspondences. Yet the most immediate context in which to grasp (figuratively and literally) the *guinomi*, which is after all a drinking vessel, is that of gastronomy, the art of the table. While table settings in the West tend to consist of matched sets of identical dishes, Japanese cuisine valorizes unmatched ensembles chosen not only to celebrate the beauty and rarity of individual objects, but also according to numerous ambient exigencies: the complexities of seasonal cuisine (where many foods are traditionally matched to specific forms of pottery); the unique decor of the restaurant (including woodworking, painting, calligraphy, ikebana, kimono fabric patterns); the seasonal state of the local and regional landscape. Most spectacular are the platings, where food often appears as miniature landscapes: sometimes the entire plate, sometimes just a minute detail, might evoke the decor and exterior landscape. Murata Yoshihiro, chef of the famed Kikunoi restaurant in Kyoto, offers a definition of *kaiseki* cuisine, the multi-course meals originally related to the tea ceremony, having over the years become not only the refined cuisine particular to Kyoto but also typical of Japanese haute cuisine in general. He quite simply says that it is 'eating the seasons'.[5] Another Kyoto chef, asked by a Zen monk about the reasoning behind his cuisine, responded, as had so many ikebana masters before him, 'To reflect nature precisely'.[6]

Kaiseki is an elaborate meal the complexity of which, always attuned to locale and season, offers a microcosm of Japanese cuisine. It will typically include dishes representing all styles of cooking (boiled, braised, sautéed, fried, grilled, steamed), all modalities of rawness (simpliciter, dried, smoked, salted, sugared, fermented), and all sources of food (mountain, field, ocean, river, sky). As in all Japanese art, such meals take part in a complex representational matrix, suggesting the landscape, season, climate and even time of day, by a subtle yet codified set of analogies and juxtapositions. The perfection of each element (food, sake, pottery and so on) is made even more complex by the dynamic and non-hierarchical relationship between the varied elements. This culinary aesthetic is manifest, in a highly condensed version, in the Japanese *bento* lunchbox which in its most sophisticated examples features *kaiseki* cuisine. The holistic-cosmological symbolism of the *bento* is evident in its form, as is attested to by the *shokado* lunchbox, whose square shape with four equal compartments approximates the kanji for rice paddy, 田, the core of Japanese agriculture. Sometimes the representational allusions are purely metaphorical, sometimes literal, as in the planked barracuda served in Kikunoi one evening in December 2009, which arrived in the form of an autumn landscape. In the cookbook from this restaurant, entitled *Kaiseki*, one of the dishes for February is *anago* (saltwater eel) with rice, where the long

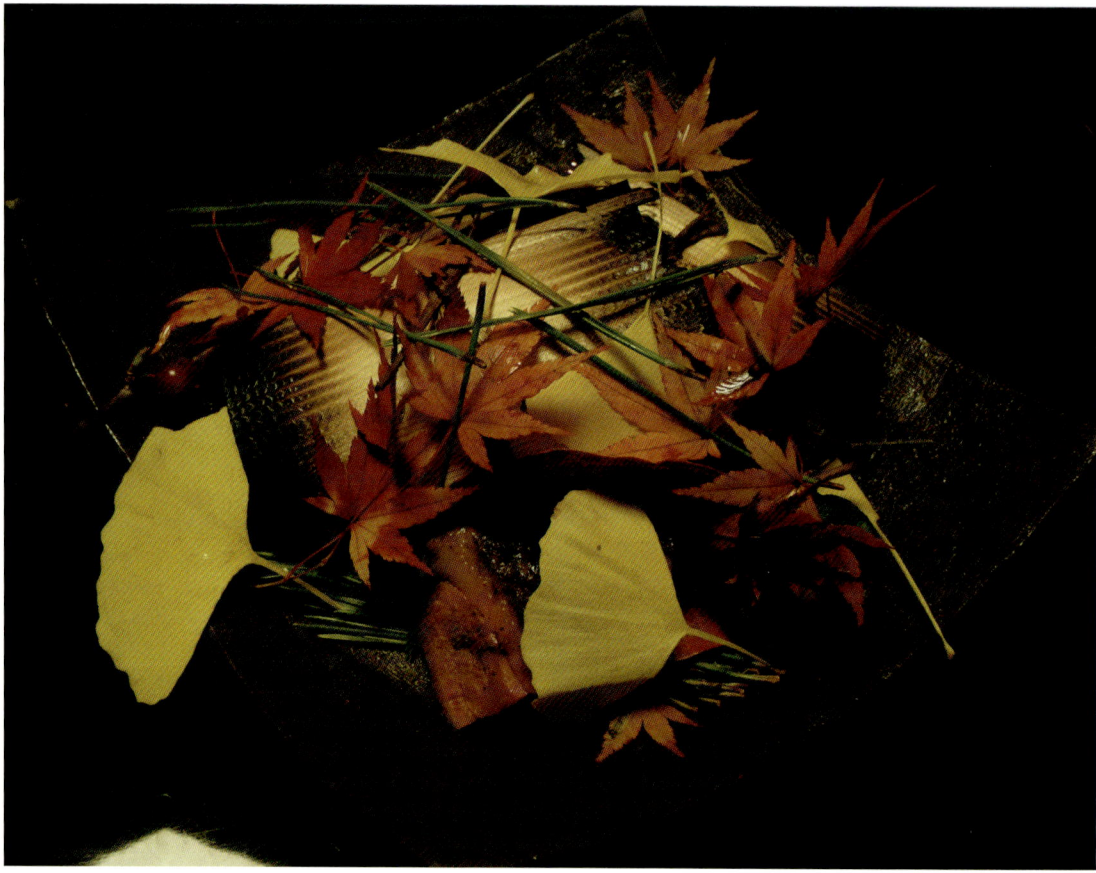

Kikunoi restaurant, Kyoto, December 2009, planked barracuda.

eel fillets are wrapped around a savoury rice mix; the accompanying photo is of the dry garden of Ryōan-ji, where the form and colour of the roofed walls surrounding the white gravel parterre is evidently homologous with the eel dish. Such correspondences are neither mannerisms nor pretensions, but an integral part of the Japanese culinary arts.

The passion for the diminutive is typical of Zen-inspired aesthetics, where the cosmos can be compressed into the form of a small garden, the garden reduced to the disposition of food on a plate, and the plated 'landscape' represented by the patterns on the plate or *guinomi*, whose constituent features derive from the macrocosmic five elements of the Shinto and Buddhist cosmos: fire (kiln), wood (ash), earth (clay), metal (glazes), water (cooling agent). Representation implies both abstraction and metaphorization, such that – just as the qualities of each morsel on a plate are enriched by the adjacent foodstuffs – the profundity of metaphor depends on both the specific beauty of each of the terms and the vast range of qualities that simultaneously link and separate them. That said, the appreciation of a *guinomi* must begin not in metaphor, but with its uniqueness as an object, not with symbol but with material. It might seem superfluous to stress that the *guinomi* has a front, back, lip, interior and foot. But since the particularities of Japanese aesthetics, especially in relation to pottery, diverge greatly from Western forms of connoisseurship, these terms take on different significance in each context. If the conventions of aesthetic judgement are different in the West and in Japan, so too are the protocols of etiquette. In the West it is generally considered ill mannered to turn over the dinner plates in order to discover their mark of origin, and to refrain from commenting on the table setting is in many circles considered a mark of refinement. In the tea ceremony, on the contrary, close observation is part of the ritual, and to neglect to do so would be disrespectful. During the much less formal situation of a dinner, in Japan standard etiquette demands that bowls be lifted to the mouth, while in the West one needs great dexterity and

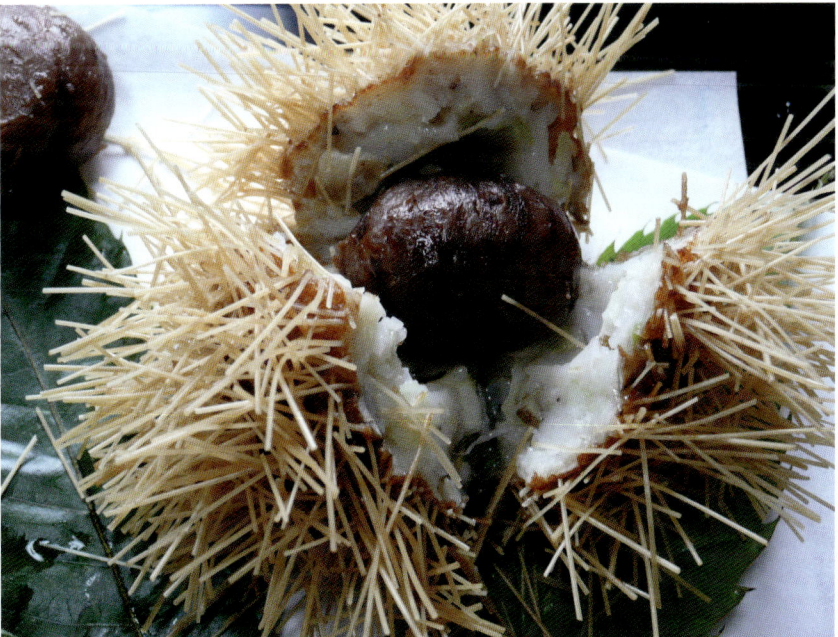

Nishiki restaurant, Kyoto, December 2009. Fish purée and fried noodles in the form of a chestnut.

subtleness to get the last drop of soup from a bowl, which should never leave the table, and never even be tilted in certain directions. This suggests that in Japan the everyday relations to utensils are of greater familiarity and ease. Politeness demands detailed, prolix examination and praise, not silent appreciation. Every aspect of the *chawan* must be observed and commented on, and contrary to most Western pottery, the foot (*kōdai*) and the interior (*mikomi*, pool) are essential. Thus, while a strictly formalized procedure does not exist for examining and appreciating *guinomi*, in fact the experience is not unlike that of examining a *chawan*, though without the ritual. Such heightened attention spans the difference between the functional and the aesthetic, bringing connoisseurship into the everyday realm. One finds, for example, that front and back are often equivocal, variously determined by visual cues on glaze patterns, by a curve or thickness appropriate for the placement of the lip, or by the very form of the piece; that the stone-like inertness of pottery is often made dynamic by an inner spiral that forms a veritable whirlpool, or through glaze drippings that suggest continual melting; that the formal features of the interior are transformed by the mobile yet transparent presence of the sake, with its shift from horizontal surface at rest to diagonal flows and eddies, as well as by its refracting and reflecting optical qualities.[7]

The aesthetics of tea bowls and sake cups demands total visibility. If we wished to reduce visibility to its rhetorical dimension, it might be said that in the West the perception of most traditional pottery depends on a unique perspective (a sort of synecdoche, where the whole is intuited from a single view), while the Japanese tea aesthetic demands panopticism and even pansensorialism, of the sort only available through manipulation of the object. These different epistemological and ontological protocols result in the fact that while much Western pottery bears only one surface meant to be primarily visible, most Japanese pottery is created to be seen from every possible angle. Furthermore, tactility is of the essence, a fact well expressed in Nooteboom's *Rituals*, when Taads first handles the tea bowl by Ryōnyū mentioned in the previous chapter:

Kawabata Kentaro,
guinomi, 2008.

there are also rules about the shape, all of which were drawn up by
Rikyu, how the bowl should feel when you hold it, its balance, the
way it feels to the lips . . . and of course the temperature. The tea must
not feel too hot or too cold to your hand when you hold it, but exactly
as you would like to drink it.[8]

Though it goes without saying that the visual is also essential, the stress on
the tactile is fundamental and profound. There is a 'beauty of intimacy'
exemplified by the fact that, as Yanagi Sōetsu (the modern philosopher
and founder of the Mingei folk craft movement) explains, the tea masters
'embraced the shape and kissed the thickness' of the *chawan*.[9] Here, the
effects of *sabi*, patination by long use, determine aesthetic value: not only
visually, not only for the implied sense of longevity connected with the
passage of time and history, but also to indicate that a tea bowl was adoringly
caressed by the lips and fingers of a great tea master, which adds immeasur-
ably to the value of the piece. The sensitivity to *sabi* effects is highly refined.
For example, the white Hagi pottery glaze is particularly prone to change after
use, and one speaks of 'the seven changes of Hagi', which include discolouration, crackling, blackening of the cracks and so on. Such discolouration is
considered a transformation rather than a stain, a poetic effect rather than a
defect. These changes may completely transform the iconography of a piece,
as when a 'snowy glaze' crackles, consequently losing the appearance of snow
as the materiality of the glaze becomes evident. This predilection is very different from the Western collector's sensibility, where damage or wear usually
diminishes value, and provenance adds mainly to the monetary, not the
aesthetic, worth. *Sabi* implies that use value augments aesthetic value: the more
famous the user, the more refined the ceremony, the more acute the aesthetic
intuition, the more valued the cup. Consequently, the use of priceless vessels
is not a sign of conspicuous consumption, but of aesthetic delectation.

This is why it would be an error to consider such drinking vessels
according to criteria specific to the appreciation of Western ceramics. Even
more crucially, this is why Eurocentric aesthetics in general is ill equipped
to interpret Japanese art. Consider, for example, Pierre Bourdieu's sociology

of art and taste, *La Distinction: Critique sociale du jugement*,[10] which distinguishes between the aesthetic sensibilities of the learned (*docte*) and the worldly (*mondaine*), played out in terms of a series of existential dichotomies: specialist / aesthete; scholar / apprentice; erudite / connoisseur; schooled / autodidact; viewing / touching; acquired taste / inherited taste. These in turn translate into metaphysical dichotomies: knowledge / experience; reflection / sensation; concept / pleasure; discourse / contemplation; comprehension / appreciation; form / substance; consciously formulated aesthetic laws / unconscious, though no less strict, apprehension of aesthetic rules. In Japan, there is decidedly less distance between art and craft, scholarship and pleasure, transcendence and immanence. Japanese connoisseurship continues to be on the side of the worldly, while modern Western art history has become more and more slanted towards the learned, the specialized, the academic, indeed the scientific. One can immediately see how the ceremonially necessary physical contact with a tea bowl greatly complicates these issues and forces not only the disintegration of such dichotomies, but also that of the distinction between art and craft so long held in the West. Yanagi expresses this in particularly pithy form: 'If we want to see a thing well, we must use it well.'[11] The beauty and use value of a *chawan* are inextricable; form not only follows function, but art follows life, and craft is indistinguishable from art. For mastery of the tea ceremony is a rite of passage into the world of *chawan* connoisseurship, where erudition is concomitant with worldliness and where tea bowls are near the summit of the Japanese aesthetic hierarchy, unlike the lowly pottery relegated to the realm of 'craft' in Western aesthetics. Such is perhaps what Nietzsche called a 'joyful wisdom', a term that would be an oxymoron for Bourdieu.

The main tenets of the *wabi-sabi-shibui* tea aesthetic inform pottery connoisseurship, privileging certain types of material effects and representational forms, guiding both the hand of the potter and the eye of the collector. Emblematic of this passion for materials is the particular importance of the favoured technique of leaving exposed areas of undecorated clay to reveal the 'clay flavour' (*tsuchi-aji*) of the work, since recognition of the type, quality and treatment of clay are keys to connoisseurship, and it is for this reason that much pottery, whatever the glaze, has at least one place, however tiny and usually on the foot, where the clay is left unglazed. This spot, safeguarded from the transformations of fire and ash, most clearly and literally reveals the potter's touch. This appreciation of clay flavour is not unlike the sense of *terroir* in French gastronomy, signifying those site-specific characteristics of taste so often evoked in wine connoisseurship. In pottery, this clay flavour is a function of the relations between earth (clay) and tree (fuel) as they interact through combustion in the kiln. For example, the preferred wood of many potters has long been black pine, because of both the high heat that can be obtained and the particular glaze effects caused by its ash. But might one not ask whether this preference is also symbolic, in some small part due to the fact that the pine is one of the most important trees in Japanese iconology? Or the irony that this evergreen, the symbol of longevity par excellence, is destroyed in the flames of the kiln? Yet beyond the many conscious manners of treating the clay – spinning, moulding, throwing, carving, cutting, incising, texturing, inlaying, impressing, dipping, dripping, trailing, glazing, under-glazing, overglazing – there also exist those accidental features so cherished in

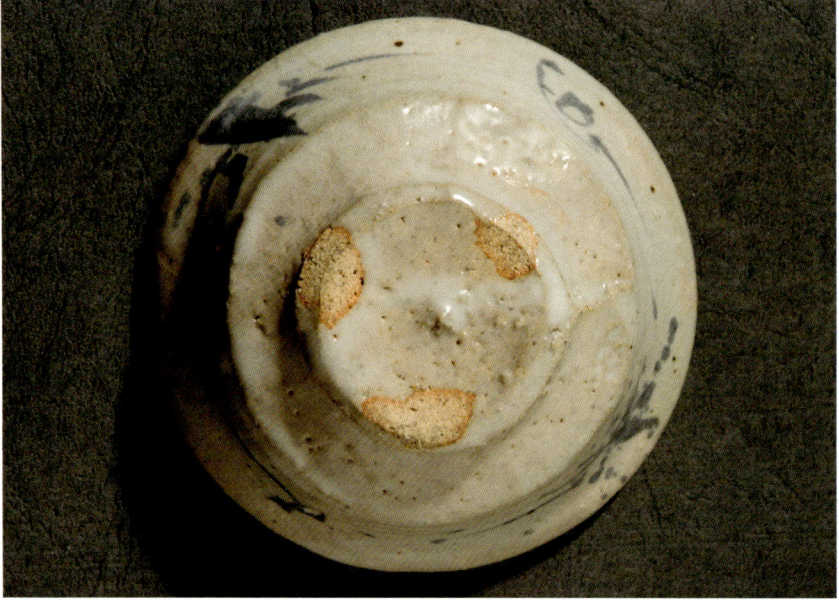

Sato Satoshi, foot (*kōdai*) of *sakazuki* on p. 168, *c.* 2007.

Zen-inspired art, a perfection of the imperfect inherent in effects particular to the art of pottery such as finger impressions, spur marks or shell imprints from stacking, scratch marks, ash deposits, firing cracks, crazing, glaze crackling, fusings from adjacent pottery, scorch and fire flash marks, breaks caused by tooling, glaze drippage, running slips.[12] Aleatory and partially indeterminable firing effects are most highly valued, as exemplified by a Shino *guinomi* made by Arimoto Kuugen, with its dripping white glaze and pitted surface.

Sake cups are produced by practically all of the over 100 major kilns (and over 50,000 minor ones) in Japan, utilizing almost every possible technique, in traditional, folk and experimental styles, ranging from the purely decorative and abstract through such stylizations as sharkskin, oilspot, hare fur and sesame spot glazes, to full-blown figuration and calligraphy done in underglaze or overglaze painting. Following the tea aesthetic, many connoisseurs prefer works from those kilns (Bizen, Hagi, Shino, Karatsu, Iga, Shigaraki) that emphasize the more or less aleatory effects caused by natural ash glaze, undecorated mineral glaze, or fire on unglazed surfaces, where figuration, if any, exists in the form of the most subtle similitudes. As Robert Yellin explains: 'Keshiki [landscape] involves how the glaze flows, stops and pools, or the color of the clay, the creating process, or how certain kiln occurrences play out on the surface.'[13] Though the figuration and symbolism in individual cases may occasionally seem either oversimplistic or unduly remote to the outsider, it must not be forgotten that the representational value of a piece, which exists in a complex aesthetic web, is but one aspect of its existence. Quite often, Japanese connoisseurs might see representational correspondences on pottery surfaces where many Western observers would only discern abstract patterns.[14] While for most of the history of Western art and aesthetics potential images have been marginal if constant features of artistic practice and discourse (such as Leonardo's interest in images seen in clouds and fire, and various sorts of anthropomorphization), modernism from Symbolism onwards has increasingly brought such equivocal and potential images into its purview, both pictorially and theoretically, though hardly to the extent that such images are recognized and sought after in Japan. This

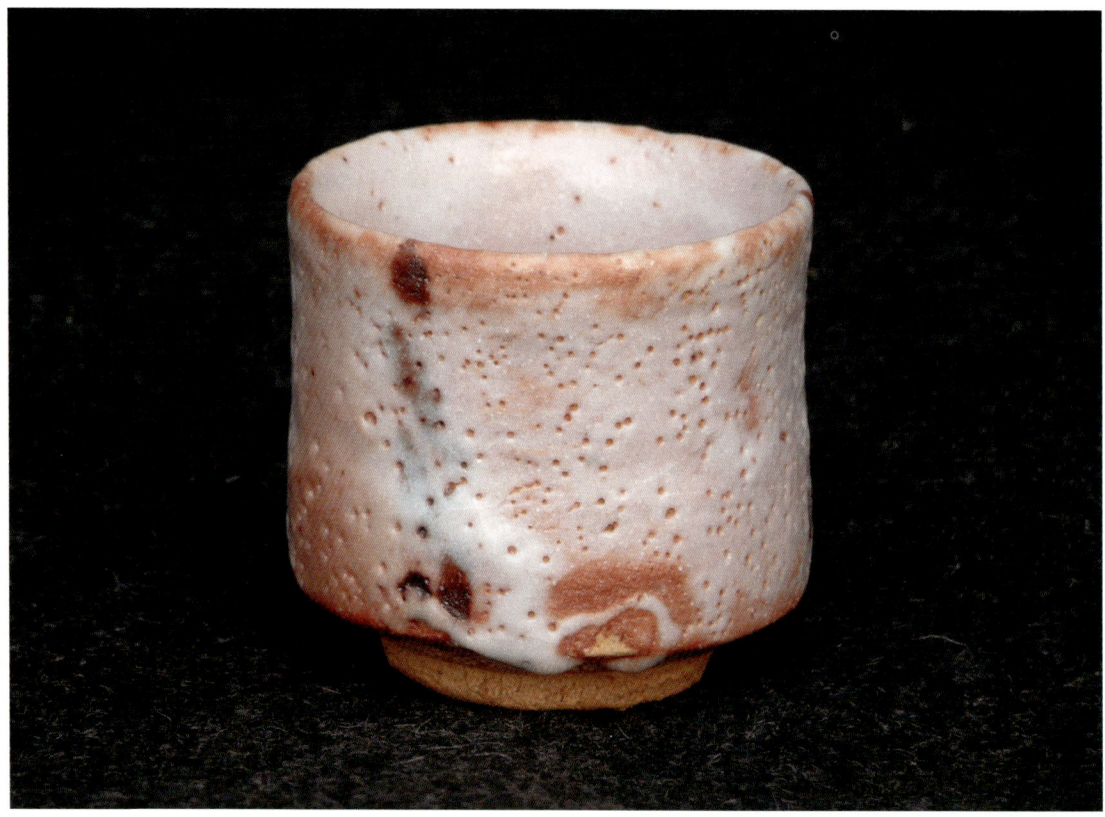

Arimoto Kuugen,
Shino *guinomi*, 2011.

has been crucial for epistemology, as the roles of appreciation, interpretation, suggestion and imaginary perception have taken on increasing importance in grasping the sort of 'open work' that has characterized so much twentieth-century art, where following Duchamp's famous dictum, the role of the spectator in completing the work of art is crucial. Figuration and abstraction are relative terms: every aesthetic system determines a different threshold between the two, and even the most blatantly representational art is founded on a non-figurative material foundation that is essential to the perception of the work.

Representation in pottery fills the entire spectrum from trace to icon, and given the potential richness of something as primary as the fissure, it is clear that Zen-inspired representation is a dynamic system oscillating between

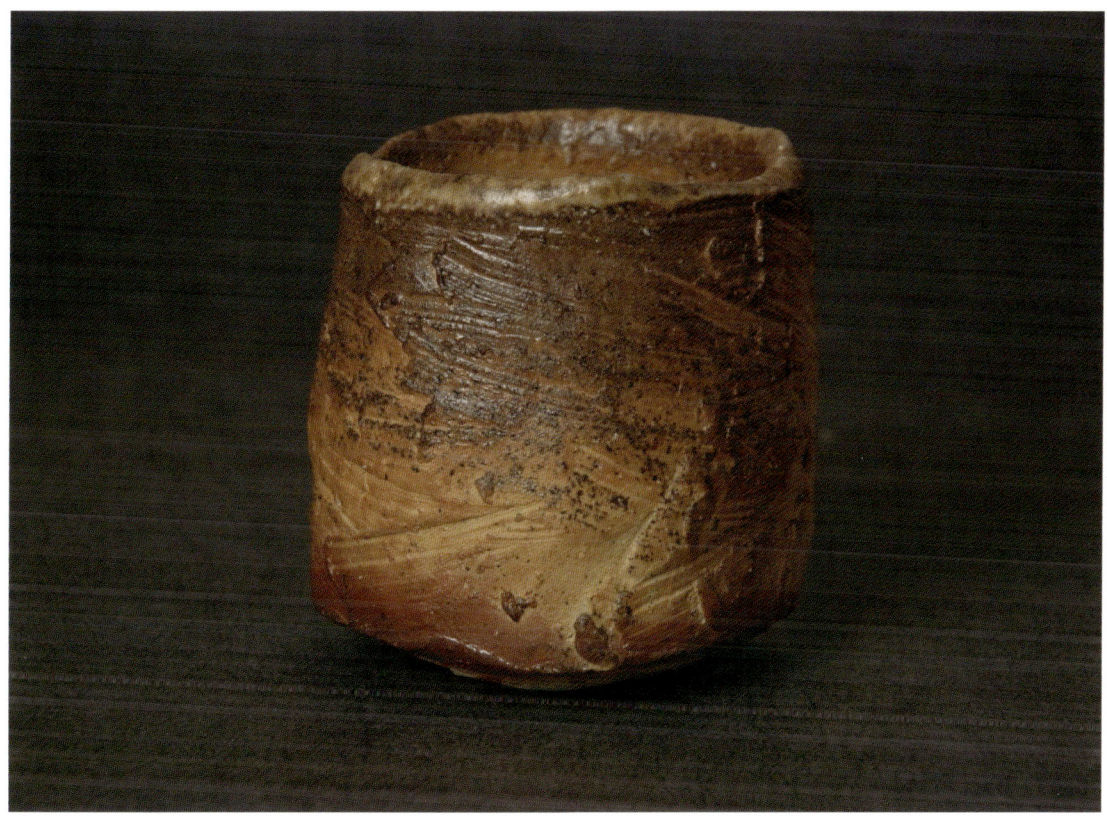

Suehiro Manabu, Bizen *guinomi*, c. 2007.

abstraction and figuration. Not only is there an aesthetic imperative to view certain traces within a representational framework, but many pieces are even named – by potter, tea master or collector – according to such resemblances, such as the famed tea bowls Fujisan and Seppo. Two contemporary examples are a Bizen *guinomi* by Kakurezaki Ryūichi named by Robert Yellin 'The Cup of Humanity' for a small crack in the form of the Japanese character for *hito*, 人 (person), and a Shigaraki *guinomi* by Matsuyama Suketoshi called 'The Grand Canyon', because its colours evoke those of the canyon walls at sunset.[15] It is interesting that, given the modernist allure of abstraction, the naming of pottery continues primarily to evoke the figurative. Perhaps this is because the longstanding Japanese passion for the materiality of pottery already implies an appreciation of abstraction, of a pure materiality prior to the imaginative function that seeks iconicity. The evocation of figuration is necessary to locate the image in a symbolic web: however abstruse, the name given to a piece or the image revealed will often have a bearing on the time of day and season in which it will be exhibited or used, which is to say on the very meaning of a work, and its relation to both nature and culture. These representational values depend on factors spanning the entire duration from production to use: the *potter's work* in conceiving and creating each piece within a specific tradition and with an individual style; the *kiln effects* that are partially planned and partially aleatory; the *potter's choice* of which pieces are worthy of display after having survived the generative violence of the flames, a choice that implies a hierarchy, consisting of works to be sold and those to be saved for museums or the potter's own collection; the *critic's discourse*, which outlines the complexities of changing taste, temporary fads, historical transformations, aesthetic revisionism and international influences within the never-ending history of pottery; and the *collector's vision* which, through the arcana of connoisseurship, contextualizes the work by positioning it within the ineluctable seasonal symbolism demanded by the tea ceremony.

We are currently in the midst of a major museological shift that has extenuated, if not totally abolished, the strict hierarchy that had so long separated art and craft in Western art history. The result is that many museums, pioneered by the Musée d'Orsay in Paris, now exhibit 'craft' and 'art' alongside each other, to the great benefit of both. This innovation in Western aesthetics, which has greatly benefitted the 'arts of the table', should help in our appreciation of Japanese art, where the line between art and craft has been drawn very differently, and with radically different consequences. Japanese conventions of viewing pottery are quite different from those in the West, and are made even more complex by the profound interconnectedness of all the arts in Japanese culture. While there are viewing protocols and modes of connoisseurship specific to pottery, pottery also shares, to differing degrees, the viewing conventions of the other arts: painting, calligraphy, sculpture, cuisine, gardens. The *chawan* or *guinomi* is both sculptural object and painterly surface: irregularities enhance figuration, curvature suggests depth, play of light evokes motion. The piece may reverberate with landscape allusions, thus playing a central role in the arts of the table by articulating food and drink, pottery and decor, ikebana and landscape. A discussion of all the possible contexts for appreciating pottery would fill an entire book, so a single emblematic example related to landscape, by the Kyoto potter Sato Satoshi, must here suffice. While determinate, central, guiding perspectives constitute a major design feature of most Western gardens, they do not necessarily imply the primacy of a single fixed viewpoint, from which the garden should be viewed. In Zen-inspired gardens there exist controlled views, framed views, partial views, multiple views, counter views, hidden views and, most famously of all, borrowed views (*shakkei*), which have entered garden design the world over. The borrowed or captured view is a manner of relating proximate and distant space, created by opening up a foreground or middle-ground perspective such that the distant landscape is precisely framed and consequently integrated into the garden. In a greatly reduced sense, the *guinomi* 'landscape' may exhibit such a borrowed view every time it is examined or drunk from. As the cup is raised, its lip serves as the 'horizon' that links the proximate scene on the front to the 'distant' landscape beyond the lake of sake within, as is the case for the cup by Sato Satoshi, where the bamboo branch forms the proximate field for viewing the distant mountains. That the sake is transformed into a cascade as the elbow is bent and the *guinomi* is tilted is rarely an unwelcome effect.

KAWABATA YASUNARI, in the preface to a book by the landscape painter Higashiyama Kaii, recounts his reaction to having seen the famous Three Pines at Kanazawa, one of the great natural sites of Japan, celebrated in painting and poetry through the ages:

> They struck me to the point that I wondered if there existed a comparable beauty anywhere in the world. I was overwhelmed with thanks for that state of mind among the Japanese that would not hesitate to consecrate centuries to transmitting the beauty of a single tree.[16]

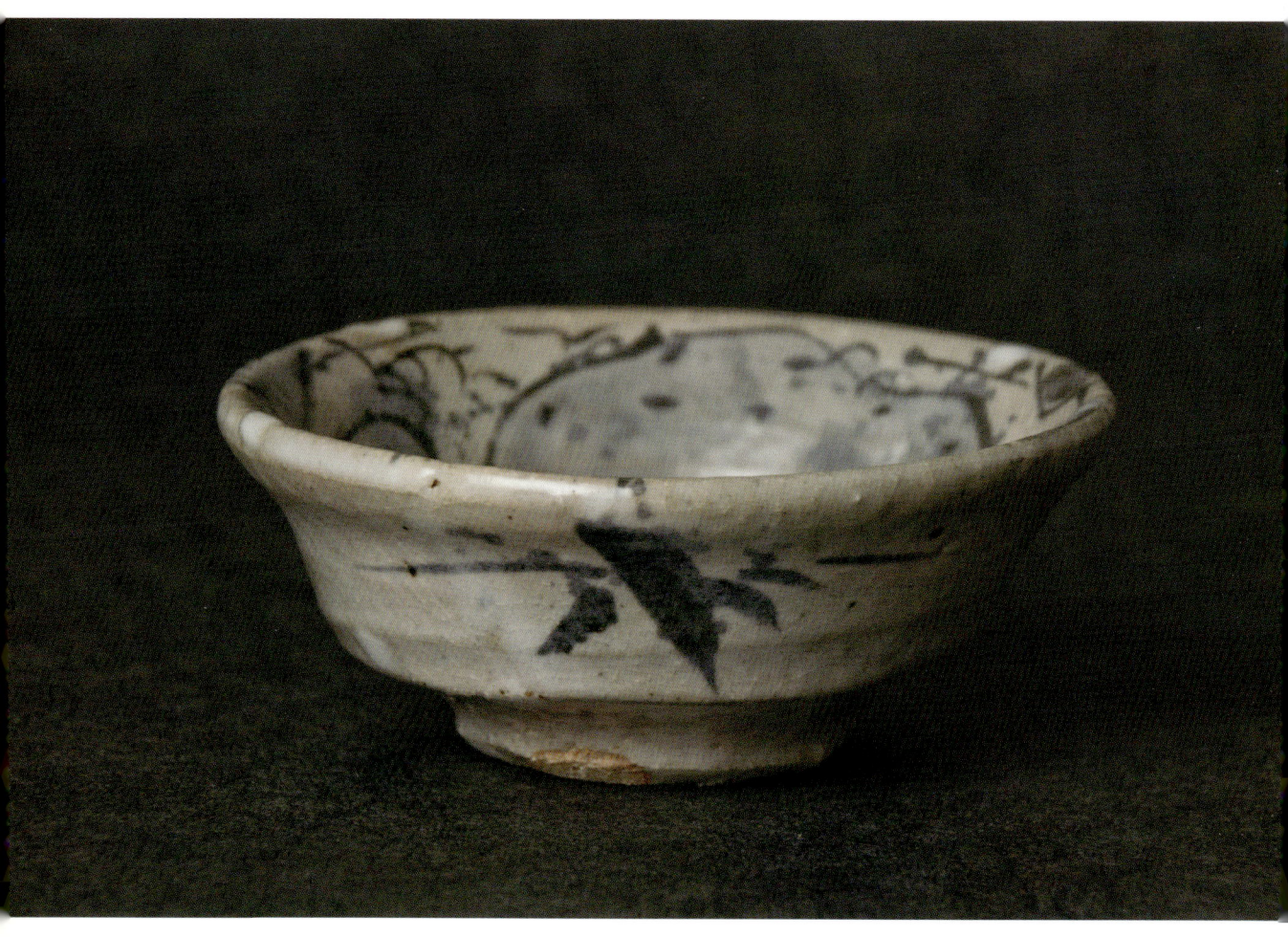

Sato Satoshi, *sakazuki, c.* 2007.

Much the same may be said concerning the beauty of a single bowl. In general, wine drinking is really about the wine and its intoxicating effects, be they euphoric, inspiring or depressing, and accounts of bacchic exploits in which the receptacle is of great importance are quite rare. On the contrary, ceremonial tea drinking is of the greatest material refinement, and is thus the source of endless discourse about the objects, such that the interrelations between the arts in tea-oriented aesthetics cannot be overestimated. Writing of the formative influence of Murata Jukō on the modern form of the tea ceremony, Louise Allison Cort explains:

> The transformation that Jukō and his associates wrought in the tea ceremony sprang from a deeply felt and widespread spiritual undercurrent – the fruit of war – that manifested itself in the forms of the other arts as well, including Nō theater, flower arranging, and poetry. The emergence of Jukō's aesthetic and of parallel aesthetics in other fields is usually explained by the dissemination of Zen Buddhist concepts. The importance of the influence of Zen Buddhism has been overemphasized, however, to the point of concealing the vital role of the perception and vocabulary developed within the tradition of classical court poetry in the form known as *renga*, or linked verse. Jukō's most lasting achievement was to apply for the first time to material objects the vocabulary – expressive of a particular and deep-rooted strain of Japanese perception – that had theretofore been developed as purely verbal imagery within the art of *renga*.[17]

Not only did this new poetic vocabulary greatly enrich the perception of pottery by establishing a vast range of imagery that provides a sort of mental grid according to which such works can be seen anew, but it also implicitly reinforced and perhaps augmented the already high status of pottery by verbally, iconographically and conceptually linking it to poetry. Within this poetic system, the natural world, and especially the most famous sites of Japan such as Mount Fuji, were transformed into veritable commonplaces (in the root sense of the term, stressing the *locus* or *topos*, the sense of place) and fully codified as poetic tropes, 'toponyms so abstracted from their geographic reality that, practically delocalized and often reduced to simple epithets, their only function was to evoke images'.[18] Thus poet and reader could travel throughout the country without ever leaving home, by means of the continual circulation between poetic allusion, pictorial image, reverie, dream. Once Rikyū established the priority of Japanese pottery, and once the great Japanese kilns became distinguishable by their clays, forms and iconography in the multitude of their specificity, such general poetic geographic tropes were concretized in the tea ceremony by the very materiality of indigenous pottery.

Tea is both performance and paradigm: each ceremony is a unique and unrepeatable event, celebrating the ephemeralness of the passing moment and the changing season, as well as a particular grouping of people whose sensibilities are attuned to the images, objects and allusions of the instant. Yet simultaneously, each ceremony is also a formal structure – inspired by previous ceremonies and perhaps destined in turn to influence the future of tea – with only minor variants in gesture and choreography, and where certain objects may reappear and accrue new significations. Tea is thus an aesthetic paradigm stressing spiritual concentration and psychological interiorization, based on the synaesthetic inmixing of the arts. It is also a form of etiquette that is formalized by a veritable choreography of gestures, as well as that attention to detail particular to connoisseurship as a form of material knowledge. Tea also imposes social and ethical imperatives, as the eighteenth-century tea master Zuihosai Issoku summarized by the principles of harmony, reverence, purity, calm: 'The guest must fully realize the pains taken by the host, and try to give him as little trouble as possible. The ideal relation between them is a mutual understanding and appreciation that needs no words to express.'[19] The appreciation of the effort need not be articulated, but that of the objects demands precise, even poetic, commentary. Of course, the foundations of such understanding and appreciation are erudition and connoisseurship, which establish a vast range of acceptable allusions. Eccentricity, exoticism, bizarreness and excessive obscurity are to be avoided, which is the reason that, for example, many tea masters insist that only flowers that are generally familiar and sung about by the poets are permitted in the *tokonoma*. The degree of connoisseurship, as well as the level of proficiency in the ceremony, indicates the appropriateness of certain objects.

Tea proposes not only an aesthetics and an ethics, but an epistemology. In the tea world, the arts are all linked through a metaphoric and synaesthetic imperative. To begin with a *chawan* in the palm of one's hand and end up imagining a garden, poem or painting reveals the richness inherent in Japanese culture.

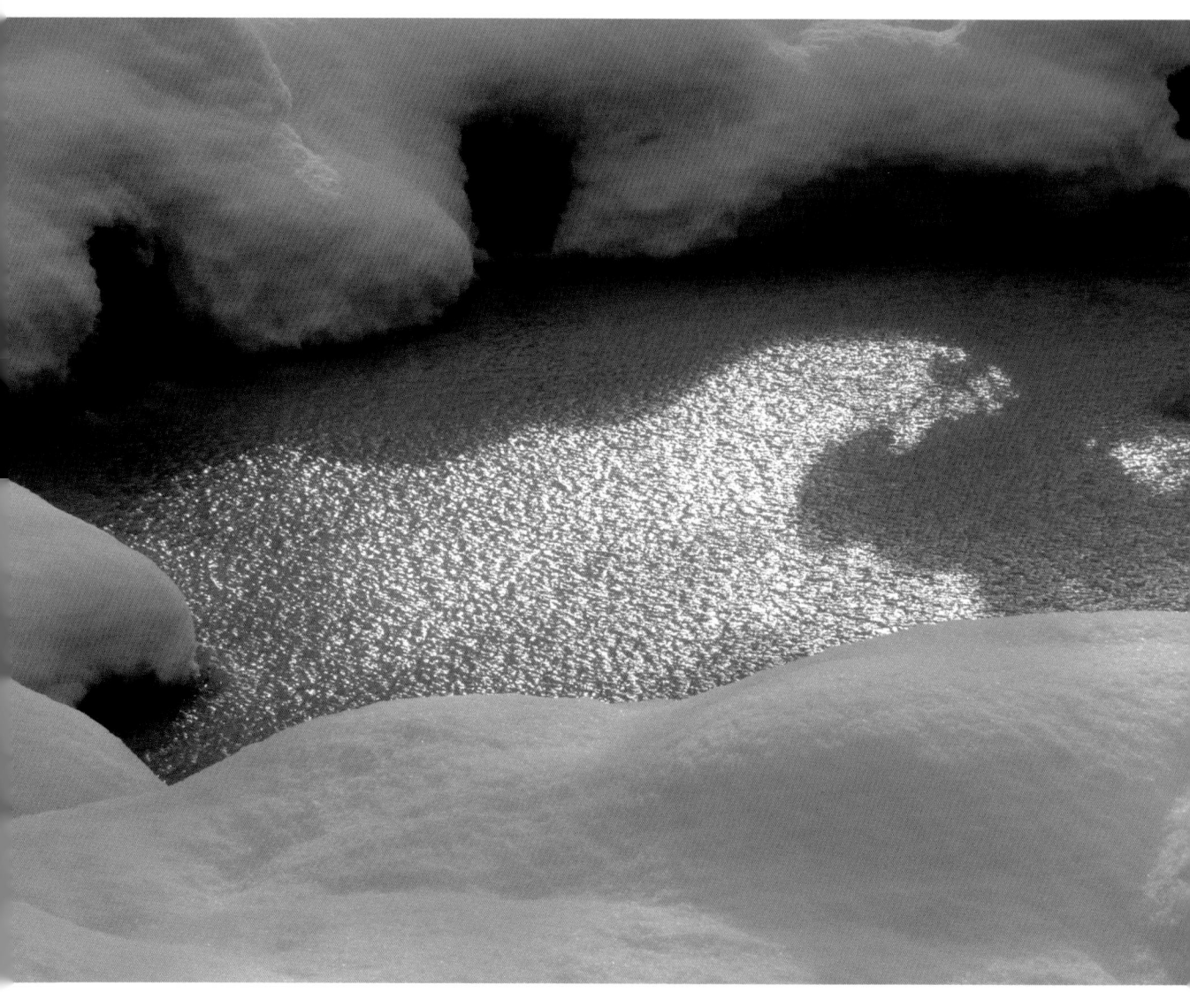

Jikkō-in, Ohara.

SIX

THE TEA BOWL AND THE TOILET BOWL

In 1968 the potter Koie Ryōji produced a work that would call into question centuries of received opinion. Scheduled to exhibit in the Nagoya Museum of Modern Art, the show was cancelled due to a demonstration by the radical Zero Dimension art group. He nevertheless created a work on the site, *Return to the Earth*: a series of small mounds made of the powder obtained from pulverized white ceramic toilet bowls, each of which carried an impression of his face moulded by a mask, the images becoming successively less and less distinct, so that the final one was indistinguishable from a simple mound of powder. While the work is superficially related to the serialism and minimalism central to the Western avant-garde of the period, this radical gesture more pointedly highlights the tensions and contradictions in the contemporary world of Japanese pottery, which may be outlined as follows:

Mass-produced / handmade. For centuries Japanese art had been centred on the tea ceremony, which defined the major aesthetic codes and hierarchies. With the tea bowl at the summit of the arts, no greater audacity, indeed sacrilege, could be imagined than creating a work made of toilet bowls, if not the gesture of pulverizing them – a spoof of the sacrosanct nature of the handmade – to create a new sort of raw material that remains, after all, within the category of ceramics.

Damage / perfection. The Japanese pottery aesthetic cherishes all sorts of accidental surface effects and even partial breakage, often accentuated in the repair. Thus the choice of imperfect toilet bowls (discarded because of high Japanese industrial quality standards) is doubly ironic: the imperfections constitute a fatal flaw rather than an attractive detail, and the transformation into powder eradicates, rather than accentuates, the flaw.

Found object / created work. Most accounts of *Return to the Earth* allude to Marcel Duchamp's *Fountain* (a urinal presented as an artwork in 1917) and

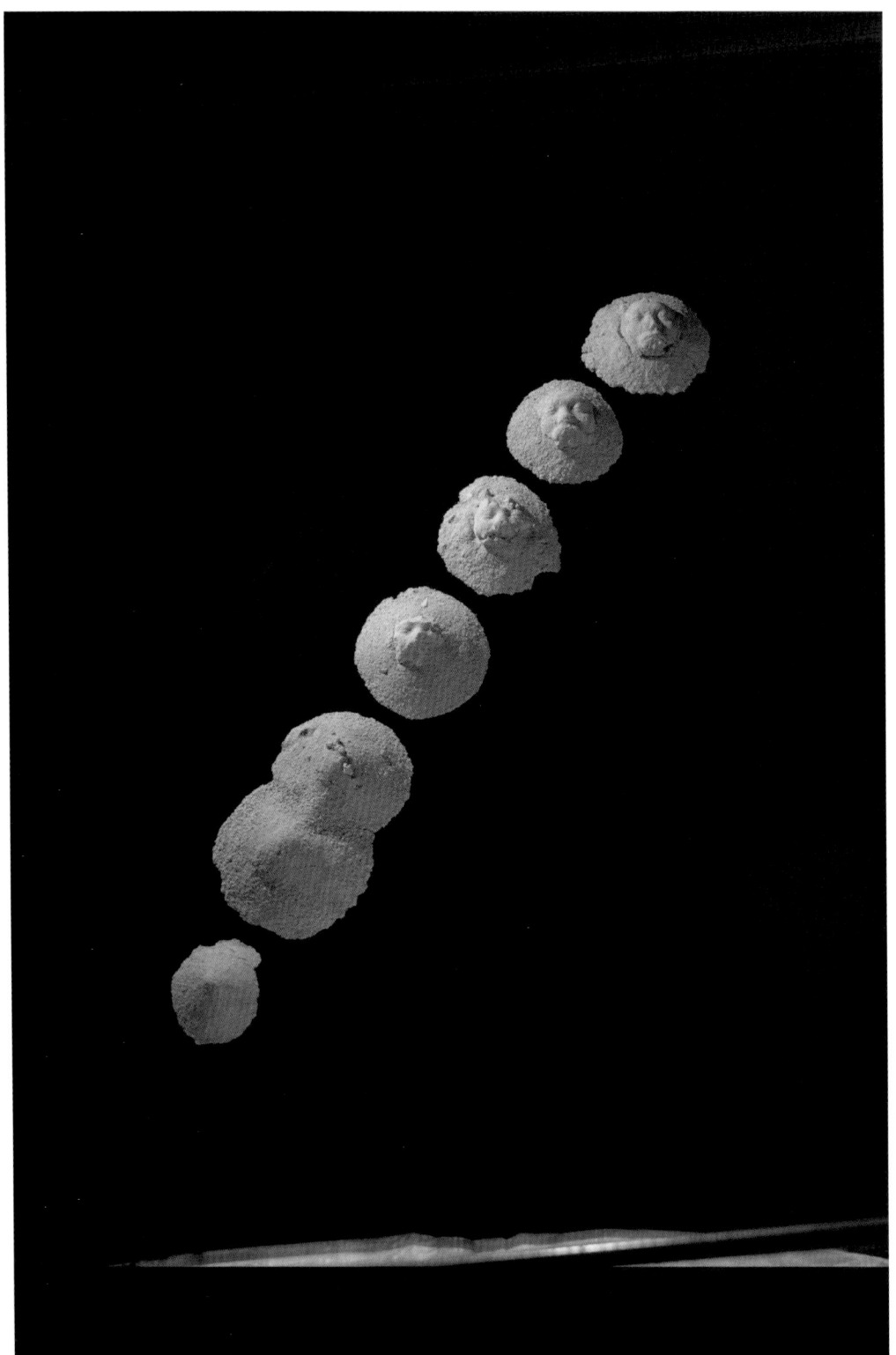

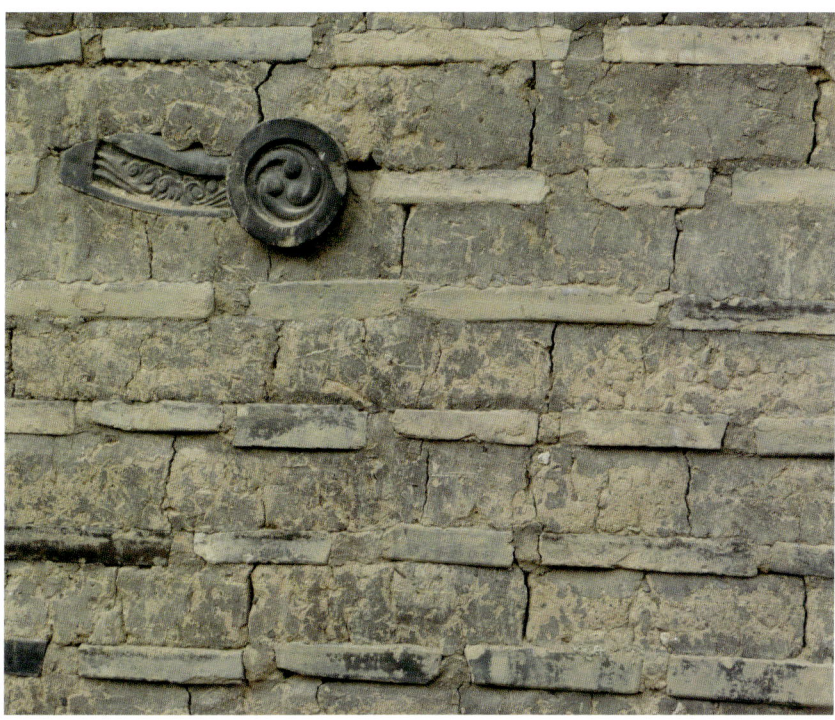

*Tenryū-ji,
mitate-mono.*

the tradition of the readymade, which brought the industrialized object into the field of art in the context of a critique of individualist handmade creativity. While the Arts and Crafts movement in the West and Mingei in Japan offered critiques of industrialization and a valorization of handmade craftsmanship, Duchamp simultaneously produced a critique of the industrial *and* the handmade via the ironies implicit in his exhibition of mass-produced objects, chosen not because of their design aesthetic, but despite their formal and physical qualities. This was the beginning of a conceptualism which would have untold ramifications on art history and aesthetic theory. Yet the significance of Koie's gesture is quite different, since the found object had existed in Japan for centuries in the form of *mitate-mono*, which literally means 'selected' or 'appraised' objects, specifically referring to the use of unnoticed or discarded objects and fragments in art, decor and architecture, such as the recuperation of decorated roof tiles set in clay and stone walls, or foundation stones and millstones recycled as garden ornaments.[1] While the Duchampian aesthetic of the readymade achieved the ultimate voiding of self-expression, *Return to the Earth* proffers the iconic presence of the artist and its gradual absorption into the prime matter of the work, a veritable

*Koie Ryōji, Return
to the Earth, 1971
version, powdered
ceramic sculpture.*

175

allegory of the new-found role of self-reflection in the world of contemporary Japanese pottery.

Materiality / expression. Duchamp's urinal was chosen in disregard of its material qualities (though its provocative nature cannot be discounted), Koie's because of them (an equally provocative gesture). Given that the regionally specific quality or 'flavour' of the clay is a key element in Japanese pottery, the choice of standardized or 'flavourless' industrial porcelain is a provocative statement, and the transformation of such waste matter into a self-portrait that itself dissolves back into that matter is a conundrum worthy of a Zen master. (Today, the widespread availability and use of commercially produced clays, cosmopolitan pottery studios and technical colleges, international trade and competitions, have all impacted on the regional specificity of Japanese pottery.)

Tradition / innovation. In the Japanese pottery world, one enters into the traditional order (both aesthetic and sociological) by a long period of apprenticeship so as to master matter and technique, with the goal of reworking elements, processes and forms within the traditional and regional context. Innovation is founded on tradition, individuality circumscribed by collectivity and self-expression subsumed by the exigencies of local matter, stylistic lineage, historical precedent. But what transpires when the matter and technique themselves are radically new and hyperbolically unaesthetic? There is also a historical contingency that played a major role in the transformation of Japanese pottery. In 1962 the country passed the Soot and Smoke Regulation Law, strengthened in 1968, which effectively closed all of the huge wood-burning climbing kilns in urban pottery centres like Kyoto. This motivated many potters to switch to small electric or propane kilns, with the result of fostering creativity by freeing the individual from the collective. Potters could now work in total privacy, on their own schedule, with ample kiln space, and in the manner they wished.[2]

Aesthetic agency exists as much in extra-human kiln effects and in the connoisseurship of tea masters as it does in the craft of the potter, such that, for example, certain anonymous utilitarian works like those Korean rice bowls beloved by early Japanese tea masters could find a new use as a *chawan* and be raised to the level of absolute masterpieces by the mere act of being chosen and used by a great tea master. This system was ultimately challenged in the years after the Second World War, when the aesthetic values of Japanese ceramics began to approximate those of the international art world, and the potter-artist came to the fore.

The logic of *Return to the Earth* profoundly depends on the distinction between pottery and sculpture, since this dichotomy operates in both international modernism and traditional Japanese art. While the West maintains a strong hierarchical sense of the difference between art (non-utilitarian) and craft (utilitarian) – such that a teacup would be near the bottom of the aesthetic hierarchy – in Japan, where pottery is almost as highly regarded as painting and calligraphy, for centuries the borderline between the art and craft distinction existed in a very different manner, if at all. It is generally agreed that the first instance of a non-functional object in the context of Japanese pottery was Yagi Kazuo's *The Walk of Samsa* (1954), a sort of abstract wheel hub to which numerous pipes were attached. Despite the allusion to Kafka and the formal influence of the clay sculptures of Isamu Noguchi, Yagi self-consciously and polemically wished to remain within the tradition of Japanese pottery, which had no means of categorizing such objects. Whence the creation of the term *obuje-yaki* (fired object; derived from the French word *objet*), in distinction to the traditional word for pottery, *yakimono* (fired thing). The motivation behind *The Walk of Samsa* stemmed from a double tension – the threat of industrial production to the Japanese handicraft tradition, and the threat of the international art world to the primacy of pottery in Japan – from which ensued a contradiction that would inform and transform the future of Japanese pottery.[3]

To counter industrialization, both traditional and avant-garde potters would celebrate ancient artisanal qualities (clay types, kiln effects, regional styles), all the while remaining wary of the reactionary use that this folkloric discourse had served in the name of wartime imperialist nationalism. To respond to the pressures of international modernism, the Japanese avant-garde would need to adopt the Western distinction between ceramics (both *yakimono* and *obuje-yaki*) and art, simultaneously in order to maintain the prestige of the field of ceramics and so that the radical novelty of their creations would not be diluted by being misplaced in and subsumed by the international domain of sculpture.[4]

The crux of the matter is that Japanese pottery had always been utilitarian, whence the primacy of the sense of touch and the importance of hands-on examination. The postwar influx of Western museum practices – whether in the context of exhibitions or of juried salons – brought the opposite phenomenon, an art that is primarily viewed, and where touching is forbidden. The new and radically different viewing conditions had vast aesthetic and epistemological consequences. Traditionally, tea ceremony pottery had been part of private, temple and tea school collections, and pieces were exhibited or used one by one, placed either in the *tokonoma* (alcove) or on the *tatami* (mat)

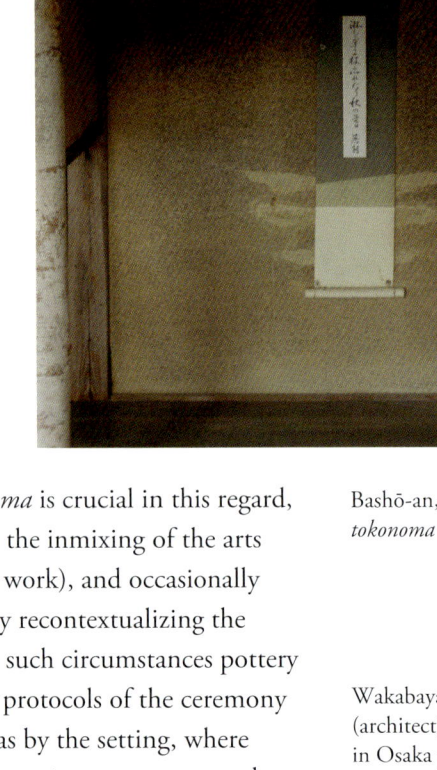

Bashō-an, Konpuku-ji *tokonoma* (alcove).

Wakabayashi Hiroyuki (architect), *tokonoma*, in Osaka prefecture residence, 1998; note the use of a steel beam on the left to replace the traditional wooden pillar. The untitled calligraphy (part of a classic Chinese poem) is by Kawabe Tsutsumi, 2008.

during the ceremony. The function of the *tokonoma* is crucial in this regard, since it focuses the attention, serves as a stage for the inmixing of the arts (painting, calligraphy, pottery, ikebana, bamboo work), and occasionally operates a secularization of sacred iconography by recontextualizing the sacred images and texts within the tea setting. In such circumstances pottery is given maximum attention, accentuated by the protocols of the ceremony which demand discussion of the objects, as well as by the setting, where attention is concentrated by the diminutive space, quietness, austere and monochromatic decor, understated architecture and subtle lighting of the tea room (where much is left in shadow), as well as by the codified comportment of the guests, for whom courtesy, respect and connoisseurship are essential. Handling is a form of both pleasure and knowledge, accentuated by ceremonial gesture and solemn ambiance. The practical and spiritual exigencies of the tea ceremony foster the practice of meticulous examination

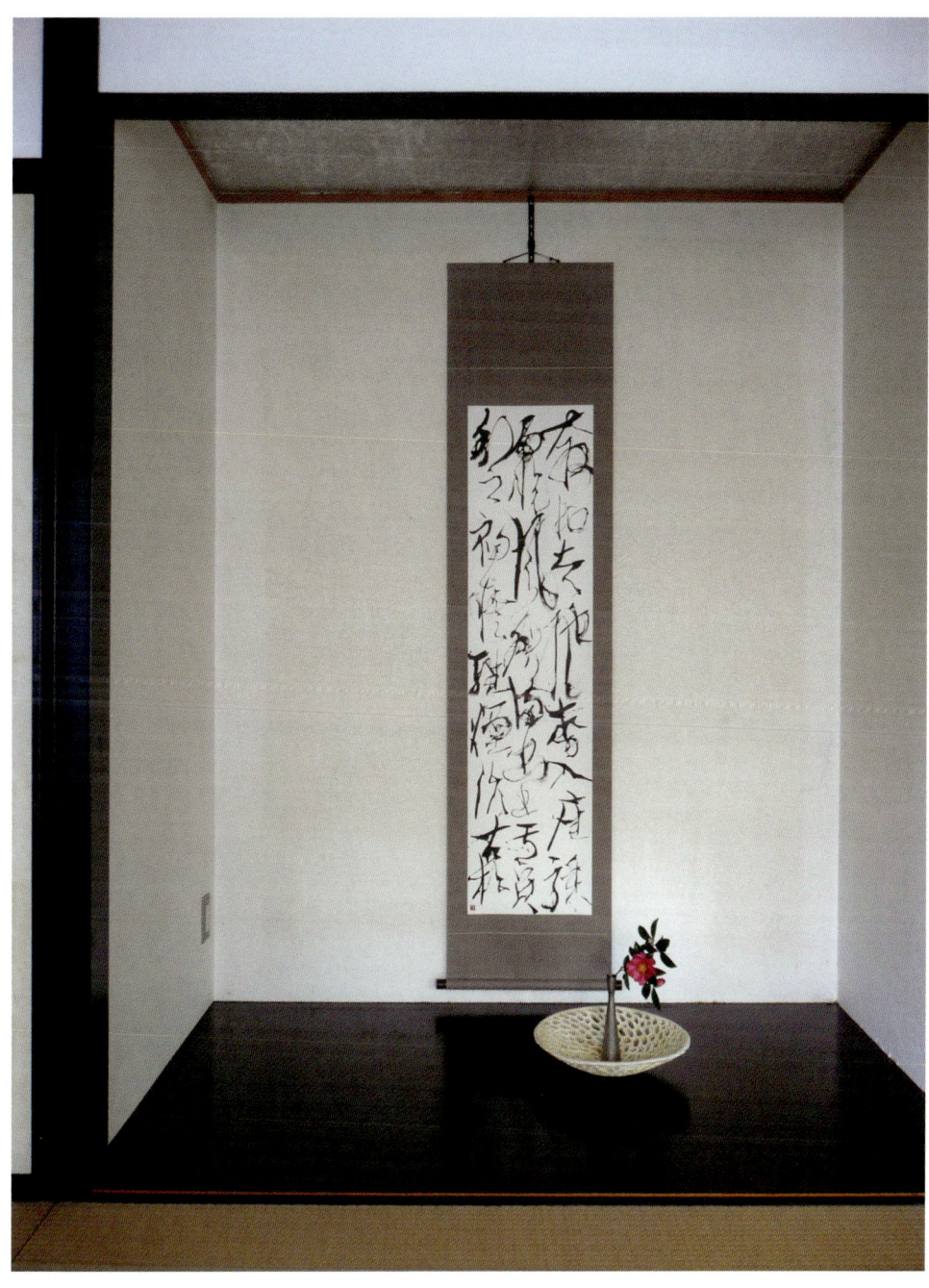

and its corresponding judiciousness of description and praise. The form of the tea garden, the design and lighting of the room, and the staging of the ceremony are all intended to separate the participants from the everyday world within a utopian space of aesthetic perfection and social harmony. Attention is concentrated by removal from the cares of everyday reality, by the forms of the ritual and by the physical aspect of the room, the smallest of which is a mere one and a half *tatami* in size.[5] Such close quarters have a crucial effect on connoisseurship, since direct contact with tea paraphernalia and the ritualistic requirement of close-up examination of the objects both used in the ceremony and on display in the *tokonoma* establish a hyper-sensitive attention to detail.

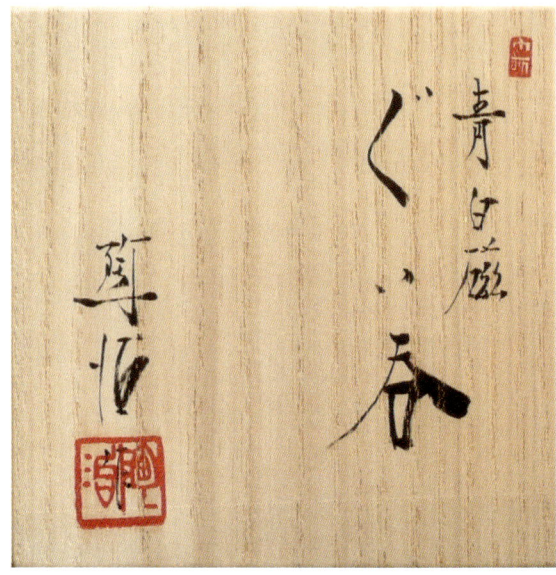

Fukami Sueharu, *tomobako* (wooden box) for the *guinomi* on p. 219, 2009.

The extraordinary discretion of Japanese connoisseurship demands that very few objects be visible at a given time, and that an important work of pottery will be seen but rarely. When not in use, each precious work is stored in a wooden box (*tomobako*) that bears calligraphy and seals noting the name of the artist, the provenance, style and sometimes history of the piece. When used during a tea ceremony, a work will be examined to the fullest extent possible, and at all other times it will remain strictly invisible and inaccessible. According to the understatement typical of the *wabi* sentiment, the more precious an object, the less often it will be displayed, and the very rarest pieces will eventually be withdrawn from use and protected in special boxes, only to be shown on the most noteworthy of occasions. Rarefaction replaces ostentation and, paradoxically, value accrues from both use and concealment. When the box itself becomes valuable because of the historical celebrity of the inscriber, it will be placed in another box which in turn is inscribed, and so on and so forth, so that certain of the rarest works are protected by what amounts to a *mise en abyme* of boxes. The results are the hyperbolic valorization of use value and concealment. Scrupulous examination over-compensates for long-term dissimulation. In *The Book of Tea* (1906), Okakura Kakuzo reminds us that

> the tea-masters guarded their secrets with religious secrecy, and it was often necessary to open a whole series of boxes, one within another, before reaching the shrine itself, – the silken wrapping within whose soft folds lay the holy of holies. Rarely was the object exposed to view, and then only to the initiated.[6]

D. T. Suzuki recounts that when a certain Jisen Iyehara came into possession of Rikyū's famous Onjōji bamboo vase, a friend asked him to see it, and he made the friend wait an entire year, until he could finish a tea room constructed without any bamboo, so as better to display the vase. This tale speaks to the principles of discretion, concealment and aesthetic reverence central to *chanoyu*. Such inaccessibility is not only a manner of augmenting value, but also a means of steeping the work in that aura of mystery (*yūgen*) at the core of Zen spirituality.[7]

Initiation is a key to the sacred in all cultures, and the tea ceremony is profoundly informed by Zen Buddhism, from the core of its aesthetics to the form of its gestures. The sacred is often the secretive. In *The Narrow Road to the Deep North* Bashō writes of his ascent of Mount Nikkō to visit its sacred shrine, but actually reveals very little, explaining: 'to say more about this shrine would be to violate its holiness'.[8] In describing his visits to three other mountains, Haguro, Gassan and Yudono, he explains concerning the latter: 'I saw many other things of interest in this mountain, the details of which, however, I refrain from betraying in accordance with the rules I must obey as a pilgrim.'[9] This silence is elliptical and respectful, poetic and religious. The logic of both tea room and Zen garden design makes extensive use of all sorts of barriers: stone and mud walls, bamboo gates and partitions, sliding paper cloisons (*shōji*), and often a simple small stone with a black rope tied around it (*sekimori ishi*) – recalling the ritually tied straw ropes (*shimenawa*) that indicate the sacred nature of certain rocks and trees – placed in front of a

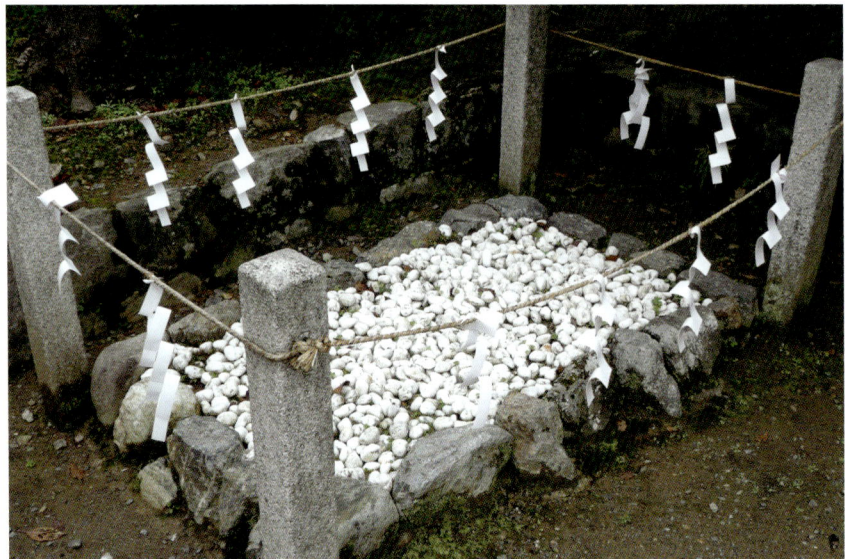

Matsuo Shrine,
sacred pebbles.

doorway or path to indicate restricted entry. The tea room has its own forms
of closure, restriction and secrecy – beginning with the small hatched crawl-
space (*nijiriguchi*) that serves as an entry – including the protocols that
determine the rituals of examining works, and thus the forms and limits of
connoisseurship. (It is precisely this system of values that had long restricted
scientific modes of examining pottery, which demand very different, and
generally non-aesthetic, protocols.)

Before the age of photography, this meant that the most cherished
pieces of pottery were known mainly through hearsay, and many a tea master
could only dream of using a particularly famous bowl without ever having
seen it. Representation was a function of imagination, anticipation and remin-
iscence. That a particular piece might be seen but once in a lifetime, and then
for but a very brief moment, is most appropriate to the tea ceremony, which
aims at creating a unique, unrepeatable, harmonious, once-in-a-lifetime
experience organized according to the time of day, season, choice of utensils,
kaiseki menu, grouping of participants. Consciousness of the condensation
of space and the briefness of time creates an atmosphere of acutely enhanced
observation, where minute details (pottery 'landscapes', wood grain, play of

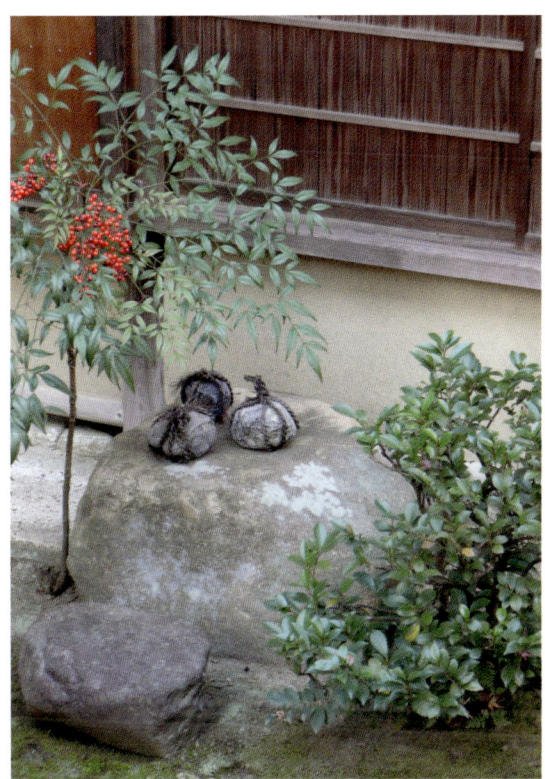

Zuihō-in, *sekimori ishi* (stone marker).

light, the sound of boiling water) take on great value. Zen masters and tea masters have summed up the epistemologically transformative effects of the ceremony in many ways, though perhaps never as succinctly as Okakura Kakuzo when he describes the tea house:

> It is an Abode of Fancy inasmuch as it is an ephemeral structure built to house a poetic impulse. It is an Abode of Vacancy inasmuch as it is devoid of ornamentation except for what may be placed in it to satisfy some aesthetic need of the moment. It is an Abode of the Unsymmetrical inasmuch as it is consecrated to the worship of the Imperfect, purposely leaving some thing unfinished for the play of the imagination to complete.[10]

The tea room is thus a stage where a hyperbolic aestheticization of objects takes place in a highly condensed utopian space and a hyper-acute consciousness of time. The effects on connoisseurship are both aesthetic and epistemological, as Murielle Hladik so astutely explains:

> the traces left by the passage of time, signs of wear and use, the traces of finger marks (*teaka*), offer so much micro-information, mini-histories for us to reinterpret. Starting from these minute details, our imagination can reconstitute tales and narratives. Thus these traces of time and use confer a superior degree of beauty upon things, one which transcends quotidian beauty within an aesthetic of contemplation.[11]

These traces not only indicate the melancholic sense of things lost and time passed (*mono no aware*), but also create a sense of harmony among the participants of the tea ceremony, as each person adds his or her fingerprints and lip marks to those already there, deepening the history of the tea bowl by adding to its provenance. Hladik's claim that 'the tea ceremony constitutes the paradigm of the valorization of matter' paradoxically implies that the positive sense of degradation inherent in this aesthetic is precisely what creates a form of surplus value.[12] One might add that the tea ceremony also constitutes the paradigm of the valorization of time, but a time nuanced and complex, polychronic and polyvalent, spiritualized and aestheticized.

On the contrary, modern museology tends to alienate pottery from its practical and ceremonial functions, transforming a performative object into a static work by placing it in a vitrine, where it can be seen but not touched. In the very best of display conditions, one can walk around a free-standing vitrine to see all four side of the piece, and even occasionally look down into it, but almost never (except with the rare use of a plate glass and mirror system on which the piece is set) are we able to see the all-important foot, so essential to the aesthetics of Japanese ceramics. Thus, in contradistinction to tea, where a piece is rarely revealed but when finally seen is thoroughly handled, in the museum the works are only partially visible – though often for long periods – but handling is always prohibited. Furthermore, in the tea room a single bowl will be shown, thus concentrating attention, while in the museum concentration is dissipated among the many works on display. Perhaps the most dramatic difference between *tokonoma* and vitrine is the lighting. Traditionally, the tea room is lit either by indirect sunlight filtering through paper screens (*shōji*), by moonlight entering a transom or by oil lamps, while museum lighting has always been electric (generally flourescent in Japan), contrary to traditional practices of Japanese design. Tanizaki Jun'ichirō presents the most famous elegy of the subtleties of Japanese forms of lighting in his classic *In Praise of Shadows*, and nearly every account of the tea ceremony also makes apparent how essential lighting is to mood and symbolism. While *chanoyu* is calculated to accord with the changes of light according to time of day, season and meteorological conditions, museum lighting is generally constant, though current advances in lighting design make possible increased use of natural light and its fluctuations. The degree of subtlety and refinement of lighting in relation to the appreciation of pottery is made evident in the claim, prominently displayed in a wall text describing the state-of-the-art lighting in the newly refurbished Museum of Oriental Ceramics (Osaka), that 'it has been said that to appreciate fully the color of celadon, it should be viewed at ten in the morning on a sunny autumn day, in a room facing north, with one shoji sliding paper door.' This is not sheer aesthetic affectation, for in preparation for a proper tea ceremony, every aspect of the event is given the most careful consideration, so as to maximize the harmony between all the constituent parts. Perhaps nothing sets the overall mood, and modulates all the objects, more than the lighting. What this perfectionism – one might say oversensitivity, finickiness or even obsessiveness – concerning lighting suggests is the degree to which connoisseurs seek the optimum conditions for enjoying each work, and that different sorts of work demand different viewing conditions. This is precisely the reason that such care is taken to choose the pieces appropriate to the season, type of ceremony, and so forth.

While the tea ceremony offers a range of exhibition possibilities in a performative setting, the muscological context is exhibitive and fundamentally static. All told, once a piece of pottery is taken out of circulation, its use value is reduced to mere exhibition, and there can be no fully satisfactory display situation, however elaborate and up-to-date the setting. Until recently, standard museological practice worldwide amounted to the use of artificially lit vitrines, occasionally located near windows so as to combine natural and artificial light, with displays changing seasonally. In Japanese museums a model tea room is usually added somewhere. However, the use of dim lighting levels to try and approximate tea room lighting only exacerbates the problem, because very often the pieces are too dimly lit to be properly seen. One often sees visitors in Japanese museums using monoculars, both to read the writing on distantly hung works and to examine details on poorly lit pottery. The irony is that reduced visibility due to dim lighting during the tea ceremony is overcompensated for by the possibility, indeed the necessity, of taking the work in hand. It is true that many of the museums that house the great collections of tea objects have a functioning tea room, as is the case in the Nomura Museum in Kyoto, where private tea ceremonies are held. This exception to the rules of standard museum display, while concerning only very select private groups, is nevertheless an ideal situation where pottery once again comes to life, but this hardly mitigates the frustrations of the average visitor. Until the post-Second World War epoch, *chanoyu* had primarily been an elitist occupation. The irony is that its democratization, along with the rise of public and private museums, has resulted in the near impossibility of the vast majority of practitioners ever even dream of using the most admired works. Furthermore, the fact that many such objects are housed in those bastions of tradition that are Buddhist temples is no guarantee that they will be accessible for customary use, since certain of them have become so precious as to have been named National Treasures or Important Cultural Properties, and have consequently been taken out of circulation. There are some that are even deemed too precious to be seen except on certain rare occasions, much less used.[13]

The Museum of Oriental Ceramics in Osaka, which houses one of the world's premier collections of Asian pottery, has gone to great lengths to try and alleviate this situation by the installation of state-of-the-art lighting. Their wall panel cited above, which suggests the ideal lighting conditions for celadon ceramics – a prelude to laud their revolutionary lighting system – ends up being unintentionally ironic and quite disconcerting. Here, the use of a complex system of skylights and mirrors channels diffused sunlight into the vitrines, which are themselves made of non-reflective glass, with supplemental artificial light to compensate for adverse meteorological conditions. The ingeniousness and complexity of this system, itself a distraction, brings it even further from the conditions of the tea room, and the artificiality of the increased visual presence of the pottery is all the more frustrating. One feels as if there were fewer barriers between the viewer and the work, but of course it is still impossible to handle the pottery, examine the pool and the foot, and put it to use. Furthermore, this new form of visibility hardly accords with sunlight at ten in the morning on a sunny autumn day, in a room facing north, illuminated through one sliding paper door – or with whatever optimal natural lighting might be appropriate for a given work. (While these observations obtain a fortiori for traditional types of pottery, it is certain that many modernist works were conceived to be seen in the artificial and often glaring lighting typical of contemporary architecture and design.) The prime case in point is the museum's prize possession, a Chinese Jian ware *tenmoku* (silver oil-spot glaze) tea bowl of the Southern Song dynasty (twelfth–thirteenth centuries), a National Treasure. This is the first object seen after reading the wall panel in question, and its presence comes as something of a shock. For rather than in any way approximating what would be optimal lighting for the tea ceremony (in any case an impossible, even paradoxical ideal in the museum context), this display epitomizes a certain museological ideal, that of maximal presence and the aura of rarity, not unlike the high-tech displays of the most exclusive jewellery and fashion shops. While this lighting is indeed at least partially 'natural', it is a nature denatured by the use of glass skylights, mirrors and non-reflective glass, all of which focus the light on the bowl in such a way that it is perfectly visible, a condition not at all desirable according to traditional Japanese aesthetics. The irony is that traditional tea rooms are also often lit by skylights, though to very different effect. Even more disconcertingly, at times the highly reflective *tenmoku* glaze sends out a brilliant streak of light, unthinkable in a tea room. Such lighting has nothing to do with the performance of tea, and everything to do with the drama of contemporary museum exhibitions. It has a place in the history of optical gadgets, not in the annals of tea.

There are, however, different forms of museum scenography, and different modes of compensation for the discrepancies between tea hut and museum. The Musée Tomo, Tokyo, is a newer venue specializing in contemporary ceramics that has created a unique exhibition situation, the antithesis of the Museum of Oriental Ceramics. Here, in dimly lit rooms with predominately black walls and partitions, the works are individually placed on display stands without vitrines, and dramatically lit by state-of-the-art spotlighting systems. The visual presence is greatly accentuated by the lighting and the overall presence is heightened by the lack of barriers. While one is obviously not allowed to handle the works, the pieces may be examined from extremely close up, and all but the foot becomes visible.

One can almost, but not quite, touch the works and one's breath can nearly fog over the glaze. The temptation to touch is so great, the sense of tactility so acute, that one often witnesses the gesture of people holding up two cupped hands in front of a bowl to imagine how it would fit in their palms. Since the museum is devoted to contemporary pottery, works from the same firings as those exhibited are often available in galleries, and thus potentially for use, as was the case for the recent retrospective of Shino ware by Living National Treasure Suzuki Osamu. This situation certainly blurs the distinction between museum and gallery, but the display and circulation of art has always been, in one manner or another, a form of business.[14]

The most extreme museological solution addressing these problems is found at the Raku Museum in Kyoto, which pushes both the visual and tactile logics to the limit. The museum is of limited scope, dedicated to works by all fifteen generations of the Raku family. This collection is of monumental importance for several reasons: Chōjirō, founder of the Raku dynasty and collaborator of Sen no Rikyū, was at the origin of Japanese tea pottery; the subsequent history of the major tea schools was intimately linked to the successive generations of Raku potters; and the current representative of the dynasty, Raku Kichizaemon XV, is one of the most admired potters in Japan.[15] Each exhibition (whether thematic, showing works by successive generations or monographic) is of the same format, consisting of very dramatically lit individual pieces in vitrines (with an occasional mirror positioned to show the rear of the piece), the epitome of contemporary museum practice. The pieces, however sensually presented, are experienced as untouchable, by dint of their isolation and preciousness. However, the extreme stress on the visual aspect of this museum-going experience is compensated for by something quite rare, indeed almost unique, in contemporary museums, a 'tangible museum' programme that includes handling sessions, tea ceremonies, and even special children's sessions. Raku pottery thus participates in both the museum and the tea world, an ideal solution.

Coming from Raku Kichizaemon XV, this radical solution is not so surprising, since he was the first of his lineage to take an avant-garde turn, one directly inspired by modernist art and literature, both Western and

Japanese. While he continues to cite ancient Chinese and Japanese poetry and theatre as sources of inspiration, he also celebrates a group of authors, artists and works discovered in the Europe of his youth, as he enumerates in the flyer to his commemorative exhibition (2010): Sartre, Kafka, Dostoevsky, Rimbaud, Freud, Camus, Bataille, Bachelard, Merleau-Ponty; Miyazawa Kenji, the Rigveda, the *Tibetan Book of the Dead*, Abe Kōbō, Dazai Osamu, Ōe Kenzaburō, Mishima Yukio, Yoshimoto Takaaki, Haniya Yutaka; Bakunin, Stirner, Marx; Bosch, Giacometti, Kandinsky, Brancusi, Duchamp, Rothko, Pollock, Picasso; Berg, Takemitsu, Hijikata (a rare reference to Butoh by a Japanese artist working in a traditional context); Godard, Resnais, Antonioni, Pasolini; Michelangelo's *Slaves* and Grünewald's *Isenheim Altarpiece*. These inspirations mark a radical, almost unimaginable and certainly contentious paradigm shift in the sensibility of the tea ceremony. But above all there is Goya, specifically one of the black paintings, in front of which he felt that 'I had found that within me which responded viscerally and immediately, unmediated by received ideas about value and meaning.'[16] These influences became increasingly evident in his works as the years passed and as he broke from Raku tradition to create pottery that is at the forefront of Japan's avant-garde. The passion for Goya is emblematic, manifested in his works – with their tortured forms, expressionist applications of glaze, and spectacularly saturated colours on deep black backgrounds – as well as in the dramatic museum lighting. Referring to the black tea bowl named Saidō Fūki (1990, 'Human Soul in the Shape of a Demon'), a work inspired by Zeami, and the first in the Raku lineage with applied gold and silver, Raku Kichizaemon xv explains: 'I had a feeling that if I could reach the other extreme of Chōjirō's bowls by boldly breaking the ban, that is, stepping further beyond to the excessive decorativeness, I would be able to find something.'[17] Indeed, he has been continuously creating works that may be deemed the antithesis of his family tradition, with the latter's emphasis on the traditional subtleties of the *wabi-sabi-shibui* aesthetic. In his *Father and Son* catalogue (2003), referring to the same tea bowl, he offers a poem that includes the following: 'cut sharply, deform heavily, splash colors on black, extremity of excess'.[18] The very term 'excess' is an indication of his rupture with tradition, and his excess had gone

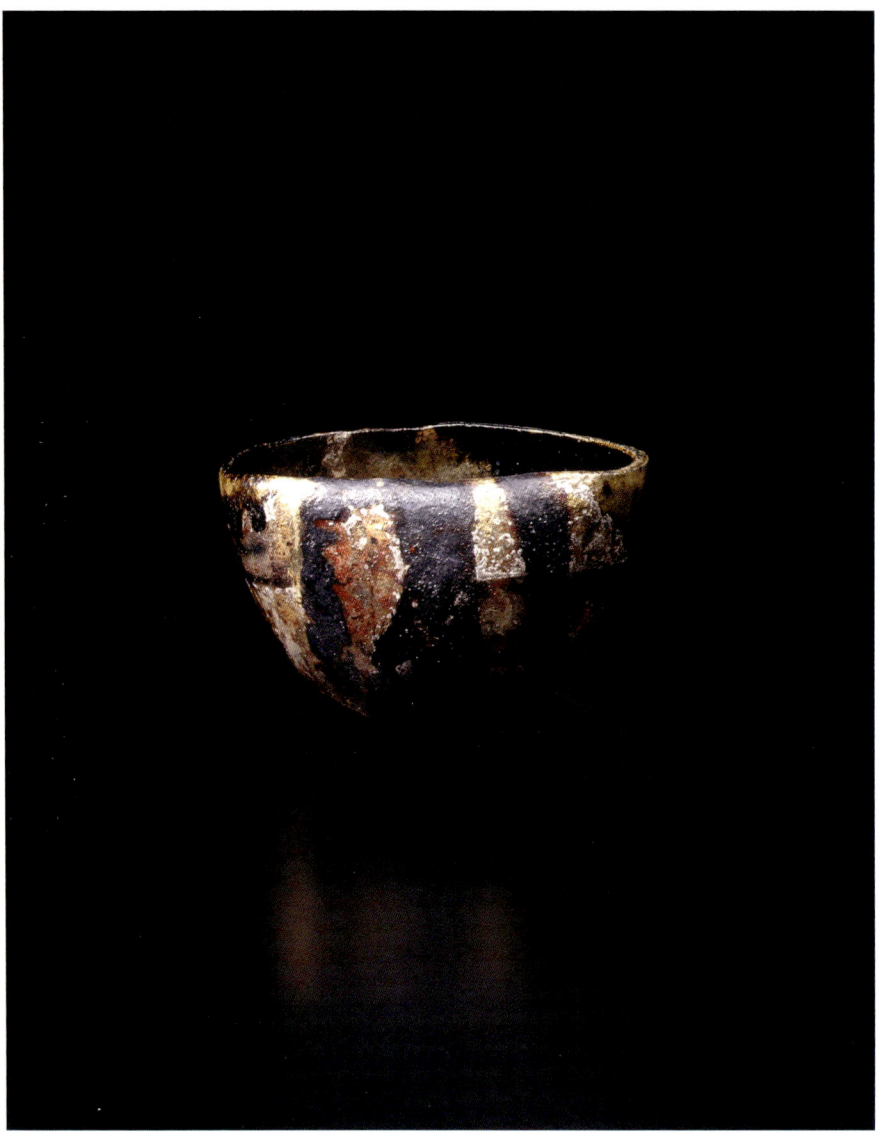

Raku Kichizaemon xv, *chawan* named *Saidō Fūki* ('Human Soul in the Shape of a Demon'), 1990.

so far that by the time of his breakthrough 'Tenmon' exhibition (1990), many people would complain that his bowls were maladapted to the tea ceremony, whether because their decorativeness would not permit them to match other, more classic utensils, or that their bizarre, non-traditional shapes would damage the tea whisk or would make it difficult to wipe the bowls clean using traditionally prescribed gestures. In a certain sense, Raku Kichizaemon xv's dual exhibition methods – hyperdramatic vitrine presentations and hands-on workshops and ceremonies – emphasize the avant-garde complexities of his works and their ultimate practicality respectively.

The museum website for the 2010 Raku Kichizaemon xv retrospective opened with a series of five larger-than-life-size moving images of surface details of tea bowls. The scale, saturated colours, abstracted detail and motion all served to maximally transform object into image, and if one happened on these photos out of context, they would just as likely be taken to represent sculptures or even abstract paintings as tea bowls. (Such might be seen as a postmodern remake of Domon Ken's photographic revolution in representing pottery.) It is not until the fifth image – the only one to be shot from above, thus clearly showing the object as a bowl – that the context is visually clarified, with a caption revealing the bowl's true monumentality: 'Microcosm within your hands. RAKU WARE'. Nowhere could the paradoxes of contemporary pottery display be more apparent than in this image, a veritable ontological transformation, where the reduction of clay object to moving image obviates all possibility of our taking it into our hands. Such is an allegory of, or perhaps rather a warning about, the situation of pottery in the museum setting, calling into question certain key issues of representation central to the practice of tea. For centuries, the famous tea utensils were known only to a select few, and one might spend an entire lifetime harbouring the futile wish to have the privilege to use once a tea bowl never seen and ultimately never to be seen. In such instances, the bowl was known only through descriptions offered either in conversation or through written tea diaries. However, with the modern advent of photographic reproduction and electronic diffusion, depiction not only supersedes description but it often overcompensates for the improbability of ever using or even seeing a particular bowl.

This new epoch in the history of tea pottery opened in 1965 when the photographer Domon Ken shot the images for his book *Shigaraki Ōtsubo*, dedicated to large ancient jars from this classic pottery-producing region. It is interesting that in the very brief notes in English at the end of the book, Koyama Fujio states:

> Only in recent years did the general public begin to divert their attention from tea-ceremony utensils and return to a more detailed study of earlier Shigaraki ware. The solid shapes and ruddy hues of this early pottery remind people of an autumnal sunset glow and were found most appealing and refreshing to the modern mind.[19]

It is interesting that even in this context, unrelated to *chanoyu*, the writer felt obliged to determine the subject with a seasonally charged landscape metaphor, so as to give added symbolic and poetic dimensions to what might otherwise appear as rather technical documentary images. This landmark volume for the first time emphasized and accentuated the tactile quality of pottery surfaces by the use of extremely detailed close-ups. It is no accident that the subject of this work is Shigaraki pottery, which of all the old kilns of Japan probably most demands tactile appreciation, since this high-fired unglazed stoneware is characterized by cracks and impurities caused by embedded quartz, by a very subtle ash glaze best made visible by picking up the piece and turning it in the light, and by occasional fingerprint traces that seem to summon one's own touch. The use of extreme close-ups has since become a standard feature in pottery books and on websites such as that of the Raku Museum. One particularly striking example is the catalogue of Living National Treasure Miwa Jusetsu's recent retrospective exhibition of Hagi pottery. The extreme visual complexity that characterizes his *oni-hagi* technique is often portrayed here in larger-than-life-size images of surface details of brilliant clarity and excellent colour reproduction by photographer Takemoto Haruji.[20] Such photographs, like Domon's, are aesthetic artefacts in themselves, existing at the limits of visual-haptic synaesthesia, where abstracted detail is raised to the level of monumentality. However, such hyperbolically increased visibility can never truly compensate for lost tactility, and we enter a new domain of pottery connoisseurship, divorced from the domain of tea, where appreciation is limited by the manner in which the strictures of pure visibility contradict the exigencies of unmediated tactility.

The diminution of tactility, valorization of visibility and transformation of use value contemporaneous with the post-war rise of museums motivated the creation of non-utilitarian forms in modernist pottery. As Bert Winther-Tamaki explains:

> While the privileged hand-clay contact of the *user* of a ceramic vessel was threatened by the modern exhibition culture, a compensatory increase of concern arose for the hand-clay contact of the *potter* in the act of making the clay object.[21]

This contradiction yielded a shift in artistic agency, from the connoisseur whose aesthetic intuition traditionally determined value, to the potter whose individual craft would henceforth create new forms. It also diminished the attraction of the fire that creates the aleatory kiln effects (*yōhen*) of traditional pottery for the sake of greater technical control.[22] Here, the agency of the artist is brought in line with modernist aesthetic paradigms. It is for this reason that in 1963 Yagi Kazuo began to work in a smoky-black glazeless ceramic with minimal aleatory effects due to the low firing temperature, which afforded more control over the results of firing. This choice was congruous with the desire to realign forms of consciousness with forms of matter by balancing newfound modes of expression in ceramics with expanded technical means.

Yagi's oft reiterated claims that 'I am a tea bowl maker' and 'a tea bowl is also an art object' must not be understood as false modesty, but rather as a means of contextualizing his work at the intersection of a Japanese pottery tradition pushed beyond its limits and an international modernist art world destined to include pottery within its domain. Koie too began to practise in the same mode – influenced by the Sōdeisha group, founded by Yagi – and it is most probable that in creating the hyperbolically white *Return to the Earth*, Koie was in part reacting to Yagi's predilection for white and black

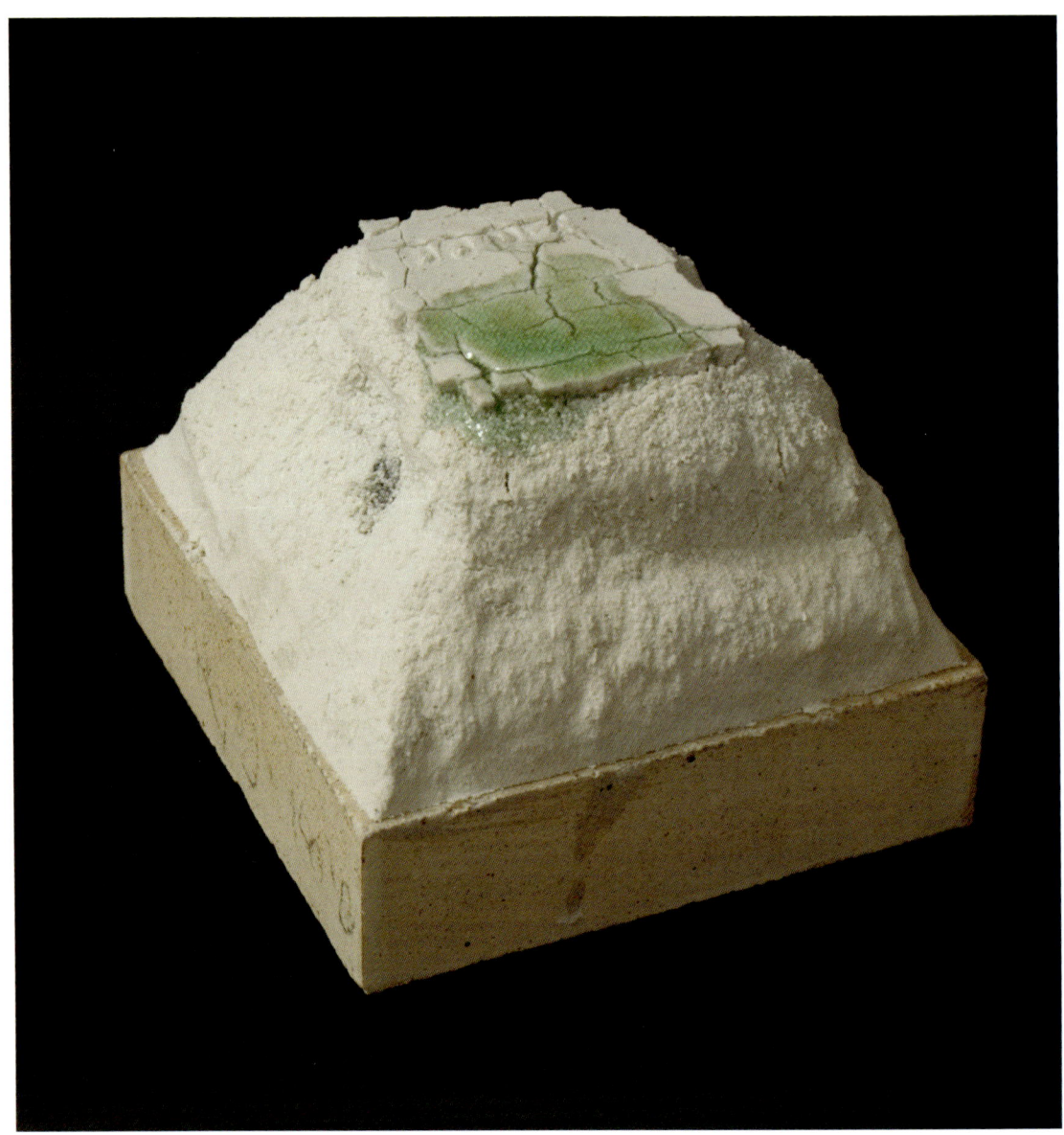

Koie Ryōji, from the *Chernobyl* series, 2006, porcelain sculpture.

glazes, all the while seeking the limits of expressionless surfaces, ironically in order to use them to increase the means of expression in the ceramic arts. Yet while the two artists posed the question 'What is ceramics?' rather than 'What is art?', their answers differed radically. Yagi remained within the context of traditional ceramics, opting for low temperatures that increase artistic control, while Koie sought the most extreme limits of pottery by reformulating the question more specifically as 'At what firing temperature does something become ceramic?' and 'Need something be fired to be ceramic?' The answer to these questions resulted in the production of such formally provocative works as *Return to the Earth*, where the prime matter, the ceramic toilets, was indeed fired, though not by the artist's hand, while the resulting ceramic powder was not refired to produce the artwork itself, but only moulded. Yagi worked to transform pottery by extending the limits of tradition; Koie rethought it in relation to the ontological limits of fire.

As a schoolboy, Koie worked for a time in a home-town (Tokoname) factory that made ceramic toilet bowls and clay sewerage pipes, which suggests at least one of the sources of his iconography and his iconoclasm. He went so far as to suggest that a sewage pipe is more interesting than a Katō Tōkurō tea bowl worth 10 million yen.[23] Yet despite his creative acts based on the extreme transformative violence of fire, he is also a potter capable of creating the most delicate works, such as the *guinomi* illustrated here from an autumn 2008 firing, characterized by the pottery specialist and tea aficionado Umeda Mitsuko simply as 'snow', the familiar sort of metaphoric seasonal correspondence that indicates appropriate forms of appreciation and privileged moments of contemplation. This work evinces the most classic *shibui* aesthetic (understatement, restraint, refined simplicity, noble austerity), with its elegant and subtly irregular form, pure white Shino glaze and even an uncharacteristic lack of those slash marks that have become Koie's signature in recent years. It does, however, bear a tiny spot of exposed clay scorched red by the flames, a mark of its origin and a symbol of its provenance. Looking at this piece, it is difficult not to think of the even purer whiteness of the pulverized toilet bowls of *Return to the Earth*, difficult not to imagine that the tactility of one is informed by the conceptuality of the other, that the beautiful, joyful utilitarianism of the cup conceals the bleak underside of modernity, ravaged by unthinkable forms of fire (a new manifestation of the sublime, expressed in *No More Hiroshima, Nagasaki* and *Chernobyl*), making of this *guinomi* the oxymoron of a joyful memento mori. Koie has interiorized the extremes of fired things, from the most classically beautiful objects through provocative avant-garde creations to the most horrendous manifestations of modern inhumanity. His works suggest a new way of appreciating the previously unmentionable dark and morbid side of existence. From the ritualized formality of tea to the quotidian *joie de vivre* of sake, from pottery to sculpture, he has created objects that cross aesthetic, formal and international boundaries.

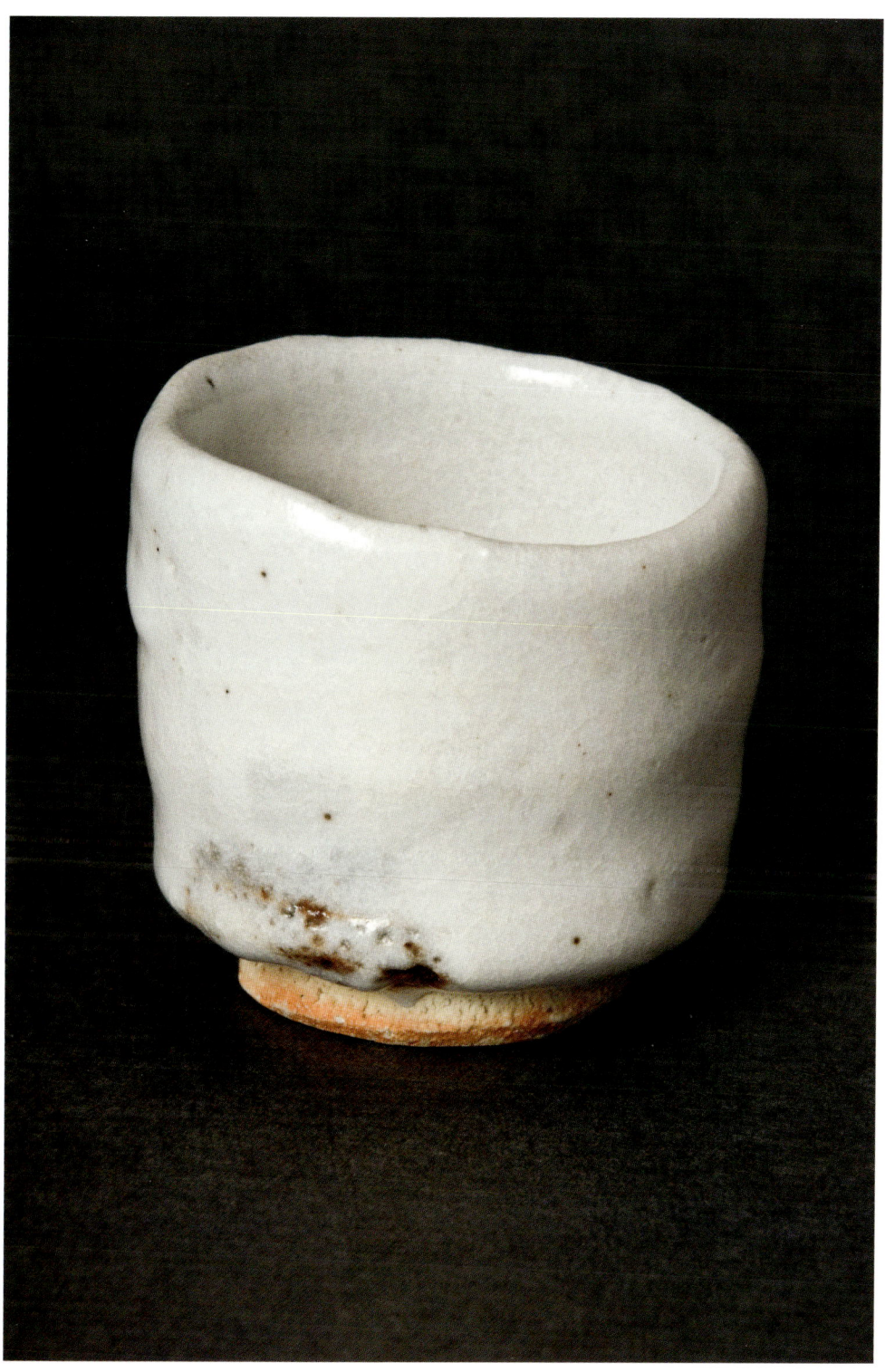

Koie Ryōji, Shino *guinomi*, 2008.

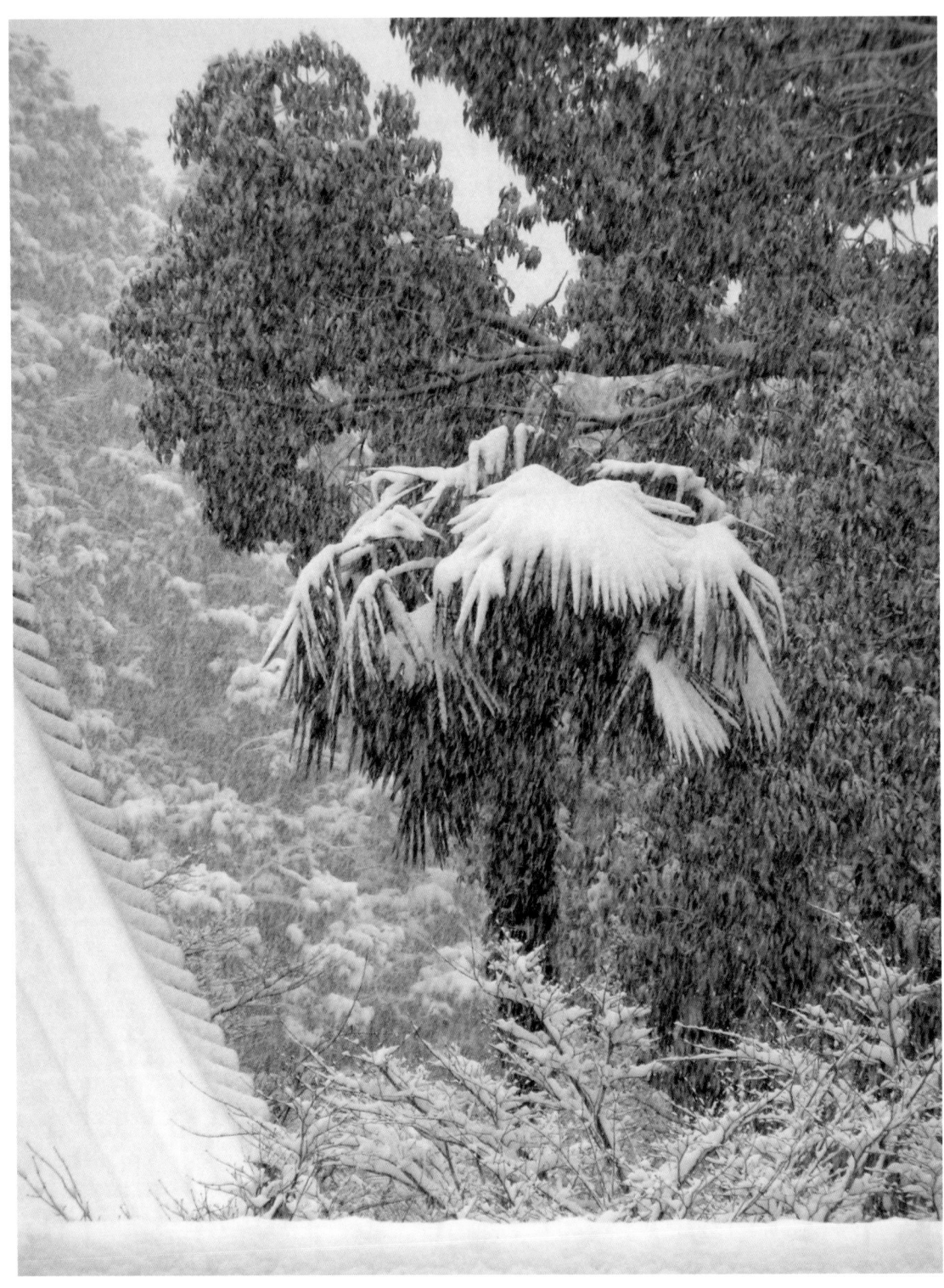

Ryōan-ji, view beyond the dry garden, 31 December 2010.

SEVEN

IMPOSSIBLE POSSIBLES

In an article entitled 'Paul Claudel exégète du Japon', Maurice Pinguet tempers his homage to his illustrious predecessor Claudel with a list of errors contained in his writings, among which we find: 'he sees fifteen stones in the garden of Ryōan-ji which only has fourteen.'[1] That none of my acquaintances who know both the article and the garden in question noted Pinguet's error, and that no corrective footnote is offered, is symptomatic. For the garden of Ryōan-ji was conceived to foster precisely this type of confusion. Nearly everybody who visits Ryōan-ji believes that from any given vantage point, only fourteen of the fifteen stones are visible. Whatever may be the sublime meditative heights attainable in this garden, the main activity of the myriad of schoolchildren who visit it is reduced to counting the stones over and over as they move across the veranda, with the inevitable unabashed astonishment to discover what they already knew: that they will never arrive at a full count of fifteen. This is because they do not know the secret. It is true that from any given *zazen* (seated meditation) position along the veranda only fourteen stones can be seen. However, if viewed from the right corner pillar of the temple by a person over 6 feet tall, all fifteen stones become, at least partially, visible. In any case, the children are not tall enough to attain this viewpoint, as would also have been the case for most Japanese until the post-Second World War era. The other secret is that all the stones are also visible if viewed from approximately the middle of the altar room, with the *shōji* open to create the proper sight lines, though tourists are generally forbidden to enter the temple rooms. It is telling that the only totalizing viewpoints are one that is improbable if not quite impossible, being just beyond the reach and the knowledge of most visitors, and another that is forbidden to all but the initiated and the invited. This is not to mention the a priori all but impossible bird's-eye view that would reveal all the stones, with its consequent valorization of the ground plan, a transcendent viewpoint of an omniscient observer, always on the aesthetic horizon of theologically inflected Western gardens such as Versailles, but unthinkable in the traditional Japanese context. (Of course aeroplanes and Google Earth have somewhat transformed this situation, but the effect of such long-distance views on the experience and imagination of gardens still needs to be examined. Shigemori Mirei, for example, has created gardens that are ideally viewed from above, such as the Garden of the Peaceful Heart at Kōsei-ji, where the rocks and moss form the kanji for the word 'heart', 心, *kokoro*, and the raked gravel simulates watermarks on paper.) There is yet one more impossible viewpoint, one more secret: two signatures, most probably of the *kawaramono* stoneworkers who crafted the garden, appear on the back of the leftmost rear stone. But the time is long past when one can enter this garden. Thus the garden's design plays on the equivocation of a series of incomplete views, complicated by two facts: the laws of visual gestalts reveal that most people cannot easily intuit the number count of fifteen assembled objects, and the usual viewing protocols of Zen gardens limit the possible viewpoints, since one cannot enter most *karesansui*. These factors conspire to transform this sublime garden into a visual conundrum based on the undecidability between the multiple ostensible viewpoints and the secret perspectives.

So much landscape study suffers from a narrowly construed sense of representation, where gardens are imagined as pictures to be seen rather than fields to be entered, according to analyses that promote a static ontological model based on perspectival projections, rather than a dynamic one founded on kinaesthetic transformations. These heuristic issues are complicated by the particularity of the dry Zen garden that it usually cannot be entered, and many of which indeed undergo the most minimal seasonal changes, both factors that seem to imply certain perspectival and iconographic limitations. However, their situation is quite complex, and according to their disposition within the temple complex, Zen gardens may be viewed from one, two, three or four sides. Some may even be walked *over* by means of a corridor that serves as a bridge. Others may be walked *through* on a series of stepping stones, contingent on the caution of a rite of passage. Furthermore, in the relatively rare instances when considerations of motion are considered, it is

Zuiho-in, a subtemple of Daitoku-ji, garden created by Shigemori Mirei, 1961.

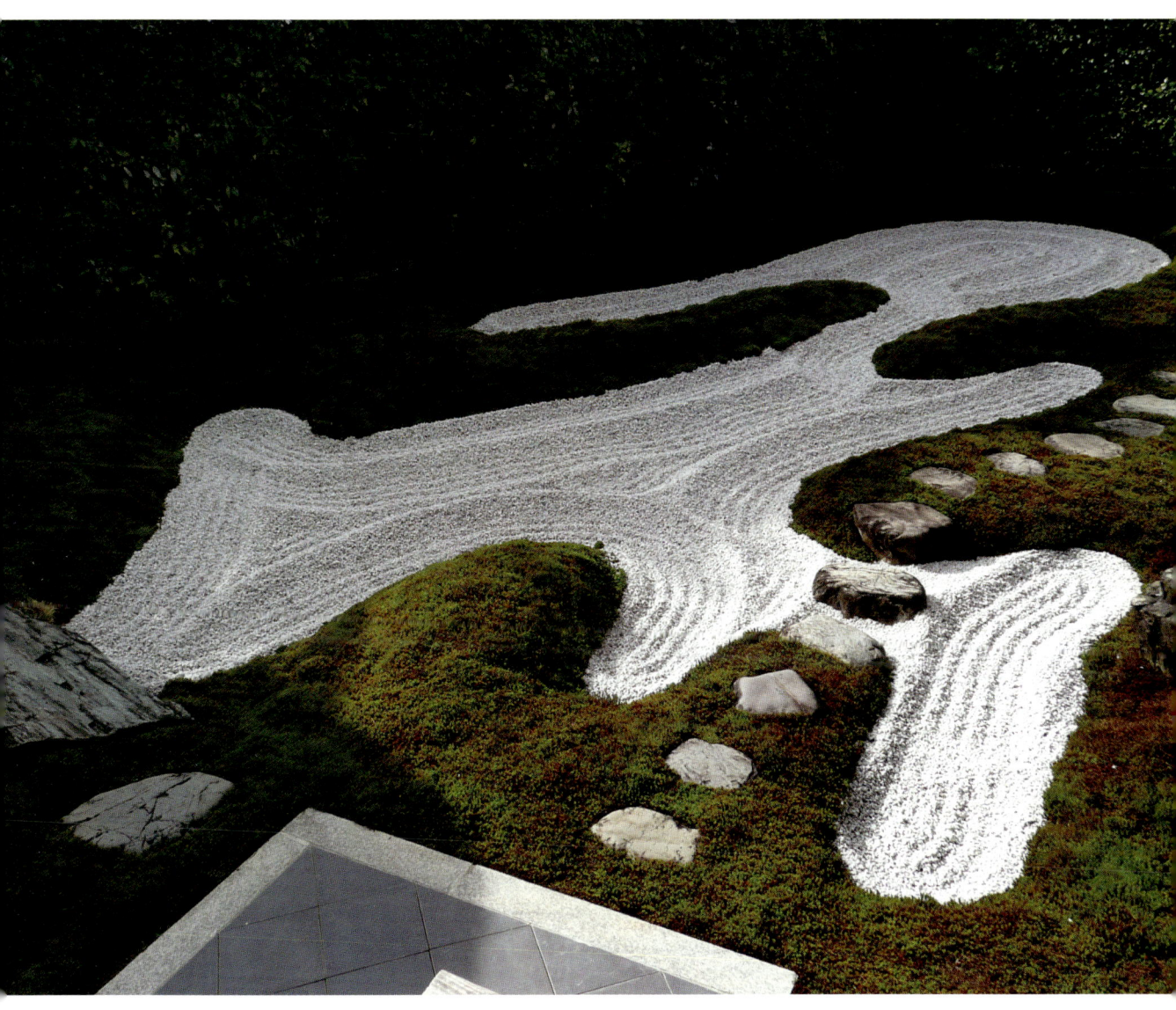

usually forgotten that the body moves not only laterally and in depth, but also vertically, as it ascends and descends staircases and ramps, or changes from a standing to a sitting position. While walking has been a source of poetic inspiration throughout history (witness Bashō, Rousseau, Thoreau, Baudelaire, Breton, Debord, among so many others), the *zazen* position of seated meditation, usually in the lotus position, is crucial to Zen. Furthermore, it should be stressed that the seated position is in itself conducive to meditation, Zen and otherwise, as explained by the landscape specialist David A. Slawson:

> The frontal posture in particular presents a symmetrical triangle where the lateral forces are in a state of equilibrium. No wonder this seated posture has been the traditional one for meditation or contemplation – it fosters alertness and at the same time minimizes bodily tension. In the Japanese garden, while the effect of the whole upon the senses is likely to be one of restful equilibrium, there is typically a dynamic, highly engaging interaction of forces among the various elements of the design. The object, after all, is to entice and reinvigorate the viewer, but not to tire or alienate him. To understand how this is achieved, we need to know how the simplest shapes can create a sense of movement.[2]

Both walking and sitting are integral to the Zen sensibility, and both are fully integrated into Zen garden design. The wooden corridors or galleries that surround and connect buildings – serving as walkways between the various buildings of a temple, and as verandas when they pass in front of an altar, tea room, abbot's private quarters or inner sanctum – often have no banisters and are of a height that invites the visitor to sit and contemplate the garden. The corridors are simultaneously walkways and seats, and have a double role in defining the spatiality of these gardens, much as the floor (also used for walking and sitting) always does in Japanese architecture and design. Mobility is inscribed in the design of Ryōan-ji, and the perpetual play of dissimulation and revelation (*mie-gakure*) is essential. Thus interior screens and exterior walls do not simply delimit, but simultaneously conceal

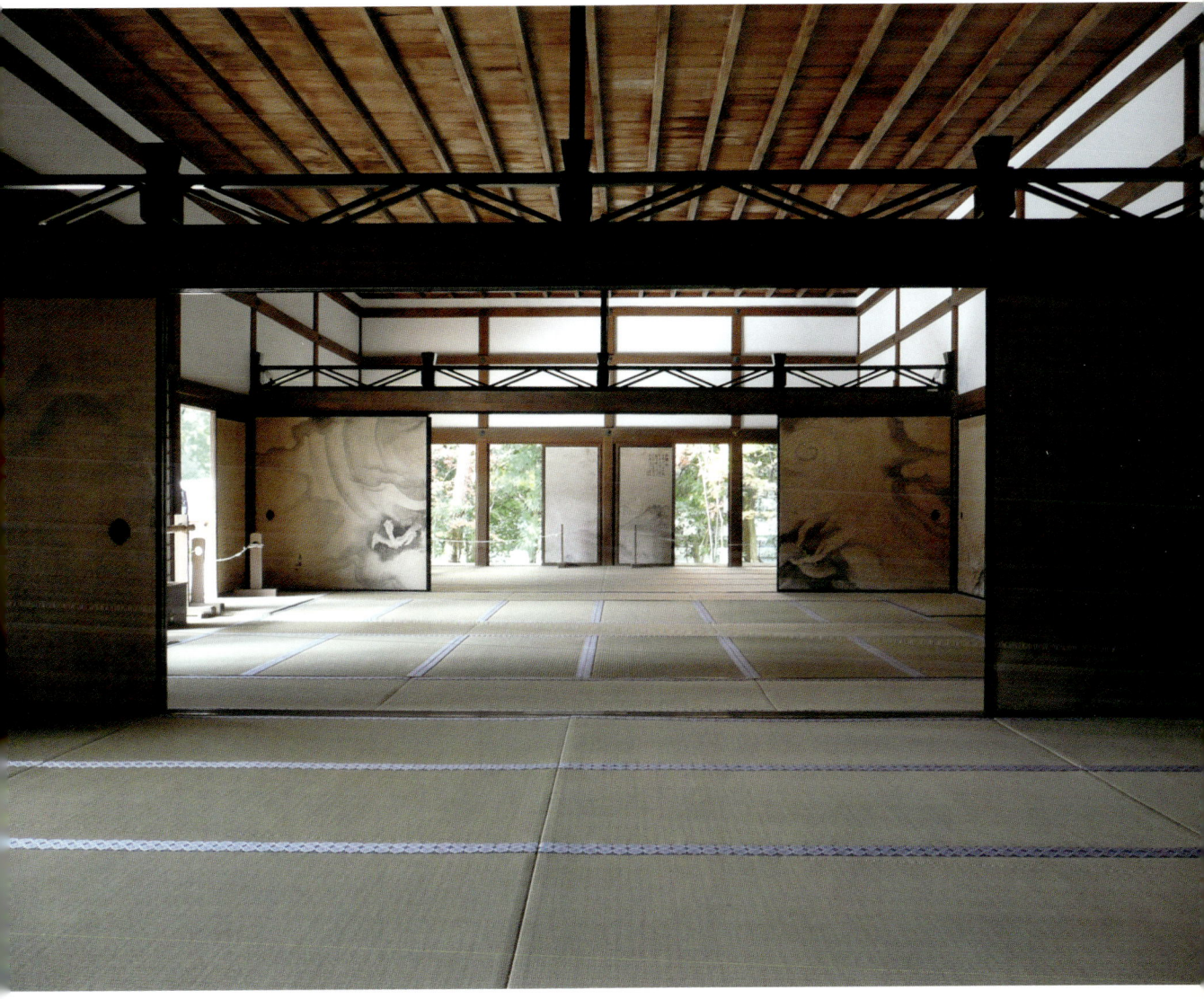

Ryōan-ji, interior of the *hōjō* (main building), with the dry garden to the left.

and reveal, such that certain objects beyond the *karesansui* walls are nevertheless integral parts of the garden, such as the splendid cherry, palm and maple trees at Ryōan-ji. Given such paradoxes, equivocations and complexities, the aesthetic coherence of such gardens does not stem from a unified geometry of perspectival projections (as in many Western gardens), but rather from the innate sense of proportion that is a result of the modularity unique to Japanese architecture and design.[3] Thus, Günter Nitschke is correct in centring his analysis of the Zen garden on the tension between natural accidents and artificial types, between unique irregular natural objects (often worshipped as the abodes of spirits) and refined artificial perfection (revered as the height of craft).[4] The key forms of the latter are modularity and the right angle, and its exemplar is the *tatami*, the ubiquitous bamboo floor mat, the proportions of which establish both conscious and unconscious grids according to which every room, house, scene and garden is experienced. Architecture serves as the visual frame of the *karesansui*.

The spatiality of the veranda-corridor is bifunctional, and thus potentially equivocal. Typical of the errors caused by this equivocation is one by art historian Dore Ashton, in what is otherwise a rather perspicacious discussion of Ryōan-ji: 'The single viewing point – the veranda from which the more austere Zen gardens are to be viewed – is implicit in painting.'[5] In fact, the dry garden usually has many possible viewpoints: there is no single ideal seated position at the edge of the veranda, and at least a dozen people can comfortably sit side-by-side at Ryōan-ji. Such gardens are so small that the visual difference between viewpoints is enormous; one may observe the garden sitting or standing, from the edge of the veranda or from within the facing rooms, still or walking, and many of these gardens, such as Daisen-in, are L-shaped. There even exist some garden plans that reveal a form of sequential notation, noting appropriate ways of traversing the space.[6] Furthermore, to propose scroll viewing as a model for experiencing gardens is certainly appropriate, but this is never a matter of single viewpoints or one-point linear perspective. On the contrary, traditional Chinese and Japanese landscape paintings are not articulated by a single viewpoint, and furthermore, long horizontal scrolls need to be unrolled in order to see the image through a progression of viewpoints. Such is not an instantaneous vision, but a gradual unfolding over time, as François Cheng reminds us: 'in China, the unrolling and the contemplation of a masterpiece, taking hours, constitutes a nearly sacred ritual.'[7] One might add that the complexities of this experience are certainly accentuated by the often mysterious and dynamic cosmologies that underlie such imagery.

A stunning example of the role of motion is to be found in the garden at Konchi-in, where a vast expanse of raked gravel separates the temple from the rest of the garden, which is a complex formal dry garden of stones and moss set amidst a semi-formal green landscape, the entirety focused on a huge flat central stone, a sort of intense concentration and condensation of the field of gravel. The extreme rarity of a central focus in Zen-inspired art suggests the extraordinary nature of the stone in question, and its profound metaphorical, perhaps even metaphysical, value. When viewed from the front of the veranda, the entirety of the scene (foreground, mid-ground, background) is visible, but when seen from further back in the middle of the temple room, from the point of view of the altar, the architecture delimits the scene by precisely framing the formal part of the garden. The formalism is emphasized by intensified focus; the field of view condensed by precise framing; the point of view exaggerated by calculated retreat in perspective; the lighting amplified by contrast between garden light and altar shadow; the horizon dramatized by an architecturally formed horizon line. In short, a new view is created by retreating just a few steps from the veranda towards the altar, as if the proximity of the sacred focused vision and transformed design.

In general, the Zen garden is a perpetual play of thresholds and passages, statics and dynamics, pictorial views and abstract spaces. The effects of movement (whether lateral, vertical or in depth) are amplified within these gardens due to their extremely small size, some existing within but a few square metres, like the extraordinary Totekiko-in, a modern garden that is one of the smallest *karesansui* in Japan, found within Ryōgen-in (a subtemple of Daitoku-ji). The angles of vision, relationship between elements, implied horizon lines, effects of closure, degree of framing, play of thresholds, narrative

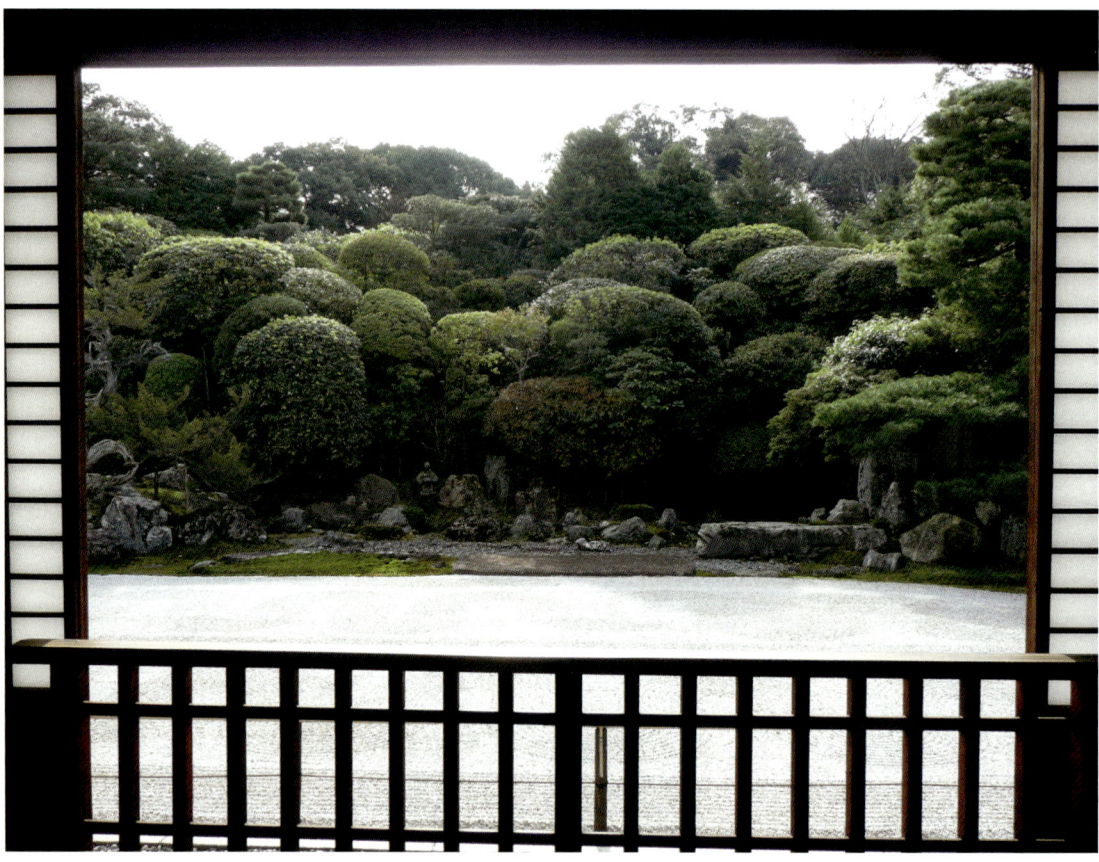

Konchi-in.

allusions and symbolic implications are all transformed not only by the particular point of view chosen along the corridor, but also according to whether one is sitting, standing or walking (all appropriate attitudes for Zen meditation). Due to the small scale of most *karesansui*, the viewpoint changes radically as one moves about, and since the corridors are only approximately 1 metre from ground level, the mere difference between sitting and standing often entails a prodigious change in perspective, which may alternately (and often simultaneously and equivocally) be frontal, oblique or aerial – if these terms still have any meaning in such a context, which is doubtful. Indeed, these considerations complicate relations between the planar and the volumetric aspects of these gardens, given the fact that the apparent forms of

Totekiko-in garden at Ryōgen-in, a subtemple of Daitoku-ji.

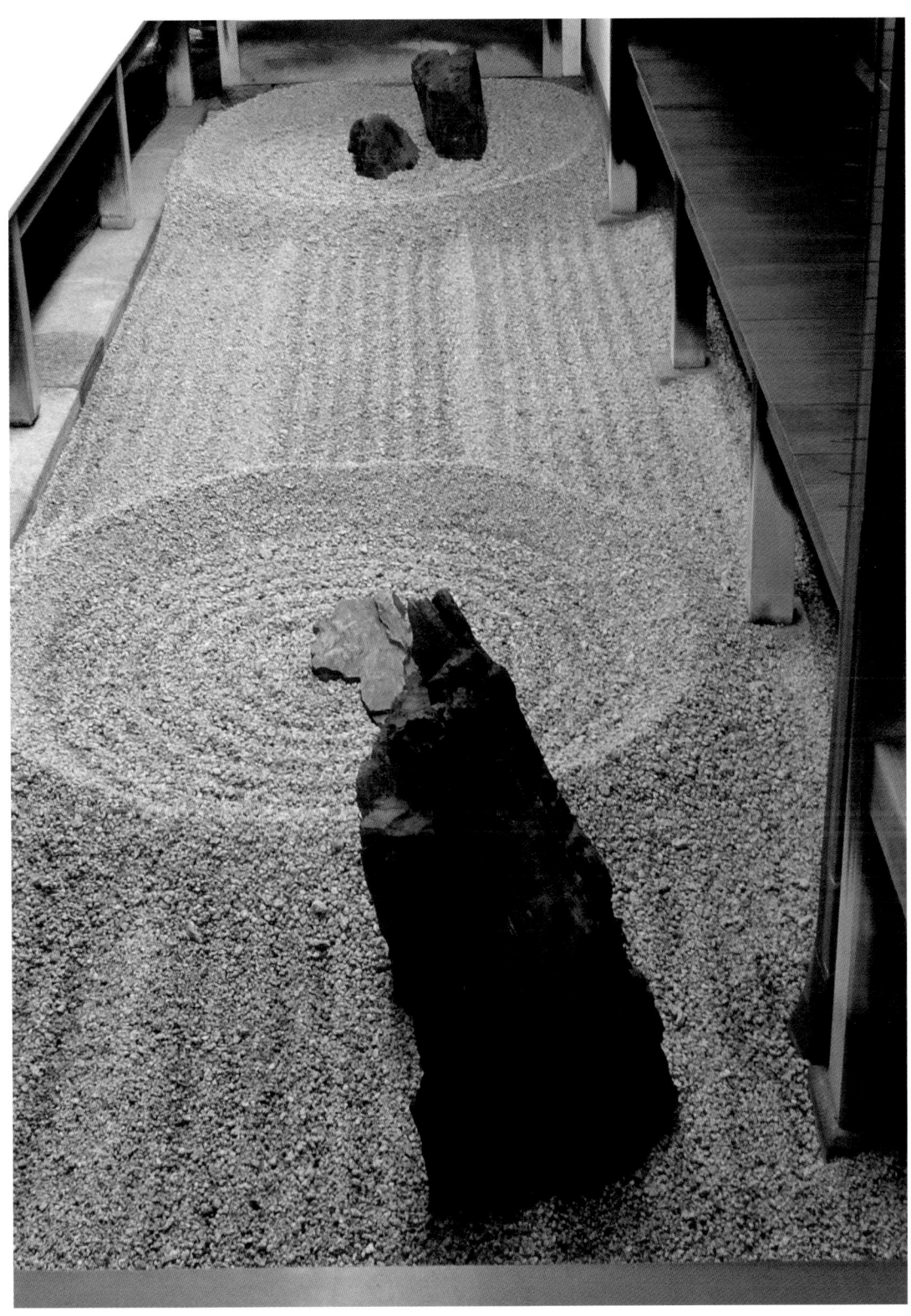

walls and stones, for example, change so greatly with even the slightest movement. In the extremely restricted space of the dry Zen garden, a mere few steps, even the tilt of the head may effect transformations of cosmic dimensions. Some of these gardens are narrower than the height of an average person, and one's shadow may well cover an entire landscape. Others are so subtle that they may not be immediately recognizable as gardens, and literally passed over as one crosses a walkway or enters a building. In other instances, a particular architectural feature may, under certain circumstances, be construed as a garden, or at least inspire new landscape forms.

For example, the thatched rooftops of houses and gateways, like the spectacular one at Hōnen-in near the 'Philosopher's Walk' in Kyoto, are often overgrown with moss, ferns and other plants, and appear as gardens in the sky. In the nineteenth century Edward S. Morse noted one house near Yezo with a flat ridge on its thatched roof from which sprouted a luxuriant growth of lilies, and remarked that plants, weeds and mosses growing on thatched roofs were a form of protection against fire.[8] These might well have inspired recent ecologically oriented constructions, like Fujimori Terunobu's 1997 design of a Tokyo rooftop plantation of 1,000 potted chive plants.[9] Other details might seem too trivial to be noticed, much less to warrant the name 'garden', but they may be revelatory, such as the posts supporting the astonishing wall at the Saishō-in subtemple of Nanzen-ji (Kyoto), the tops of which support growths that can be related to the tradition of bonsai (miniature tree plantings) and *suiseki* (miniature rock arrangements). A garden or not a garden, that is the question.

THE SORTS OF EQUIVOCATION inspired by Zen and long inscribed in Japanese gardens and painting did not, however, effect forms of pottery, which were rather transformed by the influence of Western modernism, effecting a different form of contradiction. As we have seen, Western museum practices would soon motivate the creation of a new sort of object, neither pot nor sculpture, works no longer destined for the tea room but for the museum. Meanwhile, the burgeoning art and technical schools promulgated novel forms, modern techniques (most importantly increased firing precision,

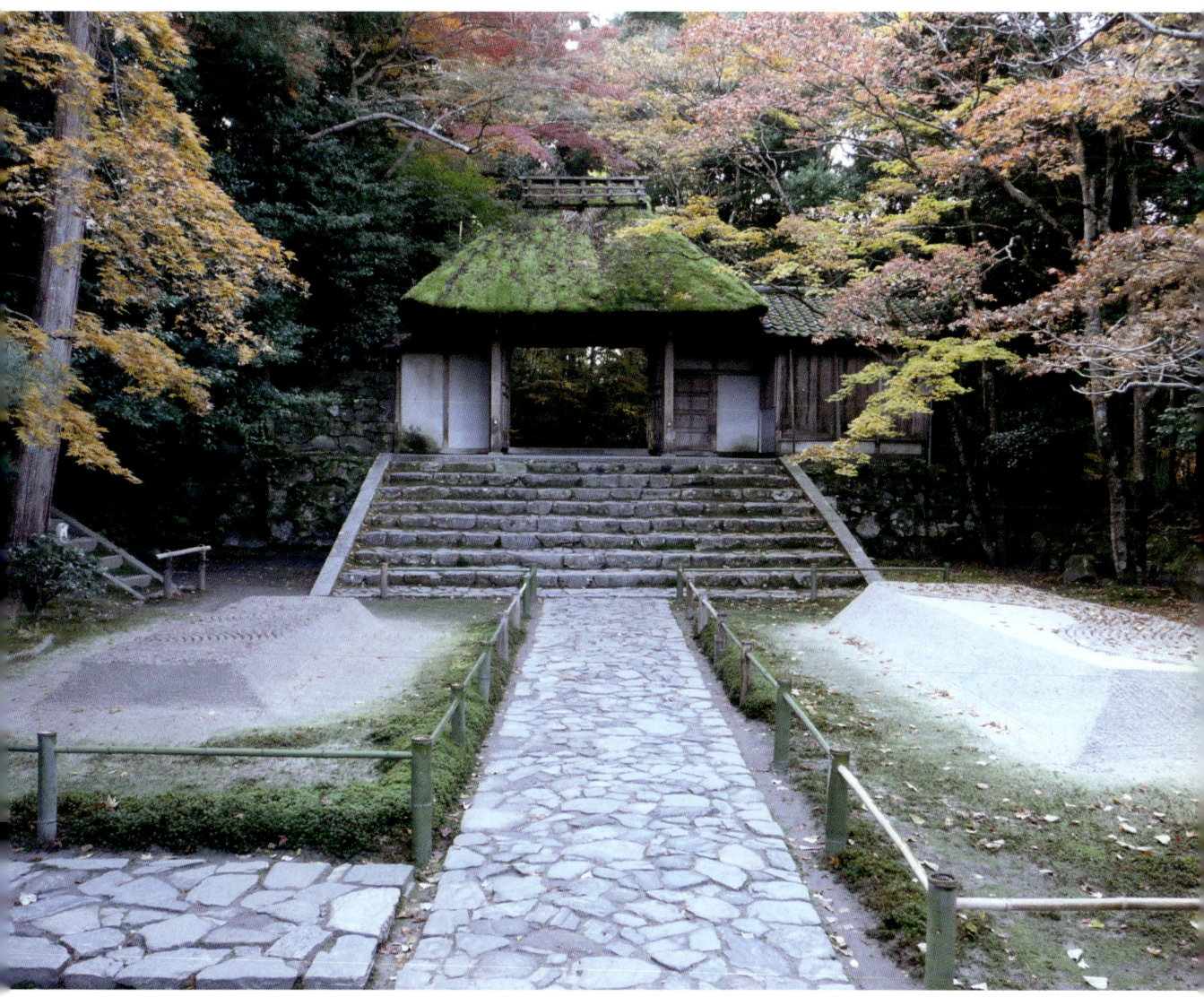

Hōnen-in.

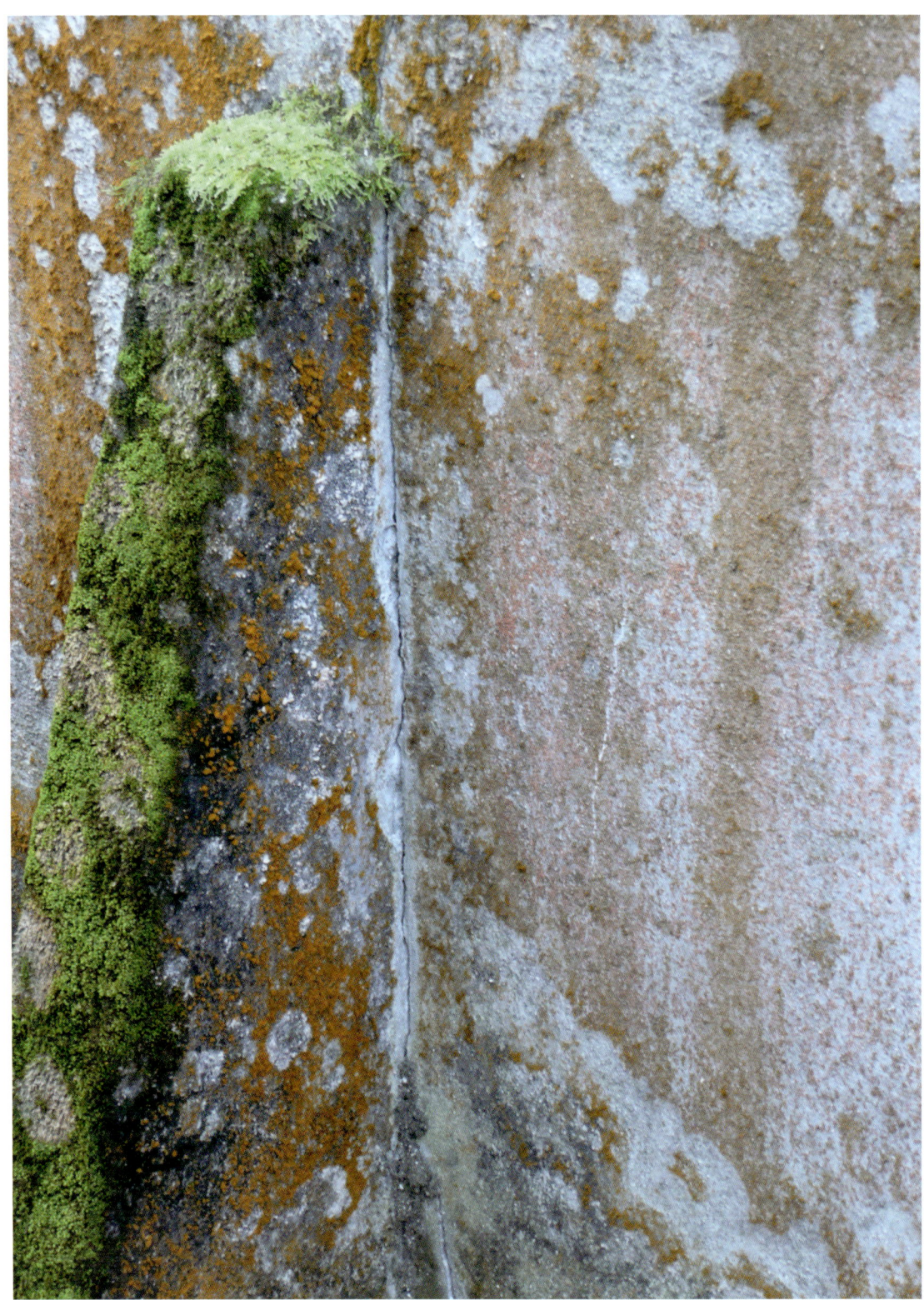

so as to ensure greater control over surface effects), new materials (notably artificial glazes and commercial clays of consistent, standardized quality), the taste for experimentation and an openness to aesthetic internationalism.

The year 1950 was fateful for Japanese pottery. Until then, a Japanese potter simply made pots. However, unlike in the West, where pottery was always deemed a craft aesthetically inferior to the 'fine' arts due to its utilitarian nature, in Japan the appreciation of pottery, always utilitarian, had been linked for half a millennium to the Zen-inspired tea ceremony, thus raising certain works of pottery to the top of the aesthetic hierarchy. Yet in the years after the Second World War, the situation changed since the American occupation rapidly accelerated a process of cross-cultural influences that had begun with the opening of Japan to the West during the Meiji period (1868–1912). In 1957, at the height of the first wave of the post-war pottery avant-garde, Kawai Kanjirō, among the greatest of early modernist Japanese potters, noted his own transformation during the year 1949: 'Is released from conventional ceramics, and simultaneously enters the realm of indeterminate forms.'[10] The tensions between the traditional and the modernist were soon exacerbated, a fact emblematized by two major events in 1950. On the one hand, the Japanese government promulgated the Law for the Protection of Cultural Properties, which supported traditional culture by not only protecting certain antiquities (in terms of ceramics, all of the works in question were utilitarian), but also by fostering certain skills designated as Intangible Cultural Properties. The emphasis soon shifted to the artisans who possessed those skills, holders of Important Intangible Cultural Properties, commonly referred to as Living National Treasures. Examination reveals that most craftsmen named Living National Treasures produced works linked to the tea ceremony, thus maintaining the centrality of traditional *chanoyu* aesthetics within this modern system of values. On the other hand, contemporary Japanese potters began to confront European modernism, emblematized by the exhibition at the Musée Cernuschi in Paris, 'Japon: Céramique Contemporaine' (1950), which also travelled to the pottery town of Vallauris, famed for its association with Picasso. The show, which included traditionalist, independent and avant-garde potters, was co-curated by the

Saishō-in, wall supports showing weathering and lichen.

director of the Musée Cernuschi, René Grousset, and the influential pottery specialist Koyama Fujio, curator of ceramics at the Tokyo National Museum. Among the avant-garde potters featured were members of the Sōdeisha group, one of whose founding members was Yagi Kazuo, as well as the already famous Isamu Noguchi, who during an extended stay in Japan in 1952 had a major pottery exhibition in the Museum of Modern Art at Kamakura, which would seal his position as the greatest modernist influence on the emerging Japanese ceramics avant-garde.

While the conceptual conflict at the core of most modernist art theories has long been between representation and abstraction, in the field of pottery it was between utilitarianism and non-utilitarianism. To put it in the most fundamental terms, a pot is an object with a hole capable of holding water, and the critical moment in the history of Japanese pottery was the first time a potter sealed off that hole. That potter was Yagi Kazuo, and it is not without interest that while he came from a traditional Kyoto family of potters, during his time at art school in the 1930s he studied not only Japanese ceramics but also, quite atypically, European-style ceramic sculpture. He had thus already internalized the dichotomy in clay that would be manifested in the post-war pottery revolution.

There is an anecdote that speaks to this issue. The young Yagi studied ceramic sculpture with Numata Ichiga, who one day asked him to comment on one of his own pieces, an incense burner. Yagi reproached him by exclaiming: 'Its form is splendid, but unfortunately there is only one hole so the smoke would build up and choke the fire out.'[11] Ironically, approximately two decades later, it would be Yagi who would finally close off all the holes by creating what is generally claimed to be the first non-functional work in the history of Japanese pottery, *Mr Samsa's Walk* (1955), a roughly formed, circular object of wood-ash glazed clay, like the rim of a wheel, from which emerge numerous hollow tubes, both forming the rim and sticking out from it. This work instantiated the contemporary tensions that perturbed the Japanese pottery world at that moment: tradition / innovation; functionality / non-functionality; craft / art; ceramics / sculpture; symmetry / asymmetry; wheel-thrown / hand-built (with the major exception of Raku, most traditional

Japanese pottery is thrown on the wheel). In this piece, the functional openings of traditional pottery are replaced by a myriad of useless holes, 'a multitude of tiny "mouths" leading nowhere',[12] as Louise Allison Cort describes them; and the wheel-thrown parts are rearranged and attached in such a manner that while the wheel is instrumental in creating the parts, it does not determine the total form. Japanese pottery would never be the same.

There is a further complication in this history, one that has for the most part escaped the purview of Western art history, since it deals with an art form that simply does not exist as such in the West: ikebana, flower arranging. In the immediate post-war years, while a potter such as Kitaōji Rosanjin resuscitated traditional forms and techniques so as to create ceramics that would further enhance the arts of the table, the most radical form of artistic transformation in Japan was probably, in the hands of Teshigahara Sōfū, the art of flower arranging. Just as Yagi freed pottery from the pot, Teshigahara liberated flowers from the vase. Traditional ikebana – derived from temple offerings and developed in relation to the tea ceremony – were frontal, vertical, highly codified in form, and set indoors in a vase or other receptacle. Teshigahara's creations were brought into galleries or removed to outdoor spaces, meant to be seen in the round, often laid out horizontally and placed directly on the ground, and were either arranged in unconventional containers he himself created, in avant-garde vases or occasionally even unconventionally set in other artists' sculptures not initially intended as vases, such as those of his friend Noguchi. He extended this logic to create ikebana without the use of either containers or even water, acts that he described in 1952 as 'flower arranging with an invisible container', and in many cases the landscape itself, whether garden or beach, served as receptacle.[13] From vase as garden to garden as vase. He would go even further in this logic: 'Somebody once asked me what I would do if I lived in a place like Manchuria where there were no flowers or plants, to which I replied that I would probably arrange the earth',[14] foreshadowing Koie's act of firing the earth with a blowtorch and considering it pottery, and aligning ikebana with the burgeoning land art movement. Just as Yagi was to transform pottery by the multiplication of useless holes, Teshigahara would revolutionize ikebana with his open metalwork sculptural forms that appear as a matrix of nothing but holes, useless in the context of traditional flower arranging. No longer would ikebana be bound by the ancient precept of arranging flowers to appear as if reproducing natural forms; now the very artificiality of the art was grasped as the key to its creativity. Furthermore, certainly influenced by the post-war shift from object-making to performance, he insisted that 'ikebana is a preordained drama played out between man and flowers.'[15] In the hands of Teshigahara Sōfū, ikebana was aligned with the new arts of installations and happenings, since he did not only reproduce nature or create formal arrangements, but stressed the performative aspect of the art.[16]

This transformation was taking place in the much broader context of radical artistic experimentation in the immediate post-Second World War period, when Teshigahara Sōfū's continued collaborations with his son, film-maker Teshigahara Hiroshi, placed him near the centre of the nascent Japanese avant-garde. At the time that Hiroshi filmed *Ikebana*, the documentary on his father's work, he also collaborated on the creation of a building for their ikebana school that opened in 1958, permitting an ambitious programme of invited artists. They subsequently commissioned the architect Tange Kenzō to design a new building that opened in 1978, and Hiroshi succeeded his father as headmaster in 1980. Teshigahara Hiroshi was one of the founders of the Seiki no Kai (Group of the Century) in 1949, whose members included writer Abe Kōbō, who would later collaborate, along with the composer Takemitsu Tōru, on Hiroshi's most celebrated film, *Woman in the Dunes* (1964). It should be stressed that Sōfū was not only an ikebana artist, but also a painter, calligrapher and sculptor, just as Hiroshi was a film-maker, potter, tea master and stage designer, as well as an ikebana artist. While historically the interrelations between the arts in Japan occasionally set the stage for such polyvalent artists, as in the case of the great potter and painter Ogata Kenzan (1663–1743), the interdisciplinarity of Teshigahara father and son existed in a new context that would not only permit such art to flourish but would transform the very nature of aesthetics. Given their own artistic polymorphousness, it is not surprising that they became patrons of the new arts: Sōfū entrusted Hiroshi to develop the lecture, performance, screening and exhibition programmes at the Sogetsu school, so that it became, in the words of critic Tōno Yoshiaki, 'the epicenter of the avant-garde', both Japanese and international.[17] Emblematic of this watershed moment is the work of another group, the Jikken Kōbō (Experimental Atelier), whose first public performance took place in 1951 at the Takashimaya department store in Tokyo in conjunction with a Picasso exhibition. The event consisted of a synthesis of several interactive yet autonomous components, which high-lighted formal innovations in each field, abolished the traditional divisions between genres and established a new type of performative art (just as potters, sculptors and ikebana artists were seeking new forms of objects): music by Takemitsu Tōru, costumes and sculptures by Fukushima Hideko and Kitadai Shōzō, poetry by Akiyama Kuniharu and lighting by Imai Naoji. It is notable that this performance occurred a year before the famed Black Mountain College event that is generally cited as the major source of multi-media art happenings.[18]

Emblematic of this new nexus of the arts is the project that Isamu Noguchi, long-time collaborator and friend of Teshigahara father and son, realized for the entrance to the new Sogetsu building in 1978. It is difficult to say whether this huge multi-level stone structure with streams of water running through it – which can be walked through and used as a performance and exhibition space – is an indoor garden, conceptual playground or vast sculpture. The very ambiguity of its genre is certainly coherent with both Noguchi's lifetime experimentation across art forms, as well as with the interdisciplinary core of the Sogetsu aesthetic.[19] Indeed, one might even see this work as one of the largest ikebana in existence, for stemming from the front of the stone structure is a single huge dead tree trunk, recalling in hyperbolically modernist manner the essence of *wabi-sabi* aesthetics. Teshigahara Sōfū had long used dead plants in his ikebana, and had also created ikebana 30 metres high at both the Grand Palais in Paris and the Rockefeller Center in New York, and Teshigahara Hiroshi would eventually renew the art form with his vast bamboo installations for gardens, theatre, opera and tea ceremony, a form of landscape art inspired by his father's ikebana aesthetics.[20]

To push this logic to the limit, one might make the somewhat outlandish suggestion that *Mr Samsa's Walk* be used as an ikebana vase. The fact that this piece has become so identified as *the* iconic instance of non-functional pottery certainly works against such iconoclastic fantasies. Yet it is tempting to think of an alternate destiny for this revolutionary work, one that returns it to its utilitarian function via the contemporaneous revolution in flower arranging. Teshigahara Sōfū often used Yagi's works for his ikebana, and even started making pottery under Yagi's tutelage. As Yagi overthrew the functional in pottery, Teshigahara eliminated strictly utilitarian receptacles in ikebana, precisely by finding new uses for seemingly non-utilizable objects. The ground-breaking move from functional to non-functional tubes, evidenced in the difference between Yagi's 1950 work *Vase with Two Small Mouths* (a closed, elongated, footed vessel with Miro-inspired designs, whose openings consist of two tubes) and *Mr Samsa's Walk* (with its tubes that do not open into an interior) might well have been inspired by Teshigahara's elimination of the need for open pots, that is to say, for holes.[21] Had *Mr Samsa's Walk* been appropriated for use in ikebana, the history of Japanese ceramics might have taken a somewhat different course. In the end, both Yagi and Teshigahara taught the same lessons: that holes need not have a function, that a pot need not have a hole, and that hole and pot are simultaneously entity and metaphor.

Such complexities and contradictions (double binds, one might even say) galvanized the Japanese pottery world, and inaugurated a period of the richest innovation that has become more and more audacious with time and has continued to this day. However, appreciation of the widespread creativity and occasional extravagences of modernist pottery should not obscure earlier moments of great change in relation to traditional forms, notably those established by the progressive taste and occasional idiosyncrasies of the greatest tea masters. The critic Kumakura Isao reminds us of a particularly extreme instance:

Oribe's aesthetic taste was based on the extremely deformed – for example, a misshapen tea bowl in which it was difficult to use a whisk or a water pitcher with large cracks which, although of extremely inter-esting shape, leaked when water was poured into it – and the need to destroy even the functional qualities of a tea article as a work of craft.[22]

Might we imagine that in Oribe's time, which marked one of the heights of tea, certain tea masters began to conceive of an aesthetic that transcended the practical and material exigencies of the ceremony, thus moving towards a conceptualism that directly engaged certain paradoxical forms of beauty? Might we not see this as a prefiguration of the aesthetic upheavals in the Japanese pottery world of the 1950s and 1960s? Might these moments not highlight the inextricable connection between those diverse qualities that in the West we differentiate as art and craft?

Currently, one of the most admired potters is Fukami Sueharu. Born in 1947 into a Kyoto pottery family and early on inspired by the Sōdeisha group, he soon developed a signature style of sleek, minimal, light-blue porcelain of almost archetypal forms, created by a delicate process of air-compressed moulded slip casting to create flawless contours, ultra-fine surfaces and subtle colouration. He resuscitated an ancient glaze, transform-ing it through modern techniques into modernist forms. These abstract blue-glazed porcelain pieces suggest broad metaphoric possibilities: 'the beauty of sweeping temple rooflines' (specifically those of the Tōfuku-ji temple that he admired as a child), the horizon line, ocean waves and the less visual but equally sweeping 'pleasantly painful breeze while on the shore of a beach during winter'.[23] We are reminded of the fact that as a small child in Chigasaki, Noguchi made his very first sculpture in the form of a wave glazed blue.[24] The unique colour of Fukami's *seihakuji* glaze, derived from ancient Chinese pottery – neither celadon (*seiji*) nor white porcelain (*hakuji*), but rather fluctuating between the two – perhaps best corresponds to a sky that the famed interpreter of Japanese culture, Lafcadio Hearn, saw over

Fukami Sueharu, *Tenku <Sho>* ('Heaven <Soar>'), 2010, porcelain sculpture with wood base, 18 × 94.5 × 10.5 cm.

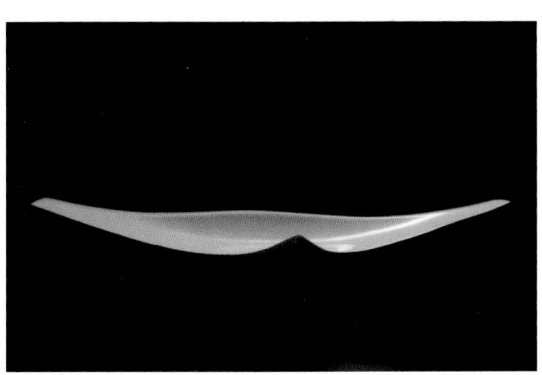

Hyōgo in May 1895: 'a cloudless splendor of tint that seems the ghost of azure rather than azure itself.'[25] Fukami's titles for his works support these descriptions: Distant View, Seascape, Distant Seascape, Windy Seascape, Firmament, Clarity, Soaring, Sky, Infinity, all bearing witness to a desire to seek metaphor in even the most extreme abstraction, as is the case for the stones of Zen gardens. If Fukami's forms resemble anything in the history of art, it is surely the work of Noguchi's teacher, Constantin Brancusi, exemplified by *Bird in Space* (1923). However, Fukami explicitly explains that 'if the pieces were made of metal, it would not be as beautiful nor would it project or convey a sense of fragility or insecurity'.[26]

In the contemporary pottery equation, one must never forget the troubled relationship between sculptor and potter, art and craft, artisan and industry. Fukami specifically refers to his works as 'ceramic sculpture', and maintains this equivocation in the very composition of the work. His slip casting technique was refined so as to remove all warping, imperfections and traces of handling during the firing.[27] Thus, though these works are handmade with the most exacting of techniques, their formal regularity and surface perfection make them appear to be produced by machines, unlike most other art pottery. Though most of Fukami's works are abstract sculptures, he does continue to make a small number of functional pots, including several forms of sake cups. Here, the contradictions between form and function, sculpture and pot, take a most subtle turn. Although spouted *guinomi* and *chawan* exist in traditional pottery, Fukami's case is particular, for he produces at least three styles: spout, inverted spout (where a spout-like form points towards the inside of the cup) and split spout (which appears cracked). The very fact that his *guinomi* and *sakazuki* have spouts is already the sign of a conundrum, for in such small drinking vessels, these minuscule spouts are totally ineffectual, even counterproductive, since the resultant flow of sake is far less than satisfying and the feel on the lips rather unpleasant. The result, whether intended or unintended, verges on the comic, due to the disproportion between form and function. One is tempted to drink from the other side, turning spout into handle, equally disproportionate and ineffectual as this may be. These counter-intuitive

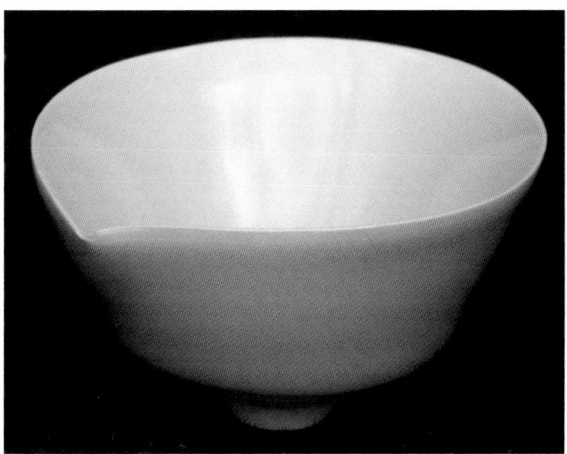

Fukami Sueharu,
guinomi, 2009.

formal characteristics – implying a double uselessness due to size and non-functionality – suggest that such are purely formal signs that allude to and call into play the very contradictions that have haunted modern Japanese pottery. What normally serves a tactile function is reduced to sheerly visual interest, such that the roles of haptic and optic are reversed. This suggests that these seemingly functional objects should in fact be regarded as sculptures, for if sculptures can occasionally be used as vases or cups (as Teshigahara Sōfū was wont to do), there is no reason to believe that sculptures cannot also take the very forms of pots and cups. But in these cases there must be some sign, whether intrinsic or extrinsic, that the utilitarian function has been diverted, subverted or obliterated. One such indication consists of the split and apparently damaged spouts of certain Fukami cups, yet another mark of 'imperfection' as a form of perfection, a miniscule sculptural effect on an otherwise utilitarian object, the tiniest sign of a momentous aesthetic statement.

Lest it be thought that these issues are only the concern of the fine arts, it might be amusing to consider those sorts of sake cups called *bekuhai*, in their formal simplicity resembling the world's oldest pottery, those oblong, baseless Jōmon vessels that needed to be set in the earth to stand upright. *Bekuhai* (可杯) are so named because of the particularity of the way the kanji for the word is formed, signifying the improbability and impracticality of a cup that has no usable bottom, a sort of *Alice in Wonderland* object.[28] Such *guinomi* with either rounded or pointed bottoms thus have no foot (*kōdai*), that most important part of traditional Japanese pottery, where one may observe the 'flavour' of the clay and the touch of the potter's hand. But for true tipplers these *guinomi* indeed have a decided advantage related to the etiquette of sake drinking, where an empty cup is to be refilled by a drinking partner. Bottomless, they can not be set down on the table, and must remain constantly in hand, eliciting not simply a 'good pour' but better yet, a perpetual pour. The literal and the figurative coincide, such that the cup without a bottom is a bottomless cup.

But there are more radical contradictions in form that test and transform the limits of the pot. Unlike Fukami's sake cups, whose ethereal and contradictory forms do not totally obviate their utilitarian possibilities, and the *bekuhai* that actually enhance them, certain recent works take the form of practical utensils, but are fundamentally unusable. Among these are Niisato Akio's porcelain *chawan* that are deemed by some too fragile to use, and Miwa Jusetsu's recent *oni-hagi chawan* that are too large to be practical. Hypotrophy and hypertrophy of a given physical aspect may lead to grotesqueness, but it may also be a sign of 'art'. In a sense, one need only transform a single parameter of a pot – be it size, substance, form – beyond usefulness for a utensil to become not a failure, but an artwork.[29] Most extreme in this regard are the spiky beakers of the London-based ceramic artist Iwamoto Ikuko, which mark the threshold between the sculptural and the functional in a nearly sadistic format. These pieces are clearly thrown as cups, while the rows of sharp spikes that protrude inside, outside or atop the rim make drinking from them strictly impossible, since either the liquid would pour through the spikes, or the spikes would injure the lips and hands. These works are pure aberrations, visual conundrums that are an ultimate extrapolation of the ontological conundrums resulting from utilitarian pottery entering the museum, works that call into question the very aesthetic system that supports them. High modernism would have form following function, while post-postmodernism revels in form belying, contradicting or mocking function. Might we need to imagine these cups in some alternate universe, where the laws of etiquette, physiology and perhaps even gravity have no correspondance to our own?

Concerning the Zen dictum which states that before enlightenment a mountain is just a mountain, during the quest a mountain is everything but a mountain, and after enlightenment a mountain is once again just a mountain, we might add to our previous comments that this is not just an

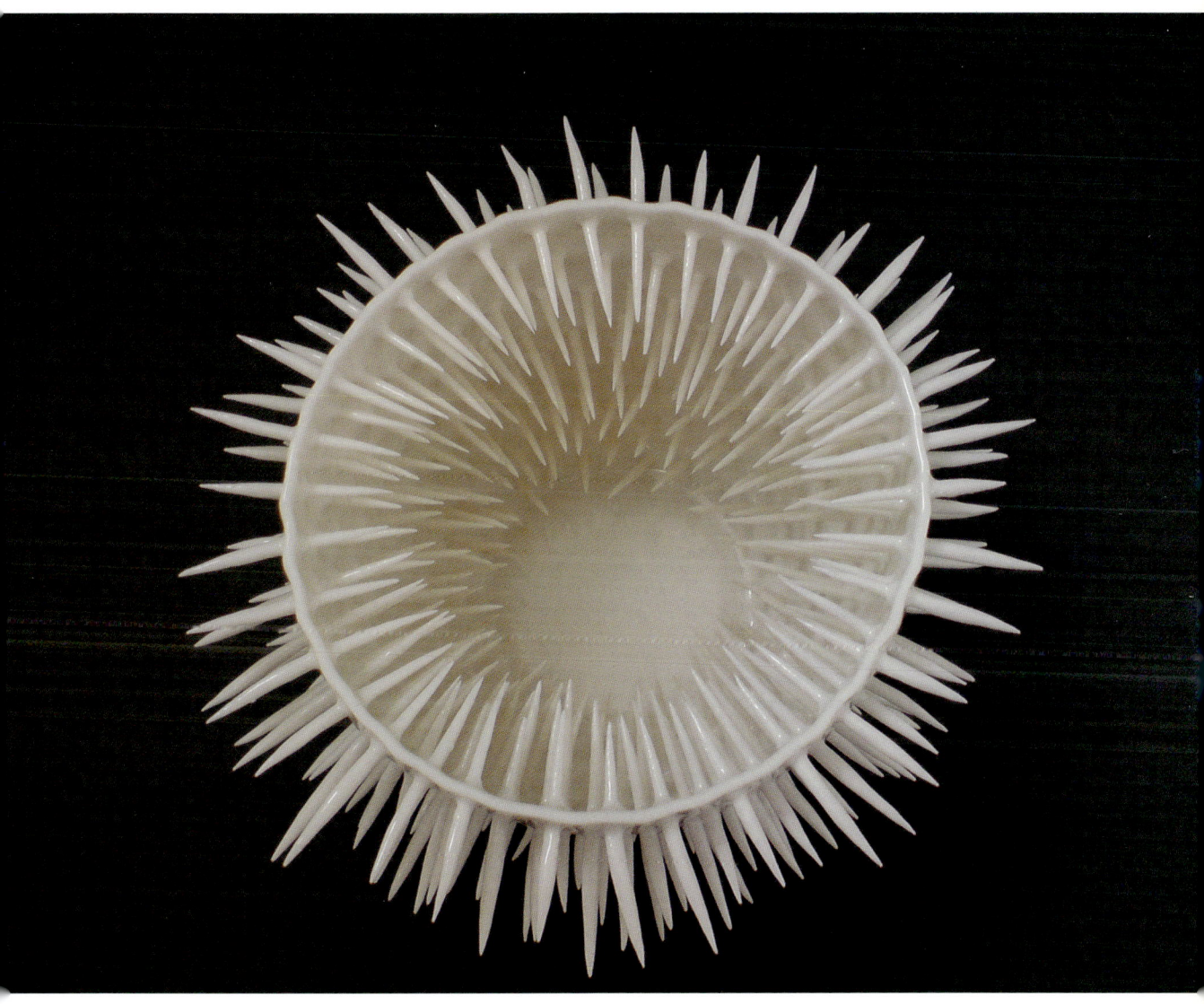

Iwamoto Ikuko, *Spikyspiky Bowl*, 2009.

allegory of the process of metaphorization, condensation and equivocation at the core of Japanese aesthetics, but that it also holds true for the ontological status of concrete objects, such as the stone 'mountains' of Zen gardens. By substituting the word 'pot' for 'mountain', this precept would also do justice to the aesthetic status of contemporary pottery. Equivocation is articulated across history in many forms. In the Zen tradition – where metaphorization and miniaturization are key design features – we are occasionally given to wonder whether a site is or is not a garden. We are also occasionally confronted with ambiguous objects that might or might not be pots. Perhaps it would be more appropriate not to use an exclusive disjunction but rather an inclusive one, and say that there exist objects that simultaneously are and are not pots, are and are not gardens, works that have internalized the contradictions inherent in the modern and postmodern epochs. Throughout the last century, the traditional doctrines of tea ceremony connoisseurship were challenged by the encroachments of modernism. Today, the ambiguities of modernism have inflected the very form of our epistemology. This transformation, and all the equivocations that it entails, were already prefigured in Ryōan-ji, that garden which is the most traditional and the most modern, the most symbolic and the most abstract, the most mysterious and the most familiar.

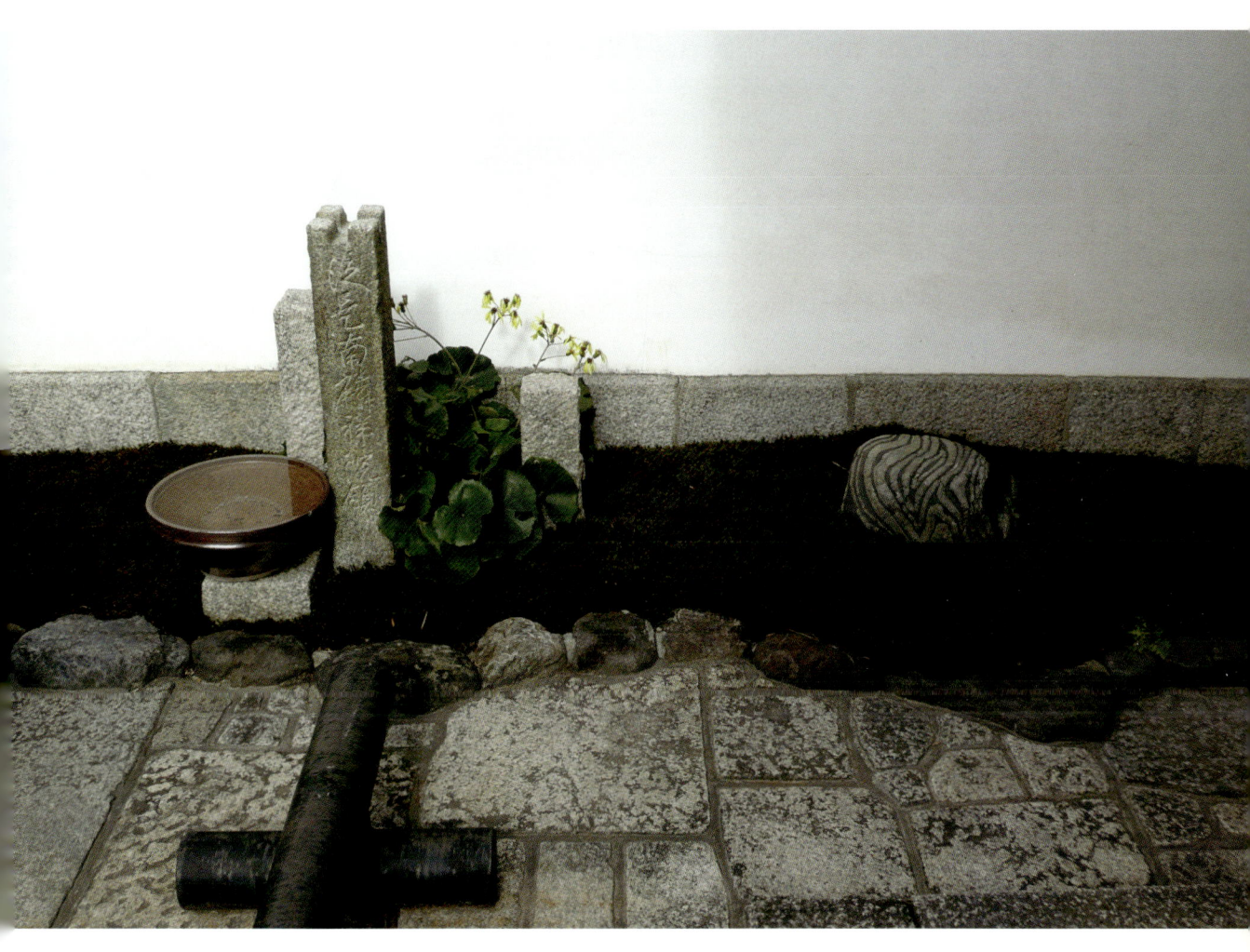

Taizō-in, a subtemple of Myōshin-ji.

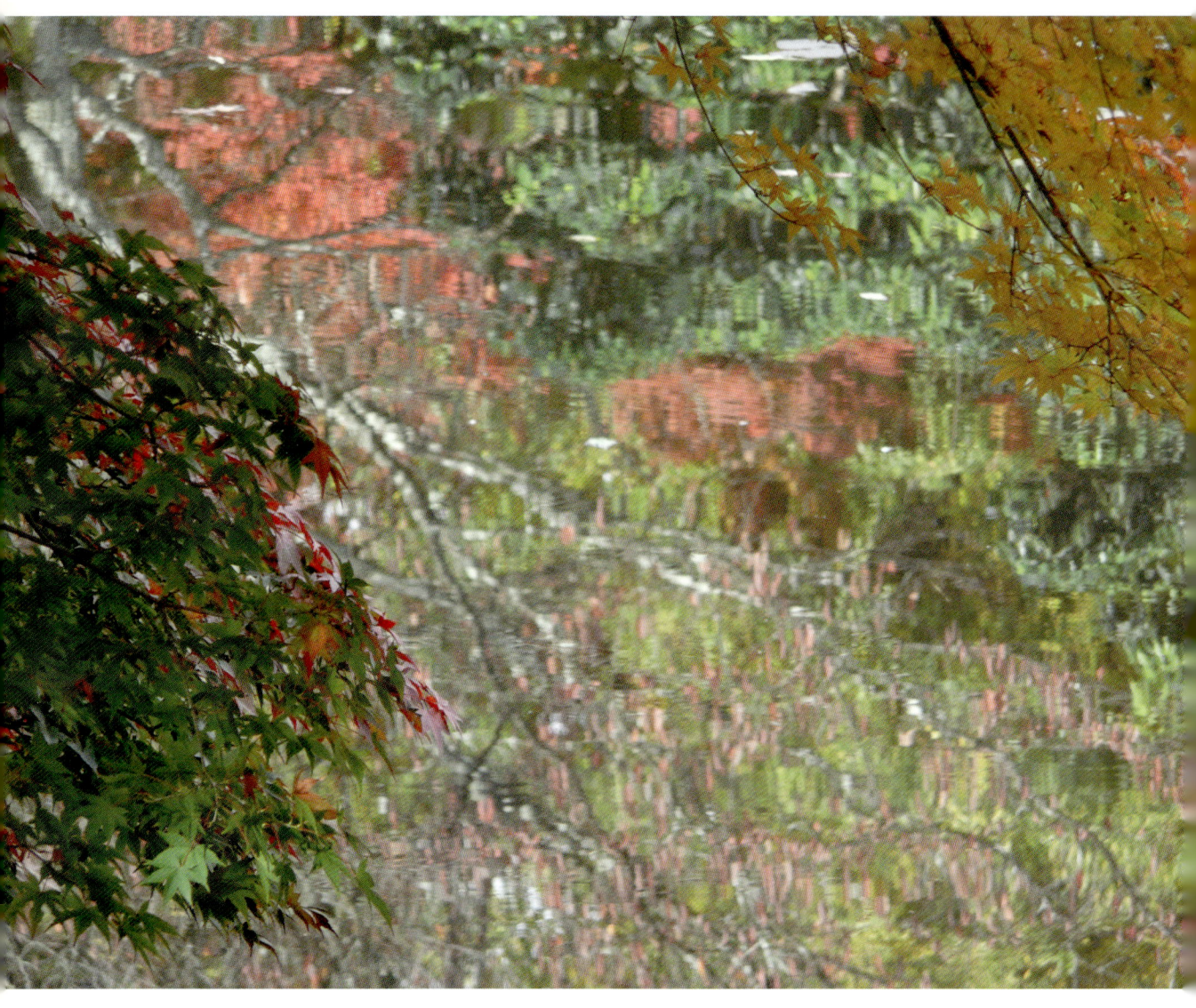

Ryōan-ji, Kyōyōchi Pond.

POSTSCRIPT

A Leaf

In a certain sense, the Zen garden is like a haiku. The very intuition of the instant is a form of narration, abstracted from the flux of time's passing, yet revealing the poignancy and profundity of the ephemeral. Equivocal spatiality and polymorphous temporality are unified and surpassed in a flash of inspiration, where metaphors ultimately disappear. Such intuition takes the narrative form not of the epic or the romance but of the haiku, depicting the few seconds that it takes a leaf to fall within the confines of the most durable gardens in history. The Zen garden is variously described as the site that makes possible such intuition, a symbol of this intuition, or as a manifestation of the intuition itself. It is all this, and more.

There is an oft-told story about Sen no Rikyū that exists in many versions, perhaps most famously in Okakura Kakuzō's *The Book of Tea*. One autumn day Rikyū watched as his son Shōan swept and watered the garden path. 'Not clean enough', insisted the master, time and again. After an hour, his son replied: 'Father, there is nothing more to be done. The steps have been washed for the third time, the stone lanterns and the trees are well sprinkled with water; moss and lichens are shining with a fresh verdure; not a twig, not a leaf have I left on the ground.' In response Rikyū exclaimed: 'Young fool, this is not the way a garden path should be swept', upon which he shook a maple tree, randomly scattering its crimson leaves.[1] Rikyū's famed pupil, Oribe, one of the greatest tea masters, went so far in his mannerism as to sweep his garden clean of leaves, and then sprinkle pine needles under deciduous trees. These tales have never been forgotten.

My first visit to Ryōgen-in took place early one morning in December 2007. The garden, brilliant in the matinal sunlight, revealed a curious detail: a single crimson maple leaf lay just alongside the left-most rock group. It is almost inconceivable that this could have been an omission during the morning cleaning because the autumnal maple leaf is revered in Japan, the subject of the greatest attention and admiration. Furthermore, nature herself could not have brought this gift, since the entire morning was of the utmost calm. One could only deduce that the novice, monk or gardener entrusted with cleaning and raking the garden that day – conscious or not of the famed tale of Rikyū – had placed this leaf on the otherwise immaculate gravel surface, perhaps in imitation of the unpredictable quality of nature, perhaps as a minimal and mannerist aesthetic gesture. This single leaf refocused the entire garden, not unlike the jar on a hill in Tennessee celebrated in the first stanza of Wallace Stevens's poem, 'Anecdote of the Jar'.[2] According to Zen aesthetics, the presence of this solitary leaf might suggest a drastic, even if ephemeral and aleatory, reconstitution of this garden's already sublime aesthetics. The brief moment of its fall unveils the potentiality of time, and its short trajectory traces the malleability of space. In the Zen garden, the fall of a leaf, a sudden rain, a ray of sunlight, a moonbeam, may offer aesthetic, religious or utopian possibilities hitherto unimaginable.

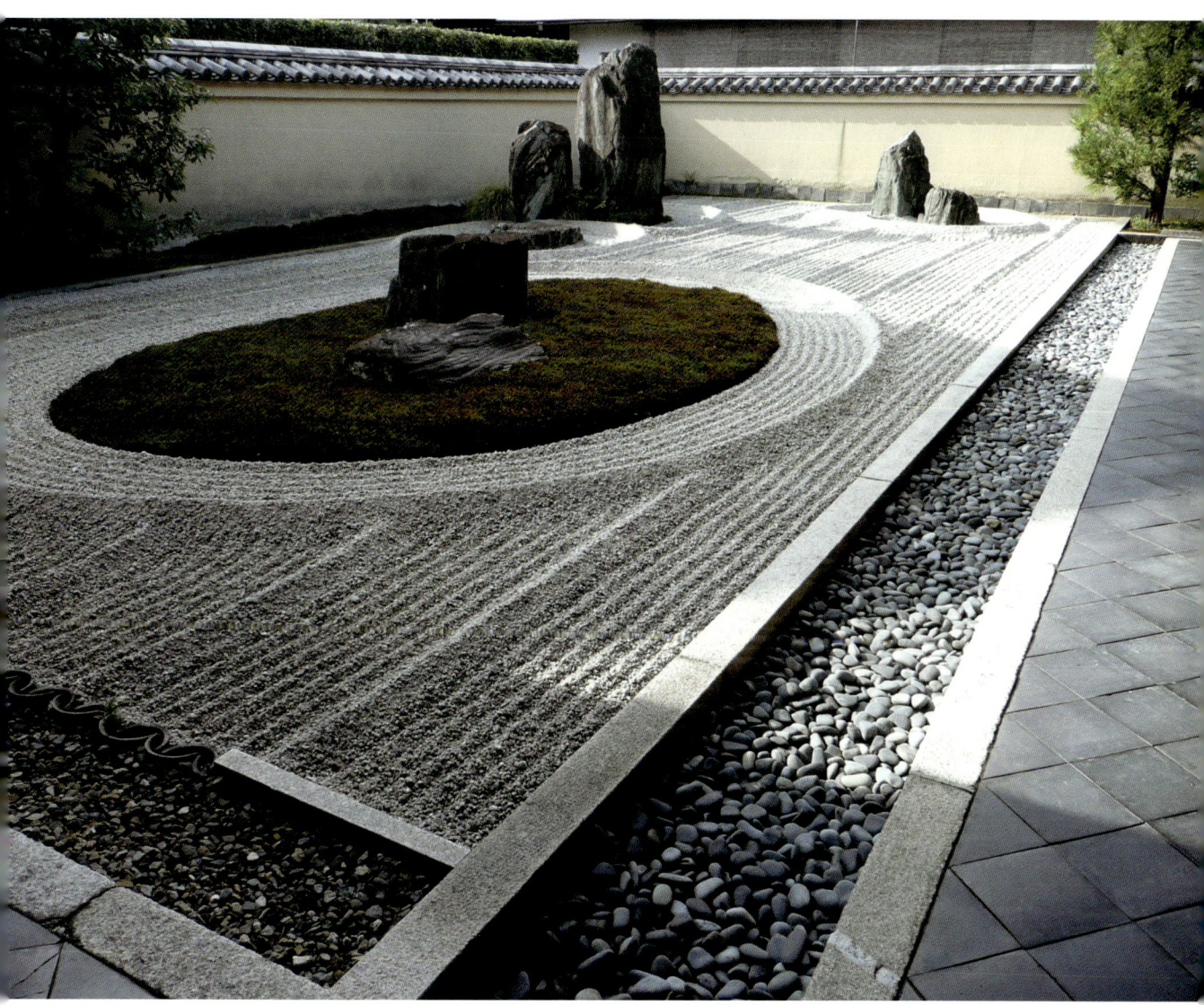

Ryōgen-in, a subtemple of Daitoku-ji.

REFERENCES

In the body of the text and in the Index, Japanese names follow the Japanese convention of family name first; in the References and Select Bibliography, names are listed as they appear in the publications, generally following the Western convention of family name last.

All gardens are located in Kyoto. All ceramics are post-2000 and from private collections, unless otherwise specified. Rather than note the exact size, which is often difficult given the irregular shape of much pottery, I would simply mention that all sake cups can fit comfortably into the palm of one hand, and most tea bowls into two cupped hands. (Several of the sake cups appear larger than life-size, and the tea bowls are all smaller than their actual size.)

INTRODUCTION TRANSFORMATIONS OF VISION

1 See Allen S. Weiss, *Mirrors of Infinity: The French Formal Garden and 17th-century Metaphysics* (New York, 1995); *Unnatural Horizons: Paradox and Contradiction in Landscape Architecture* (New York, 1998); *The Wind and the Source: In the Shadow of Mont Ventoux* (Albany, NY, 2005); *Varieties of Audio Mimesis: Musical Evocations of Landscape* (Los Angeles, 2008).

2 Throughout this book I refer to the Japanese dry garden (*karesansui*) as a Zen garden. I am well aware of the current revisionist trend that denies the influence of Zen on this tradition, and I hope that my work will add to the debate. Shoji Yamada, in *Shots in the Dark: Japan, Zen and the West*, trans. Earl Hartman (Chicago, 2009), argues that there is no historical evidence that the dry garden is a manifestation of Zen culture, and that this interpretation is a modern construct. While he convincingly reveals the lack of textual evidence for what has become a commonplace belief, it is nevertheless hard to believe that these gardens – originating in Zen temples and an integral part of their decor, framed by tea rooms and represented in paintings inspired by Buddhist iconography – are not integral to Zen-inspired culture. Here, a positivist concern with lack of textual evidence unfortunately obviates all other forms of hermeneutic endeavour. In response: (a) Why would everything in a temple complex *except* their gardens – commissioned by the priests at significant expense and requiring great effort in their creation, and occasionally designed by Zen priests themselves – be Zen inspired? (b) In any case, all Japanese art forms were a result of a vast syncretism, of which Zen is only a part, so to narrow down the issue to this degree is already to ask the wrong question. (c) There is a hermeneutic fallacy in reducing evidence uniquely to the textual and verbal, especially as the issue at stake concerns an iconic system, which is even more of a problem given that Zen is decidedly anti-cognitive. (d) Following the work of Aby Warburg, Irwin Panofsky, Ernst Cassirer and others, the symbolic implications of non-linguistic icons must certainly be taken into account.

3   Christine M. E. Guth, *Art, Tea, and Industry: Masuda Takashi and the Mitsui Circle* (Princeton, NJ, 1993), p. 64. For an excellent introduction to tea culture, see Jennifer L. Anderson, *An Introduction to Japanese Tea Ritual* (Albany, NY, 1991).

4   Haga Kōshirō, 'The *Wabi* Aesthetic Through the Ages', in *Tea in Japan*, ed. Paul Varley and Kumakura Isao (Honolulu, 1989), p. 197.

5   The term *chashitsu* means 'tea room' while *chaseki* more generally signifies 'a place for tea', which can be either a room, hut, pavilion or house, of varying dimensions.

6   Rupert A. Cox, *The Zen Arts: An Anthropological Study of the Culture of Aesthetic Form in Japan* (London, 2003).

7   Joseph D. Parker, *Zen Buddhist Landscape Arts of Early Muromachi Japan (1336–1573)*, (Albany, NY, 1999), p. 111.

8   Cited in Gregory P. A. Levine, *Daitokuji: The Visual Cultures of a Zen Monestary* (Seattle, 2005), p. 158.

9   Donald Keene, 'Japanese Aesthetics', in *Japanese Aesthetics and Culture*, ed. Nancy G. Hume (Albany, NY, 1995), p. 29.

10 Haga, 'The *Wabi* Aesthetic', pp. 195–9; D. T. Suzuki, *Zen and Japanese Culture* [1959] (New York, n.d.), p. 284.

11 See Edward S. Morse, *Japanese Homes and Their Surroundings* [1886] (New York, 1961), pp. 34 and 199.

12 Donald Richie, *A Tractate on Japanese Aesthetics* (Berkeley, CA, 2007), pp. 44–6.

13 An excellent recent study discusses the relation between the aesthetic and culinary significance of astringency in Japanese culture, Ryoko Sekiguchi, *L'Astringent* (Paris, 2012).

14 Suzuki, *Zen and Japanese Culture*, p. 285.

15 In conversation, Michael Lazarin has pointed out that only things that were once exquisite can acquire *wabi-sabi*, for example, a ceramic doll, but not a plastic doll. But not all exquisite things can become *wabi-sabi*: jade can but not diamonds; the concrete walls of Andō Tadao are from the start *shibui*, but concrete can never become *wabi-sabi*. Thus, a *chashitsu* made of *hinoki* and *sugi* can become *wabi-sabi*; a knotty-pine cabin will not likely ever be *shibui* or become *wabi-sabi*.

16 See Cox, *The Zen Arts*.

17 Suzuki, *Zen and Japanese Culture*, pp. 304–5.

18 Richard L. Wilson, *The Art of Ogata Kenzan* (New York, 1991), p. 195.

19 See the essays in Varley and Isao, eds, *Tea in Japan*, and Hume, ed., *Japanese Aesthetics and Culture*.

20 Louise Allison Cort, *Shigaraki: Potters' Valley* (Bangkok, 2001), p. 129.

21 Ibid., p. 128. Recent revisionist research has suggested that the relation between Rikyū and Chōjirō is more originary myth than historical fact, but this hardly mitigates the vast importance of the relationship, whatever be the ratio of fact to fiction, within the history of the tea ceremony. See the exemplary historical study, Morgan Pitelka, *Handmade Culture: Raku Potters, Patrons, and Tea Practicners in Japan* (Honolulu, 2005), to which this section of my book is indebted.

22 Ostentation is of course relative; compared to traditional Chinese forms as interpreted by the Heian court, the tea ceremony under the regent and the shoguns might appear austere, but at the same time, compared to *wabi-sabi* tea, the gold tea room and tea set owned by Hideyoshi, and his tea ceremony for thousands of connoisseurs at Kitano, cannot but be deemed extremely flamboyant.

23 Robert Smithson, 'Discussions with Heizer, Oppenheim, Smithson' [1970], in *Robert Smithson: The Collected Writings*, ed. Jack Flam (Los Angeles, 1996), p. 251.

24 Allen S. Weiss, 'In Praise of Anachronism', in *Unnatural Horizons: Paradox and Contradiction in Landscape Arcitecture* (New York, 1998), pp. 108–53.

25 See Robert D. Mowry, ed., *Worlds Within Worlds: The Richard Rosenblum Collection of Chinese Scholar's Rocks*, exh. cat., Harvard University Art Museums, Cambridge, MA (1997).

26 See Vincent T. Covello and Yuji Yoshimura, *The Japanese Art of Stone Appreciation: Suiseki and Its Use with Bonsai* (Rutland, VT, 1984).

27 Parker, *Zen Buddhist Landscape Arts*, p. 136.

28 See the engraving from Akisato Rito, *Illustrated Guide to Famous Gardens in Kyoto* [1799], reproduced in Hiroshi Onishi, Takemitsu Oba and Sondra Castile, *Immortals and Sages: Paintings from Ryoanji Temple* (New York, 1993), p. 14. Sāno Touemon is mentioned in Dore Ashton, *Noguchi: East and West* (New York, 1992), p. 43.

29 The revision of the iconographic history of Ryōan-ji proposed in the revelatory publication by Onishi, Oba and Castile, *Immortals and Sages*, is quite recent, based on the discovery in 1989 that four previously unidentified Momoyama-era (1570–1610) sliding wall-panel paintings acquired by the Metropolitain Museum in New York had originally been created for the Abbot's temple of Ryōan-ji. My analysis is totally indebted to this groundbreaking work.

30 Hiroshi Onishi, 'Chinese Lore for Japanese Spaces', in Onishi, Oba and Castile, *Immortals and Sages*, p. 41.

31 Parker, *Zen Buddhist Landscape Arts*, pp. 190–96; see this work for a detailed study of Zen syncretism, especially in relation to its Chinese origins, and for a discussion of the theological implications of aesthetic miniaturization.

ONE TRANSIENT SYMBOLS

1 D. T. Suzuki, *Zen and Japanese Culture* [1959] (New York, n.d.), pp. 339–40.

2 Cited ibid., p. 258.

3 Ibid., p. 393.

4 Murata Shukō, cited in Haga Kōshirō, 'The Wabi Aesthetic Through the Ages', in *Tea in Japan*, ed. Paul Varley and Kumakura Isao (Honolulu, 1989), p. 197.

5 Yoel Hoffmann, trans. and ed., *Japanese Death Poems* (Rutland, VT, and Tokyo, 1986), p. 138.

6 Theodor W. Adorno, 'Cultural Criticism and Society', in *Prisms*, trans. Samuel and Shierry Weber (Cambridge, MA, 1967), p. 19. On the most recent catastrophe, see Michaël Ferrier, *Fukushima: Récit d'une catastrophe* (Paris, 2012).

7 John Felstiner, *Paul Celan: Poet, Survivor, Jew* (New Haven, CT, 1995), p. 31.

8 Shikibu Murasaki, *The Tale of Genji* [11th century], trans. Royall Tyler (New York, 2000), p. 178.

9 Edward S. Morse, *Japanese Homes and Their Surroundings* [1886] (New York, 1961), pp. 286–7.

10 Cited in David A. Slawson, *Secret Teachings in the Art of Japanese Gardens: Design Principles, Aesthetic Values* (Tokyo, 1987), p. 146.

11 Hijikata performed at Sōgetsu several times, beginning in 1961.

12 In conversation, Michael Lazarin suggests that the atomic bomb was not just a destruction in space but also through time, since generations live as pariahs due to fear of radiation-induced genetic defects, and he fears that the same will be true for the victims of Fukushima. On the topic, see the recent book by Michaël Ferrier, *Fukushima: Récit d'un désastre* (Paris, 2012).

13 Isozaki Arata, *Japan-ness in Architecture* (Cambridge, MA, 2006), p. 87.

14 Ibid., p. 88.

15 Ibid.

16 Donald Richie, *A Tractate on Japanese Aesthetics* (Berkeley, CA, 2007), pp. 44–6.

17 Isozaki, *Japan-ness in Architecture*, p. 88.

18 Ibid., pp. 99–100.

19 Cited in Louise Allison Cort, *Shigaraki: Potters' Valley* (Bangkok, 2001), p. 297.

20 Ibid.

21 Bert Winther-Tamaki, 'The Ceramic Art of Isamu Noguchi: A Close Embrace of the Earth', in *Isamu Noguchi and Modern Japanese Ceramics: A Close Embrace of the Earth*, ed. Louise Allison Cort and Bert Winther-Tamaki, exh. cat., Arthur M. Sackler Gallery of the Smithsonian Institute, Washington, DC (Berkeley, CA, and London, 2003), p. 63.

22 Cort, *Shigaraki*, p. 112.

23 Ibid.

24 Yasushi Inoue, *Le Maître de thé* [1981] (Paris, 2009), p. 150 (translation by Allen S. Weiss). One of the best accounts of the life of Rikyū is given in the recent novel by Kenichi Yamamoto, *Le Secret du maître de thé*, trans. Yoko Kawada-Sim and Silvain Chupin (Paris, 2012).

25 A. L. Sadler, *The Japanese Tea Ceremony* (Rutland, VT, 2008), p. 30.

26 See Hoffman, *Japanese Death Poems*.

27 Yokoya Hideko, 'Interview with Koie Ryoji' (2002), published on Robert Yellin's website www.e-yakimono.net; republished on www.ceramicstoday.com.

28 I would like to thank Michael Lazarin for this observation.

29 Teiji Itoh, *Space and Illusion in the Japanese Garden* (New York, Toyko and Kyoto, 1973), p. 73. The Japanese taste for miniaturization is evident in the little-studied art of *suiseki*, miniature landscapes resembling diverse forms of Japanese gardens, created around pebble-sized stones. The term *suiseki*, or 'water stone', is a contradiction in terms which is at the core of the symbolism of the Zen garden.

30 Paul Claudel, *L'Oiseau noir dans le soleil levant* [1929] (Paris, 1974), p. 191. The earthquake occurred on 1 September 1923; Japan traditionally followed a unisolar calendar (until the Gregorian calendar was adapted during the Meiji period in 1873), thus at Claudel's time the

September moon and its poetic symbolism would still have been considered that of early autumn. The discrepancy between these two calendars occasionally creates confusion, especially in modern descriptions of ancient scenes.

31 Murasaki Shikibu, *The Tale of Genji*, p. 11.

TWO ON THE CIRCULATION OF METAPHOR

1 Charles Baudelaire, letter to Armand Fraisse, 19 February 1860, cited in Walter Benjamin, *Paris, capitale du XIXe siècle*, trans. Jean Lacoste (Paris, 1993), p. 336.

2 Gary Snyder, *The Practice of the Wild* (New York, 1990), p. 17.

3 Cited in François Cheng, *Souffle-Esprit: Textes théoriques chinois sur l'art pictural* [1989] (Paris, 2006), pp. 37–8 (translation by Allen S. Weiss). In the West, we would need to await Monet, Turner and Whistler for such images.

4 Maurice Pinguet, 'Paul Claudel exégète du Japon' [1969], in *Le Texte Japon*, ed. Michaël Ferrier (Paris, 2009), p. 99 (translation by Allen S. Weiss).

5 Michel Foucault has shown how the medieval European system of classification of the natural world was in fact a function of resemblances, a worldview transformed by the beginnings of scientific investigation and the new order of things that resulted. See the section on classifying in *The Order of Things* [1966] (New York, 1970), pp. 125–65.

6 See Matsuo Bashō, *Friches*, trans. René Sieffert (Paris, 1992), pp. 72 and 200, and Mrs Paul Kincaid, *Japanese Garden and Floral Art* (New York, 1966), pp. 47–50, for precise details about the seven grasses; certain aliments, such as the highly prized sea bream, even bear a different name for each season.

7 Augustin Berque, *Le Sauvage et l'artifice: Les Japonais devant la nature* (Paris, 1986), pp. 21–4.

8 Ibid., p. 77 (translation by Allen S. Weiss).

9 Joseph D. Parker, *Zen Buddhist Landscape Arts of Early Muromachi Japan (1336–1573)* (Albany, NY, 1999), p. 18.

10 Ibid., p. 19.

11 Yoshi Oida and Lorna Marshall, *The Invisible Actor* (London, 1997), p. 48.

12 Shikibu Murasaki, *The Tale of Genji* [11th century], trans. Royall Tyler (New York, 2000), p. 117.

13 Ibid., p. 137.

14 Berque, *Le Sauvage et l'artifice*, pp. 288–91 (translation by Allen S. Weiss).

15 Paul Claudel, *L'Oiseau noir dans le soleil levant* [1929] (Paris, 1974), p. 172.

16 Cited in Christine M. E. Guth, *Art Tea and Industry: Masuda Takashi and the Mitsui Circle* (Princeton, NJ, 1993), p. 61.

17 Sasaki Sanmi, *Chado, The Way of Tea: A Japanese Tea Master's Almanac*, trans. Shaun McCabe and Iwasaki Satoko (Rutland, VT, 2005), p. 87.

18 Ibid., pp. 86 and 91.

19 See Hiroichi Tsutsui, 'The Development of Formal Tea Cuisine', *Chanoyu Quarterly*, L (1987), pp. 40–57.

20 Murata Yoshihiro, *Kaiseki: The Exquisite Cuisine of Kyoto's Kikunoi Restaurant* (Tokyo, 2006), p. 16.

21 Michaël Ferrier, *Sympathie pour le fantôme* (Paris, 2010), pp. 94–6 (translation by Allen S. Weiss).

22 Cited in Dore Ashton, *Noguchi: East and West* (New York, 1992), p. 256.

23 The metaphoricity is even more precise, as there are also numerous subcategories of *keshiki*, for example *sekkei*, snowy landscapes. See Robert Yellin's extremely informative website www.e-yakimono.net. It is interesting to note that in English-language catalogues on Japanese pottery, such metaphoric landscape effects are downplayed, if not completely ignored. This is a prime example of how the exigencies and limits of one aesthetic and epistemological system skew the understanding of another.

24 Louise Allison Cort, *Shigaraki: Potters' Valley* (Bangkok, 2001), p. 5.

25 Kakuzo Okakura, *The Book of Tea* [1906] (New York, 1964), p. 59.

26 Illustrated in Gabriele Fahr-Becker, *Ryokan: A Japanese Tradition* (Königswinter, 2005), p. 45.

27 Sōfū Teshigahara, *This Boundless World of Flowers and Form* (Tokyo, 1966), p. 109.

28 Murata, *Kaiseki*, pp. 106–7 and 138–9; see also Kenji Ekuan, *The Aesthetics of the Japanese Lunchbox* (Cambridge, MA, 1998). An excellent volume on Japanese food presentation and its relation to pottery is Yoshio Tsuchiya, *The Fine Art of Japanese Food Arrangement* (Tokyo, 2002); for more avant-garde possibilities, see Hisayuki Tekeuchi, *Nouvelle cuisine japonaise* (Paris, 2003).

29 Paul Ricoeur, *Temps et récit* (Paris, 1983), vol. I, p. 76 (translation by Allen S. Weiss); on metaphoricity in landscape, see Allen S. Weiss, *The Wind and the Source* (Albany, NY, 2005).

30 For an excellent introduction, see Louise Boudonnat and Harumi Kushizaki, *Traces of the Brush: The Art of Japanese Calligraphy*, trans. Charles Penwarden (San Francisco, 2003).

31 Joseph M. Kitagawa, 'The Japanese *Kokutai* (National Community): History and Myth', *History of Religions*, XIII (1974), p. 224; cited in *Tea in Japan*, ed. Paul Varley and Kumakura Isao (Honolulu, 1989), p. 91.

32 Morgan Pitelka, 'Rikyō and Chōjirō in Japanese Tea Culture', in *The Culture of Copying in Japan*, ed. Rupert Cox (New York, 2008), p. 129.

33 I came to the same conclusion concerning representation in music and sound art, as expressed in Allen S. Weiss, *Varieties of Audio Mimesis: Musical Evocations of Landscape* (Los Angeles, 2008).

34 Gregory P. A. Levine, *Daitokuji: The Visual Cultures of a Zen Monestary* (Seattle, 2005), p. 254.

35 Thomas Hoover, *Zen Culture* (New York, 1977), p. 105.

36 Ibid., p. 110.

37 François Berthier, *Reading Zen in the Rocks*, trans. Graham Parkes (Chicago, 2000), pp. 63 and 41.

38 D. T. Suzuki, *Zen and Japanese Culture* [1959] (New York, n.d.), p. 220.

39 Ever since the landmark exhibition 'The Spiritual in Art: Abstract Painting, 1890–1985', Los Angeles County Museum of Art, 1986, until the 'Aux origines de l'abstraction, 1800–1914' (Paris, Musée d'Orsay, 2003), even the most seemingly recondite abstraction

has been seen to contain some level of representation, whether physical or metaphysical. The earliest allegorical readings of the stone arrangements at Ryōan-ji claim that it represents a mother tiger crossing a river with her cubs, taken from an ancient Chinese myth. This univocal sort of interpretation seeking absolute clarity, long abandoned, is at the antipodes of the current iconoclastic ones, intended to plunge us into Zen paradox.

40 Berque, *Le Sauvage et l'artifice*, p. 27 (translation by Allen S. Weiss). Consider in this regard the ground-breaking exhibition at the Centre Pompidou in Paris by Arato Isozaki, 'Ma: Space-Time in Japan' (Paris, 1978), discussed in his book *Japan-ness in Architecture*, trans. Kohso Sabu (Cambridge, MA, 2006), pp. 93–100. There exist nine levels of Noh performance, with snow falling in a silver bowl the seventh and the sun shining at night the highest. Translations of such terms are always complex: *kū* is literally 'sky', so the void here might be taken in the sense of aether; *mu* connotes nothingness as transience rather than privation.

41 Murasaki, *The Tale of Genji*, p. 373.

42 William Theodore de Bary, 'The Vocabulary of Japanese Aesthetics', in *Japanese Aesthetics and Culture*, ed. Nancy G. Hume (Albany, NY, 1995), p. 53.

43 Cited in Haga Kōshirō, 'The Wabi Aesthetic Through the Ages', in *Tea in Japan*, ed. Paul Varley and Kumakura Isao (Honolulu, 1989), p. 214.

44 Rupert A. Cox, *The Zen Arts: An Anthropological Study of the Culture of Aesthetic Form in Japan* (Abingdon and New York, 2003).

45 See Daniel Charles, 'Gloses sur le Ryōan-ji', in *Gloses sur John Cage* (Paris, 1978), pp. 269–88.

46 Günter Nitschke, *The Architecture of the Japanese Garden: Right Angle and Natural Form* (Cologne, 1991), p. 115.

47 Ibid., p. 92.

THREE ZEN MOUNTAINS, ZEN WATER

1 The modern garden at Zuihō-in, created by Shigemori Mirei, is extremely innovative. One striking feature is the form of the fields of gravel, which strongly resemble sand traps on golf courses. This seemingly iconoclastic observation is in fact not too strange, given that Shigemori designed many residential and commercial gardens and that landscape architecture has always incorporated quotidian as well as symbolic forms. The extent to which golf courses have come to dot the post-war Japanese landscape is striking, and it should not be surprising to find their unique forms incorporated into gardens.

2 Lafcadio Hearn, *Kokoro: Hints and Echoes of Japanese Inner Life* [1895] (Rutland, VT, 1972), p. 260.

3 Ibid., p. 214.

4 André Leroi-Gourhan, *Le Geste et la parole* (Paris, 1964), vol. II, p. 214 (translation by Allen S. Weiss).

5 Ibid., p. 214.

6 Jim Holt, 'The Mind of a Rock', *New York Times Magazine*, 18 November 2007, pp. 19–20.

7   Günter Nitschke, *The Architecture of the Japanese Garden: Right Angle and Natural Form* (Cologne, 1991), p. 119.

8   Teiji Itoh, *Space and Illusion in the Japanese Garden* (New York, Tokyo and Kyoto, 1973), p. 48.

9   François Cheng, *Souffle-Esprit: Textes théoriques chinois sur l'art pictural* [1989] (Paris, 2006), pp. 69–70, 129; see also François Cheng, *Vide et plein: Le Langage pictural chinois* (Paris, 1991), p. 133.

10 Cheng, *Souffle-Esprit*, p. 166.

11 Loraine Kuck, *The World of the Japanese Garden* (New York and Tokyo, 1968), p. 153.

12 Bernard Rudofsky, *The Kimono Mind* (New York, 1965), p. 234. An egregious error is to be found on pp. 236–7, namely a two-page reproduction of an engraving bearing the following caption: 'The notorious sand garden of Ryôanji Temple near Kyoto. The dotted lines of the woodcut convey the eerie beauty of the sand patterns far better than do photographs. From an undated garden book.' Apparently Rudofsky's sense of 'architecture without architects' (to cite the title of his most famous book) was far more accurate than that of his eye for gardens with gardeners, as neither the sand patterns, the stone formations and groupings, nor even the form of the garden, resemble Ryōan-ji. Even if the error is in the engraving, it is also in his eye.

13 Cited in Graham Parkes, 'The Role of Rock in the Japanese Dry Landscape Garden', postface to François Berthier, *Reading Zen in the Rocks*, trans. Graham Parkes (Chicago, 2000), p. 104. This passion continued into modern times, as evidenced by the small fortunes paid for extraordinary stones, for example the huge *sajiishi* stone from Tottori prefecture that painter Kaho Akira waited twenty years to obtain and for which he paid 20 million yen, as recounted in Michael Freeman, *The Modern Japanese Garden* (Rutland, VT, and Tokyo, 2002), p. 45.

14 Marc Peter Keane, *The Art of Setting Stones* (Berkeley, CA, 2002), p. 134. See also his *Japanese Garden Design* (Tokyo and Boston, MA, 1996).

15 Cited in David A. Slawson, *Secret Teachings in the Art of Japanese Gardens: Design Principles, Aesthetic Values* (Tokyo, 1987), pp. 146–7. On the creation of dry waterfall scenes, see Masuno Shunmyo, 'Arranging a "Dry Waterfall"', in *The New Zen Garden*, ed. Joseph Cali (New York and Tokyo, 2004), pp. 58–9.

16 Steve McCaffery, 'A Chapter of Accidents', *Public*, 33 (2006), p. 69.

17 In Katsuhiko Mizuno, *Landscapes for Small Places: Japanese Courtyard Gardens*, trans. John Bester (Tokyo, 2002), pp. 100 and 67 respectively, we find both a contemporary version of a mythical landscape, namely the floating island of Mount Sumeru in the garden of Hashimoto Teru Orimono, and a representation of the contemporary Japanese landscape in the garden of the Matsumura residence, where all the materials come from the Kyoto area, and the garden itself represents the Kyoto basin.

18 Itoh, *Space and Illusion*, p. 27.

19 Isamu Noguchi, 'Guggenheim Proposal', in *Isamu Noguchi: Essays and Conversations*, ed. Diane Apostolos-Cappadona and Bruce Altshuler (New York, 1994), pp. 16–17.

20 Bert Winther-Tamaki, 'The Ceramic Art of Isamu Noguchi: A Close Embrace of the Earth',

in *Isamu Noguchi and Modern Japanese Ceramics*, ed. Louise Allison Cort and Bert Winther-Tamaki, exh. cat., Arthur M. Sackler Gallery of the Smithsonian Institute, Washington, DC (Berkeley, CA, and London, 2003), p. 63.

21 Jeff Shapiro, email communication with the author, 2008.

22 See Masakazu Kusakabe and Marc Lancet, *Japanese Wood-fired Ceramics* (Iola, WI, 2005), p. 57.

23 Winther-Tamaki, 'The Ceramic Art of Isamu Noguchi', p. 52.

24 Cited in Shoji Yamada, *Shots in the Dark: Japan, Zen and the West*, trans. Earl Hartman (Chicago, 2009), p. 167.

25 Gary Snyder, *The Practice of the Wild* (New York, 1990), pp. 101–2.

26 Augustin Berque, *Le Sauvage et l'artifice: Les Japonais devant la nature* (Paris, 1986), p. 75.

27 Cheng, *Souffle-Esprit*, p. 174.

28 Cited ibid., p. 76.

29 Cited ibid., p. 58.

30 Cited in Slawson, *Secret Teachings*, p. 71.

31 Cited ibid., p. 74.

32 Cited in Dore Ashton, *Noguchi: East and West* (New York, 1992), p. 260.

33 Since photography is generally not permitted at Daisen-in and Obai-in, the accompanying illustration is of Tōfuku-ji.

34 One site which was designed specifically to be viewed from the sky is Shigemori Mirei's garden for the castle of Kishiwada-jo near Osaka, created in 1953; see Christian Tschumi, *Mirei Shigemori: Modernizing the Japanese Garden* (Berkeley, CA, 2005), pp. 34–43

35 On the aesthetics of moss, see Véronique Brindeau, *Louange des mousses* (Paris, 2012).

36 Cited in David Toop, *Haunted Weather: Music, Silence and Memory* (London, 2004), p. 46. It was John Cage who first incorporated 'small sounds', those needing amplification in order to be heard, into music; many contemporary musicians, Japanese and others, are fascinated by sonic extremes, both loud and soft, as discussed in David Toop, *Ocean of Sound: Aether Talk, Ambient Sound and Imaginary Worlds* (London, 1995).

37 Toop, *Haunted Weather*, p. 46.

38 Yasunari Kawabata, 'The Hat Incident' [1926], in *Palm-of-the-Hand Stories*, trans. Lane Dunlop and J. Martin Holman (San Francisco, 1988), p. 65.

39 Hiroshi Teshigahara, cited in Dore Ashton, *The Delicate Thread* (Tokyo and New York, 1997), p. 95.

40 Leonard Bernstein, *The Unanswered Question* (Cambridge, MA, 1976), p. 424. The magnum opus on the chthonic basis of music remains Friedrich Nietzsche, *The Birth of Tragedy* (1872). For a broad assessment of the symbolism of music, see Victor Zuckerkandle, *Sound and Symbol: Music and the External World*, trans. Willard R. Trask (Princeton, NJ, 1956), and Allen S. Weiss, *Varieties of Audio Mimesis: Musical Evocations of Landscape* (Los Angeles, 2008).

41 Shikibu Murasaki, *The Tale of Genji* [11th century], trans. Royall Tyler (New York, 2000), p. 641. In traditional Japanese culture, cricket listening was a classic early autumn activity, and even today bamboo cricket cages can be found in markets everywhere. This interest led

to particular discrimination in their musical qualities, such that the different sorts of crickets – notably pine crickets and bell crickets – were evaluated for the beauty of their song; see Murasaki, *The Tale of Gengi*, pp. 709–16.

42 A. L. Sadler, *The Japanese Tea Ceremony*, (Rutland, VT, 2008), p. 67.

43 Yasunari Kawabata, *Snow Country* [1956], trans. Edward G. Seidensticker (New York, 1960), p. 127.

44 Kakuzo Okakura, *The Book of Tea* [1906] (New York, 1964), p. 35.

45 Sadler, *The Japanese Tea Ceremony*, p. 152.

46 Murasaki, *The Tale of Genji*, p. 471.

47 Ibid., p. 471, n. 18.

48 D. T. Suzuki, *Zen and Japanese Culture* [1959] (New York, n.d.), p. 274.

49 Cited in Kumakura Isao, 'Sen no Rikyū: Inquiries into His Life and Tea', in *Tea in Japan*, ed. Paul Varley and Kumakura Isao (Honolulu, 1989), p. 62.

50 John Cage interviewed by Daniel Charles, in John Cage, *For the Birds: John Cage in Conversation with Daniel Charles* (Boston, MA, 1981), p. 222.

51 This is perhaps best illustrated by Cage's *Williams Mix* (1952), a work of *musique concrète* consisting of a micro-montage of very short segments of assorted taped sounds. The nearly regular metre caused by the rapid cuts frames the infinitely rich and varied metres of the taped sounds; see Allen S. Weiss, *Phantasmic Radio* (Durham, NC, 1995), pp. 35–55.

52 The turning point in the plot of *Woman in the Dunes* is when the protagonist discovers that what he had intended as a crow trap – a small covered barrel buried in the sand – actually functions as a well, which motivates him to remain in the village. Fascinated by the discovery of water, he abandons the plot to attach a call for help to a crow's leg. It is interesting that this apparatus appears as and functions like a *suikinkutsu*, and that this is one of the rare moments in the film when the soundtrack is somewhat aquatic.

53 The quotation is from two emails received from Steven Feld in 2008; the work was released on his album *Suikinkutsu* (VoxLox 106, 2006).

54 From a letter from Steven Feld to the author dated 30 September 2008.

55 Okakura, *The Book of Tea*, p. 64.

56 Matsuo Bashō, *The Narrow Road to the Deep North* [1694], trans. Nobuyuki Yuasa (London, 1966), p. 123.

four Cracks

1 Cited in David A. Slawson, *Secret Teachings in the Art of Japanese Gardens: Design Principles, Aesthetic Values* (Tokyo, 1987), p. 146.

2 Recounted in Teiji Itoh, *Space and Illusion in the Japanese Garden* (New York, Toyko and Kyoto, 1973), p. 28. On climate and gardens, see Allen S. Weiss, 'Obituary to the Trees of Versailles', *Architecture New York*, 27 (2000), n.p., accompanied by Toby Glanville's photographs depicting the destroyed trees of Versailles in January 2000. On a somewhat more gentle note, I would once again point to the remarkable photographs of Mizuno Katsuhiko,

who has depicted the Zen garden under varied meteorological conditions, including the always picturesque fog and the rarely represented snow.

3 Cited in Slawson, *Secret Teachings*, p. 173.

4 This would suggest the incursion of a Shinto *kami* into the Buddhist garden. However, this is not as far-fetched as it may appear, given the syncretism of Japanese religion. We are told that in the eighth century the god Hachimen revealed through an oracle that he wished to be moved from Usa in western Japan to the capital. This transfer was made with great pomp, and he was installed in a specially constructed shrine in one of the palaces, officiated over by Buddhist priests. G. B. Sansom, *Japan: A Short Cultural History* [1931] (Stanford, CA, 1978), p. 183.

5 Murielle Hladik, *Traces et fragments dans l'esthétique japonaise* (Wavre, 2008), p. 180. The 'house surgery' was most probably inspired by Arata Isozaki's writings, curatorial work and architectural practice, as described in the chapter '*Ma* [Interstice] and Rubble', in Isozaki, *Japan-ness in Architecture*, trans. Kohso Sabu (Cambridge, MA, 2006), pp. 81–100.

6 The best English-language source for visualizing Japanese pottery surface effects is Masakazu Kusakabe and Marc Lancet, *Japanese Wood-fired Ceramics* (Iola, WI, 2005).

7 Kaii Higashiyama, *Les Quatre saisons de Kyôto* [1969], trans. Ryōji Nakamura and René de Ceccatty (Paris, 2007), p. 188.

8 In this regard, art theories inspired by gestalt psychology are particularly useful, notably Hans Prinzhorn, *Artistry of the Mentally Ill* [1922], trans. Erik von Brockdorff (Berlin, 1968).

9 There were, of course, crackled glazes in Korea and Vietnam, but such considerations are beyond the reach of this study.

10 Miyeko Murase, ed., *Turning Point: Oribe and the Arts of Sixteenth-century Japan* (New York, 2003), pp. 108–9; it is perhaps not by coincidence that Christianity was strongly present in the Kyoto tea milieu of the period, and it is believed that Oribe himself might have converted.

11 Cited in A. L. Sadler, *The Japanese Tea Ceremony* (Rutland, VT, 2008), p. 112.

12 See Yanagi Sōetsu, *The Unknown Craftsman* [1972], adapted by Bernard Leach (Tokyo and New York, 1989), p. 190. One might also note the importance of broken forms in pottery historiography: the most ancient of all Japanese pottery, the cord-patterned Jōmon works (the earliest-known pottery in the world, dating from the fourteenth millennium BCE, which along with the later Yayoi period pottery is widely considered to be one of the paradigms of Japanese artistic forms) is known mainly from fragments.

13 Kumakura Isao, 'Kan'ei Culture and *Chanoyu*', in *Tea in Japan*, ed. Paul Varley and Kumakura Isao (Honolulu, 1989), p. 141.

14 Compiled from Sadler, *The Japanese Tea Ceremony*, pp. 79, 127, 130, 153, 201, 204.

15 There are many reasons for wilfully damaging pottery. Katagiri Sadaaki, a tea master and antiques connoisseur, once found a very fine antique Chinese chamber pot in an old inn. After much insistence he bought it from the owner, only to have his assistant destroy it, claiming that he wanted to avoid the possibility that some other connoisseur might mistake it for a water jar and purchase it at a high price, and then use it in the tea ceremony, where its former uncleanness would make it an abomination. Ibid., p. 201.

16 Yanagi, *The Unknown Craftsman*, p. 224.

17 Cited in Yoshiaki Inui, *Hiroshi Teshigahara: Works, 1978–1987* (Tokyo, 1987), p. 255.

18 Email communication with Robert Yellin, 2008, see his extremely rich website on Japanese pottery, www.e-yakimono.net.

19 Cees Nooteboom, *Rituals* [1980], trans. Adrienne Dixon (Baton Rouge, LA, 1983), p. 133.

20 Ibid., p. 143. We find a similar gesture at the end of Kenichi Yamamoto's novel, *Le Secret du maître de thé*, trans. Yoko Kawada-Sim and Silvain Chupin (Paris, 2102), where we find that after the suicide of the tea master, his wife smashes his most cherished possession, a tea caddy that was given to him by his first love.

21 Compare the innovative exhibition curated by James Bernauer at the McMullen Museum of Art in Boston, 'Fragmented Devotion: Medieval Objects from the Schnütgen Museum, Cologne' (2000), where the religious objects are exhibited in three different settings to reflect their complex destiny: public and private devotional settings of the Middle Ages; a room simulating Schnütgen's own nineteenth-century private exhibition space; and a white cube recalling the modern space of the Schnütgen Museum created in 1932.

22 Yasunari Kawabata, *Thousand Cranes* [1958], trans. Edward G. Seidensticker (New York, 1981), p. 140.

23 Ibid., p. 72.

FIVE POTTERY LANDSCAPES

1 M.F.K. Fisher, 'Serve it Forth' [1937], in *The Art of Eating* (New York, 1976), p. 41. We tend to refer to sake as rice wine, but it is technically brewed more like a beer. While there exist sparkling sakes, unfiltered sakes of milky opacity, and even red sakes coloured by a particular strain of rice, they constitute a tiny minority.

2 An excellent introduction to Zen art is Stephen Addiss, *The Art of Zen* (New York, 1989).

3 This brings up the issue of the recent trend of drinking chilled sake. Until well into the second half of the twentieth century, probably around the 1980s, sake had always been drunk warm, even hot (hot sake is called *atsukan* or *joukan*, warm sake *nurukan*, chilled sake *reishu*, and the relatively rare sake over ice is called 'cold falling snow'). Certainly one of the reasons was the fact that Japanese habitations were so sparely heated in winter that any means of getting warm was most welcome. Warm sake also enters the bloodstream somewhat more quickly, and thus hastens inebriation. The trend of drinking chilled sake would seem to have three major reasons: the widespread modern heating of buildings; the taste for white wine that developed with increased culinary interchange following the inception of French nouvelle cuisine, which was itself deeply influenced by Japanese cuisine (with many culinary interchanges between the two countries beginning in the 1960s); and the discovery of sake as another domain in which luxury and prestige goods could be produced, since drinking sake chilled permits much greater taste discrimination.

4 Among the most informative sources in English on contemporary Japanese pottery, including many examples of *guinomi* and *chawan*, is Anneliese Crueger, Wulf Crueger and Saeko Itō,

Modern Japanese Ceramics: Pathways of Innovation and Tradition (New York, 2004).

5 Murata Yoshihiro, *Kaiseki: The Exquisite Cuisine of Kyoto's Kikunoi Restaurant* (Tokyo, 2006), p. 12.

6 Rafael Steinberg, *The Cooking of Japan* (New York, 1976), p. 198.

7 In one instance, while I was examining a *tenmoku* (oil spot) *guinomi* by the Kyoto potter Kamada Koji, the gallerist filled it with water and insisted that I take it outside into the sunlight, which effectively transformed the piece.

8 Cees Nooteboom, *Rituals* [1980], trans. Adrienne Dixon (Baton Rouge, LA, 1983), pp. 134–5.

9 Cited in Yanagi Sōetsu, *The Unknown Craftsman* [1972], adapted by Bernard Leach (Tokyo and New York, 1989), p. 193.

10 Pierre Bourdieu, 'Titres et quartiers de noblesse culturelle', in *La Distinction: Critique sociale du jugement* (Paris, 1979), pp. 9–106.

11 Yanagi, *The Unknown Craftsman*, p. 178.

12 An excellent introduction to the material and technical aspects of Japanese ceramics is Herbert H. Sanders with Kenkichi Tomimoto, *The World of Japanese Ceramics* (Tokyo, 1967).

13 Robert Lee Yellin, 'Keshiki: Ceramic Landscapes', at www.e-yakimono.net. See Yellin's website for a detailed, illustrated list of such effects. Given the types of effects and degree of metaphorization at stake, it would seem that the gestalt theory of perception, especially where it deals with issues of pattern recognition, in the hands of an art historian such as Ernst Gombrich, might serve as an extremely useful tool for the study of pottery.

14 See Dario Gamboni, *Potential Images: Ambiguity and Indeterminacy in Art*, trans. Mark Treharne (London, 2002). This is the most far-ranging and detailed study on the topic of ambiguous and indeterminate images in Western art.

15 Robert Lee Yellin, *Ode to Japanese Pottery* (Tokyo, 2004), pp. 26–7 and 54. This is one of the rare texts in English devoted to *guinomi* and *tokkuri* (sake flasks).

16 Yasunari Kawabata, 'L'Image de Kyôto – tout au fond de mon coeur', preface to Kaii Higashiyama, *Les Quatre saisons de Kyôto* [1969], trans. Ryōji Nakamura and René de Ceccatty (Paris, 2007), p. 9.

17 Louise Allison Cort, *Shigaraki: Potters' Valley* (Bangkok, 2001), p. 110.

18 Augustin Berque, *Le Sauvage et l'artifice: Les Japonais devant la nature* (Paris, 1986), p. 228.

19 Cited in A. L. Sadler, *The Japanese Tea Ceremony* (Rutland, VT, 2008), p. 101.

SIX THE TEA BOWL AND THE TOILET BOWL

1 Edward S. Morse notes a particular predilection for integrating weathered wooden fragments of shipwrecks as architectural features: Edward S. Morse, *Japanese Homes and Their Surroundings* [1886] (New York, 1961), p. 69.

2 Hans Bjarne Thomsen, 'Individuality in a Communal Setting: Kyoto Ceramics and the Tradition of Innovation', in *Fukami: Purity of Form*, ed. Andreas Marks, exh. cat., Clark Center for Japanese Art and Culture, Hanford, CA (2011), pp. 26–39.

3 The period between the two world wars saw the rise of the Mingei movement, a celebration of Japanese folk crafts, created in reaction to increased industrialization and internationalization, not unlike the earlier Arts and Crafts movement in Britain. The theoretical debates that developed from this reconsideration of traditional forms would inform the post-Second World War pottery debates, though the latter would be centred on questions of international modernism.

4 This discussion is indebted to Bert Winther-Tamaki, 'Yagi Kazuo: The Admission of the Nonfunctional Object into the Japanese Pottery World', *Journal of Design History*, XII/2 (1999), pp. 123–41.

5 The modern *tatami* measures: Edoma (Tokyo) 175.8 × 87.9 cm; Kyoma (Kyoto) 191 × 95.5 cm.

6 Kakuzō Okakura, *The Book of Tea* [1906] (New York, 1964), p. 46. One might compare these series of boxes within boxes with the *jūnihitoe*, which are the twelve superposed kimonos traditionally worn by the empress during certain court ceremonies.

7 On the practical application of such strategies, see Richard L. Wilson, *The Art of Ogata Kenzan: Persona and Production in Japanese Ceramics* (New York and Tokyo, 1991). There are those, including Tanazaki, who claim that the calligraphy scrolls are placed in the *tokonoma* precisely so that the shadows make it difficult to decipher. On the Rikyū vase see D. T. Suzuki, *Zen and Japanese Culture* [1959] (New York, n.d.). p. 326.

8 Matsuo Bashō, *The Narrow Road to the Deep North* [1694], trans. Nobuyuki Yuasa (London, 1966), p. 100.

9 Ibid., p. 126.

10 Okakura, *The Book of Tea*, pp. 30–31.

11 Murielle Hladik, *Traces et fragments dans l'esthétique japonaise* (Wavre, 2008), pp. 95–6.

12 Ibid., p. 99.

13 Two related issues have been suggested to me by Michael Lazarin concerning the temporality and spatiality of the tea ceremony: first, that the traditional *iemoto* system of apprenticeship practically guarantees that one cannot use or even touch certain great works until a quite advanced age; second, in terms of both the feel of a *chawan* and the proper gestures to be made within a tea hut, the rapid increase in the height and size of the Japanese in the modern, and especially post-war, epochs has almost certainly problematized the proportions of traditional architecture and objects. It would be interesting to survey the average sizes of *chawan* in traditional and modern periods.

14 See Christine M. E. Guth, *Art, Tea, and Industry* (Princeton, NJ, 1993) for a detailed account of the business of art and antiquities in the tea context.

15 See the Raku Museum website at www.raku-yaki.or.jp.

16 Flyer for the exhibition 'Raku Kichizaemon XV: To Celebrate the 60th Anniversary, Part 1: From the Succession to "Tenmon"', Raku Museum, Kyoto, September–December 2010.

17 Exhibition label from the exhibition 'Raku Kichizaemon XV: To Celebrate the 60th Anniversary, Part 2: From "Tenmon" to Today', Raku Museum, Kyoto, January–March 2011.

18 Ibid.

19 Koyama Fujio, Domon Ken and Kobayashi Hideo, *Shigaraki Ōtsubo* (Tokyo, 1965).

20 *Jusetsu Miwa: A Retrospective* (Tokyo, 2006).

21 Bert Winther-Tamaki, 'Yagi Kazuo: The Admission of the Nonfunctional Object into the Japanese Pottery World', *Journal of Design History*, XII/2 (1999), p. 129.

22 For a theorization of agency in art, see Allen S. Weiss, 'The Trench and the Dump', in *Existed: Leonardo Drew*, ed. Claudia Schmuckli, exh. cat., Blaffer Gallery of the Art Museum of the University of Houston (2009), pp. 19–25.

23 See Kenji Kaneko, 'The Work of Ryoji Koie: A Proud Return to Earth', in *The Works of Ryoji Koie* (Tokyo, 1994), pp. 18 and 21.

SEVEN Impossible Possibles

1 Maurice Pinguet, 'Paul Claudel exégète du Japon' [1982], in *Le Texte Japon*, ed. Michaël Ferrier (Paris, 2009), p. 81. Another example of this confusion is to be found in Hiroshi Onishi, Takemitsu Oba and Sondra Castile, *Immortals and Sages: Paintings from Ryoanji Temple* (New York, 1993), p. 11, where the ground plan of the garden details only fourteen stones.

2 David A. Slawson, *Secret Teachings in the Art of Japanese Gardens: Design Principles, Aesthetic Values* (Tokyo, 1987), p. 98.

3 See Heino Engel, *Measure and Construction of the Japanese House* [1964] (Clarendon, VT, 1985); and Virginia Ponciroli, ed., *Katsura Imperial Villa* (Milan, 2005).

4 Günter Nitschke, *The Architecture of the Japanese Garden: Right Angle and Natural Form* (Cologne, 1991), p. 12.

5 Dore Ashton, *Noguchi: East and West* (New York, 1992), p. 112.

6 Nitschke, *The Architecture of the Japanese Garden,* p. 185.

7 François Cheng, *Vide et plein: Le Langage pictural chinois* (Paris, 1991), p. 107.

8 Edward S. Morse, *Japanese Homes and Their Surroundings* [1886] (New York, 1961), pp. 59 and 64.

9 See Michiko Rico Nosé, *The Modern Japanese Garden* (Rutland, VT, and Tokyo, 2006), pp. 165–7, and Arata Isozaki, Tadao Ando and Terunobu Fujimori, *The Contemporary Tea House* (Tokyo and New York, 2007), pp. 88–91.

10 Cited in Louise Allison Cort, 'Japanese Encounters with Clay', in *Isamu Noguchi and Modern Japanese Ceramics*, ed. Louise Allison Cort and Bert Winther-Tamaki, exh. cat., Arthur M. Sackler Gallery, Smithsonian Institution, Washington, DC (Berkeley, CA, and London, 2003), p. 118. I am indebted to this article for the information concerning Japanese pottery in the immediate post-war period.

11 Cited in Bert Winther-Tamaki, 'Yagi Kazuo: The Admission of the Nonfunctional Object into the Japanese Pottery World', *Journal of Design History*, XII/2 (1999), p. 128.

12 Cort, 'Japanese Encounters with Clay', p. 168.

13 Ibid., p. 147.

14 Sōfū Teshigahara, *This Boundless World of Flowers and Form* (Tokyo, 1966), p. 8.

15 Ibid., p. 104. That he made this claim in 1966 might suggest some influence of the

avant-gardism of his son's generation, though in fact it is coherent with his lifelong project of expanding the boundaries of ikebana.

16 Though ikebana is intimately related to tea (*chabana* is the specific form of flower arranging for *chanoyu*), most major tea schools would not share the passion for these new forms of experimentation. In the post-war period, the revolution in tea was more sociological than aesthetic, centred on a vast democratization and on creating a new base of women practitioners, who had traditionally been more or less excluded from the ritual of tea. It would still be quite a while before the major tea schools began to valorize the use of modernist utensils, and as for the performative aspects of the art, they are still for the most part directly linked to their original forms, instituted by Rikyū and his immediate successors.

17 Cited in Dore Ashton, *The Delicate Thread: Teshigahara's Life in Art* (New York and Tokyo, 1997), p. 73 Among those who appeared at Sogetsu were Butoh pioneers Hijikata Tatsumi and Ōno Kazuo, John Cage, David Tudor, Merce Cunningham, Yoko Ono, Robert Rauschenberg and Jasper Johns. The films of the vanguard of the American experimental cinema were also shown, such as those of Kenneth Anger, Stan Brakhage and Jack Smith.

18 Michael Lucken, *L'Art du Japon au vingtième siècle* (Paris, 2001), pp. 165–70.

19 Noguchi met landscape architect, tea aficionado and ikebana specialist Shigemori Mirei (who had long collaborated with Teshigahara Sōfū in creating an avant-garde form of ikebana) in 1957, and they subsequently collaborated on the UNESCO garden project in Paris. Certain works of both artists could well be characterized as sculpted landscapes.

20 An anecdote of interest, mentioned in Ashton, *The Delicate Thread*, p. 70, tells that when Teshigahara Sōfū visited Salvador Dalí at Porto Ligato in 1959, he was so taken with the Surrealist that he offered him an ikebana of driftwood in a lacquer bowl.

21 Ibid., pp. 163 and 169, for illustrations of these two works.

22 Kumakura Isao, 'Kan'ei Culture and *Chanoyu*', in *Tea in Japan*, ed. Paul Varley and Kumakura Isao (Honolulu, 1989), p. 140.

23 Cited in Robert Yellin, 'Suehara Fukami: Porcelain Horizons, Modern Monoliths', in *Japan Times*, 31 August 2005, available at www.e-yakimono.net; see also Hans Bjarne Thomsen, *Sueharu Fukami: Visions from the Shards of Sennyūji* (New York, 2008).

24 Bert Winther-Tamaki, 'The Ceramic Art of Isamu Noguchi', in *Isamu Noguchi and Modern Japanese Ceramics*, ed. Cort and Winther-Tamaki, p. 41.

25 Lafcadio Hearn, *Kokoro: Hints and Echos of Japanese Inner Life* [1895] (Rutland, VT, 1972), p. 87. On the myriad tones of the sky, see Hervé Chandès, *Azur*, exh. cat., Fondation Cartier, Jouy-en-Josas, France (1993).

26 Cited in Maezaki Shinya, 'New Horizons of Ceramic Sculpture', in *Fukami: Purity of Form*, ed. Andreas Marks, exh. cat., Clark Center for Japanese Art and Culture, Hanford, CA (2011), p. 24.

27 Ibid., p. 21.

28 Mark Halpern was kind enough to offer the following explanation of *bekuhai*: 'The sake cup you describe is called *bekuhai*, written in Chinese characters as 可杯. The (apparent) meaning derivation is interesting and came from Chinese into Japanese. The second character,

杯 (pronounced *hai* or *pai*), is often used to denote a cup or cupful, as in *ippai nomimashou* (let's have a drink; literally, "let's drink one cup") or as in the toast *kanpai* ("dry cup"). The basic meaning of the first character, 可 (here pronounced *beku*, but more usually *ka*), is possibility. This character is frequently combined with other characters to form words. But in such combinations, 可 is apparently (at least in Chinese) never the last character in the word. And since Chinese is written top to bottom, 可 can never be the "bottom". Thus, *bekuhai*, a cup which has no usable bottom.' Email from Mark Halpern, 2012. One might add that certain sculptures also bear the same form, such as Fukami Sueharu's *Midair V-1* (2003), illustrated in Marks, ed., *Fukami*, p. 132.

29 Both doll's house miniatures and gigantic shopfront pots offer examples of different use values of works done in unusual scales.

POSTSCRIPT A Leaf

1 Kakuzo Okakura, *The Book of Tea* [1906] (New York, 1964), p. 36.

2 Wallace Stevens, 'Anecdote of the Jar', in *Harmonium* [1923], reprinted in *The Collected Poems* (New York, 1982), p. 76.

SELECT BIBLIOGRAPHY

All the titles mentioned in the references are of interest, though often in relatively narrow domains of study. The following English-language works are recommended for those who would like to have a manageable list of readings, either in preparation for a trip to Japan or simply as an extended introduction.

Addis, Stephen, *How to Look at Japanese Art* (New York, 1996): one of the most intelligent introductions to the subject.

——, *Zen Art* (New York, 1989): a sumptuously illustrated, erudite study.

Bashō, Matsuo, *Narrow Road to the Interior* [1694], trans. Sam Hamill (Boston, MA, 2000): the classic travelogue by the great haiku poet.

Benedict, Ruth, *The Chrysanthemum and the Sword* [1946] (New York, 2005): the *locus classicus* on Japanese behaviour and psychology.

Cort, Louise Allison, *Shigaraki: Potters' Valley* (Bangkok, 2001): probably the most detailed study in English on a single type of Japanese pottery, this work is also an extraordinarily rich source on the art form's more general practical and aesthetic aspects.

Crueger, Anneliese, Wulf Crueger and Saeko Itō, *Modern Japanese Ceramics* (New York, 2006): a detailed and fully illustrated book offering an overview of the many regional types of contemporary Japanese pottery, with extensive practical information.

Holborn, Mark, *The Ocean in the Sand: Japan, from Landscape to Garden* (Boulder, CO, 1978)

Mizuno, Katsuhiko, and Tom Wright, *Zen Gardens: Kyoto's Nature Enclosed* (Kyoto, 1990): or any other book on Kyoto gardens by photographer Katsuhiko Mizuno, for beautiful images of gardens, many of which are closed to the public.

Murasaki, Shikibu, *The Tale of Genji* [early 11th century], trans. Royall Tyler (New York, 2000): the origin of Japanese literature and a treasure trove of cultural information.

Nitschke, Günter, *Japanese Gardens* (Cologne, 2003): one of the most comprehensive, well-illustrated studies.

Okakura, Kakuzō, *The Book of Tea* [1906] (New York, 1964): the classic introduction to the subject.

Richie, Donald, *A Tractate on Japanese Aesthetics* (Berkeley, CA, 2007): the most succinct statement on Japanese aesthetics, by one of the foremost Japan specialists.

Sadler, A. L., *The Japanese Tea Ceremony* [1933] (Rutland, VT, 2008): a fascinating compendium of tea lore.

Sei, Shōnagon, *The Pillow Book* [1002], trans. Meredith McKinney (London and New York, 2006): this journal of encyclopedic form by a court lady contemporary of Murasaki

Shikibi, including portraits, anecdotes, poems, tales and lists, is one of the earliest psychological self-portraits, offering a rare glimpse into the secret life of the Heian court.

Slawson, David A., *Secret Teachings in the Art of Japanese Gardens* (Tokyo, 1987): an excellent design-oriented study by a landscape architect, this book includes a translation of Zōen's classic *Illustrations for Designing Mountain, Water, and Hillside Field Landscapes* (15th century).

Tanaka, Sen'ō, and Sendō Tanaka, *The Tea Ceremony* (Tokyo, 2000): an excellent primer on contemporary tea aesthetics and practice.

Tanizaki, Jun'ichirō, *In Praise of Shadows* [1933], trans. Thomas Harper and Edward Seidensticker (Stony Creek, CT, 1977): a classic by one of Japan's most celebrated modern novelists.

Treib, Marc, and Ron Herman, *A Guide to the Gardens of Kyoto* (Tokyo, 2003): the best pocket guide to the gardens.

Yasuda, Kenneth, trans. and ed., *The Japanese Haiku* (Rutland, VT, 1957): a rich, annotated volume of haiku.

In addition, I have found the following pottery-oriented websites to be particularly useful:

www.e-yakimono.net
The extraordinarily informative site of Robert Yellin's Yakimono Gallery (Kyoto), with especially fine photographic documentation.

www.g-utsuwakan.com
Minoru and Mitsuko Umeda's outstanding and innovative Utsuwakan Gallery (Kyoto), specializing in non-traditional contemporary pottery.

www.mirviss.com
Joan B. Mirviss Ltd (New York) is perhaps the foremost dealer of modern Japanese ceramics outside Japan.

www.yufuku.net
Wahei Aoyama's Yufuku Gallery (Tokyo), with excellent commentary on contemporary Japanese pottery and other crafts.

ACKNOWLEDGEMENTS

I would like to thank Michael Leaman, for his support of my work and his extraordinary bibliophilic sense; the Japan Foundation (New York), for their generous support of this project; Michaël Ferrier, for sharing his vast erudition concerning Japanese culture as well as his *joie de vivre*; Mark Halpern, for all the pleasures he made possible in my discovery of Tokyo and for his invaluable reading of the manuscript; Michael Lazarin, for his extreme generosity and matching erudition; Sekitani Kazuhiko and Kawabe Tsutsumi, for their extraordinary hospitality which revealed so many subtleties of Japanese refinement and beauty; Karen Shimakawa, for all the inspiring discussions; Umeda Minoru and Umeda Mitsuko, for introducing me to the marvels of Japanese pottery and cuisine; Robert Yellin, for his erudition, enthusiasm and kindness; Ikeba Kumi, for her generosity and the remarkable precision of her research into art history; and above all to Chantal Thomas, for sharing so many things with so much joy. Thanks also go to all those others who helped me in so many ways, notably: Aoyama Tom, Aoyama Wahei, François Bizet, René de Ceccatty, Murielle Hladik, Hosokawa Shuhei, Koie Ryōji, Sylvia Lachter, Masuda Makoto, Mori Chikako, Nakamura Ryōji, Ofer Shagan, Jeff Shapiro, Abbot Yamada Sōshō of Shinju-an; also the Cavin-Morris Gallery, Jukō-in, Omote Senke, the Japan Foundation Kyoto Office, and special thanks to Raku Kichizaemon XV and the Raku Museum.

Portions of this book were published in earlier forms in the following journals: 'Cracks', *artUS*, 29 (2010); 'Dry Mountain Water', *Cabinet*, 38 (2010); 'Guinomi', *Cabinet*, 30 (2008); 'Guinomi', *Gastronomica*, X/1 (2010); 'Impossible Possibles', *Log*, 19 (2010); 'The Limits of Metaphor: Ideology and Representation in the Zen Garden', *Social Analysis*, LIV/2 (2010); 'On the Circulation of Metaphors in the Zen Garden', *AA Files*, 60 (2010); 'Seeing the Unspeakable', *artUS*, 32 (2012); 'The Toilet Bowl and the Tea Bowl', *artUS*, 27 (2009).

PHOTO ACKNOWLEDGEMENTS

The author and publishers wish to express their thanks to the below sources of illustrative material and/or permission to reproduce it:

Photo courtesy of the Cavin-Morris Gallery, New York: p. 194; photo courtesy of Contemporary Applied Arts, London: p. 221; photo Gakuji Tanaka, courtesy of Aoyama Wahei and the Yufuku Gallery, Tokyo: p. 217; photo courtesy of Ginza Kuroda Touen Gallery, Tokyo: p. 54; photo © Isozaki Arata (digital image © The Museum of Modern Art, New York / Licensed by SCALA / Art Resource, NY): p. 49; from Mrs Paul Kincaid, *Japanese Gardens and Floral Art* (New York, 1966): p. 109; photos Sylvia Lachter: pp. 61, 159, 162, 165, 168, 197; photo courtesy of Miyamoto Katsuhiro: p. 137; photo Nagata Yo, courtesy of Utsuwakan Gallery, Kyoto: p. 59; photo courtesy of the National Museum of Modern Art, Kyoto: p. 174; photo K. Noble © 2012 The Isamu Noguchi Foundation and Garden Museum, New York / Artists Rights Society (ARS), New York: p. 102 (top); photo Prudence Cuming Associates, London (provided by the Hayward Galleries, courtesy of the John Cage Trust): p. 82; photos courtesy of Raku Kichizaemon XV: pp. 20, 190; photo courtesy of Robert Yellin, Yakimono Gallery, Kyoto: p. 138. All other photographs are by Allen S. Weiss, taken between 2008 and 2011.

INDEX